Elementary
Korean

Elementary Korean

by Ross King, Ph.D. and Jae-Hoon Yeon, Ph.D.

TUTTLE PUBLISHING
Tokyo • Rutland, Vermont • Singapore

Published by Tuttle Publishing, an imprint of Periplus Editions (HK) Ltd., with editorial offices at 364 Innovation Drive, North Clarendon, Vermont 05759 and 61 Tai Seng Avenue #02-12, Singapore 534167.

ISBN-13: 978-0-8048-3614-2

Distributed by:

North America, Latin America & Europe
Tuttle Publishing
364 Innovation Drive
North Clarendon, VT 05759-9436
Tel: 1 (802) 773 8930; Fax: 1 (802) 773 6993
Email: info@tuttlepublishing.com
www.tuttlepublishing.com

Japan
Tuttle Publishing
Yaekari Building, 3rd Floor
5-4-12 Osaki, Shinagawa-ku
Tokyo 141-0032
Tel: (81) 3 5437 0171; Fax: (81) 3 5437 0755
Email: tuttle-sales@gol.com

Asia Pacific
Berkeley Books Pte. Ltd.
61 Tai Seng Avenue #02-12
Singapore 534167
Tel: (65) 6280 1330; Fax: (65) 6280 6290
Email: inquiries@periplus.com.sg
www.periplus.com.sg

11 10 09 08
11 10 9 8 7

Printed in Singapore

TUTTLE PUBLISHING® is a registered trademark of Tuttle Publishing, a division of Periplus Editions (HK) Ltd.

Contents

Reference Section

Preface

This textbook began naively as a simple remake of Martin and Lee's *Beginning Korean* (1969). Because *Beginning Korean* is entirely in Yale Romanization, we believed Martin's system would be better appreciated if only the book were in Han'gŭl. The idea was to scan it onto disk, convert the Korean bits to a Korean font, and reissue the textbook. Ross King and Hyoshin Kim began scanning *Beginning Korean* onto disk at Harvard in 1989. Hyoshin Kim also did much of the initial hard work of creating the Microsoft Word™ files on the Apple Macintosh™ and converting the Korean fonts. She has been an excellent informant and critic throughout the project.

When we started teaching from *Beginning Korean* at the School of Oriental and African Studies (SOAS) in autumn 1990, we soon found that much needed updating, correcting, shortening, or throwing out. Much was also missing. We continued to write new dialogues, and rework and revise the grammar notes throughout the academic year 1991–92, during which time we taught first-year Korean not from *Beginning Korean,* but from the new Korea University textbooks. The Korea University books have given us many ideas, and we are grateful to the authors. We are also grateful to other textbooks for various ideas here and there: the Myongdo textbooks, Namgui Chang and Yong-chol Kim's *Functional Korean,* the Republic of Korea (ROK) Ministry of Culture's *Korean I-III,* and Adrian Buzo and Shin Gi-hyon's *Learning Korean: New Directions I* (Pilot Edition 5). Ho-min Sohn's recent descriptive grammar, *Korean* (1994), has also been of assistance.

In the nine years that have passed since this project began, the textbook has changed radically. While still owing much of its grammatical apparatus to the original *Beginning Korean,* this book has become a different creature. This is why, at the urging of Samuel Martin, we have changed the title to *Elementary Korean* and listed just our names as coauthors.

We would like to thank those who have helped make this textbook possible. Several cohorts of SOAS students have helped us—Chris Murphy and Eunice Brooker, who suffered through the first chaotic revision of *Beginning Korean;* Janet Poole and Denise Chai, who put in long hours during the summer of 1992 editing, organizing, and retyping the text; Flora Graham, Simon Hayward, Youngsoon Mosafiri, Natalie

Lemay-Palmer, Satona Suzuki, Lars Sundet, and Mark Vincent (the 1992–93 cohort); Tom Hunter-Watts, Sakura Kato, Stefan Knoob, Andrew Pratt, Andy Wong, Erin Chung, Charlotte Hørlyk, Stephen Matthews, and Pernille Siem (the 1993–94 cohort); Andrew W. Oglanby, Adam Barr, Steven Conroy, Sung Khang, Sue Perkins Morris, Alex Calvo, Meher McArthur, Aileen Baker, Ethan Bond, and Edith Hodder (the 1994–95 cohort); Akiko Maeda, Masamichi Yasuda, Daniel Choo, Fedor Tsoi, Yu Maeda, Reiko Yamazaki, Nakako Takei, and Izumi Nakamura (the 1995–96 cohort). Two British Foreign and Commonwealth Office (FCO) diplomats on the Korean Long Course at SOAS also used the second pilot version and gave us valuable feedback: Colin Crooks and Patrick Butler. Most recently, the University of British Columbia (UBC) Korean 102 (Elementary Korean) cohorts for the academic years 1995–98 have provided valuable feedback, especially Jeff Armstrong, Jenny Cho, Brian Choi, Chinfai Choi, Clara Choi, Dian Choi, Karen Choi, Mina Chung, Ted Kim, Hannah Joe, Janette Kim, Claudia Kwan, Jowan Lee, Marina Lee, Miyoung Lee, Tammy Lee, Victor Lim, Liza Park, Delphine Tardy, David Thumm, Ryo Yanagitani, and Jenny Yim. All have provided valuable comments and criticism for which we are grateful.

In particular, the authors wish to single out SOAS students Mark Vincent and Youngsoon Mosafiri for special thanks. Mark clocked nearly 100 hours revising, formatting, editing, and proofing the second pilot version on the Macintosh in May and June of 1993. He continued to provide excellent suggestions on fonts, formatting, style, content, and presentation in the 1993–94 academic session. Youngsoon performed the tedious, but important task of retyping all of the Korean in the new TrueType™ fonts on the Macintosh in the summer of 1994.

We have also benefited from the comments and criticisms of some of our colleagues. Seungja Choi was foolhardy enough to teach from the second pilot version during the 1993–94 academic session at Yale. She and her students raised many helpful points. SOAS Korean lectors Youngjoo Lee, Jiyong Shin, and Jae-mog Song also provided valuable input. David Moon and Yoon-Suk Chung at the University of California-Berkeley both made many useful criticisms, and Bjarke Frellesvig at the University of Oslo, Norway, gave valuable feedback too. In addition, some of our colleagues at the Korea Foundation–sponsored conference on "Collaborative Korean as a Foreign Language (KFL) Textbooks Development" in Seoul, December 1993, made some useful criticisms of the second version: Chŏngsuk Kim of Korea University, Dong-jae Lee of the University of Hawaii, and Young-mee Yu Cho of Stanford. More recently, the manuscript has benefited from excellent criticisms and suggestions by UBC Korean Language Instructor Insun Lee, who has taught from the book at

UBC since 1996, and from UBC Korean 102 teaching assistans Jee-Weon Shin and Soowook Kim, who taught from the book during the 1996–1997 and 1997–98 academic sessions, respectively. UBC students Victor Song, Gabriel Gervey, and Paul Liu made valuable suggestions during thie 1996–1997 academic year, and Sally Foster and Sunah Park Cho compiled the answer key to exercises.

The recordings for this book were made in December of 1996, shortly before Tuttle Publishing underwent a series of managerial and editorial staff changes that have significantly delayed the appearance of this book. The technical aspects of the recording sessions were expertly supervised by Clay Dixon of UBC's Crane Production Unit in the Crane Resource Centre. Native speaker voices were cheerfully volunteered by Mr. Ilsung Lee, Mrs. Sunah Park Cho, Nam-lin Hur, Yunshik Chang, Miseli Jeon, Suk-man Jang, Hyoshin Kim, and a supporting cast of Korean visiting scholars and their families too numerous to name individually. We are grateful to them all.

Financial support for this project at SOAS came from the Korea Research Foundation through its generous annual grants to the SOAS Centre of Korean Studies. The authors also would like to thank the SOAS Research Committee for providing funds for research assistance on this project; and the Center for Korean Studies, University of California-Berkeley, for providing Ross King with the opportunity to convert the manuscript into NisusWriter™ as well as finish the pre-publication revisions while on a Korea Foundation post-doctoral fellowship during the 1994–95 academic year. Financial support for preparation of the final camera-ready copy at UBC came from the UBC Faculty of Arts, UBC's Centre for Korean Research, and the SOAS Centre of Korean Studies. The authors were also pleased to win an Honorable Mention in the 1995 Tuttle Language Prize. We have used the prize money to support work on the textbook.

We would be delighted to hear more feedback, positive or negative, from future users of this book. Please contact us at these addresses.

Ross King
Department of Asian Studies
Asian Centre
1871 West Mall
Vancouver, B. C. (Canada)
email: jrpking@unixg.ubc.ca
fax: (604) 822-8937

J. H. Yeon
Centre of Korean Studies
SOAS, University of London
Thornhaugh Street, Russell Square
London WC1H OXG (U.K.)
email: jy1@soas.ac.uk
fax: (171) 323-6179

About this Book

Like other Korean language textbooks on the market, this textbook has its strengths and weaknesses. The authors have tried to write a book that will appeal to a broad range of learners, including individuals working on their own, professional people working with a tutor, and university students in a classroom setting. The following remarks are aimed at teachers contemplating using the textbook with learners of the latter type.

Main Objective

This course consists of two volumes, of which *Elementary Korean* is the first. The sequel volume, tentatively called *Korean: A Continuing Course*, should appear within a year of this volume. The main objective of the two volumes comprising this course is communicative competence in contemporary spoken Korean through a systematic and streamlined introduction to the fundamental patterns of the language. Most lessons in the sequel volume also contain a "Reading Passage," and both volumes introduce a number of patterns more relevant to written language than spoken. In such cases, the student is advised as to the spoken vs. written language status of the pattern in question. Thus, *Elementary Korean* and *Korean: A Continuing Course* do not aim at oral competence alone.

In terms of the American Council of Teachers of Foreign Languages (ACTFL) Proficiency Guidelines, the authors believe that *Elementary Korean* and *Korean: A Continuing Course* together provide enough material for a student to attain an Intermediate-Low to Intermediate-Mid proficiency level. Of course, this is also dependent on the number of contact hours and the quality of "act-related" instruction provided.

Basic Methodology

This textbook is unabashedly structuralist and eclectic in its philosophy and methodology. Some teachers versed in the latest task-based and proficiency-oriented approaches to language teaching may find the book's structuralist approach reminiscent of the grammar translation method and the audio-lingual method. Such teachers should remember one point: the book does not teach the course in the classroom.

The authors believe the textbook is amenable to any number of language-teaching approaches and styles in the classroom; yet, we see it primarily as an out-of-class reference tool to ready the students for whatever activities their teacher has prepared for them in class. The grammar notes are richer (though still concise) than those in other textbooks for at least two reasons:

1. to help those students working on their own without recourse to a teacher
2. to reduce the amount of class time needed for "fact" (as opposed to "act").

About the Exercises

The exercises at the end of each lesson are designed primarily as written homework, not as oral exercises for the classroom. We have deliberately omitted oral pattern drills from the lessons because we feel such drills take up unnecessary space and are easily constructed by the teacher. Thus, one major shortcoming of the textbook is the lack of a teacher's manual with ideas and guidance for both task-based classroom activities and pattern drills. The lack of a teacher's manual or activity book places an additional burden on the teacher, but in this respect our textbook is no different from other Korean textbooks currently available. Insun Lee at the University of British Columbia is currently working on a combination teacher's manual-and-activity book; look for it in the near future. In the meantime, we encourage teachers using the book to share their ideas and supplementary materials with us.

About the Dialogues: Themes and Situations

The dialogues were written after the authors had determined which patterns were to appear in which sequence in the course. This increases the risk of producing dialogues that become mere vehicles for the structural items being introduced. Keeping this risk in mind, we have tried to write dialogues that succeed at once in illustrating each new structural point in the lesson and in introducing tasks and situations likely to be of immediate use to a beginner. We have tried to keep the conversations natural and colloquial and, where possible, humorous.

The dialogues cover the themes of daily academic life in Korea, business, and travel. Most of the dialogues center around two middle-aged foreigners (Chris and Eunice Murphy) and their two university-aged children (Eric and Sandy). The authors hope these characters will enhance the functional range and potential market for the book.

Situations and functions covered in the two volumes include: greetings and good-byes, classroom expressions, identifying things and introducing people, existence, location and possession, asking for directions, buying tickets and other travel-related situations, discussing one's studies and one's language abilities, telling time, ordering at a restaurant, asking for people on the telephone, shopping, social drinking, etc. Though our treatment of situations is by no means comprehensive, most situations and tasks necessary for attaining basic proficiency are covered.

About Transcription

The first four lessons include broad phonetic transcriptions of the Korean material. The transcriptions are *not* romanization—students can learn the McCune-Reischauer and Yale romanizations in a Korean studies course. The transcriptions are there for students who want them and are presented *separately* from the Korean-script renditions (in Lessons One and Two). Teachers and students who want or like transcription can use it, while others have the option to ignore it.

About Teaching the Korean Script

Some Korean teachers proudly teach the Korean script from day one. Others prefer to wait a few weeks while working in an exclusively oral-aural mode. *All* Korean teachers have their own way of teaching the Korean script, and thanks to the genius of the script itself, they all work. This is why our textbook does not dwell on the script; we simply give the basics rather than force one or another scheme on the teacher and student.

The authors prefer to wait at least a week or two before introducing the Korean script. We keep practicing the basic expressions from Lessons One and Two while hammering home the various pronunciation points treated in Lessons Three and Four until everyone is ready for Lesson Five. Lessons Three and Four are more akin to reference lessons—points to come back to again and again over the course of an entire academic year—than to lessons for formal, systematic presentation in the classroom. We find it most useful to treat Lessons One to Four as an organic whole, the contents of which can be covered in any number of ways.

Lessons One and Two introduce approximately seventy daily and classroom expressions, which at first blush seems a lot. But recall that these expressions are the raw material around which the pronunciation points in Lessons Three and Four are to be reinforced. Thus, students actually have four lessons' worth of time to practice these expressions in class.

About Contact Hours

Most university Korean courses in the United States, Canada, United Kingdom, Australia, and New Zealand meet four or five hours per week. At this pace, the authors would recommend covering one lesson for every eight to ten classroom hours, in which the students have at least a 30-minute quiz at the end of every other week. But the authors recognize that different students and different courses proceed at different paces; thus, anywhere from six to ten hours per lesson is possible, depending on the circumstances. The authors believe the book is particularly well-suited for an intensive course of eight to ten contact hours per week, in which case it would be possible to finish both *Elementary Korean* and *Korean: A Continuing Course* (forthcoming) in one academic year.

About Vocabulary

This textbook introduces a lot of vocabulary, some one thousand items in all. The authors are skeptical of statistical frequency list approaches to introducing vocabulary, since these frequency lists are never based on the vocabulary needs of university students, businessmen, or travelers learning Korean. Our book includes many sophisticated adult, intellectual vocabulary items—the sorts of words that mature adults would like to be able to say early in their Korean learning career. Furthermore, since Korean does not give the English speaker as many shortcut vocabulary "freebies" as does French or Spanish or German, it is a hard fact of life that students need to spend more time on vocabulary building.

It is also the view of the authors that some vocabulary items cost more than others to learn. This view is reflected in the layout of the vocabulary sections, where certain words are indented beneath others to indicate that these items are related to the main vocabulary item in question, and thus cost less to learn.

Other features of the vocabulary sections to be born in mind are these: (1) starting with Lesson Seven, all verb bases are given in the special notation which students learn in this lesson; (2) processive and descriptive bases are distinguished from each other by their English glosses—descriptive verbs are always preceded by *be* (*blue*, *sad*), while processive verbs are not; (3) vocabulary is broken up into sections according to part of speech—verbs, nouns, adverbs (although the classification of verbal nouns is often arbitrary); (4) we have tried to provide more exemplification of the vocabulary items than is typical of other textbooks. Example sentences using a particular vocabulary item in context are indented below the main word.

About Verbs and Lesson Seven

Lesson Seven is the "heartbreak hill" of the course—if the students don't survive it, they will not survive the course (or ever learn Korean, for that matter). Lesson Seven is unusual in two ways. First, it covers more or less all major verb types in one fell swoop (sort of the way they do it in intensive university Latin and Greek courses). Crucially, it includes those verbs traditionally called irregular: p~w verbs and t~l verbs. The authors have found that it is usually possible to ask for and get more effort from students at the beginning of the course when they are still fresh and excited from the initial exposure to the language. Lesson Seven is to verbs as Lessons Three and Four are to pronunciation: it is important to master the basics early, after which one can keep coming back to problem points.

The second important feature of Lesson Seven is its *treatment* of the so-called irregular verbs. Our analysis follows Samuel E. Martin's style in turning the traditional analysis on its head. This is most significant for the p~w verbs and t~l verbs, but also applies to the L-extending verbs. In Martin's system, the p~w verbs are bases ending in *w*, and the students learn a rule that changes *w* to *p* (ㅂ) before consonants, e.g., *hot* 더 w ˉ + -다 → 덥다 (see below for use of linguistic symbols in this book). The *w* counts as a consonant, and students also learn the rule that *w* + 으 gives 우: 더 w- + -으세요 → 더우세요.

In the case of verbs like 듣다 *listen*, Martin takes the form with ㄹ as the base (들-), and students learn a rule which changes ㄹ to ㄷ before consonants: 들- + -다 → 듣다. Verbs like 살다 *live* are treated as a special kind of L-extending vowel base (사-ㄹ-) that requires the addition of an ㄹ in front of certain verb endings.

Our analysis of the p~w verbs actually saves the student one rule in comparison to the traditional treatment, and in general the analysis completely disposes of the traditional Korean notion of irregular verbs for these conjugation classes. It is this prejudicial notion of irregular verbs that leads some Korean teachers (and students) to regard them as difficult, and tackle them far too late in a student's career.

About Speech Styles and Honorifics

Our book introduces Polite Style 해요 first, beginning in Lessons Five and Six (copula -이에요, 있어요 and 없어요), followed by a comprehensive overview of Polite Style for most major verb classes in Lesson Seven. This is directly related to the Martinesque analysis of those verbs traditionally called irregular by Korean grammarians (Martin chops off everything to the left of the infinitive vowel -아 ~ -어 and calls it the base). The honorific suffix -(으)시- is introduced in Lesson Eight, and Formal Style 합니다 is introduced in Lesson Eleven. Apart from the basic expressions in Lessons One and Two, which are presented without analysis for rote memorization, the student will not see honorific forms until Lesson Eight and Formal Style forms until Lesson Eleven. This seems a small price to pay for a systematic, streamlined, and sequenced introduction to the structures.

About Orthography

Some teachers are finicky about spelling and conforming to the latest official orthographic guidelines. We are not. Whether one writes 할 거예요 or 할 거에요, for instance, seems to have little or no bearing on how well students assimilate this pattern. Our book uses the latter spelling, even though it is now nonstandard orthography, because (1) this is how it is actually pronounced, and (2) students have already learned the simple rule for the copula that the -이- drops regularly in colloquial speech after a vowel. They can learn about the vagaries and idiosyncrasies of official Korean orthography at a later stage, once they actually know the patterns.

About the English Translations and Glosses

In a number of cases the English translations of Korean expressions and patterns are structured to resemble as closely as possible the Korean meaning. In some cases, students and teachers may feel that certain English renditions are not typical English usage. For example, the authors are well aware that 'wanna' is not considered good English. However, this contracted form is used for pedagogical reasons (the form in question is also historically derived from a contraction in Korean), and seems to work as a mnemonic device, too. The authors ask for indulgence on this matter.

About Linguistic Symbols

Both authors received their primary training in linguistics, and this background is reflected in the analyses in the book and in the use of certain linguistic symbols. Our use of linguistic symbols amounts to a special kind of code that is designed to streamline the learning process for the student, and to streamline the book's presentation. Once the teacher and students have mastered the few simple symbols below, they should have no trouble following the exposition in the book.

Symbol	Comments
- (Times), - (Apple Myungjo)	The hyphen is used to demarcate boundaries and bound forms. Because the abstract Korean verb stems (we call them bases) to which students must attach endings are all bound forms (that is, they cannot be used and do not occur in real speech without some ending), verbs in each lesson's Vocabulary List are listed as a base, that is, as a bound form, followed by a hyphen to its right (e.g., 사-ㄹ- *live*). The same goes for all verb endings in Korean—they are abstract notions that only occur in Korean when attached to a verb base; they are bound forms, and always appear in the book with a hyphen to their left. We continue to refer to verb bases and endings in the grammar notes in this way, too.
+ (Times), + (Apple Myungjo)	The plus sign means 'plus' 'added to' 'in combination with'.

/.../ vs. [...]	Phonemic notations are enclosed by slash brackets and phonetic notations by square brackets. Most examples of slash brackets have been purged from the book, but we often use square brackets to indicate the phonetics, i.e. actual pronunciation of a Korean form when this is not indicated in the Korean orthography. Another usage of the square brackets is to indicate optional material.
*	The asterisk is used to mark grammatically unacceptable utterances.
→	This arrow sign means 'becomes', 'gives', 'yields', 'produces'.
←	This arrow sign means 'comes from', 'is a product of', 'derives from'.
~ (Times), ~ (Apple Myungjo)	The tilde is used to represent an alternation, and means 'in alternation with'.

Note the following example:

$$\text{w-} \quad + \quad \text{-으} \quad \rightarrow \quad \text{우}$$

Here, the w- identifies a particular verb class in Korean (p~w verbs), learned in Lesson Seven (think of it as a kind of code—this is how we teach it in class). The hyphens indicate boundaries, the + indicates "plus", and the arrow means 'yields, gives'. This particular example is as complicated as our 'code' gets, and makes sense in the context of the lesson in which it is introduced.

Cast Of Characters

The Murphy Family:

Christopher Murphy, a middle-aged British businessman in charge of the Seoul
    office of a Yorkshire textiles firm
Eunice, his Australian wife who teaches piano at an International School in Seoul;
Eric and **Sandy**, their 21-year old twins, both attending the International Division at
    Korea University

The Kim family:

Mr. Ch'ang-gi Kim, Chris Murphy's Korean teacher, a middle-aged Korean
his wife, a full-time housewife active in their local church
Chin-yŏng, their 21-year old daughter
Chin-sŏp, their twenty-year old son, both attending Korea University

Others:

Miss Lee, Christopher Murphy's secretary, a woman in her mid-twenties
할머니 (halmŏni), the grandmother living across the hall from the Murphy's place
Mr. Kang, a senior employee of Han'guk Sŏmyu, a Korean textiles firm based in Pusan, a
    middle-aged man who is a long-time business associate of Chris Murphy
Mr. Nam, another business associate of Chris Murphy
Yŏngch'ŏl, a friend of Eric's from Korea University
Sŏngman, a friend of Sandy's from Korea University
Miss Kwak, a waitress befriended by Eric

The list above is given to clarify the gender, age, status and inter-relationships of the
various characters in the book, since this affects the style of Korean which they use in
addressing each other.

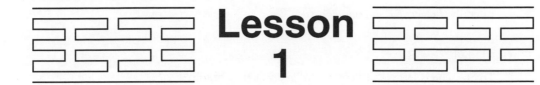

Lesson 1

In this lesson you will learn the first of two sets of Basic Expressions that you will use constantly in everyday life in Korea and that you will need in the classroom. The purpose of memorizing these expressions is to help you come to grips with Korean pronunciation. You needn't worry at this stage about the grammar or about how things are written. They are expressions of greeting and general politeness for the most part. We also introduce you to some of the fundamental features of all Korean sentences.

Basic Expressions I: Korean Script

Shortly you will learn the Korean alphabet, at which time you should use this section to review the basic expressions. Until then, you may find it helpful to have a simple Roman-script indication of how the sentences sound. Therefore, we have provided in the following section a transcription of the same set of basic expressions in a phonetic notation to give you a guide to pronunciation.

	Korean	English
1.	네 or 예	*Yes.*
2.	아니오	*No.*
3.	김선생님, 안녕하세요?	*How are you, Mr. Kim?*

Explanation: 김 (a family name); 선생 *teacher, Mr. or Mrs. or Ms.*; 선생님 *revered teacher, Mr., Mrs. or Ms.*; 안녕하세요? *Are you peaceful (well)?*

4.	네. 안녕하세요?	*Fine, how are you?*
5.	. . . 입니다.	*I'm . . .*

6. 만나서 반갑습니다. *Nice to meet you; nice to see you.*

   Literally: *I meet you, so I am pleased.*

7. 안녕히 가세요. *Good-bye!*

   To one who is leaving. Literally: *Go in peace* (i.e., health).

8. 안녕히 계세요. *Good-bye!*

   To one who is staying. Literally: *Stay in peace* (i.e., health).

9. 수고하십니다. *Hello!* (to someone working)

   수고하세요. *Good-bye!* (to someone working)

   수고하셨어요. *Thank you for helping me* or *Well done!*

   Explanation: 수고 *hard work*, i.e., *You're doing a great job*; *Keep up the good work*; and *Well done.*

10. 처음 뵙겠습니다. *Pleased to make your acquaintance.*

    Literally: *I see you for the first time* (formally) i.e., *How do you do?*

11. 또 뵙겠습니다. *See you later!* (FORMAL)

    Explanation: 또 *again*, 뵙겠습니다 *will humbly see / meet*. Literally: *I will humbly see you again.*

12. 고맙습니다 or 감사합니다. *Thank you.*

13. 천만에요 or 괜찮아요. *You're welcome!* or *Don't mention it!*

    Literally: *It's one of ten million* (words).

14. 어서 오세요! *Welcome!*

    Literally: *Come (in) right away!*

15. 들어오세요! *Come in!*

    Literally: *Please enter.*

16. 앉으세요. *Please take a seat / sit down.*

17. 실례합니다. *Excuse me* (for what I am doing).

    Literally: *I am committing a discourtesy.*

실례했습니다.　　　　　　　　　*Excuse me* (for what I did).
Literally: *I have committed a discourtesy.*

실례하겠습니다.　　　　　　　　*Excuse me* (for what I'm about to do).
Literally: *I am about to commit a discourtesy.*

18.　미안합니다 or 죄송합니다　　　*I'm sorry* or *Excuse me.*
Literally: *I feel uneasy.*

19.　아니오, 괜찮아요.　　　　　　*Not at all, it's all right; No, thanks.*
Explanation: 아니오 *No*; 괜찮아요 *It makes no difference, it doesn't matter, it's okay.*

20.　여보세요!　　　　　　　　　　*Hello!* or *Hey there!*
Hello on the telephone, or when peering into a dark house. Also means *Look here!*

21.　시간이 다 됐습니다.　　　　　*It's time* (to begin or stop).
Explanation: 시간 *time*; 시간이 *time* (as subject); 다 *all, completely*; 됐습니다 *it has become . . .*

22.　또 봐요.　　　　　　　　　　*See you later!* (POLITE)
Literally: *See you again.* This is less formal than item 11.

23.　그래요?　　　　　　　　　　*Is that so? Really?*

　　　그래요.　　　　　　　　　　*That's so. Really.*

Basic Expressions I: Transcription

You are meant to master the basic expressions of Lessons One and Two before learning the Korean alphabet. Some students will be able to do this through practice and listening to the tape alone. Other students will prefer the visual mode for memorization. As a memory aid in the first few days before you learn the Korean alphabet, we reproduce below the basic expressions you have just seen this time in phonetic transcription, followed by a chart explaining the transcription symbols. This transcription writes the basic expressions **roughly** as they sound—use it to jog your memory, not as a crutch.

1. ne. or ye.
   Yes.

2. anio.
   No.

3. kim sɔnsæŋnim, annyɔŋ[h]ase yo?
   How are you, Mr. Kim?

4. ne. annyɔŋ[h]ase yo?
   Fine, how are you?

5. . . .imnida.
   I'm. . .

6. mannasɔ paŋgapssɨmnida.
   Nice to meet you; nice to see you.

7. annyɔŋ[h]i gase yo.
   Good-bye! (to one who is leaving)

8. annyɔŋ[h]i gese yo.
   Good-bye! (to one who is staying)

9. sugohašimnida!
   Hello! (to someone working)

   sugohase yo!
   Good-bye! (to someone working)

   sugohašɔssɔ yo.
   Thank you for helping me or *Well done.*

10. čʰɔɨmb[w]epkkessɨmnida.
    Pleased to make your acquaintance.

11. tto b[w]epkkessɨmnida.
    See you later! (FORMAL)

12. komapssɨmnida. or kamsa[ha]mnida.

    Thank you.

13. čʰɔmmaney yo. or kwænčʰana yo.
    You're welcome or *Not at all.*

14. ɔsɔ ose yo!
    Welcome!

15. tɨrɔ ose yo!
    Come in!

16. andžɨse yo.
    Please take a seat; please sit down.

17. šilʸle[h]amnida.
    Excuse me (for what I am doing).

    šilʸle[h]æssɨmnida.
    Excuse me (for what I did).

    šilʸle[h]agessɨmnida.
    Excuse me (for what I'm about to do).

18. mian[h]amnida. or čwesoŋ[h]amnida.
    I'm sorry or *Excuse me.*

19. anio, kwænčʰana yo.
    Not at all; it's all right.

20. yɔbose yo!
    Hello! or *Hey there!*

21. šigani ta d[w]essɨmnida.
    It's time (to begin or stop).

22. tto b[w]a yo.
    See you later!

23. kɨræ yo?
    Is that so? Really?

    kɨræ yo.
    That's so. Really.

Guide to the Phonetic Transcription System
in Lessons One to Four

Phonetic Symbol	Approximate Sound Value
a	*a* as in father
æ	*a* as in bat
č	relaxed *ch* as in chill
čʰ	aspirated *ch* as in chop!
čč	tense *tch* as in matchmaker
dž	*dg* as in edge
e	*e* as in bet
ɨ	*u* as in pull but without lip rounding
i	*ee* as in feet
h	*h* as in hope
k	relaxed *k* as in kitten
kʰ	aspirated *k* as in kill!
kk	tense *k* as in skill
l	*l* as in lamp
lʸ	soft *l* as in eel
m	*m* as in mom
n	*n* as in nice
ŋ	*ng* as in sing
o	*o* as in poke with lip rounding
ɔ	*aw* as in thaw or *uh* as in uh-oh
p	relaxed *p* as in park
pʰ	aspirated *p* as in pow!
pp	tense *p* as in spa
s	*s* as in sigh
ss	tense *s* as in stop
š	*sh* as in sheet
t	relaxed *t* as in tall
tʰ	aspirated *t* as in talk!
tt	tense *t* as in star
u	*oo* as in boot with lip rounding
w	*w* as in wide
y	*y* as in yard

Lesson Notes

1.1. Styles of Speech

Korean is characterized by an intricate system of social styles; you have just had a glimpse of the system in the basic expressions. This characteristic is so pervasive that it is impossible to speak more than a few connected words in Korean without becoming involved with HONORIFICS and politeness; yet, there is nothing in English which corresponds to it. Of course, in English there are also times when we select different speaking styles to suit the social setting. Compare, for example, the impersonal or official-sounding *What is your native country?* and the conversational *Where are you from?* To attract someone's attention, we might say under certain circumstances *Pardon me, Sir!* and under certain others *Hey you!* However, in the Korean language these speaking styles are more formally codified. **Every** Korean sentence can be adjusted to each of several hierarchical styles in a regular and systematic way. This is done chiefly by changing the endings on the verbs. Occasionally, stylistic implications in Korean are conveyed in the vocabulary itself: two words denoting the same thing differ in social connotations. For the most part, however, the style factors appear not in the words themselves but in verb endings.

Two considerations are significant in the Korean speech styles:

When talking *to* a person:
> Words have different endings attached to them, determined by the social relationship between the speakers.

When talking *about* a person:
> Words and parts of words are changed to their Honorific form to show special respect to the person discussed. Honorific forms are never used by the speaker to refer to himself or herself.

The following chart presents the major styles you will be learning in *Elementary Korean*:

Major Speech Styles in this Book

	(Regular)	Honorific
Polite	해요	하세요
Formal	합니다	하십니다

Most of the basic expressions of this lesson are in the Honorific Polite 하세요 (haseyo) style, but a few of the more stylized greetings and expressions are in the Formal 합니다 (hamnida) style. Most of the Korean you will learn in this course will be in the Polite 해요 (hǽyo), Honorific Polite 하세요 (haseyo), Formal 합니다 (hamnida) or Honorific Formal 하십니다 (hašimnida) styles, the most useful styles for everyday conversation.

1.2. Word Classes

Korean words, like those of every other language, fall into several different kinds or classes; the words are classified according to the way they are used in sentences.

Korean VERBS (the words at the **end** of nearly every basic sentence in this lesson) are INFLECTED WORDS: they consist of a basic part, the BASE, to which various ENDINGS are attached in order to make them mean different things. For example, we have already had the following three sentences:

24. 실례합니다. *Excuse me* (for what I am doing).
    šil^yle[h]amnida

    실례했습니다. *Excuse me* (for what I did).
    šil^yle[h]æssɨmnida

    실례하겠습니다. *Excuse me* (for what I'm about to do).
    šil^yle[h]agessɨmnida

The verb in each case is the same. Here, it means *do*, and its basic part is 하- [ha-]. Only the endings are different, and it is these that give the changes in meaning.

Here are a few sentences of another kind (you are not meant to learn those you haven't seen—just look at them).

25.   용서하세요   *Please forgive me.*
       yoŋsɔhaseyo.

26.   안녕히 가세요   *Good-bye (Go in peace).*
       annyɔŋ[h]i gase yo

27.   안녕히 계세요   *Good-bye (Stay in peace).*
       annyɔŋ[h]i gese yo.

28.   책을 보세요   *Please look at your books.*
       čʰægɨl bose yo.

These sentences all have different verbs, but the verbs all end the same way: –세요 [-seyo]. This ending (a combination of suffixes) makes each verb express a polite request.

Korean NOUNS, on the other hand, are not inflected; they can be used with no endings attached to them. Instead, PARTICLES are optionally added to show the relationship between the noun and the rest of the sentence, much as prepositions are used in English. The great majority of Korean nouns correspond to English words which are also nouns, e.g. 책 [čʰæk] *book*, 질문 [čilmun] *question*, 영어 [yɔŋɔ] *English*, etc. This is not always the case, however!

As a vocabulary item, 책 [čʰæk] means *book*. In sentences, however, we translate it variously: *book, a book, the book, some books, any books, the books,* and *books*. This is another way of saying that Korean has no words corresponding to *a(n)*, *the*, *some*, *any*, and that Korean nouns may have a plural meaning without any explicit sign that they are plural. To be sure, it is possible to make Korean nouns unambiguously plural, as we will learn later, but it is not imperative to do so, as it is imperative with most English nouns. In English, *book*, for example, is specifically singular; whereas, *books* is specifically plural. This rule applies every time they are used.

Exercises

Exercise 1: English Equivalents

Give English translations of the following Korean sentences, and practice them until you recognize them and can pronounce them fluently.

1. 그래요?
2. 고맙습니다.
3. 또 뵙겠습니다.
4. 김 선생님, 안녕하세요?
5. 수고하십니다.
6. 만나서 반갑습니다.
7. 여보세요!
8. 실례했습니다.
9. 처음 뵙겠습니다.
10. 들어오세요!

Exercise 2: Korean Equivalents

Give the Korean equivalents of the following English sentences. You may like to do this as a written drill when you have learned the alphabet, but you should also do it orally, as fast as you can.

1. Pleased to meet you!
2. Well done! (Thanks for doing such a good job.)
3. How are you, Mr. Lee?
4. Welcome!
5. Don't mention it!
6. It's time to stop.
7. See you later.
8. Do excuse me!
9. Good-bye. (As you are leaving, to someone staying behind.)
10. Good-bye. (To someone who is working.)

Exercise 3: How Do You Respond?

Picture yourself in the following situations. What would be the correct response to make, in Korean?

1. Someone crashes into you in the supermarket and apologizes profusely.
2. The phone rings. You pick it up.
3. Your boss introduces you to a friend of his whom you have not met.
4. What might the friend respond?
5. You are told some unusual news. How might you express your surprise?
6. You meet a friend in the street and wonder if she is well.
7. Someone visits your house, and you tell them to come in and sit down. How do you say that?
8. Class is nearly over, but your teacher seems oblivious to the time. What could you say to him?
9. You cut across the view of several Koreans watching television on your way through a room.
10. Someone gives you flowers.
11. You are asked whether or not you are married. Say *yes* or *no*, as appropriate.
12. You arrive late for an appointment. (Find a different expression to the one you used for number 9.)
13. Your friend leaves your house. Say good-bye to him.
14. What other expression might you have used?
15. If he were someone with whom you were on formal terms, how might you have said good-bye?

Lesson 2

In Lesson Two we have the second set of Basic Expressions, most of which would be used in the classroom. In the Lesson Notes you will find out more about the characteristics of Korean sentences, plus there is a section on Korean names. The exercises cover both Lesson One and Lesson Two. Once again, the key expressions are given in the Korean script, then again in romanized transcription to help you memorize them.

Basic Expressions II: Korean Script

	Korean	English
1.	하나 둘 셋 넷 다섯	1, 2, 3, 4, 5
	여섯 일곱 여덟 아홉 열	6, 7, 8, 9, 10

Note: 여덟 *eight* is actually pronounced 여덜.

2.	시작할까요?	*Shall we start?*

3.	시작합시다.	*Let's begin.* (teacher to students)

4.	책을 보세요.	*Please look at your books.*

Explanation: 책 *book(s)*; 책을 *book(s)* (as direct object); 보세요 *please look* (at it).

5.	첫 페이지를 보세요.	*Please look at the first page.*

Explanation: 첫 *the first*; 페이지 *page*; 보세요 *please look* (at it).

6.	책을 보지 마세요.	*Please don't look at your books.*

7.	다음 페이지를 보세요.	*Please look at the next page.*

8. 듣기만 하세요.   *Just listen, please.*

Explanation: 듣기 the act of *listening*; 듣기만 *only listening*; 하세요 *please do it.*

9. 따라 하세요.   *Please repeat (after me).*

Explanation: 따라 *following, repeating* 하세요 *please do, please say.*

10. 다 같이.   *All together.*

Explanation: 다 *all; everyone;* 같이 *togethe*r (pronounced 가치)

11. 다시 한번.   *One more time.*

Explanation: 다시 *again, once more;* 한번 *once, one time*

12. 대답하세요.   *Please answer.*

13. 말하세요.   *Please say it* or *Please talk.*

Explanation: 말 *language, word(s), speech, talking*; 말(을) 하세요 *please speak; please say it.* 말씀하세요 is even more polite.

14. 다시 말씀해 주세요.   *Please say it for me again. Please repeat.*

Explanation: 다시 *again, once more;* 해주세요 *Please favor me by doing it, i.e., Please do it for me.*

15. 크게 말씀해 주세요.   *Please say it loudly.*

Explanation: 크게 *so that it is big; loudly.*

16. 천천히 말씀하세요.   *Please say it slowly.*

17. 한국말로 하세요.   *Please say it in Korean.*

Explanation: 한국말로 *in Korean;* 하세요 *Please say it.*

18. 영어로 하지 마세요.   *Please don't say it in English.*

Explanation: 영어로 *in English;* 하지 마세요 *Please do not do it.*

19. 알겠어요?   *Do you understand?*

Literally: *Will you know? Might you know? Would you know?*

20. (네) 알겠어요.   *(Yes,) I understand.*

Literally: *I will know. I would know. I'll probably get it.*

21. 아니오, 모르겠어요.　　　　*No, I don't understand.*

　　　Literally: *I don't or wouldn't know.*

22. 질문 있어요?　　　　*Any questions?*

　　　Explanation: 있어요? *Does there exist . . . ?* or *Do we/you have . . . ?* 질문 *question*

23. 네. 있어요.　　　　*Yes, I have (a question).*
　　　　　　　　　　　　Yes, there are.

24. 아니오. 없어요.　　　　*No, I haven't.*

　　　Explanation: 없어요 *There does not exist* or *I/we/one does not have.*

25. 십분만 쉽시다.　　　　*Let's rest for ten minutes.*

　　　Explanation: 십 *ten* (a different word, but with the same meaning as 열); 분 *minute*; 십분
　　　10 minutes; 십분만 *(to the extent of) 10 minutes*; *ten minutes (only)*; 쉽시다 *Let's rest.*

26. 늦어서 죄송합니다.　　　　*Sorry I'm late.*

　　　Explanation: 늦어서 *I am late, and so . . . Because I am late, . . .*

Basic Expressions II: Transcription

1. hana, tul^y, set, net, tasɔt
　　1, 2, 3, 4, 5

　　yɔsɔt, il^ygop, yɔdɔl^y, ahop, yɔl^y
　　6, 7, 8, 9, 10

2. šidžak hal^ykka yo?
　　Shall we start?

3. šidžak hapššida.
　　Let's begin.

4. čʰægɨl bose yo.
　　Please look at your books.

5. čʰɔp pʰeidžirɨl bose yo.
    Please look at the first page.

6. čʰægɨl bodži mase yo.
    Please don't look at your books.

7. taɨm pʰeidžirɨl bose yo.
    Please look at the next page.

8. tɨkki man hase yo.
    Just listen, please.

9. ttara hase yo.
    Please repeat.

10. ta gačʰi.
    All together.

11. taši hanbɔn.
    One more time.

12. tædap hase yo.
    Please answer

13. mar[h]ase yo.
    Please say it.

14. taši malʸssɨm[h]ædžuse yo.
    Please say it for me again.

15. kʰɨge malʸssɨm[h]ædžuse yo.
    Please say it loudly.

16. čʰɔnčʰɔn[h]i malʸssɨm[h]ase yo.
    Please say it slowly.

17. hanguŋmalʸlo hase yo.
    Please say it in Korean.

18. yɔŋoro hadži mase yo.
    Please don't say it in English.

19. alʸgessɔ yo?
    Do you understand.

20. [ne] alʸgessɔ yo.
    Yes, I understand.

21. anio, morɨgessɔ yo.
     No, I don't understand.

22. čilʸmun issɔ yo?
     Any questions?

23. ne, issɔ yo.
     Yes, I have (a question).

24. anio, ɔpsɔ yo.
     No, I haven't.

25. šippun man šwipššida.
     Let's rest for ten minutes.

26. nɨdžɔsɔ čwesoŋ[h]amnida.
     Sorry I'm late.

Lesson Notes

2.1. Korean Sentence Patterns

The basic sentences of Lessons One and Two give you an opportunity to observe, over and over, a basic characteristic of Korean sentences: the verb expression comes at the end. This means, of course, that in a great many cases the order of things in a Korean sentence is different from the English order. Translated directly, Sentence Twenty-one of Lesson One, for example, 시간이 다 됐습니다 is *The time all has-become;* Sentence Fourteen of this lesson, 다시 말씀해 주세요 is *Once again saying-please give* and so on.

In Korean sentences, the order of the various parts is determined not by grammatical function, as it is in English, but by importance: the closer a word is to the end of a Korean sentence, the more important it is. At the very end comes the one element that is indispensable: the verb. Many Korean sentences contain nothing but a verb.

먹었어요.   *I've eaten.*
mɔgɔssɔyo

This verb says in a formal way that someone *ate*, past tense; that is all it specifies. But the sentence is grammatically complete. It would not be wrong to add a subject and/or an object, but it would be superfluous.

Aside from commands, it is a rare English sentence that has no subject. Telegram, postcard, or diary style are special cases: *Arrive 9 a.m. Monday. Will bring George. Saw a movie last night. Having a wonderful time.* Even commands not uncommonly have subjects: *You stop that! You boys get out of here!*

As a general rule, the nearer a word or phrase appears to the beginning of a Korean sentence, the less essential it is—the more readily expendable. The order of such elements as subject, object, time, place, is determined by the emphasis assigned to each; and one thing that makes them less necessary is earlier mention in a context.

A conversation beginning with a sentence like *John bought a new suit* could continue in Korean without further mention of either *John* or *the suit*. Notice that in English both of these must reappear, as pronouns if not in their original form: *When did **he** buy **it**?* The Korean equivalent could say simply *When bought?* and still be complete.

In other words, old information, if repeated at all, comes at or near the beginning of a Korean sentence, while newly supplied information clusters near the verb. If subject and object both offer new information, the object is more likely to come next to the verb.

2.2. Korean Names

In Sentence Three of Lesson One you saw the expression 김 선생님 [kim sɔnsæŋnim] *Mr. Kim.* This illustrates another difference in English and Korean word order: the title is used **after** the name.

김 [kim] *Kim* is a family name. As a general pattern, a Korean has two names: first of all the family name, then this is followed by a personal or given name. Most of the family names have one syllable, though there are some which have two: for example, 황보 [hwaŋbo], 독고 [tokko]. If the family name has one syllable, the personal name most commonly has two: 이승만 [isɨŋman] *Syngman Rhee,* 김일성 [kimilsɔŋ] *Ilsung Kim.* If the family name has two syllables, the personal name has only one, so that either way there are usually three syllables in the full name. There are exceptions to this pattern, and a number of Korean names have only two syllables: for example, 허웅 [houŋ], 백철 [pækčʰɔl], 김구 [kimgu] etc. The following table shows some common Korean surnames:

김	이	박	최	장	남
kim	i	pak	čʰwe	čaŋ	nam

홍	허	서	배	조	노
hoŋ	hɔ	sɔ	pæ	čo	no

정	전	임	오	강	안
čɔŋ	čɔn	im	o	kaŋ	an

한	심	윤	송	신	문
han	šim	yun	soŋ	šin	mun

It is often possible to guess the gender of person on the basis of the syllables used in their given name. Some syllables tend to occur only in males' names, others only in females' names.

Syllables used typically in names for males: 철 [čʰɔl], 호 [ho], 태 [tʰæ], 석 [sɔk], 준 [čun], 훈 [hun], 섭 [sɔp], 식 [šik], 범 [pɔm]. For example:

철민	철수	진호	철호
čʰɔlmin	čʰɔlsu	činho	čʰɔrho

호철	석헌	홍석	석준
hočʰɔl	sɔkhɔn	hoŋsɔk	sɔkčun

혁준	태경	재훈	정호
hyɔkčun	tʰægyɔŋ	čæhun	čɔŋho

태호	춘섭	익섭	규식
tʰæho	čʰunsɔp	iksɔp	kyušik

Syllables used typically in names for females: 미 [mi], 희 [hɨy], 나 [na], 애 [æ], 자 [ča], 혜 [he], 선 [sɔn], 경 [kyɔŋ], 숙 [suk] . For example:

수미	미나	경애	승자
sumi	mina	kyɔŋæ	sɨŋdža

진희	희정	민희	정희
činhɨy	hɨydžɔŋ	minhɨy	čɔŋhɨy

경자	미경	은미	혜경
kyoŋdža	migyoŋ	ɨnmi	hegyoŋ

경숙	미선	지선	윤미
kyoŋsuk	mison	čison	yunmi

This is only a general rule of thumb. Some syllables (like 희 [hɨy]) can occur in both male and female names.

A title always comes at the very end, and can be used with a full name (surname plus given name) or just a given name, in the case of 씨, or with full name or just surname, in the case of 선생님.

김복동 씨
kimboktoŋ šši

Poktong Kim (a male's name), or

복동 씨
poktoŋ šši

장진희 씨
čaŋdžinhɨy šši

Chinhee Chang (a female's name), or

진희 씨
činhɨy šši

김복동 선생님
kimboktoŋsonsæŋnim

Mr. Poktong Kim (Honorific)

김 선생님
kim sonsæŋnim

Mr. Kim (Honorific)

Unless you are on intimate terms with somebody, it is usual to refer to that person in Korean by their name plus a title. One of the most commonly used titles is the little word 씨, which comes after a person's full name, or just after the given name. This is the title you should use when referring to your peers.

When talking to, or about, children, it is customary to attach the diminutive suffix -이 [i] to given names ending in a consonant. Thus, if 김복동 [kimboktoŋ] is a small boy, you would refer to him as just 복동이 [poktoŋi], without a title. If the child's name ends in a vowel, as in the girl's name 진희 [činhɨy], it simply stays the same. No diminutive suffix is added.

선생 [sɔnsæŋ] is a word that, on its own, means *teacher*. With the honorific particle 님 [nim] after it, it functions as a title of respect honoring the person whose name it accompanies. You should use this title with the names of people to whom you wish to show courtesy. You should **not** use it with your own name. When you introduce yourself, for example, simply give your name *My name is Adams* or *I'm Helen Baker* with no title. 님 [nim] is an honorific suffix which you can add to titles (but not to 씨 [šši]) to show an added degree of respect or deference. Nowadays, Koreans seem to use 선생님 [sɔnsæŋnim] more than plain 선생 [sɔnsæŋ].

When otherwise unspecified, the title 선생님 [= sɔnsæŋnim] is usually translated *Mr.*, but sometimes the context tells you that *Mrs.* or *Miss* would be more appropriate. To say specifically *Mrs.* or *Miss* you have to say something like *Mr. Kim's wife* 김 선생님 부인 [kim sɔnsæŋnim buin] or *Mr. Kim's daughter* 김 선생님 딸 [kim sɔnsæŋnim ttal], or else you can simply do it in English 미세스 김 [misesɨgim], 미스 김 [misɨgim]. If the Kims are parents, an informal way of saying *Mrs. Kim* is to refer to her as the eldest child's mother, e.g., 복동이 어머니 [poktoŋi ɔmɔni] *Mrs. Kim (who is Poktong-i's mother)*, and similarly *Mr. Kim* may be referred to as 복동이 아버지 [poktoŋi abɔdži] *Mr. Kim (who is Poktong-i's father)*. Foreigners sometimes mistranslate *Mrs. Kim* as 김부인 [kimbuin] rather than 김 선생님 부인 [kim sɔnsæŋnim buin]. In Seoul you will often hear 사모님 [samonim] used for *Mrs.* or *Madam* (instead of so-and-so 선생님 부인). 사모 [samo] is an elegant word that originally means *one's teacher's wife*, but it can be used to refer to the wife of your superior or of any prominent man. The usual way for you to refer to your teacher's wife is 사모님 [samonim].

There are a number of ways to say *you* in Korean, and the most polite way is by using a title or name plus title. As your study of the language proceeds, you will notice that Korean is in many respects less direct than English. Sentence Three of Lesson One (김 선생님 안녕 하세요?) is an example of such indirectness; it seems to say *How is Mr. Kim?*, but it means *How are you, Mr. Kim?*

주의! *Caution!*

While it is acceptable to use either the Western order or the Korean order when giving a Western name, you should always use the Korean order with Korean names, e.g.,
애니 스미스입니다 or 스미스 애니입니다 *I'm Annie Smith,*
but only
김복동입니다 *I'm Poktong Kim.*

Exercises

Exercise 1: Practicing Responses

Which response(s) are appropriate to the sentence given? First read aloud the sentence itself, then all the responses given. Finally, read the initial question or sentence along with the correct response(s) and translate.

1. 안녕하세요?
   a. 네, 안녕하세요.
   b. 괜찮아요.
   c. 천만에요.

2. 처음 뵙겠습니다.
   a. 실례합니다.
   b. 만나서 반갑습니다.
   c. 미안합니다.

3. 미안합니다.
   a. 들어 오세요.
   b. 수고하세요.
   c. 아니오, 괜찮아요.

4. 고맙습니다.
   a. 네.
   b. 천만에요.
   c. 또 만나요.

5. 안녕히 가세요!
   a. 안녕히 가세요!
   b. 안녕히 계세요!
   c. 또 뵙겠습니다.

6. 질문 있어요?
   a. 없어요.
   b. 있어요.
   c. 다시 말해 주세요.

7. 알겠어요?
   a. 네, 알겠어요.
   b. 아니오, 모르겠어요.
   c. 네, 있어요.

8. 시작할까요?
   a. 시작합시다!
   b. 괜찮습니다.
   c. 시간이 다 됐습니다.

9.   실례했습니다.

　　　a.　　미안합니다.

　　　b.　　아니오, 괜찮아요.

　　　c.　　천만에요.

10.　수고하셨어요.

　　　a.　　천천히 말하세요.

　　　b.　　천만에요.

　　　c.　　시간이 다
　　　　　　됐습니다.

Exercise 2: Match the Appropriate Response

Match each sentence in the left-hand column with an appropriate response from the right-hand column. You may use some responses more than once; others not at all.

1.	고맙습니다.	a.	안녕히 가세요!
2.	안녕하세요?	b.	네, 있어요.
3.	질문있어요?	c.	아니오, 괜찮아요.
4.	실례했습니다.	d.	천만에요.
5.	알겠어요?	e.	네, 고맙습니다.
6.	그래요?	f.	네, 그래요.
7.	안녕히 계세요.	g.	모르겠어요.
8.	미안합니다.	h.	네, 안녕하세요?
9.	실례했습니다.	i.	네, 알겠어요.

Exercise 3: Remember the Korean Equivalent

Give the Korean equivalents of the following English expressions.

1.	Shall we start?	2.	Excuse me.
3.	Yes, let's begin.	4.	All together. Please say it in Korean.
5.	Do you have any questions?	6.	Please don't look at your books.
7.	Could you repeat, please?	8.	Say it loudly, please.
9.	Please answer. Do you understand?	10.	Please look at the next page.
11.	Please speak slowly.	12.	I don't understand.
13.	Yes, I understand.	14.	Really?

15.	Let's rest for ten minutes.	16.	Please don't talk in English.
17.	1, 2, 3, 4, 5, 6, 7, 8, 9, 10	18.	Let's rest for ten minutes (again!).
19.	Just listen, please.	20.	I'm sorry I'm late.
21.	Please look at the first page.	22.	Please repeat after me.
23.	Thank you.	24.	Good-bye!

Exercise 4: Practice with Korean Names

Practice reading the following Korean names. Can you guess whether the person is male or female?

1. 김정호	2. 이석헌	3. 박은미	4. 최홍석
5. 장혜경	6. 남경자	7. 홍진호	8. 허미선
9. 서지선	10. 배경희	11. 조철민	12. 노호철
13. 정재훈	14. 임석준	15. 오경애	16. 강승자
17. 안철호	18. 한수미	19. 심진희	20. 윤철수

Exercise 5: Vocabulary Drill

The vocabulary items you have learned at this point are not easy to separate from the short sentences in which they appear. One way you can drill yourself on the words is to make use of a technique that will be valuable throughout the lessons.

After you have completed the job of memorizing the basic sentences, copy each one on a 3-by-5-inch index card or slip of paper. Write the Korean on one side, the English on the other, with one sentence to a card. Shuffle the cards thoroughly, arranging them so that you see only the Korean side. Run through them as rapidly as you can, reading aloud the Korean and immediately calling off the English equivalent.

Reshuffle and repeat, looking only at the English. See whether the Korean comes instantly to your mind. By this method, you can be the judge of whether you have completed your work on Lessons One and Two.

Lesson 3

Korean Writing and Basic Pronunciation

By the time you reach this lesson, it is time to learn the Korean writing system. This section is not intended as a complete training course on writing with the Korean alphabet, but the lesson gives you important information about Korean pronunciation and the way in which the written signs are tied to the spoken sounds. It is important that you take pronunciation seriously. Your aim should ultimately be to sound like a native Korean speaker. Good pronunciation of Korean is difficult, but the rules formulated in this and the following lesson should help you a great deal throughout your Korean studies, if you take time to learn them properly. The rules are demonstrated by Korean words, most of which you won't have seen before. You are not intended to learn all these off by heart; they are there merely to illustrate the different sounds of Korean. In the exercises there is plenty of practice with both writing and pronunciation.

한글 The Korean Writing System

Han'gŭl, the Korean writing system (한글 in Korean), is one of the most scientifically designed and efficient scripts in the world. Promulgated in 1446 by the sage King Sejong 세종 under the title Hunmin Chŏng'ŭm 훈민정음 (meaning The Correct Sounds for the Instruction of the People), han'gŭl was the product of deliberate, linguistically informed planning. The Korean script is remarkably original and has resisted all attempts to prove its relationship to this or that other system of writing.

As you will soon see, Han'gŭl is also quite easy to learn; the Korean language, on the other hand, is quite difficult. We have so far avoided the term *alphabet*. Han'gŭl is usually referred to as an alphabet, and that it is, but with one special quirk: rather than arranging its letters in a row from left-to-right and writing on-line, e.g., ㅎㅏㄴㄱㅡㄹ for han'gŭl, han'gŭl has always written Korean words in syllable blocks 한글.

Now let us look at the letter shapes that comprise the alphabet and learn how to pronounce Korean. To the left of each of the letters we have given an English sound approximation. This is not intended as a rigorous romanization system, but merely as a rough equivalent in English of the Korean letter. Always imitate your Korean instructor.

The Vowels

Korean has the following vowel signs.

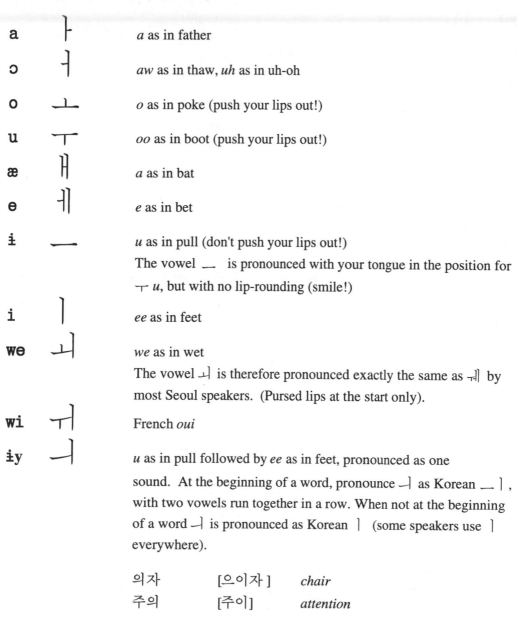

a ㅏ   *a* as in father

ɔ ㅓ   *aw* as in thaw, *uh* as in uh-oh

o ㅗ   *o* as in poke (push your lips out!)

u ㅜ   *oo* as in boot (push your lips out!)

æ ㅐ   *a* as in bat

e ㅔ   *e* as in bet

ɨ ㅡ   *u* as in pull (don't push your lips out!)
The vowel ㅡ is pronounced with your tongue in the position for ㅜ *u*, but with no lip-rounding (smile!)

i ㅣ   *ee* as in feet

we ㅚ   *we* as in wet
The vowel ㅚ is therefore pronounced exactly the same as ㅔ by most Seoul speakers. (Pursed lips at the start only).

wi ㅟ   French *oui*

ɨy ㅢ   *u* as in pull followed by *ee* as in feet, pronounced as one sound. At the beginning of a word, pronounce ㅢ as Korean ㅡㅣ, with two vowels run together in a row. When not at the beginning of a word ㅢ is pronounced as Korean ㅣ (some speakers use ㅣ everywhere).

의자   [으이자]   *chair*
주의   [주이]   *attention*

By adding a stroke to the first six vowel signs above, the Koreans produced the combination *y* plus VOWEL. For example, ℮ (as in get) becomes y℮ (as in yes).

ya	ㅑ	*ya* as in yard
yɔ	ㅕ	*yo* as in yonder
yo	ㅛ	*yo* as in yoga (push your lips out!)
yu	ㅠ	*yu* as in yuletide (push your lips out!)
yæ	ㅒ	*ya* as in yap or Yankie
y℮	ㅖ	*ye* as in yep

Finally, the following combinations give *w* plus VOWEL.

wa	ㅘ	the first vowel sound of wide or wow
wɔ	ㅝ	*wo* of wonder
wæ	ㅙ	*wa* of wax
w℮	ㅞ	*we* of wet (that is, it has the same pronunciation as ㅚ above)

This concludes all the vowel sounds possible in Korean.

Any written syllable in 한글 (han'gŭl) must begin with a consonant sign. In order for these vocalic signs to form the nucleus of a syllable (remember that the Koreans write in syllable blocks), they must attach to the side of or below a consonant sign. This means that even when the syllable contains no spoken consonants (when it begins with a vowel in pronunciation), you still have to start the syllable with the little circle ㅇ representing a zero consonant.

To put it another way, when a spoken syllable begins with any of the vowel sounds above, Han'gŭl treats the initial consonant as a zero and writes it as such.

a 아 wa 와 ya 야

The Consonants

We begin by continuing to look at the ○ symbol. This zero sign has a clever alter ego: whereas at the beginning of a syllable (before a vowel) it functions as **zero** (telling the reader "Don't pronounce me!"), at the end of a syllable it represents the sound *ng* as in English <u>singer</u>. When it is not zero (before a vowel sound) this sound is always as *ng* in English <u>sing</u>, never as in <u>finger</u> (<u>fing-ger</u>). E.g.,

oŋ   옹   aŋ   앙

Since Korean has no basic syllables of the type ŋ plus VOWEL (ŋa, ŋu, etc.), this is quite a clever economy and one good example of the ingenuity of Han'gŭl.

Now look at the rest of the consonants.

p	ㅂ	*p* as in park, but relaxed
pʰ	ㅍ	*p* as in pow! with lots of aspiration (air)
pp	ㅃ	*p* as in spa, tense, tight, no aspiration
t	ㄷ	*t* as in tall, but relaxed
tʰ	ㅌ	*t* as in talk! with lots of aspiration
tt	ㄸ	*t* as in star, tense, tight, no aspiration
k	ㄱ	*k* as in kiss, but relaxed
kʰ	ㅋ	*k* as in kill! with lots of aspiration
kk	ㄲ	*k* as in skill, tense, tight, no aspiration
č	ㅈ	*ch* as in chill, but relaxed
čʰ	ㅊ	*ch* as in change! with lots of aspiration
čč	ㅉ	*tch* as in matchmaker, tense, tight, no aspiration
m	ㅁ	*m* as in mother

The sounds n, l, h, s and ss require a bit more explanation and a bit more care in learning to pronounce them.

n   **ㄴ**   *n* as in no

For ㄴ *n* the tongue tip touches the upper teeth, as in most continental European languages. Be sure to make your double *nn* and double *mm* double!

몸	*body*	논	*paddy field*
아마	*perhaps*	아니	*no*
삼만	*thirty thousand*	언니	*older sister of a female*

l   **ㄹ**   *l* as in lamp and feel or *r* as in Spanish

The Korean consonant ㄹ will sound different to you in different environments.

a)   At the beginning of a syllable (in foreign words only), it is rolled like Japanese or Spanish *r*.

    라디오   *radio*

b)   Between vowels (including *w/y* plus vowel) or vowel and *h* (which often drops), it is also rolled (like the Spanish *r*).

아래	a-ræ	*below*
일원	i-rwɔn	*one wǒn* (Korean currency)
설화	sɔr[h]wa	*tale, legend*

c)   When double, make a **long**, and somewhat soft *l*.

몰라요	*I don't know*
실례 〔실레〕	*discourtesy*

d)   When before a consonant, or final before a pause, you will hear a clear, soft *l* as in English <u>feel</u>.

물	*water*
실망	*disappointment*

h **ㅎ**   *h* as in hope

    a.   An initial *h* is made with friction in the throat, as when blowing to steam up glasses.

        하나   *one*

    b.   But before *y* or *i*, the friction may be between the middle front of the tongue and the hard palate, giving a soft sound close to the German *ich*.

        혀   *tongue*

        힘   *strength*

    c.   And between voiced sounds (*m*, *n*, *l* and vowels) the *h* is weak, and often drops, especially when preceded by ŋ (the *ng* sound in *singer*) or *n* and followed by *i* or *y*.

시험	〔시험 or 시엄〕	*examination*
안녕히	〔안녕이〕	*in good health*
많이	〔마니〕	*much, lots*
전혀	〔저녀〕	*[not] at all*

s **ㅅ**   *s* as in soul, but relaxed and somewhat weak.

ss **ㅆ**   *s* as in soul (but more tense and tighter than the single *s*)

    a.   The single ㅅ is very weak, something less than an English *s*, and often followed by a little puff of local air. You should practice trying to make your Korean ㅅ breathy. The double ㅆ is very strong, something more than an English *s*, with tension in the throat and tongue.

        살   *flesh*

        쌀   *hulled rice*

    b.   Before 이 and 위, most speakers change the *s* to a soft *sh*. Some speakers do this also for the tense *ss*.

        시   *poem*

        씨   *seed*

        쉽시다   *let's rest*

More on the Three-way Consonants

As you have seen above, for the sounds like p, t, k, č, Korean exploits a three-way contrast based on aspiration and tenseness where English exploits just a two-way contrast based on voicing. That is, where English has just *pig/big*, *tug/dug*, *kit/git*, *choke/joke*, Korean has three types of consonants in each position. The question of voiced/voiceless (English *p* vs. *b*, *t* vs. *d*, *k* vs. *g* and *ch* vs. *j*) is irrelevant to Korean: it is not distinctive.

The basic series in Korean is:

p   ㅂ   t   ㄷ   k   ㄱ   č   ㅈ

By doubling each of these consonants, the Koreans write the tense, unaspirated series:

pp   ㅃ   tt   ㄸ   kk   ㄲ   čč   ㅉ

The best way to master their pronunciation is to start off pronouncing an s-cluster, e.g., spa, and then suppress the *s*. Alternatively, it is useful to fake a French or Spanish accent when pronouncing these: French and Spanish *p*, *t*, *k* are much less aspirated than in English.

Next, by adding a stroke to the basic plain series, the Koreans write their lax, aspirated series:

p^h   ㅍ   t^h   ㅌ   k^h   ㅋ   č^h   ㅊ

These sound like English **p**ike, **t**ake, **k**ite, **ch**eat, but with more aspiration than in English. If you hold a piece of paper three inches from your mouth, it should jump away when you pronounce the aspirated sounds. On the other hand, if you hold a piece of paper three inches from your mouth and pronounce the tense, unaspirated (double) sounds, the paper should not move at all. When you pronounce plain p, t, k, č, the piece of paper should move slightly, but not nearly as much as with the aspirated sounds. It is useful to practice producing these consonants one after the other, with one of each three types.

We can now draw out the comparison between the three different types of consonants for each one in turn.

Three kinds of initial *p*:

Lax	Lax Aspirated	Tense Unaspirated
불 *fire*	풀 *grass*	뿔 *horn*

Three kinds of initial *t*: (Tongue tip touches upper teeth!)

Lax	Lax Aspirated	Tense Unaspirated
달 *moon*	탈 *mask*	딸 *daughter*

Three kinds of initial *k*:

Lax	Lax Aspirated	Tense Unaspirated
개 *dog*	캐 *digs out*	깨 *sesame*

Three kinds of initial *č*:

Lax	Lax Aspirated	Tense Unaspirated
자요 *sleeps*	차요 *is cold*	짜요 *is salty*

The Alphabet in a Dictionary

Korean dictionaries employ a bewildering variety of han'gŭl alphabetizations. However, they can be divided into two broad types. The first is most common in South Korea, the second is official in North Korea. The South Korean dictionaries imbed all the vowel signs under the letter ㅇ ;whereas, the North Korean dictionaries relegate the letter ㅇ in its zero reading (i.e., preceding vowels) to the back of the dictionary. In the early stages of your course you will not need to consult a dictionary often, but later you will. do so considerably. You will probably want to refer to this section at a later stage.

1. Republic of Korea (South Korea)

(Read from left to right.)

Consonant Order

k ㄱ   (kk ㄲ)   n ㄴ   t ㄷ   (tt ㄸ)

l ㄹ   m ㅁ   p ㅂ   (pp ㅃ)   s ㅅ

(ss ㅆ) ∅-/ŋ ㅇ   č ㅈ   (čč ㅉ)   čʰ ㅊ

kʰ ㅋ   tʰ ㅌ   pʰ ㅍ   h ㅎ

Note: For an explanation of the letters in parentheses, see the next page.

Vowel Order (within the zero consonant sign ∅-/-ŋ ㅇ)

a 아   æ 애   ya 야   yæ 얘

ɔ 어   e 에   yɔ 여   ye 예

o 오   wa 와   wæ 왜   we 외   yo 요

u 우   wɔ 워   we 웨   wi 위   yu 유

ɨ 으   ɨy 의   i 이

There are three variations on the South Korean ordering:

1.   Ignore double consonants except where entries are otherwise the same.

2.   Ignore double consonants except where entries are otherwise the same, but keep a difference for final double consonants analogous to that of the singlets:

k	ㄱ	kk	ㄲ	ks	ㄳ	n	ㄴ	nč	ㄵ
l	ㄹ	lk	ㄺ	lm	ㄻ	lp	ㄼ	ls	ㄽ
lth	ㄾ	lph	ㄿ	lh	ㅀ	p	ㅂ	ps	ㅄ
s	ㅅ	ss	ㅆ						

3.   Recognize double consonants both initially and finally, making separate places for the initial double consonants (as in parentheses on the preceding page), and keeping the final double consonants in the order shown in item two.

2 Democratic People's Republic of Korea (North Korea)

In North Korea, the doubled consonants and all the vowel signs are placed at the back of the dictionary:

Consonant Order

k	ㄱ	n	ㄴ	t	ㄷ	l	ㄹ		
m	ㅁ	p	ㅂ	s	ㅅ	-ŋ	ㅇ	č	ㅈ
čh	ㅊ	kh	ㅋ	th	ㅌ	ph	ㅍ	h	ㅎ
kk	ㄲ	tt	ㄸ	pp	ㅃ	ss	ㅆ	čč	ㅉ

Vowel Order (within the zero consonant sign ㅇ)

a 아   ya 야   ɔ 어   yɔ 여

o 오   yo 요   u 우   yu 유

ɨ 으   i 이

æ 애   yæ 애   e 에   ye 예

we 외   wi 위   ɨy 의

wa 와   wɔ 워   wæ 왜   we 웨

How To Write Korean

Stroke Orders

It is important to learn correct stroke orders from the beginning. Let's begin with two general principles of Korean writing.

1. Everything horizontal moves from left to right. This applies to the movement of individual strokes, as well as to writing a sequence of letters (e.g., the consonant first, then the vowel).

2. Everything vertical moves from top to bottom.

How to combine a consonant with a vowel:
Any written syllable in 한글 must begin with a consonant sign. This means that even when the syllable contains no spoken consonants (i.e., when it begins with a vowel in

pronunciation), you still have to start the syllable with the little circle ○ representing a zero consonant, as you have learned.

A vowel letter is placed to the right of, or below the initial consonant. Possible patterns, therefore, are as follows:

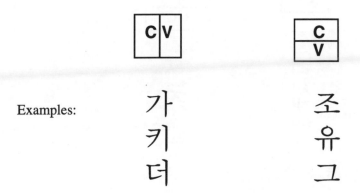

Examples:

The final consonant of a syllable (if it has one) is placed directly below the preceding consonant and vowel, regardless of how they are arranged (i.e., whether horizontally or vertically).

The possible combinations are:

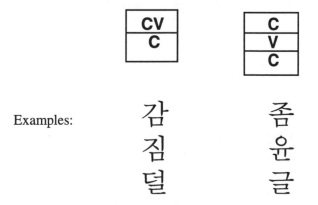

Examples:

A block forming a syllable with three letters (C - V - C) will naturally be more congested than a block with two letters (C - V). However, each syllable (or block) should be approximately of the same size, regardless of the number of letters contained in it. It is, therefore, necessary to make the size of the letters smaller when a syllable contains three or four letters, as you can see in the examples below (don't worry about how to pronounce these for now—they are here to demonstrate written syllable composition). Those syllables with four signs in them will have the shape:

Examples:

Structure of Written Syllables

These notes concern the **written** structure of syllables, that is, how syllables are recorded and dealt with in the writing system, **not** how they are pronounced.

1. If the vowel letter has a long vertical stroke, then the vowel letter is written to the right of the initial consonant sign.

김	남	섬	박
kim	nam	sɔm	pak

한	가	머	시
han	ka	mɔ	ši

2. If the vowel letter has a long horizontal stroke, then the vowel letter is written below the initial consonant letter.

송	문	동
song	mun	tong

노	두	조
no	tu	čo

3.   If the vowel letter has both a long vertical stroke and a long horizontal stroke, then the (diphthong) vowel letter is written in such a way as to fit under and to the right of the initial consonant letter.

곽   권   위   원
kwak   kwɔn   wi   wɔn

쥐   줴   죄
čwi   čwe   čwe

4.   It is possible to have a written syllable with two consonant letters filling the final position.

있   묶   앉   젊
it--   muk--   an--   čɔm--

But note that in the pronunciation, the double *ss*, double *kk*, *nč* and *lm* at the end of each syllable are reduced to *t*, *k*, *n*, *m* respectively. This is because no vowel yet follows, and so the Korean is stuck on a consonant which he cannot yet release.

Structure of Pronounced Syllables

The following notes concern only the structure of pronounced syllables, not written forms.

1.   Sometimes, Korean pronounced syllables follow Korean written syllables closely, if we ignore the technicality that an initial ㅇ is a consonant, but not pronounced.

하나 (CV -CV)   어머니 (V -CV - CV)
hana   ɔmɔni

제이 (CV - V)   여기 (V- CV)
čei   yɔgi

사과 (CV- CV)
sagwa

교수 (CV - CV)
kyosu

가방 (CV - CVC)
kabang

도서관 (CV - CV -CVC)
tosɔgwan

창문 (CVC - CVC)
čʰangmun

칠판 (CVC - CVC)
čʰilʸpʰan

2. At other times, the written structure tries to preserve consistency where, in pronunciation, changes occur. Thus, the final consonant of a preceding syllable is pronounced as the initial consonant sound of the following syllable when the following syllable begins with a vowel.

받아요 CVC-V-V in writing, CV-CV-V pa-da-yo in pronunciation

먹어요 CVC - V -V in writing, CV-CV-V mɔ-gɔ-yo in pronunciation

Note that in earlier times, when the Korean spelling system was less consistent, these would have been written 바다요 and 머거요.

산이나   CVC - V - CV in writing, CV -CV -CV sa-ni-na in pronunciation

있어   VC - V in writing, V-CV i-ssɔ in pronunciation

3. If the syllable has two different final consonants before a vowel-initial syllable, then the first of these closes the first phonetic syllable, and the second begins the following phonetic syllable.

읽어요   VCC-V-V in writing, VC-CV-V ilʸ-gɔ-yo in pronunciation

젊어요   CVCC-V-V in writing, CVC-CV-V čɔlʸ-mɔ-yo in pronunciation

Exercises

Exercise 1: The Korean Script—Review and Practice

Practice your writing and stroke orders in the empty boxes under Practice.

1. The Vowels

Letter Shape	Sound Value	Name	Practice		
ㅏ	a	아			
ㅑ	ya	야			
ㅓ	ɔ	어			
ㅕ	yɔ	여			
ㅗ	o	오			
ㅛ	yo	요			
ㅜ	u	우			
ㅠ	yu	유			
ㅡ	ɨ	으			
ㅣ	i	이			

2. The Consonants

Letter Shape	Sound Value	Name	Practice			
ㄱ	k, -g-	기역				
ㄴ	n	니은				
ㄷ	t, -d-	디귿				
ㄹ	l/r	리을				
ㅁ	m	미음				
ㅂ	p, -b-	비읍				
ㅅ	s/š, -t	시옷				
ㅇ	Ø-/-ŋ	이응				
ㅈ	č, -dž-, -t	지읒				
ㅊ	čʰ, -t	치읓				
ㅋ	kʰ, -k	키읔				
ㅌ	tʰ, -t	티읕				
ㅍ	pʰ, -p	피읖				
ㅎ	h, -t	히읗				

Exercise 2: Recognizing Country Names

The following Korean words written in Han'gŭl are the names of countries which you should be able to recognize. To practice your writing in Han'gŭl, copy each one out three times and then write down the English equivalent.

1. 케냐
2. 프랑스
3. 파키스탄
4. 멕시코
5. 라오스
6. 그리스
7. 이라크
8. 핀란드
9. 뉴질랜드
10. 싱가폴
11. 덴마크
12. 네덜란드
13. 타이
14. 폴란드
15. 칠레
16. 스웨덴
17. 리비아
18. 브라질
19. 인도네시아
20. 캐나다
21. 말레이시아
22. 니카라구아
23. 쿠바
24. 베트남
25. 리히텐슈타인
26. 레바논

Exercise 3: Recognizing Loans from English

The following Korean words have been borrowed from English, and you should be able to recognize them. To practice your writing in Han'gŭl, copy each one out three times and then write down the English equivalent.

1.	라디오	2.	버스
3.	택시	4.	피아노
5.	캥거루	6.	토스트
7.	테니스	8.	바나나
9.	카메라	10.	쏘세지
11.	레몬	12.	째즈
13.	케이크	14.	아이스크림
15.	카세트	16.	인터뷰
17.	호텔	18.	골프
19.	토마토	20.	나이트클럽
21.	텔레비젼	22.	타이어
23.	컴퓨터	24.	햄버거
25.	트럭	26.	샌드위치

Exercise 4: Practicing Consonant Contrasts

Practice pronouncing the two-way and three-way consonant contrasts in the words below. Do not worry about the meanings—many are nonsense words anyway.

1.	탈 딸 달	2.	팔 빨 발	3.	칼 깔 갈	4.	찰 짤 잘
5.	키 끼 기	6.	피 삐 비	7.	초 쪼 조	8.	터 떠 더
9.	차차 짜짜 자자	10.	코코 꼬꼬 고고	11.	피피 삐삐 비비	12.	투투 뚜뚜 두두
13.	아차 아짜 아자	14.	위퀴 위뀌 위귀	15.	우추 우쭈 우주	16.	어퍼 어뻐 어버
17.	안카 안까 안가	18.	온파 온빠 온바	19.	인차 인짜 인자	20.	원차 원짜 원자

Lesson 4

Further Pronunciation Guidelines

There are certain pronunciation rules which you must learn for the Korean language and it is best to get these out of the way towards the start of the course. Words may be pronounced differently than they appear. Nonetheless, there are a number of rules that apply universally when certain letters appear together, and learning these rules will help you not to make those mistakes that betray you as a foreigner! You may need to refer to the various sections in this lesson again later in the course—they will provide a valuable reference.

4.1. Automatic Voicing of Plain ㅂ, ㄷ, ㅈ, ㄱ

The normally voiceless sounds shown by the single ㅂ, ㄷ, ㅈ, ㄱ p, t, č, k (which have a light puff of local air when they are at the beginning of a word) are voiced between voiced sounds (i.e., vowels, y, w, m, n, ŋ, l) so that they will sound like b, d, dž, g.

아버지	a-bɔ-dži	*father*
닫아요	ta-da-yo	*closes it*
애기	æ-gi	*baby*
담배	tam-bæ	*cigarettes, tobacco*
안동	an-dong	*(name of a city)*
중국	čuŋ-guk	*China*
갈비	kalʸ-bi	*ribs*
안주	an-džu	*food to go with alcoholic drinks*

4.2. Non-release of Final Consonants

Korean never allows its speakers to release a consonant at the end of a syllable unless they have to. Korean speakers have to release a consonant at the end of a syllable when the word is followed by (1) a particle or ending that begins with a vowel, or (2) by the special verb –이에요 *it is . . . .*

In the case of final unreleased p, t, k, it is often difficult for English speakers to hear the consonant—it sounds as though the Koreans swallow their consonants.

Final /-P/		**Final /-K/**		**Final /-T/ (usually from /ㅅ/)**		
굽	*hoof*	국	*soup*	굿	kut	*exorcism*
곱	*pus*	옥	*jade*	옷	ot	*garment*
입	*mouth*	목	*throat*	못	mot	*pond; nail*

4.3. The Gang of Seven: ㄹ ㅁ ㄴ ㅇ ㅂ ㄷ ㄱ

The only consonants that can be pronounced at the end of a syllable in Korean are the following seven: ㄹ ㅁ ㄴ ㅇ l, m, n, ŋ (see above) and ㅂ ㄷ ㄱ p, t, k (but remember: Korean doesn't allow you to release them unless you have to).

When the basic form of a word ends in something else other than these seven consonants, the "something else" must be reduced to one of these seven consonants, unless the word is followed by (1) a particle or ending that begins with a vowel, or (2) by the special verb – 이에요 *it is . . . .*

앞에 apʰe	*in front*	앞 ap	[압]	*front*
값은 kapsɨn	*as for price*	값 kap	[갑]	*price*
밖에 pakke	*outside*	밖 pak	[박]	*outside*
닭이에요 talʸgieyo	*it's a chicken*	닭 tak	[닥]	*chicken*

부엌이에요 puɔkʰieyo	*it's a kitchen*	부엌 puɔk	[부억] puɔk	*kitchen*
옷이에요 ošieyo	*it's a garment*	옷	[ot] ot	*garment*
밭에 patʰe	*in the field*	밭	[받] pat	*field*
낮에 nadže	*in the daytime*	낮	[낟] nat	*daytime*
꽃이에요 kkočʰieyo	*it's a flower*	꽃	[kkot] kkot	*flower*

The reduction rules are as follows.

Original sounds		Reduce to	
ㅂ, ㅍ, ㅃ	→	ㅂ	(or to *m*; see section 4.5 below)
ㄱ, ㅋ, ㄲ	→	ㄱ	(or to *ŋ*; see section 4.5 below)
ㄷ, ㅌ, ㅈ, ㅊ, ㅅ, ㅆ, ㅎ }	→	ㄷ	(or to *n*; see section 4.5 below)

Note how many different consonant sounds an unreleased *t* can disguise. In particular, note that an unreleased *s* gets pronounced as *t*. In fact, most unreleased *t*-sounds you will hear in Korean are really a final *s* in disguise.

4.4. Other Gang of Seven Situations

The final-reduced forms in p, t, k and l, m, n, ŋ are used not only when the word is before a pause, but also before words beginning with consonants and even before words beginning with vowels, provided the following word is not a particle (e.g., the subject particle 이 or the locative particle 에) or the special verb -이에요 *it is* . . . .

닭고기 → 닥고기	[다꼬기] takkogi	*chicken (as meat)*

밭도 → 받도	[바또] patto	*the field too*
밭안 → 받안	[바단] padan	*inside the field*
옷 안 → ot + an	[오단] odan	*garment lining*
옷도 → ot + to	[오또] otto	*the garment too*

4.5. When the Gang of Seven Gets Up Your Nose

When **p, t, k** precede m or n (or l pronounced as n due to the rule in section 4.6 below), they (that is, **p, t, k**) are pronounced as m, n, ŋ, respectively.

Remember that in Korean, p, t, k cannot be released in this position. When you have an unreleased p before a nasal sound like m or n and want to pronounce the next syllable, the p has nowhere else to go but up your nose. Once a p goes up your nose, it becomes an m. The same logic holds for unreleased t turning into n and unreleased k turning into ŋ.

합니다	[함니다] hamnida	*does it* [Formal style]
닫는다	[단는다] tannɨnda	*closes it* [Plain style]
먹는다	[멍는다] mɔŋnɨnda	*eats it* [Plain style]
십륙	[심뉵] šimnyuk	*sixteen*
독립 → 독닙 →	[동닙] toŋnip	*independence*
합리 → 합니 →	[함니] hamni	*rationality, reason*

Note that this rule also applies to any t which has been reduced from t^h, č^h, č, s, ss, or even h:

밭 + 만	→	〔받만〕	→	[반만] *the field only* panman

숯 + 만	→	〔숟만〕	→	[순만] *the charcoal only* sunman
낮 + 만	→	〔낟만〕	→	[난만] *daytime only* nanman
벗- + -네	→	〔벋네〕	→	[번네] *he's taking it off!* pɔnne
있었- + -네	→	〔있얻네〕	→	[이썬네] *she had it!* issɔnne

The case of h changing to (t and then) n like this is an unusual one, and we will alert you to it again when you learn about verbs that end in final h.

넣- + -네	→	[넌네] *they're inserting it!* nɔnne

주의! Caution!

If you wish to conceive of this nasalization process in terms of written 한글 symbols, note that the symbol ㅇ can only count as zero following a preceding syllable-final consonant. Thus, the sequence 먹어요 *eats* can only be pronounced mɔgɔyo and not *mɔŋɔyo.

4.6. Peculiarities of the Korean ㄹ

1. When n is next to l (n.l or l.n, where the period represents a syllable break) a double ll is pronounced.

일년	[일련] illyɔn	*one year*
신라	[실라] šilla	*Silla* (ancient Korean state)

2. When preceded by a consonant other than l or n, the l is pronounced as n.

심리	[심니] šimni	*psychology*

| 상류 | [상뉴]
saŋnyu | *upper reaches of a river* |

3. When followed by t, č, or s in words borrowed from Chinese, the l has the effect of doubling these to tt, čč, and ss, respectively.

철도	[철또] čʰoltto	*railway*
결정	[결쩡] kyolččoŋ	*decision*
설사	[설싸] solssa	*diarrhea*

Because you have no way of telling which words are originally from Chinese and which are not, and because the Korean writing system ignores these differences between spelling and actual pronunciation, we will alert you to any such pronunciation details (by rewriting the pronunciation in 한글 in square brackets) when you first learn new words in the vocabulary lists at the beginning of each lesson.

4.7. Automatic Doubling

If the final sound of the preceding syllable is p, t, or k, the single voiceless consonants p, t, č, k, s ㅂ, ㄷ, ㅈ, ㄱ, ㅅ are automatically doubled in pronunciation so they sound like pp, tt, čč, kk, ss ㅃ, ㄸ, ㅉ, ㄲ, ㅆ.

약방	[약빵] yakppang	*drugstore*
작다	[작따] čaktta	*is little* [Plain style]
먹자	[먹짜] mokčča	*let's eat* [Plain style]
덥다	[덥따] toptta	*is hot* [Plain style]
입자	[입짜] ipčča	*let's wear it* [Plain style]
십삼	[십쌈] šipssam	*thirteen*

Lesson Four / 49

4.8. Leap-frogging ㅎ h

The Korean ㅎ h can leap over a following plain ㅂ, ㄷ, ㅈ, ㄱ to yield a corresponding aspirated sound in pronunciation (ㅍ, ㅌ, ㅊ, ㅋ). In other words, the aspirated consonants ㅍ, ㅌ, ㅊ, ㅋ can be considered as equivalent to combinations of ㅂ + ㅎ (or ㅎ + ㅂ), ㄷ + ㅎ (or ㅎ + ㄷ), ㅈ + ㅎ (or ㅎ + ㅈ), ㄱ + ㅎ (or ㅎ + ㄱ), respectively. Here are some examples.

ㅎ + ㄱ → ㅋ: 좋- + -고 → 좋고, pronounced 조코 *is good, and . . .*
ㅎ + ㄷ → ㅌ: 좋- + -다 → 좋다, pronounced 조타 *is good*

4.9. Pronunciation of ㅌ before i

The Korean ㅌ (aspirated tʰ) is palatalized to ㅊ when it occurs at the end of a morpheme or word and is followed by 이.

같이	*together*		is pronounced	가치
밭	*field*	+ 이 (subject marker)	is pronounced	바치

4.10. Long and Short Vowels

Many Koreans distinguish words by pronouncing a vowel as long or short: 일 il *one*, 일 īl (i.e., with a long vowel) *affair, work*. But even for those speakers, vowel length is often suppressed, especially when not at the beginning of a phrase, so that you will often hear short vowels in words that have basically long vowels.

Modern Korean spelling does not indicate the long vowels, and we do not show them in the body of this textbook. But you should at least be aware of this contrast. Here are some examples.

SHORT VOWELS		LONG VOWELS	
밤	*evening*	밤	*chestnut*
굴	*oyster*	굴	*cave*
말	*horse*	말	*words, speech*
눈	*eye*	눈	*snow*

In the case of long and short 어, many speakers pronounce the long 어 with the tongue in a considerably higher position than it is in for the short 어, as something resembling English *uh* in *uh-oh*. Many speakers hollow the back of the tongue to make the short 어 so that it sounds rounded like the vowel sound that many people use in English *saw*, *song*, *dawn*.

SHORT VOWELS		LONG VOWELS	
거리 "kawrie"	*street*	거리 "kuhri"	*distance*
연기 "yawn'gi"	*postponement*	연기 "yuhn'gi"	*performance*

4.11. The Names of the Korean Letters

The han'gŭl vowel signs do not have special names of their own. Instead, they are called by the sounds they represent. For example, ㅘ is called "wa". Each han'gŭl consonant sign, however, has its own name based on the ingenious mnemonic device of beginning and ending the name with the consonant letter in question.

Letter	Name	Pronunciation
ㄱ	기역	kiyɔk
ㄴ	니은	niɨn
ㄷ	디귿	tigɨt
ㄹ	리을	riɨl
ㅁ	미음	miɨm
ㅂ	비읍	piɨp
ㅅ	시옷	šiot
ㅇ	이응	iɨng
ㅈ	지읒	čiɨt
ㅊ	치읓	čʰiɨt
ㅋ	키읔	kʰiɨk
ㅌ	티읕	tʰiɨt
ㅍ	피읖	pʰiɨp
ㅎ	히읗	hiɨt

The tense, or 'doubled' consonants, have the same name as the corresponding plain series consonant, preceded by 쌍 *double*.

Letter	Name	Pronunciation
ㄲ	쌍기역	ssaŋgiyɔk
ㄸ	쌍디귿	ssaŋdigɨt
ㅃ	쌍비읍	ssaŋbiɨp
ㅆ	쌍시옷	ssaŋšiot
ㅉ	쌍지읏	ssaŋdžiɨt

Exercises: Pronunciation

Exercise 1: Voicing Practice

1. 가방
2. 안주
3. 지도
4. 방법
5. 감자
6. 만두
7. 두부
8. 공장
9. 모자
10. 구기
11. 군대
12. 아기
13. 담배
14. 공기
15. 구두
16. 수제비

Exercise 2: Non-release of Final Consonants

Practice pronouncing the following (mostly nonsense) syllables, first saying each one alone, then saying it again, followed by the subject particle 이.

1. 각
2. 멀
3. 짖
4. 난
5. 갖
6. 셋
7. 칩
8. 짇
9. 깊

10.	킬	11.	탑	12.	볏
13.	작	14.	날	15.	닺
16.	넥	17.	녈	18.	캡
19.	덮	20.	설	21.	만
22.	상	23.	밥	24.	빗

Exercise 3: Nasal Assimilation Practice

1.	합니다	2.	한국말
3.	닫는다	4.	초등학교
5.	먹는다	6.	독립
7.	밥맛	8.	독립문
9.	앞문	10.	압록강
11.	숙녀	12.	십리
13.	못난이	14.	삽만
15.	작문	16.	부엌문
17.	붙는다	18.	꽃만
19.	빗만	20.	옛날
21.	옷만	22.	찾네

Exercise 4: Cluster Reinforcement Practice

1.	잡지	2.	목소리
3.	십자가	4.	엽서
5.	철도	6.	답장
7.	식당	8.	높고
9.	학교	10.	믿자
11.	학생	12.	걷자
13.	역사	14.	국방
15.	국수	16.	국비
17.	설사	18.	결정

Lesson 5

우리 집사람이에요.

We now begin the lessons proper. In this first one you will find out how to introduce and address people, identify things and ask simple questions. We also learn vocabulary for countries, nationalities, etc. In the Lesson Notes we cover pronouns, four essential particles, the use of the copula, and the ways in which Korean nouns are used. By now you should be comfortable with 한글, so we discontinue use of the phonetic transcription.

Korean Dialogues

Dialogue 1

Chris Murphy and his wife have gone into a Seoul coffee shop. Chris thinks he recognizes someone sitting at a table reading a newspaper:

크리스	저— 실례합니다.
김	어, 머피 선생님! 오래간만입니다!
크리스	(to Kim) 선생님, (gestures in Eunice's direction)
	— 우리 집사람이에요.
유니스	유니스에요. 처음 뵙겠습니다.
김	김창기에요. 처음 뵙겠습니다.
크리스	김 선생님은 내 한국말 선생님이에요.
유니스	아, 네. 만나서 반갑습니다.

Notes

저—	*Uh—*
어!	*Well! Ah!!*

오래간만입니다!	*Long time no see!*
우리	*we, our.*
우리 NOUN	*my* NOUN (used where 내 *my* would sound too individualistic to a Korean)
NOUN-(이)에요	*is a* NOUN
NOUN 은 ~ 는	*as for* NOUN
내	*my* (Mr. Kim is not Korean language teacher to anybody else in Chris' family, so 우리 would not be appropriate)

Dialogue 2

Chris and Eunice join 김 선생님, and they talk a while:

크리스	우리 집사람은 피아노 선생이에요.
김	아, 그래요? 머피 선생님은 영국사람이지요?
크리스	네.
김	부인도 영국분이에요?
크리스	아니오, 영국사람이 아니에요. 호주사람이에요.

Notes

NOUN -이지요?	*is a* NOUN, *isn't it? is a* NOUN, *right?* This is a special form of the copula in -(이)에요. You will learn more about the ending in -지요 later.
NOUN 도	NOUN, *too*; NOUN, *also*
NOUN 이 ~ 가	NOUN (as subject)
NOUN(이 ~ 가) 아니에요	*is not a* NOUN

Dialogue 3

They all get up and go, leaving the newspaper on the table. Chris notices an umbrella on the floor and picks it up.

크리스	(to Kim) 이거 김 선생님 우산이에요?
김	네, 제거에요. 고맙습니다.

| 유니스 | 이 신문도 선생님 거에요? |
| 김 | 아니오, 그건 제거 아니에요. |

Notes

이 NOUN	*this* NOUN
이거	*this thing* (abbreviated from 이것)
제	*my* (Humble)
제거	*mine* (= *my thing*); pronounced 제꺼
고맙습니다	*Thank you.*
선생님 거	*yours* (*your thing*); pronounced 선생님꺼
그 NOUN	*that* NOUN
그건	*that one, that thing* (as topic, old information, or contrast, and abbreviated from 그것은)

Dialogue 4

Chris and Eunice then take 김 선생님 to a special fair of imported goods which Chris has helped to organize at a nearby exhibition center.

김	그게 어느 나라의 와인이에요?
유니스	이거요? 이건 프랑스 와인이에요.
김	그럼, 저건 뭐에요?
유니스	아, 저건 영국 술이에요.
김	무슨 술이에요?
유니스	위스키에요.
김	전부 다 수입품이지요?
크리스	아니오, 저 인삼주는 한국제품이에요.

Notes

그게	*that thing equidistant from both of us* (as new information, and abbreviated from 그것이)
어느 NOUN?	*which* NOUN? *what* NOUN? (out of several)
NOUN의 NOUN	NOUN's NOUN (note exceptional pronunciation of 의 as 에!. Some speakers pronounce 의 as 으, but this is substandard.)
이거	*this thing* (abbreviated from 이것)
뭐	*what?* (abbreviated from 무엇)

무슨 NOUN?　　　　　　　*what kind of/ what sort of* NOUN?

저 NOUN　　　　　　　　*that* NOUN *over there.*

Vocabulary

Countries, Languages and Nationalities

	Country	**Language**	**Person**
러시아	Russia	러시아말	러시아사람
캐나다	Canada	영어,	캐나다사람
		프랑스말 (불어)	
일본	Japan	일본말	일본사람
		(일어)	
중국	China	중국말	중국사람
미국	America	영어	미국사람
영국	England	영어	영국사람
한국	Korea	한국말	한국사람
홍콩	Hong Kong	중국말	홍콩사람
호주	Australia	영어	호주사람
독일	Germany	독일말	독일사람
		(독어)	
프랑스	France	프랑스말	프랑스사람
		(불어)	
외국	foreign country	외국어	외국사람

People and Places

교수(님)	professor (honorific)
의사	doctor, physician
은행	bank
은행원	banker
회사	company
회사원	company employee
집	house, home
사람	person
선생(님)	teacher (honorific)
아내　or	wife (my)
집사람	

부인	wife (your/his)
남편	husband
나라	country, nation

People and Places (cont.)

사장(님)	company president (honorific)
친구	friend
학생	student
가수	pop-singer
-씨	polite title for name
외교관	diplomat
박사(님)	Dr., Ph.D. (honorific)

Things

제품	manufactured good(s)
신문	newspaper
잡지	magazine
책	book
공책	notebook
분필	chalk
연필	pencil
볼펜, 펜	ball-point pen
성냥	match(es)
담배	cigarette(s)
말	language, words
종이	paper
칠판	blackboard
와인	wine
술	any alcoholic drink
위스키	whisky
전부	the whole thing, total
다	all, everything
전부 다	everything, all of it
수입품	imported goods
인삼	ginseng
인삼주	ginseng wine
피아노	piano
우산	umbrella

Miscellaneous Vocabulary

나	I
우리	we, our
누가	who? (as subject)
누구	who? (non-subject)
무엇, 뭐	what?
아니에요	No; it is not
그렇지만	But
그러면	Then, In that case, If so
그럼	Then, In that case
이 NOUN	this NOUN
그 NOUN	that NOUN
저 NOUN	yon NOUN, that NOUN [way] over there
무슨 NOUN	which/what kind of NOUN?
어느 NOUN	which/what (one/NOUN)?
-곳	place
-분	person (honorific)

Lesson Notes

5.1. Pronouns in Korean

In general, Koreans use pronouns much less in conversation than we do in English. When they **do** use pronouns, they have to choose between a number of different words depending on the social relationships of the people involved (this is probably why they avoid using them in the first place).

Korean has the following first-person pronouns:

I	We
나	우리
저 Humble	저희 Humble (pronounced 저이)

It is always considered more polite to use the humble forms in polite conversation with people you may not know very well or with people deserving of deference for whatever reason.

> ### 주의 Caution!
> Of all the pronouns, Koreans avoid words for *you* the most,
> and so should you.

The following table shows some of the ways to say *you*.

너	Intimate	FIRST NAME/FULL NAME + 씨	Polite
당신	Polite	자네	Semi-Formal
TITLE (+ 님)	Polite	SURNAME/FULL NAME + 선생님	Polite

You are always safest using no pronoun at all. If unavoidable, try title (+ 님) or surname + 선생님. Of the items above, you should avoid less polite terms like 너, 자네, and 당신. The latter pronoun tends to be used mostly between spouses, but some Koreans occasionally address foreigners in this manner (as a kind of translation equivalent for English *you*), so you may hear it directed at yourself, too. When talking about or addressing your student peers, whether here or in Korea, the safest pattern is name + 씨, e.g. 만호 씨 *he* (Manho) or *you* (Manho).

Technically speaking, Korean has no proper third-person pronouns at all. Instead, for *he, she, it, they*, Korean uses an expression equivalent to *that person, that woman, that thing, those people*, etc. For now, what you need is:

그 사람   *that* [aforementioned] *person*

                            (*he, him; she, her; they, them*)

그것   *that* [aforementioned] *thing*, same as *it*

5.2. Sentence Subjects and Topics

As you have seen, Korean nouns commonly appear in particle-marked phrases. The particle after a noun sometimes has no exact English equivalent but rather assigns a grammatical function to the noun.

Two such particles are the SUBJECT PARTICLE 이 ~ 가, which puts FOCUS or a spotlight on the noun before it (often the subject), and the TOPIC PARTICLE 은 ~ 는, which has three functions:

1. to mark its noun as the sentence topic (what the sentence is about)
2. to point up a contrast, or
3. to mark its noun as old or given or assumed information

Some particles have two pronunciations or shapes: one when they come after a word that ends with a consonant, the other after words ending with vowels. Except for the reversed order of things, this is completely analogous to the English indefinite article *a/an*:

Before Consonant	Before Vowel
a man	an apple
a sandwich	an orphan
a headache	an idea

The subject and topic particles are both TWO-SHAPE PARTICLES. The subject particle is pronounced 이 when it comes after a consonant and 가 when it comes after a vowel.

After Consonant		After Vowel	
책이	*book*	잡지가	*magazine*
부인이	*wife*	아내가	*wife*
제품이	*product*	내가	*I*
무엇이	*what?*	누가	*who?*
연필이	*pencil*	종이가	*paper*

주의 Caution!

나 *I*, 너 *You*, 저 *I* (Humble) and 누구 *who?* have altered shapes when they come before the subject particle 이 ~ 가. These are:
내가, 네가, 제가 and 누가.

Remember that 이 and 가 are the same word: it is a word with two pronunciations. The same is true of the topic particle, which is pronounced 은 after consonants and 는 after vowels.

After Consonant		After Vowel	
우산은	*umbrella*	의사는	*doctor*
은행은	*bank*	박사는	*Ph.D., Dr.*
일본은	*Japan*	나는	*I*
신문은	*newspaper*	친구는	*friend*
성냥은	*matches*	담배는	*cigarettes*

A Korean sentence subject (noun plus the particle 이 ~ 가) usually corresponds to an English sentence subject. So, often, does a Korean topic (noun plus the particle 은 ~ 는). They are usually interchangeable, but you should be sensitive to their different nuances, as explained below.

When you first mention a subject—when it is new information—you usually attach 이 ~ 가, the subject particle, to it. Thereafter in the same context, if you repeat the subject at all, it has become old information and usually has the particle 은 ~ 는. The following exchanges exemplify this:

1.   A. 이것이 무엇이에요?   *What's this?*
         B. 그것은 우산이에요.   *That's an umbrella.*

2.   A long, long time ago, a man [사람이] lived in the mountains. One day, he [그 사람은] came down the mountain, and . . .

Once a particular subject has been mentioned there is no requirement in Korean to keep referring to it in subsequent sentences; you can just drop it. However, if the subject **is** mentioned again, then it would be followed by the topic particle (marking the noun as old information), not the subject particle. To repeat, the subject of conversation does not need to be referred to continuously, but if it is mentioned again then it is marked as old information by the topic marker 은 ~ 는.

We can say, therefore, that the topic particle 은 ~ 는 is a particle that flags the word or phrase in front of it as the least unknown ingredient or oldest piece of information in your communication—the part you would be most likely to drop if you wanted to make your sentence brief. For this reason, the topic phrase nearly always comes at the very beginning of the sentence. As you have learned, the important things in a Korean sentence tend to accumulate toward the end, near the verb—the single indispensable element. The dispensable things are what the other person is most likely to know already and are put closer to the beginning, where they are missed the least if they are dropped out altogether.

You can create topics from (mark with 은 ~ 는) any element in the sentence (except the verb) by pulling the element out of place, saying it first, and putting 은 ~ 는 on it. To give you the feel of this de-emphasis, here is a single English sentence showing how each element might appear as the topic of a Korean sentence, and the emphasis of the resulting order:

> *That student is studying Korean at school now.*

a. That student 은 ~ 는 is studying Korean at school now

"What about that student? As for that student . . . " The new information is the nature of the activity, not who is doing it.

b. Now 은 ~ 는 that student is studying Korean at school.

Talking about what's happening now: "That student is studying Korean at school."

c. At school 은 ~ 는 that student is now studying Korean (there).

To mention what's going on at school . . .

d. Korean 은 ~ 는 that student is studying [it] at school now.

"What I want to say about the Korean language is . . . "

Another common function of the particle 은 ~ 는 is to mark CONTRAST, which occurs when each of two parallel statements (one of which may be implied rather than stated) begins with a topic. The contrast between them is pointed up.

3.　　김 선생님은 의사에요. 그렇지만 나는 회사원이에요.
Mr. Kim (he) is a doctor. But (me) I'm an office employee.

The subject particle 이 ~ 가, on the other hand, puts a spotlight on the noun it follows. It appears most often with subjects that have not been mentioned previously in the context. Certain words, by the very nature of their meaning, rarely appear as Korean topics, but frequently as subjects. These are words that inherently ask for new information, such as 누구 *who?,* 무슨 *what (kind of)?,* 무엇 *what?,* and 어느 *which?* By the same token, when you answer a question having one of these words, you use a subject to supply the new information, rather than using a topic. For example:

4.　　어느 것이 잡지에요? 저것이 잡지에요.
Which one is a magazine? That one over there is a magazine.

5.　　누가 선생이에요? 이분이 선생이에요.
Who is the teacher? This [esteemed] person is the teacher.

6.　　누가 학생이에요? 내가 학생이에요.
Who is the student? I am the student.

Of course, if the question word occurs outside of the subject or topic, then the subject and topic positions in the sentence are handled as described above. The subject upon its first mention will have 이 ~ 가 and if mentioned thereafter, 은 ~ 는. Here are some examples of this sort of sequence.

7. 이것이 무엇이에요? 그것은 잡지에요.
    This thing is what? (That thing) is a magazine.

8. 이것이 무슨 책이에요? 그것은 한국말 책이에요.
    This thing is what kind of book? (That thing) is a Korean book.

9. 한국말 선생이 어느 분이에요? 한국말 선생은 김 선생이에요.
    The Korean teacher is who? (The Korean teacher) is Mr. Kim.

5.3. The Copula and Equational Sentences

Many of the sentences in this lesson end with a special verb called the COPULA. The copula is pronounced 이에요 after consonants but generally shortened to 에요 after vowels.

After Consonants		**After Vowels**	
선생이에요	*It is a teacher.*	의사에요	*It is a doctor.*
책이에요	*It is a book.*	잡지에요	*It is a magazine.*
연필이에요	*It is a pencil.*	종이에요	*It is paper.*
성냥이에요	*It is a match.*	교수에요	*It is a professor.*

[Note: The shape 에요 is just an abbreviation of 이에요 and sometimes you will hear the full form, even after a vowel.]

The copula is different from other verbs in this respect: it cannot make a complete sentence by itself, but must always have something in front of it—most often a noun expression. It is pronounced as though it were part of its preceding word, like a suffix, and your voice should never **pause** or **hesitate** between the noun expression and the copula.

The copula translates the English verb *to be (am, are, is)* when it means *it equals* or *it is (the same thing as)*. For this reason sentences ending with the copula are called EQUATIONAL SENTENCES.

The copula is made negative by the word 아니, followed generally by the abbreviated form that is normal after vowels: 아니에요. The noun expression before the negative (but not before the affirmative) copula may, optionally, appear as a subject, i.e., it may have the particle 이 ~ 가 after it.

10.　신문(이) 아니에요.
　　　It isn't a newspaper.

11.　영국사람(이) 아니에요.
　　　He is not English.

Negative equational sentences thus can accommodate two subjects, the second of which corresponds to the English complement.

12.　누가 학생(이) 아니에요?
　　　Who is not a student?

13.　그 사람은 일본사람(이) 아니에요.
　　　He isn't Japanese.

14.　이것이 영어(가) 아니에요.
　　　This isn't English.

5.4. The Particle 도: *too, also, even*

The particle 도 means *too, also, indeed, even*. It puts emphasis on the word before it, with reference to something earlier in the context. The particle 도 (often pronounced 두) has only one shape regardless whether it follows a vowel or a consonant.

The English words that correspond to the particle 도 fall most naturally at the end of the sentence, so that they may be widely separated from the word with which they belong, as in this example:

15.　그 가수도 한국사람이에요.
　　　That pop singer is a Korean, too.

In a negative sentence, English substitutes *either* for *too*, but in Korean 도 still does all the work.

16.　이것은 한국제품이에요. 저것도 한국제품이에요.
　　　This is a Korean product. That is a Korean product, too.

17. 이것은 수입품이 아니에요. 저것도 수입품이 아니에요.
      This isn't an import. That isn't an import either.

5.5. Expressing Possession with the Particle 의

The particle that is spelled 의 (but pronounced 에) is a one-shape particle: it is always the same, whether it comes after a vowel or a consonant. Its function is to link noun expressions together in such a way that the first one modifies, describes, or limits the meaning of the second one. The instances you have observed illustrate the possessive meaning of 의.

18. 남 선생님(의) 종이에요?
      Is it Mr. Nam's paper?

19. 어느 분(의) 잡지에요?
      Whose [which esteemed person's] magazine is it?

20. 김 선생님(의) 것이에요, 의사선생님(의) 것이에요?
      Is it Mr. Kim's or is it the doctor's?

In this usage the particle corresponds to the English suffix -'s: *John's*, *Mr. Cooper's*.

English pronouns, of course, are made possessive in other ways: *I ~ my, you ~ your, he ~ his*, and so on. Even *who* plus *'s* undergoes a spelling alternation: *whose*. In Korean, the following possessive pronouns are also somewhat irregular.

MY (Plain/Intimate)	MY (Humble/Polite)	YOUR (Plain/Intimate)
내	제	네

The form 내 *my* is actually a combination of 나 *I* and the possessive particle 의 run together. Likewise, 제 is from 저 + 의 and 네 is from 너 + 의. It is also perfectly acceptable to use the unabbreviated sequences of 나의, 저의, and 너의.

> ### 주의!
>
> Note that it is *not* possible to abbreviate 나의 NOUN and 저의 NOUN *my NOUN* to 나 NOUN and 저 NOUN, respectively.

Quite often a possessive meaning is present in phrases even when there is no 의.

그 사람 우산   *that person's umbrella*

김 선생님 담배   *Mr. Kim's cigarettes*

In effect, there are three different ways to make a possessive construction, as indicated below.

a)   NOUN 의 NOUN   크리스 씨의 선생 *Chris' teacher*

b)   NOUN   NOUN   선생님 와인   *your wine*

c)   NOUN [squeeze!] NOUN   선생님 것 〔껏〕   *yours (your thing)*

주의!

By "squeeze" here is meant the following: the pronunciation of initial
ㅂ, ㄷ, ㅈ, ㄱ, ㅅ in the second member of some NOUN + NOUN
pairs like 것 *thing* in (c) can double (in pronunciation, but not in writing)
for no good reason.

An important difference between English and Korean is that Korean sentences do not usually end with possessive phrases of the kind *This is mine*, as English sentences sometimes do, because the particle 의 must have another noun expression after it. This may be the unspecific quasi-free noun 것 *the thing, the one*, which in this usage corresponds to the English possessives in such sentences as *This is the teacher's* and *Where is Mr. Dewey's?* The following examples illustrate the point.

21.   그것은 선생님(의) 위스키에요.
      That whiskey is the teacher's.   [Lit.: *That thing is the teacher's whiskey.*]

22.   그 위스키는 선생님(의) 것이에요.
      That whiskey is the teacher's (thing).

You must not say something like:

*그 위스키는 선생님의에요.

Here are some further examples of the possessive particle.

23. 이집이 영진 씨(의) 집이에요?
    Is this house Youngjin's?

24. 이것이 일본말 선생님(의) 연필이에요.
    This is the Japanese teacher's pencil.

25. 저 신문이 누구(의) 신문이에요? 제것이에요.
    Whose newspaper is that? It's mine.

26. 저 담배가 어느 분(의) 것이에요? 제 것이에요.
    Whose cigarettes are those? They're mine.

5.6. Nouns

It was pointed out in Lesson One that Korean nouns usually correspond to English nouns. Correspondence of vocabulary is one thing, and correspondence of sentence patterns is another. Korean sentences in general are less specific than English sentences. A key spot where this difference shows up is in what strikes us as an omission of pronouns from Korean sentences, particularly subjects and topics.

As emphasized already in section 5.1., it is especially important to be cautious about addressing the second person, i.e., saying *you*. The person you are addressing may be called, respectfully, 선생님 or 김 선생님. Or you may use a professional title, like 박사님 *you (who are a Ph.D.)* or 김 박사님 *you (Dr. Kim)*. All of these can also be used for the **third** person, so that a given sentence containing such an expression is, when seen or heard out of its context, ambiguous.

Korean nouns are used in sentences in one of the following four positions.

1. Before particles
   A particle after a noun shows its grammatical relationship to the rest of the sentence.
2. Before the copula
   A noun plus the copula means *is (the same thing as) NOUN,* in the formula
   X is NOUN or *It is NOUN.*

3.   Before another noun

See below for explanation.

4.   By itself (absolute)

[Note: Korean nouns are sometimes used by themselves, with nothing but a pause after them, in absolute position, usually at the beginning of a sentence like a topic. You will learn more about this later.]

Nouns are used to modify or describe other nouns. Such noun-plus-noun phrases as 김 선생 님 and 김복동 are quite familiar to you. Names of nations (e.g., 영국 *England*, 한국 *Korea*) combine in such phrases as these.

영국사람
Englishman (England-person)

한국말
Korean (Korea-language)

You have seen instances of the latter phrase, 한국말, in turn being used to modify a third noun.

한국말 책 (선생, 학생)
Korean language book (teacher, student)

Some nouns are used more frequently as modifiers of other nouns than by themselves. Then there is a special group of nouns used only before other nouns. These are PRE-NOUNS, and you have learned the following in this lesson.

무슨 (담배)	*what kind of (cigarettes)?*
어느 (것)	*which (thing)?*
이 (것)	*this (thing)*
그 (것)	*that (thing)*
저 (것)	*that (thing), yonder*

Another special group of nouns are used only *after* such pre-nouns (or after other modifying elements). These are called QUASI-FREE NOUNS, since they seem to be free to do everything except start a sentence.

(그) 것	*(that) thing*
(그) 곳	*(that) place*
(그) 분	*(that) esteemed person*

Exercises

Exercise 1: Manipulating Two-shape Particles

To practice making a quick choice of shapes when using two-shape particles, say each of the following words aloud (together with its English meaning). Say it again with the subject particle 이 ~ 가 after it; then with the topic particle 은 ~ 는 after it. Finally, add the copula in －이에요 ~ 에요 so that you have a sentence *It is . . . .* Do you remember what each word means?

아내	한국말	남편	선생
러시아사람	신문	연필	나
잡지	일본사람	분필	러시아
책	이것	부인	담배
칠판	그 사람	학생	술
종이	친구	사람	의사
선생님	중국말	영어	미국
저	홍콩	수입품	우산

Exercise 2: Complete the Sentence

Complete 김 선생님 's sentence below in Korean, using each of the expressions in the list below. Repeat the entire sentence each time. Then write each one again, making it negative as in 머피 선생님 's sentence.

김 선생님: 저 사람은 _____(이)에요.
머피 선생님: 저 사람은 _____(이 ~ 가) 아니에요.

1. Japanese [person].
2. a Korean pop-singer.
3. a banker.
4. a Russian student.
5. an American doctor.
6. a company employee.
7. Professor Kim's wife.
8. my friend.
9. my wife.
10. my husband.
11. a Chinese diplomat.
12. an English language teacher.

Exercise 3: Complete the Sentences

Now, fill in the blanks of the following two pattern sentences with each of the expressions below, again writing out the entire sequence each time.

김 선생님:　　　　이것은 _____(이 ~ 가) 아니에요. 그럼 뭐에요?
머피 선생님:　　　이건 _____이에요 ~ 에요. 누구(의) _____이에요 ~ 에요?

1.	blackboard	2.	magazine
3.	chalk	4.	matches
5.	Chinese language newspaper	6.	newspaper
7.	cigarettes	8.	paper
9.	ball-point pen	10.	pencil
11.	Japanese language magazine	12.	Russian language book

Exercise 4: Complete the Sentence

Complete this sentence by using each of the following expressions, of course writing out the whole sentence every time.

이 신문은 _____ 거에요.

1.	박 박사님's	2.	김복동 씨's
3.	his	4.	박 박사님's wife's
5.	mine	6.	만호 씨's
7.	my friend's	8.	수진 씨's
9.	my husband's	10.	my wife's

Exercise 5: Translation into Korean

Translate these sentences into Korean.

1. Is that Mr. Pak's notebook?
2. No, that's not Mr. Pak's.
3. Whose umbrella is it?
4. It's the pop star's.
5. Is Mr. Chang's wife a student?
6. No. She isn't a student. She's a Korean teacher.

Lesson Five /71

7. Is that foreign student an American?

8. No. He's not an American. He's an Australian.

9. Are these Manho's matches?

10. What country's product is this notebook?

11. That man over there is a Chinese diplomat.

12. This is the Chinese diplomat's Korean language book.

13. Which one is the Russian newspaper?

14. I don't know. Is it that one?

15. Dr. Mogami is Japanese.

16. Is your wife Russian? No, she's not Russian. She's French.

17. Who is that man? He is Professor Chang.

18. What kind of magazine is that? I don't know.

Exercise 6: Vocabulary Drill

Each of the following sets of words contains a misfit, a word whose meaning does not fit in with that of the rest. Spot the misfit, and be sure you know why it does not belong. (This drill is best done orally and rapid fire.)

1.	가수	신문	의사	은행원
2.	종이	분필	연필	은행
3.	일본	영어	영국	러시아
4.	선생	학생	교수	책
5.	중국말	일본말	영어	한국
6.	나	당신	우리	회사원
7.	성냥	의사	가수	교수
8.	남편	부인	아내	칠판

Lesson 6

실례지만, 프라자 호텔이 어디에요?

In this lesson you will learn how to ask for and buy things in a shop, and how to ask directions and locations. You will learn two important verbs of existence and location, and how to manipulate place nouns and the location particle 에. You will also learn how to make nouns specifically plural and how to answer negative questions.

Korean Dialogues

Dialogue 1

Chris Murphy has popped into a shop to buy some cigarettes.

아저씨	어서 오세요. 뭘 드릴까요?
크리스	담배 있어요?
아저씨	네, 있어요.
크리스	성냥도 있어요?
아저씨	아니오, 없어요. 라이타는 있어요.
크리스	그럼 담배하고 라이타 주세요.
아저씨	담배는 미국 거 드릴까요?
크리스	아니오, 저 (pointing behind the 아저씨)
	한국담배 주세요.
아저씨	예, 알겠습니다. 여기 있어요.
크리스	전부 얼마에요?
아저씨	천원이에요.

Notes

어서 오세요	*Welcome! (Come [in] right away!)*
뭘	Abbreviation of 무엇을 (*what?* plus object marker)
드릴까요?	*Shall I give you?* You will learn the verb and its ending in a later lesson. For now, memorize it as part of this dialogue.
주세요	*Please give me.* You will learn the verb and its ending in a later lesson. For now, memorize it as part of this dialogue.
미국 거	*American one(s).*
여기 있어요	*Here you are, Here it is, Here you go.*

Dialogue 2

Eunice is looking for the British Embassy downtown and knows it is near the Plaza Hotel. Little does she know, but she is only yards from the Embassy.

유니스	아가씨, 실례지만, 프라자 호텔이 어디에요?
아가씨	프라자 호텔요? 저기, (pointing) 시청 맞은 편에 있어요.
유니스	아, 네. 그러면 영국 대사관은요?
아가씨	영국 대사관요? 바로 이 건물 뒤에 있어요.
유니스	고맙습니다.

Notes

실례지만 . . .	*Excuse me, but . . . (It is a discourtesy, but . . .)* Memorize this as a handy expression.
-은 ~ 는요?	*What about? How about?*

Additional Text for Reading

교실 안에 학생들이 있어요.

책상 위에 신문하고 잡지가 있어요.

창문 밖에는 무엇이 있어요? 창문 밖에는 나무가 있어요.

가방 속에 담배는 없어요? 네, 없어요.

화장실이 어디에 있어요? 교실 바로 옆에 있어요.

Vocabulary

Places

학교	school
대학교	university
이대 (이화 여자 대학교)	Ewha Women's University
연대 (연세 대학교)	Yonsei University
서강대 (서강 대학교)	Sogang University
서울대 (서울 대학교)	Seoul National University
고대 (고려 대학교)	Korea University
교실	classroom
방	room
캠퍼스	campus
서점	bookstore
기숙사	dormitory, residence hall
학생회관	student union [building]
화장실	toilet, restroom, bathroom, washroom
커피숍	coffee shop
호텔	hotel
프라자 호텔	Plaza Hotel
롯데 호텔	Lotte Hotel
조선 호텔	Chosun Hotel
신라 호텔	Shilla Hotel
쉐라톤 워커힐 호텔	Sheraton Walker Hill Hotel
하이야트 호텔	Hyatt Hotel
라마다 올림피아 호텔	Ramada Olympia Hotel
대사관	embassy
영사관	consulate
건물, 빌딩	building
교보 빌딩	the Kyobo building, near Kwanghwamun
시청	City Hall
공원	park
파고다 공원	Pagoda Park
올림픽 공원	Olympic Park
도산 공원	Tosan Park
백화점	department store
현대 백화점	Hyundai Department Store
신세계 백화점	Shinsegye Department Store

미도파 백화점	Midopa Department Store
롯데 백화점	Lotte Department Store
시장	market
남대문	Great South Gate
동대문	Great East Gate
광화문	Kwanghwamun, Kwanghwa Gate
종로	Chongno (main thoroughfare in Seoul)
신촌	Shinch'on (near Ewha, Yonsei and Sogang Universities)
정문	main gate (e.g., of a university)
근처	vicinity
가게	a shop; store
역	train station
서울역	Seoul station, pronounced 서울력
여기	here
거기	there
저기	over there
어디	where

Things or Objects

책상	desk
상, 테이블	table
그림	picture
의자	chair
창문	window
문	door, gate
나무	tree
가방	bag, briefcase
라이타	lighter
텔레비전	television

People

어머니	mother
아버지	father
부모(님)	parents (honorific)
아이 ~ 애	child
아기 ~ 애기	baby

아저씨	mister (way of referring to or addressing a man old enough to be married)
아가씨	young lady (way of referring to or addressing an unmarried young woman)
남자	man
남자친구	boyfriend
여자	woman
여자친구	girlfriend

Ways to Connect Sentences

그래서 . . .	And so . . . , And then . . . , Therefore . . .
나는 학생이에요.	I'm a student.
그래서 돈이 없어요.	Therefore I have no money.
그래도 . . .	Even so; Nevertheless
그 사람은 의사에요.	He's a doctor.
그래도 돈이 없어요.	Even so, he has no money.
그리고 . . .	And also . . . , And then . . .
이대는 신촌에 있어요.	Ewha University is in Shinch'on.
그리고 연대도 거기 있어요.	And Yonsei University is there, too.
그런데 . . .	But . . . , And then . . . , By the way . . .
책상 위에 가방하고 노트가 있어요.	There is a bag and a notebook on the table.
그런데 볼펜은 없어요.	But there is no pen.

Other Items

얼마	how many? how much?
천	thousand
-원	Korean monetary unit
돈	money
노트	notebook (same meaning as 공책)
바로	just, right (below, above, etc.), straight (adverb)
있어요	it exists, there is/are
없어요	it does not exist, there is not/aren't
주세요	please give

You are also responsible for the Place Nouns listed in section 6.5.

Lesson Notes

6.1. Existence and Location with 있어요 and 없어요

The English word *be* (*am, are, is*) has a variety of meanings. These are expressed in Korean by a number of vocabulary items.

a.　*Be* in the sense that something *equals* or *is the same thing as* something else corresponds to the Korean copula –(이)에요. Lesson Five dealt with this.

b.　*Be* in the sense that something is located somewhere or is existing, on the other hand, is 있어요. The negative is a separate word 없어요 *does not exist, is not located*. These words also mean *there is/are* and *there isn't/aren't*.

Here are some pairs of sentences that contrast the meanings of these two types of verbs—equational –(이)에요 and existential 있어요 and 없어요.

1.　A.　책이에요　　　　　　　　*It's a book. They are books.*
　　B.　책이 있어요　　　　　　　*There is a book (somewhere).*
　　　　　　　　　　　　　　　　There are some books (somewhere).
　　　　　　　　　　　　　　　　(Someone) has got a book.
　　C.　책(이) 아니에요　　　　　*It's not a book.*
　　　　　　　　　　　　　　　　They aren't books.

　　D.　책이 없어요　　　　　　　*There isn't any book (somewhere).*
　　　　　　　　　　　　　　　　There aren't any books (somewhere).
　　　　　　　　　　　　　　　　(Someone) hasn't got a book.

2.　A.　학교에요　　　　　　　　*It's a school. or They are schools.*
　　B.　학교에 있어요　　　　　　*It's at school.*

　　　　　　　　　　　　　　　　They are at school. or

　　　　　　　　　　　　　　　　There's (one) at school.

　　　　　　　　　　　　　　　　There are (some) at school.

　　　　　　　　　　　　　　　　They've got one at school.
　　C.　학교(가) 아니에요　　　　*It's not a school.*

　　　　　　　　　　　　　　　　They aren't schools.
　　D.　학교에 없어요　　　　　　*It's not at school.*

　　　　　　　　　　　　　　　　They aren't at school. or

　　　　　　　　　　　　　　　　There isn't or aren't (any) at school.

3. A. 여기가 어디에요?   *What is this (place)?*
                                  [Lit.: *This place is what place?*]
    B. 여기 어디(에) 있어요?   *Where in this place is it?* or
                                  Where in this place is there (one)?

The copula - (이) 에요, then, has one meaning—identity.

The verb 있어요 and its negative 없어요 have meanings we can label EXISTENCE (*there is[n't]* or *are[n't]*) and LOCATION (*is[n't]* or *are(n't) in a place*). A third related meaning for these—POSSESSION—is discussed in the following section. Here are some further examples of the location usage.

4. 그 학생이 여기 있어요.
    The student is here.

5. 대학교 뒤에 시장이 없어요.
    There isn't any market behind the university.

6. A. 교실 안에 그림이 있어요?
       Are there any pictures in the classroom?

    B. 네, 있어요.
    B'. 아니오, 없어요.
       Yes, there are.
       No, there aren't.

7. A. 백화점이 어디(에) 있어요?
    A'. 백화점이 어디에요?
       Where is the department store?

    B. 저기 있어요.
       It's over there.

8. A. 화장실이 어디(에) 있어요?
       Where is the toilet?

    B. 왼편에 있어요.
       It's to your left.

9. A. 여기 호텔이 있어요?
       Is there a hotel here?

    B. 없어요.
       (No) there isn't.

Note that when the thing being asked about is a place, one has two ways of asking its location (see sentences 7A and 7A' above). This is not possible with nouns which do not express a location: *잡지가 어디에요? is impossible for 잡지가 어디에 있어요?

Lesson Six / 79

6.2. Possession with 있어요 and 없어요

As you have just observed, 있어요 is in one way more limited than its English counterpart. It is equivalent to *be* (*am, are, is*) in only one of its meanings.

At the same time 있어요 is too broad in scope for a single English equivalent. It is the normal Korean way of expressing possession, as conveyed by English *has* (*have*) and *has got* (*have got*).

10.	돈이 있어요?	either	*Is there money (in some place)?*
		or	*Have you [any] money?*

11.	여자친구가 없어요.	either	*There aren't any girlfriends.*
		or	*I haven't got a girlfriend.*

The above two meanings seem quite distinct to people who are accustomed to English vocabulary patterns, but Koreans do not ordinarily draw the distinction. The context usually makes it clear which English translation is more suitable in each instance.

It is not unknown for a Korean sentence of this type to have two subjects, one naming the possessor of an object, the other naming the object possessed, as follows.

12. 내가 애기가 있어요.
I have a baby.

Another kind of sentence that might have two subjects, you may recall, is a negative copula sentence: 그것이 내 것이 아니에요 *That isn't mine*.

But it is more usual in such cases for the possessor to be expressed as a topic, and the things possessed as a subject.

13. 그 사람은 가방이 있어요?
Does he have a satchel/bag?

14. 우리는 텔레비전이 없어요.
We don't have a television.

15. 만호는 종이가 없어요.
Manho hasn't got any paper.

16.   A. 성냥이 있어요?
        Have you got a match?

       B. 있어요.
        (Yes), I have.

17.   돈이 없어요.
    I haven't any money.

18.   나는 가방이 없어요.
    I haven't got a briefcase.

6.3. Location Particle 에 *in, at*

To begin with, take a look at the following examples.

19.   우리는 교실 안에 있어요.
    We're in the classroom.

20.   그 사람은 학교에 없어요.
    He's not at school.

Korean uses the particle 에 to locate things in space. This single particle 에 conveys the meaning carried by several different English prepositions relating to general location. Perhaps the hardest thing to get used to in Korean is placing the particle after the noun, to correspond to what in English appears before the noun.

After certain nouns that end in 이, 에, or 애, the particle 에 is often not heard. This can happen, for example, in these expressions.

21.   어디(에) 있어요?
    Where is it?

22.   거기(에) . . .
    (In) that place . . .

But this is not true in every case: for example, 사이에 *between* and 위에 *on top of*.

6.4. The Particle 하고 *and, with*

Another single vocabulary item in English, the connective *and*, is translated variously in Korean, depending on its usage. Between Korean nouns, the word for *and* is 하고.

23.　　담배하고 성냥
　　　　cigarettes and matches

If English speakers pause when they are giving a list, it is natural for them to do so before the *and*, but the Koreans pause after 하고. This is because 하고 is a particle, and particles are pronounced as part of the word they follow, like a suffix rather than a separate word. Until you learn Korean equivalents for *and* in other uses, such as to join sentences, you can use two separate sentences and begin the second with 그리고.

Note that the particle 하고 can also mean *with*.

24.　　A. 진영 씨는 어디(에) 있어요?
　　　　　Where's Jinyŏng?

　　　　B. 옆방에 남자친구하고 있어요.
　　　　　She's in the next room with her boyfriend.

6.5. Place Nouns

You have seen in this lesson a number of nouns denoting specific place relationships. With 에 *in, at, on* after them, they mean *in* (a certain place relationship). Here is a list.

안에	*inside*
속에	*inside*
밖에	*outside*
위에	*above, over, on (top)*
밑에	*at the bottom, below under(neath)*
아래(에)	*below, lower, down*
앞에	*in front*
뒤에	*at the back; behind*
근처에	*near, in the vicinity of*
옆에	*next to, beside*

편 (or 쪽)	side, direction
왼편 ~ 쪽에	on the left
오른편 ~ 쪽에	on the right
맞은편에	across from, opposite
건너편에	across from, opposite
사이에	between

These are PLACE NOUNS. They are most frequently used in phrases with other nouns [refer to section 5.6., noun use (3) if necessary].

대학교 앞에	in front of the university
대사관 옆에	next to the embassy

It is important to put these nouns in the right order. If the place noun comes before the other noun, the meaning is changed. The place noun modifies the noun that follows it. This point is best illustrated by example. There are many, but the following are typical.

문 앞에	in front of the door
앞문	the front door
방 옆에	next to the room
옆방	the next room

The place noun 사이 (사이에 *between*) by the nature of its meaning usually requires two nouns before it. These are linked with 하고 *and*.

학교하고 집 사이에	between the school and the house

Some place nouns are also used as time nouns: 사이 can refer to an interval of time as well as of space; 앞 can refer ahead in time (앞으로 *in future*); 안 can mean *within* (a certain time); and, 다음 most commonly means *next* (in order or time).

Corresponding to such English expressions as *where in this room* (requests for more specific
locations), there are Korean phrases like these.

이 교실 안 어디(요)?	*Where in this classroom?* [Literally: *in what place of this classroom's inside?*]
책상 위 어디(요)?	*Where on (top of) the desk?*

You may have noticed the relationship between a special set of place nouns and the set of
noun-modifying nouns you learned.

이	*this*	여기	*this place, here*
그	*that*	거기	*that place, there*
	(nearby, aforementioned)		*(nearby, aforementioned)*
저	*that (over there)*	저기	*that place, (over) there*

You will hear these words occasionally pronounced 요, 고, 조 and 요기, 고기, 조기.
These add a connotation of smallness or cuteness *this li'l* . . . or of deprecation *this ole*. Here
are further examples of the usage of place nouns.

25.　광화문 근처에는 무슨 건물이 있어요?
　　What kind of buildings are there in the vicinity of Kwanghwamun?

26.　백화점 건너편에 무엇이 있어요?
　　What is there across from the department store?

27.   대학교 정문 앞에 가방가게가 있어요?
        Is there a briefcase shop outside (in front of) the main gate of the university?

28.   이 건물 안에 커피숍이 있어요?
        Is there a coffee shop in(side of) this building?

6.6. More about the Topic Particle 은 ~ 는

This lesson offers more examples of the topic particle in its capacity for reducing or subduing the emphasis of what goes before it. We can put these usages of the topic particle into three general categories: stage setting, contrast, old business.

Stage setting occurs when the topic particle sets the stage for what the sentence is going to be about. It comes after a noun expression and sets it aside as what we are going to talk about.

29.   가방 속에는 무엇이 있어요?
        Talking about the inside of the bag, what is in there?

In the case of contrast, two noun expressions or other phrases (about which you want to make contrasting statements or offer differing information) are set aside at the beginning of their respective clauses. Each is followed by the particle 은 ~ 는, to subdue its emphasis so the way is cleared for the important contrasting statements.

30.   왼편에는 . . . 오른편에는 . . .
        On the left (guess what?!) . . . (and) on the right (guess what?!)

We have seen that one function of 이 ~ 가 is to introduce new business. The first time a subject is mentioned in context, its newness calls for emphasis through marking with the subject particle 이 ~ 가. However, if this subject reappears in the conversation, it comes under the heading of old business. In this case, it appears with the particle 은 ~ 는, which relegates it to the realm of subdued emphasis. In fact, it often happens that the subject disappears altogether.

6.7. Answering Negative Questions

If you want to answer a Korean question with yes or no, you do it just as you would in English, so long as the question is an affirmative one. If the question is negative, you use the Korean word for yes to agree with the negativeness, and the Korean word for no to disagree with the negativeness. The resulting usage is the opposite from the English.

31. 가방 속에 담배는 없어요?
Don't you have any cigarettes inside your briefcase?

    a.   네, 없어요,
           Yes, [I agree with your words] there aren't any.

    b.   아니오, 있어요,
           No, [your impression is mistaken] there are some cigarettes.

Occasionally there are exceptions, for example, when the question is put in the negative form just to be polite. Here are some further illustrations. Note carefully the difference between the Korean and the English translations.

32.   A. 그 사람은 미국사람이 아니에요?
        Isn't that man an American?

        B. 네, 아니에요. 영국사람이에요.
           No, he's not. He's English. (Yes, he's not an American.)

33.   A. 연필이 없어요?
        Haven't you a pencil?

        B. 네, 없어요.
           No, I haven't.

34.   A. 가방(이) 없어요?
        Don't you have a bag?

        B. 아니오, 있어요.
           Yes, I do.

6.8. The Plural Marker 들

Korean nouns are not specific with respect to number. The following sentence conveys information which might correspond to several English sentences.

35.   책하고 공책하고 연필이 있어요.
        I've got a book, a notebook, and a pencil.
        I've got some books, a notebook, and a pencil.
        I've got some books, a notebook, and some pencils.
        I've got some books, some notebooks, and a pencil.

And so on, until the mathematical possibilities are exhausted. But if it is really necessary, Korean can make nouns specifically plural. (Without using numerals, Korean cannot make them specifically singular.) Korean does this by placing 들, a word meaning something like *group*, after them.

선생	*teacher* or *teachers*
선생들	*teachers*

As you might expect, Korean also allows you to put 들 on pronouns, including even those which are already plural.

우리, 우리들	*we*
저희, 저희들	*we* (Humble)
너희, 너희들	*you all* (Intimate)
그 사람, 그 사람들	*he, she; they*

Particles to be used with the plural phrase come after the 들.

The word 들 is uniquely versatile. It may pop up just about anywhere in a Korean sentence except on the verb at the very end. Furthermore, 들 need not always refer to the words near it. It is used to make explicit that the speaker is talking about (or to) more than one thing (or person). Here are some examples.

36.　어서들 오세요!
　　　Welcome! (said to more than person to be explicit that all are welcome)

37.　천천히들 가세요!
　　　Go slow! (said to two or more people going too fast)

38.　A. 학생들이 어디에 있어요?
　　　　Where are the students?

　　　B. 교실에들 있어요.
　　　　They're in the classroom.

Exercises

Exercise 1: Fill in the Blanks

Fill in the blanks of the following sentences with each of the place expressions listed. Express them in Korean and practice them aloud.

1.   집 _____ 나무가 있어요.

      a.   in
      b.   outside
      c.   in front of
      d.   next to
      e.   at the back of

2.   만호 씨 공책은 가방 _____ 있어요.

      a.   on top of
      b.   in
      c.   beside
      d.   under
      e.   to the right of

3.   교보빌딩은 광화문 _____ 있어요?

      a.   at
      b.   behind
      c.   next to
      d.   in front of
      e.   in the vicinity of

Exercise 2: Sentence Construction

Make up two sentences with each of the sets of information given below, one indicating that there is something, the other that there isn't. For example, if you were given 교실 and 학생, then your two sentences would be: 교실에 학생이 있어요 and 교실에 학생이 없어요.

1.	방	책상
2.	집	텔레비전
3.	교실	학생
4.	방	의자
5.	학교	화장실
6.	가방	책
7.	대사관	그림
8.	호텔	가게
9.	백화점	커피숍
10.	대학교	은행

Exercise 3: Naming Locations

Make Korean sentences filling in each blank five times using the phrases given in (a) - (e), completing the sentences in any way you choose. Practice saying them aloud until you feel sure of them.

1.   수진 씨는 _____.

   a.   next to
   b.   to the left of
   c.   across from
   d.   between
   e.   to the right of

2.   제 책은 _____.

   a.   on
   b.   under
   c.   just beside
   d.   between
   e.   inside of

3.   은행은 _____.

   a.   beside
   b.   right across from
   c.   at the back of
   d.   to the left of
   e.   outside of

4.   _____ 공원이 있어요.

   a.   in the vicinity of
   b.   in front of
   c.   between
   d.   opposite
   e.   behind

Exercise 4: English to Korean Translation

Translate these sentences into Korean and practice them until you can say them fluently.

1. Where are my cigarettes?
2. Are they inside Manho's briefcase?
3. In my briefcase I've got some books, some papers, and a lighter.
4. But I don't have any paper.
5. Here, I have some paper. Have you got a pen?
6. The pen is on the desk.
7. I'm sorry. There isn't any pen on the desk.
8. Is it under the desk? Is it on the television?
9. There isn't any. But I have one in the next room. Excuse me.
10. Here is a pen. It's a Korean pen.
11. Are Manho's cigarettes Korean cigarettes ?
12. No. They're American (ones).
13. Professor Park's wife is between Manho and Sujin.
14. Manho is my friend. He's a Korean student.
15. Who is Sujin? Is Sujin a student, too? Is she a company employee?

Exercise 5: Korean to English Translation

Translate the following Korean sentences into English.

1. A. 학교 앞에는 나무가 있어요.
   B. 나무 밑에는 뭐가 있어요? 애기에요?
   A. 모르겠어요.
2. 영진 씨 부모님하고 영진 씨가 여기 있어요. 만호 씨는 옆방에 있어요.
3. 책상 옆에는 그림이 있어요.
4. 최 선생님은 돈이 얼마 있어요?
5. A. 얼마에요?
   B. 천원 주세요.
6. 책상 위에는 신문하고 잡지가 있어요.
7. A. 내 공책이 어디에 있어요?
   B. 미안해요. 다시 한번 말해 주세요. 그리고 천천히 말해 주세요.
8. A. 내 담배는 책상 위 어디에 있어요?
   B. 저 책 바로 밑에 있어요.
9. A. 대사관 근처에는 무슨 건물이 있어요?
   B. 왼편에는 호텔이 있어요. 그리고 맞은편에는 시청이 있어요.

Exercise 6: Possession and Plurals

This exercise is designed to practice the way to say *I have* and also the explicit plural marker 들. You should use that particle in the following questions whenever it is reasonable to do so. This is for the purposes of this exercise only. Remember that Korean does not need to mark words as explicitly plural in the way that English does.

1. I have some books and magazines.
2. Please give me those pens. I haven't got any.
3. By the way, don't you have any Korean newspapers?
4. Teacher Lee doesn't have any chalk.
5. Are there any students in this room?
6. [Three people knock at your office door]
   Please come in!
7. A. Where are the magazines?
   B. They're over there [be explicitly plural].
8. A. Doesn't Manho's friend have any books?
   B. No, he doesn't.
9. A. Do you have any pictures in (your) room?
   B. No, but my parents do in their room.

Exercise 7: Vocabulary Drill

Complete the following sentences by filling in the blanks with each of the words listed below them. Write out each entire sentence in Korean.

1. 책상 옆에 _____이 ~ 가 있어요?

a pen	a briefcase	a lighter
a notebook	a child	a TV
pencils	pictures	a desk
a door	a book	a baby
chairs	a blackboard	
1000 wŏn	matches	

2. 만호 씨 집 근처에 _____은 ~ 는 없어요?

a school	an embassy	a bank
a park	a department store	a hotel
a company	a university	a shop

Lesson 7

대전행 차표는 어디서 팔아요?

In this lesson you will learn how to ask people where they are going and what they are doing. You learn to talk a bit about eating and drinking and how to buy tickets at a railway station. Finally, the lesson introduces you to the most important verb types in Korean, the object particle 을 ~ 를, ways to say *to* and *from*, and dynamic location with 에서.

Korean Dialogues

Dialogue 1

Eunice runs into the elderly Korean lady across the hall as she leaves on her way for her morning Korean language classes.

유니스	안녕하세요?
할머니	안녕하세요? 어디 가요?
유니스	학교에 가요.
할머니	요즘 학교에 다녀요?
유니스	네, 월요일하고 수요일에 고려 대학교에 가요.
	고대에서 한국말을 배워요.
할머니	그래요? 빨리 다녀와요!

Notes

할머니	*grandmother* (term of address for any woman old enough to be a grandmother).
수요일에	*on (Mondays and) Wednesdays.* The particle 에 is used to locate things in time, as well as in space.
다녀와요!	*See you later!* (said to somebody leaving home who will be back later). [Memorize this as a useful expression.]

Dialogue 2

Later after class, Eunice runs into the elderly lady again downstairs.

유니스	다녀 왔어요.
할머니	그래, 점심은 보통 어디에서 먹어요?
유니스	학교 식당에서 먹어요.
할머니	거기는 음식을 잘 해요?
유니스	네, 불고기하고 비빔밥을 잘 해요. 아주 맛이 있어요.
할머니	술도 팔아요?
유니스	아이구, 할머니 — 학교식당에서 무슨 술을 팔아요?!

Notes

다녀왔어요!	*I'm back!* (said by someone who has just come back home from going out for a while). [Memorize this as a useful expression.]
그래	Literally: *It is so*; *really*. This is simply the elderly lady's way of saying *I've heard your greeting* (and I am much older than you are, which is why I've dropped the 요, so I can get away with this perfunctory response).
거기는 잘 해요?	Literally: *Do they do (it) well there?* This is a useful way for expressing *Are they any good? Are they good at what they do?*
아이구!	*Oh, my! Oh, dear!* This is the most ubiquitous Korean exclamation.
무슨 술을 팔아요?!	*Since when do they sell booze?* Lit.: *What sort of booze would/do they sell (none!).* Korean can use questions with 무슨 like this to make a rhetorical question with exclamatory force.

Dialogue 3

Chris Murphy has to catch the train from Seoul station to Taejŏn for a business meeting. Unsure of which queue he should be standing in, he asks somebody.

크리스	실례합니다. 대전행 차표는 어디서 팔아요?
아저씨	매표소가 저기 있어요.
크리스	감사합니다.

Chris buys the ticket.

크리스	대전행 기차는 어느 플랫폼에서 떠나요?
아가씨	첫 플랫폼에서 떠나요.

| 크리스 | 몇 시간 걸려요? |
| 아가씨 | 두 시간 걸려요. |

He then notices the agent looking for something.

크리스	뭘 찾아요?
아가씨	제 볼펜요.
크리스	아, 여기 있어요. 미안해요.

Notes

여기 있어요	*Here it is. Here you go. Here you are.*
두 시간	*Two hours.* Notice that the final ㄹ of 둘 *two* drops before the counter expression 시간 *hours.* You will learn more about numerals and counters in Lesson Eleven.
미안해요	*I'm sorry.* This is the Polite Style version of 미안합니다.

Vocabulary

Days of the Week and Related Expressions

어제	yesterday
오늘	today
내일	tomorrow
월요일(에)	(on) Monday
화요일(에)	(on) Tuesday
수요일(에)	(on) Wednesday
목요일(에)	(on) Thursday
금요일(에)	(on) Friday
토요일(에)	(on) Saturday
일요일(에)	(on) Sunday

Other Time Expressions

요즘	nowadays, these days
보통	usually, normally
날	day
아침(에)	(in the) morning; breakfast
낮(에)	(in the) daytime; noon

오후(에)	(in the) afternoon, PM
오전(에)	(in the) AM
저녁(에)	(in the) evening; supper
어제 저녁(에)	yesterday evening
오늘 저녁(에)	this evening (not *이 저녁)
밤(에)	(at) night
어제 밤(에)	last night
오늘 밤(에)	tonight (not *이 밤(에))
일찍	early (adverb)
아침 일찍	early in the morning
늦게	late (adverb)
이따가	in a while, a while later
언제	when?
지금	now
주말(에)	(on the/over the) weekend
시간	hour; time

Food, Eating and Drinking

식당	dining room, restaurant, cafeteria, refectory
음식점	restaurant
레스토랑	restaurant (somewhat upscale)
빵	bread
고기	meat
불고기	pulgogi
비빔밥 〔비빔빱〕	pibimpap, pibimbap
음식	food
밥	cooked rice
밥(을) 먹어요	eats a meal, has a meal
아침	breakfast, morning meal
점심	lunch
저녁	supper, evening meal
우유	milk
물	water
맛	taste
맛(이) 있-	be tasty, delicious (pronounced 마시이써요)
맛 없-	taste bad, not taste good (pronounced 마덥써요, 마시업써요)

Travel and Transport

PLACE-행	bound for PLACE
부산행 기차	a Pusan train, train bound for Pusan
차	car, vehicle
기차	train
비행기	airplane
자전거	bicycle
표	ticket
차표	(train, bus) ticket
매표소	ticket counter
플랫폼	platform

Miscellaneous

아버님	father (honorific)
어머님	mother (honorific)
도서관	library
슈퍼마켓	supermarket
장(을) 보-	do grocery shopping
영화	movie, film
극장	theatre (can mean both cinema and venue for a dramatic performance)
편지	letter
불	fire; light; a light
일	matter, business; work
개	dog
고양이	cat
휴지	tissue paper, Kleenex, toilet tissue
수건, 타올	towel
노래	song
노래(를) 불러요	sings a song
노래방	noraebang; Korean karaoke box
첫 NOUN	first NOUN
몇	how many?
혼자[서]	alone, on one's own, by oneself
빨리	quickly
많이	a lot (adverb)
조금	a little
잘	well; often
아주	very

Lesson Seven introduces you to many different verbs. These are listed in groups in the Lesson Notes. For that reason they have not been repeated here. The first group below gives the verb bases occurring in the Korean dialogues at the beginning of the lesson, the second group lists verbs that are formed with 하-.

배우-	learn	파-ㄹ-	sell
먹-	eat	다니-	attend, go on regular basis
있-	be; exist; have	사-	buy
떠나-	leave, depart	가-	go
걸리-	take (time)	찾-	look for (it)

공부(를) 하-	study	잘하-	do well, do (it) well
산보(를) 하- 〔삼뽀〕	stroll, take a walk	말(을) 하-	speak, talk (a language)
		미안하-	be sorry, feel sorry
일(을) 하-	work; do work	구경(을) 하-	do viewing or sightsee
영화구경(을) 하-	see a film		

Lesson Notes

7.1. Verbs: The Polite Style and the Infinitive

The Korean sentences of this lesson end with verbs of various kinds. Notice that the verbs you have learned, including 있어요 *is, exists*; 없어요 *isn't, doesn't exist*; and the copula -(이)에요 *is*, end with 요, and that before this 요, there is a vowel sound. Verbs that end this way are in the Polite Style (해요) of speech.

As you have seen earlier, the social relationship between two speakers determines what style they use when speaking to each other, i.e., what endings they will use with the verbs at the end of their sentences. If they are educated people who respect each other and yet do not feel stiff or formal together, they are apt to use the Polite Style most of the time.

The Polite Style ending is the same regardless of whether it is used with a verb that asks a question or one which makes a statement. It is usually the speaker's tone of voice, rather than the actual syllables he utters, that indicate this sort of meaning. It is similar to the way that you can turn such a sentence as *You're not going* into either a question or an announcement.

Verbs in the polite style can make suggestions *Let's . . .* or even gentle commands *Why don't you* or *How about VERBing?* All use the same verb form, ending in a vowel sound plus 요.

Korean verb forms are made up of BASES with ENDINGS on them. The present-tense forms you have seen so far are all in the Polite Style and have the particle 요 at the end to mark the style. If you remove this 요, the part that remains is called the INFINITIVE of the verb (the term has nothing to do with the denotation of infinitives in European languages). The Korean infinitive has a great many uses of its own, and in addition it is what the past tense is based on (we will look at this in the next lesson).

Here is a list of common verbs in the infinitive form (you need to learn these as part of the vocabulary for this lesson).

앉아	*sits*	찾아	*looks for; finds*
자	*goes to bed; sleeps*	좋아	*is good*
작아	*is little in size*	줘 ← 주어	*gives*
적어	*are few in number*	없어	*is nonexistent*
해	*does* [IRREGULAR]	일어나	*gets up; stands up*
빨라	*is fast*	읽어	*reads*
받아	*receives, gets*	있어	*exists; stays; has*
배워	*learns*	와	*comes*
가	*goes*	피워	*smokes*
가르쳐	*teaches*	서	*stands*
놀아	*plays*	봐 ← 보아	*looks at, sees*
커	*is large, big*	사	*buys*
기다려	*waits (for)*	살아	*lives*
끝나	*stops, ends, is over*	써	*writes*
많아	*is much; are many*	쉬어	*rests*
만나	*meets/sees (s.b.)*	닫아	*closes it*
마셔	*drinks*	들어	*hears; listens to*
먹어	*eats*	열어	*opens it*
돼 (← 되어)	*becomes*	다녀	*attends, goes regularly*
물어	*bites*	물어	*asks*

If you glance down the list, you will see that all of the infinitives end in a vowel 어 or 아 (해 *does* is irregular). The vowel at the end is in some cases an ending (to mark the infinitive), while in others it belongs to the basic part of the verb (its base) and the infinitive vowel 어 ~ 아 has been dropped or abbreviated.

You may wonder about the translation of infinitives by English forms like *does it* instead of *to do*. It is because the Korean forms can be used as sentences just as they stand: when you remove the polite-style particle 요 you have sentences in the Intimate Style (about which we will learn later).

주의

The word infinitive (like many grammar terms) does **not** mean the same thing when we talk about Korean as when we talk about English. It is simply a label or tag for the 어 ~ 아 ending in Korean, and you should memorize it as such.

7.2. Korean Verbs with Consonant Bases

Bases of Korean verbs are classified into two main types: CONSONANT BASES and VOWEL BASES. In this section we look at the former; vowel bases are discussed in Section 7.5.

Consonant-base verbs typically have the infinitive ending -어 and their infinitives consist of the base plus this vowel ending. **However, if the last vowel of the base is 오 or 아 then the ending is -아 instead of -어.** Here is a list of some consonant bases and infinitives:

Base		Infinitive	
앉-	*sits*	앉아	*sits*
작-	*be little in size*	작아	*is little in size*
입-	*wear; put on*	입어	*wears; puts on*
찾-	*look for; find*	찾아	*looks for; finds*
벗-	*take off (clothes)*	벗어	*takes off (clothes)*

Base		Infinitive	
좋-	*be good*	좋아	*is good*
없-	*be nonexistent*	없어	*is nonexistent*
읽-	*read*	읽어	*reads*
있-	*be, exist; stay; have*	있어	*is, exists; stays; has*
많-	*be much/many*	많아	*is much; are many*
먹-	*eat*	먹어	*eats*
받-	*receive, get*	받아	*receives, gets*
닫-	*close it*	닫아	*closes it*
들-	*listen to; hear*	들어	*listens to; hears*
더 w-	*be hot*	더워	*is hot*
나(ㅅ)-	*get/be better*	나아	*gets/is better*

7.3. The Dictionary Form of Korean Verbs

Korean dictionaries list verbs in a special dictionary form or citation form with the one-shape ending -다. This ending is the same for all verbs, and is not an infinitive. Remember that in English or other commonly learned Indo-European languages, the infinitive is something quite different. The rule for making the dictionary form is simple: base plus -다. The first four verb bases in the list on the preceding page will appear in a Korean dictionary as follows:

앉다   작다   입다   찾다

7.4. Three Types of Special Consonant Base

The only tricky point to remember about consonant-base verbs concerns the last three bases in the list in section 7.2. (들- *listen to*, 더 w- *be hot*, 나(ㅅ)- *get/be better*).

1. ㄹ ~ ㄷ verbs

    Verbs that end in -ㄹ change the -ㄹ to ㄷ before endings that begin with a consonant.

    들-   *listen to*   →   듣다   *to listen to* (Dictionary form)

2.   w ~ ㅂ verbs

     Verbs that end in -w change the -w to ㅂ before endings that begin with a consonant.

더 w- *be hot*   →   덥다   *to be hot* (Dictionary form)

주의

The ㅇ or zero consonant sign which gets written before any syllable beginning with a vowel does not count as a consonant for the purposes of our rules.

---

3.   S-irregular Verbs

     Verbs that end in (ㅅ) drop the ㅅ before endings that begin with a vowel.

나(ㅅ)-   *be better*   →   낫다   *to be better* [dictionary form]

                            →   나아   *is better* [infinitive form]

These are different from regular verbs in ㅅ, which keep the ㅅ in all forms.

벗-   *take off (clothes)*   →   벗어   *takes off (clothes)* [infinitive form]

                            →   벗다   *to take off (clothes)* [dictionary form]

7.5. Korean Verbs with Vowel Bases

The second major type of Korean verb entails bases that end with a vowel. Vowel-base verbs are unfortunately somewhat more complex:

1.   In one group, the infinitive is the same shape as the base. This includes bases ending in 아, 어 and 애:

자-	*sleep*	자	*sleeps*
가-	*go*	가	*goes*
비싸-	*be expensive*	비싸	*is expensive*
만나-	*meet*	만나	*meets*
사-	*buy*	사	*buys*

| 매- | *tie* | 매 | *ties* |
| 서- | *stand* | 서 | *stands* |

2.   In another group, the base ends in 이 and the infinitive ending -어 is added, but 이어 is abbreviated to 여.

가르치-	*teach*	가르쳐	←	가르치어	*teaches*
기다리-	*wait*	기다려	←	기다리어	*waits*
마시-	*drink*	마셔	←	마시어	*drinks*
치-	*strike, hit*	쳐	←	치어	*strikes, hits*

Note that the base 쉬- cannot abbreviate (there is no 한글 letter combining 위 and 어 in one syllable).

| 쉬- | *rest* | 쉬어 | | | *rests* |

3.   A similar group consists of bases that end in 우; they add the ending -어 and then the sequence 우어 abbreviates to 워 if the base is just one syllable.

배우-	*learn*	배워	←	배우어	*learns*
피우-	*smoke*	피워	←	피우어	*smokes*
주-	*give*	줘	←	주어	*gives*

4.   Vowel bases that end in 오 add the infinitive ending as -아 and then 오아 is shortened to 와.

| 오- | *come* | 와 | ← | 오아 | *comes* |
| 보- | *look at, see* | 봐 | ← | 보아 | *looks at, sees* |

[Note: In the case of *come*, the contraction from 오아 to 와 is obligatory. In the case of *see*, note that Korean pronunciation frequently drops *w* after consonants, especially labial sounds like ㅂ, so you will hear 봐 pronounced 바 in fast or sloppy speech.]

5.   Most vowel bases that end in 으 drop the 으 before adding the infinitive ending -어 (or -아, if there is a preceding syllable with 오 or 아).

크-	be large	커	is large
쓰-	write	써	writes
바쁘-	be busy	바빠	is busy

6. Most vowel bases that end in 르 not only drop the 으 but double the ㄹ before adding the appropriate infinitive ending (normally -어, but -아 when the vowel of the preceding syllable is 오 or 아).

빠르-	be fast	빨라	is fast
부르-	sing (a song); call	불러	sings (a song)
모르-	not know	몰라	doesn't know

These are called **L-doubling bases**.

7. Another common kind of vowel base is one which looks at first glance like a consonant base: it ends in a vowel before some endings, but picks up an ㄹ before others, two of which are the infinitive and the dictionary form.

Base		**Infinitive**		**Dictionary Form**
노-ㄹ-	play	놀아	plays	놀다
사-ㄹ-	live	살아	lives	살다
여-ㄹ-	open it	열어	opens it	열다
아-ㄹ-	know it	알아	knows it	알다
파-ㄹ-	sell it	팔아	sells it	팔다

For each new ending you learn, you must memorize whether the -ㄹ- of these verbs stays or drops before it. So far you have not learned any endings that require the -ㄹ- to drop. These are called **L-extending bases**.

It is vital that you keep these L-extending bases apart from the ㄹ ~ ㄷ verbs like 들- (듣다) *listen* introduced in section 7.4 above. Given an infinitive form like 물어, you do not know whether the underlying base is 무-ㄹ- (물다) or 물- (묻다). As it turns out, both bases exist.

무-ㄹ-	bite	물어	*bites*	물다	*to bite* (dictionary form)
물-	ask	물어	*asks*	묻다	*to ask* (dictionary form)

8.   Finally, there are three special infinitives we should mention.

1. Become

The infinitive of this verb usually has the same shape as the base, but is sometimes spelled, and occasionally pronounced, 돼 (though pronounced with a long vowel).

되-   *become*   되어 or 돼

2. Copula

The infinitive of the copula is irregular in that it does not abbreviate from -이어 to -여. Note also that the relationship between Polite Style and infinitive in the copula is irregular:

-이에요 (Polite Style)   -이어 (infinitive)   -이다 (dictionary form)

3. Do

The important verb 하- *do* has an irregular infinitive: 해. The literary form of the infinitive, which you may sometimes see, is: 하여 *does*.

해요 (Polite Style)   해 (← 하여) (infinitive)   하다 (dictionary form)

There are a few other kinds of verb bases that you will learn later.

7.6. The Direct Object Particle 을 ~ 를

The DIRECT OBJECT PARTICLE 을 ~ 를 is another two-shape particle, like the subject particle 이 ~ 가 and the topic particle 은 ~ 는. Its form is 을 after consonants and 를 after vowels. Here are some examples.

을 **After Consonant**		를 **After Vowel**	
물을	*water*	노래를	*song*
밥을	*cooked rice*	고기를	*meat*
빵을	*bread*	개를	*dog*

After a vowel, 를 is often abbreviated to just -ㄹ, especially in common expressions like 날 *me* and 이걸 *this thing*.

Remember that Korean requires you to pronounce most particles without hesitating, as though they were part of the preceding word, like suffixes. Much like English requires its speakers to pronounce "sandwich-es" or "boy-s" without stopping between the word and its suffix. If you need to pause and think what particle to use, it is better to do so before you begin to say the noun, not after you have said it. If you find you must pause, once you have found the right particle, go back and start from the noun again: 친구 . . . , 친구 . . . , 친구를 . . . .

Again like the subject and topic particles, 을~를 has no English translation. Rather, it marks a grammatical function: the noun before it is the direct object of the verb, the *it* of *does it.*

Since the subject and object particles flag their nouns as subject and object, the order in which these expressions come along in a Korean sentence is not crucial, as it is in corresponding English sentences where word order alone marks grammatical functions, so that *Mother sees baby* does not mean the same thing as *Baby sees mother.*

1.　　어머니가 애기를 봐요.　　　　*Mother sees baby.*
　　　애기를 어머니가 봐요.　　　　(same)

2.　　어머니를 애기가 봐요.　　　　*Baby sees mother.*
　　　애기가 어머니를 봐요.　　　　(same)

In spoken Korean, either subject or object particle may drop out. If both are omitted the sentence may become ambiguous. 어머니 애기 봐요 and 애기 어머니 봐요 can both have two opposite meanings. *Mother sees baby* and *Baby sees mother*, because Korean does not use simple word order to signal subject-object relations. If only one particle drops, of course, the sentence is not ambiguous. 어머니가 애기 봐요 and 어머니 애기를 봐요 can only mean *Mother sees baby.*

Many English verbs take objects by way of a linked preposition: 사람을 기다려요 *waits for a person*, i.e., *awaits a person.* So you can't always count on a one-to-one correspondence between transitive verbs in Korean and what are called transitive verbs in English.

In certain kinds of Korean sentences, as you have learned, a verb can have two subjects: two different nouns with the particle 이~가. There is, however, usually only one direct object to a verb. Most often, a direct object is similar in meaning to English direct objects: 책을 봐요 *reads [looks at] a book*, 편지를 써요 *writes a letter.*

7.7. Particles of Direction: *to, from*

Corresponding to English *to* are the particle 에 for places and 한테 (or also 에게) for living things:

은행에 가요	*goes to the bank*
공원에 가요	*goes to the park*
내 친구한테 줘요	*gives it to my friend*
or 내 친구에게	
만호 씨한테 줘요	*gives it to Manho*
or 만호 씨에게	

From is expressed by the same particles with 서 after them. Sometimes the original particle is omitted, and you can simply say 서. You can do this when you want to say *from (a place)*.

은행에서 학교에 가요	*Goes from the bank to school.*
or 은행서	
식당에서	*from the cafeteria*
or 식당서	

To express *from* with living things, you do the same thing you do to express *from* with nonliving things: add 서 to the directional/locational particle.

내 친구한테서	*from my friend*
or 내 친구에게서	
만호 씨한테서	*from Manho*
or 만호 씨에게서	

However, colloquial Korean allows you to use 한테 (or 에게) without 서 in the sense of *from* (a person).

3.   A.   한국말은 누구한테 배워요?
           Who are you learning Korean from?

      B.   한국사람한테 배워요.
           I'm learning from a Korean.

Here are some example sentences.

4. A. 편지는 누구한테서 와요?
Who do you get letters from?

    B. 어머니한테서 와요.
From my mother.

5. 학생이 선생에게서 책을 받아요.
The student receives a book from the teacher.

Finally, here is a chart to help you keep these various meanings and particles straight.

	TO	FROM
Living thing	에게 한테	에게서 한테서 한테 (colloquial)
Place	에	에서 서 (colloquial)

7.8. Static and Dynamic Location

Corresponding to English *in*, *at*, *on*, as you learned in section 6.3, is the particle 에 *(being) at*, with or without some specific word of location in front of it. This is a particle of STATIC location: something *is in (at, on) a place*. For DYNAMIC location, when something *happens in (at or on) a place*, Korean uses the particle 서 *(happening) at* or the combination 에서. These particles have the same English translation as 에, but are used when the verb denotes an action.

Directional 에 is used with verbs of motion like 가요, 와요.

Static location 에 is used with verbs of location like 있어요 and 없어요. This same 에 is used to locate things in time, too.

6. 월요일에 쉬어요.
On Monday(s) I take it easy.

7. 아침에 우유를 사요.
   In the morning I buy milk.

However, just as in English certain time adverbs do not take 에 (or a preposition in English): *어제에, *오늘에, and *내일에 are all unacceptable for *yesterday*, *today* and *tomorrow*.

Dynamic location 에서 is used with all other verbs to describe where an action is taking place. Here are some examples.

8. A. 만호 씨는 어디에 있어요?
    Where is Manho?

    B. 집에 있어요.
    He is at home.

9. A. 점심은 어디에서 먹어요?
    Where does he eat lunch?

    B. 음식점에서 먹어요.
    He eats at a restaurant.

10. 동호 씨는 학교에 있어요.
    Tongho is at school.

11. 내 친구는 학교에서 가르쳐요.
    My friend teaches at school.

주의!

With some verbs either 에 or (에)서 is used:
서울에 살아요 or 서울(에)서 살아요 *lives in Seoul.*

With most verbs only one of the alternatives is possible:
있어요 *is, stays* and 앉아요 *sits* take only 에.

7.9. Using Location To Express Possession

You learned in section 6.2 to use 있- and 없- for expressing possession in sentences of the type.

12.　　나는 책이 있어요.
　　　 I have a book [Literally: *As for me, there exists a book*].

Korean can also use a locational construction to express possession; whereas 에 functions to locate things in inanimate (nonliving) places, the particles 한테 or 에게 are used to locate things with living creatures, especially humans. Compare the following three sentences.

13.　　은행에 돈이 있어요.
　　　 The bank has money. [Literally: *There is money in/at the bank.*]

14.　　나한테 돈이 있어요.
　　　 I have money. [Literally: *Unto me there exists money.*]

15.　　수진 씨한테는 돈이 없어요.
　　　 Sujin has no money.

7.10. Different Kinds of Verbs

Korean verbs are either PROCESSIVE or DESCRIPTIVE. Processive verbs usually mean *does (it)*, i.e., *performs an action.* Descriptive verbs (sometimes called adjectives) usually mean *is (a certain way)*, i.e., *has some characteristic.* In the vocabulary lists for this textbook, descriptive verb bases are glossed with English *be*, e.g., 크- *be big.*

The distinction between descriptive and processive verbs will become more and more important as you advance through this book. For now, only a few are pointed out of the differences between these two types of verbs. One of the differences is that you can use the processive verbs as commands (*do it!*) and suggestions (*let's do it!*), but the descriptive verbs are limited to statements (*it is*) and questions (*is it?*). To say *let's be good* in Korean you have to turn the sentence into one that means *let's behave nicely.*

Another difference is that descriptive verbs never take an object marked with the object marker 을 ~ 를 (but this does not mean that all processive verbs *can* take the particle 을 ~ 를). Sometimes descriptive verbs mean *has one that is (a certain way)* as follows.

16.　　책이 많아요.
　　　 I have lots of books.

Notice that what corresponds to the object in English (*books*) is marked with 이 ~ 가 in Korean.

Descriptive verbs can have a subject (sometimes even two).

17.   누가 술이 있어요?
      Who has the booze?

18.   나는 이것이 좋아요.
      I like this.

19.   그 음식은 맛이 좋아요.
      The food has good flavor (tastes good).

Many processive verbs, on the other hand, can take a direct object (sometimes even two) as well as a subject, as you learned in Section 7.6. Some examples are:

20.   책을 읽어요.
      Reads the book

21.   한국말을 공부를 해요.
      Studies Korean

In addition, some processive verbs can take an indirect object marked by the particle 한테 (or 에게) for living things and the particle 에 for things or institutions. This was covered in Section 7.7.

22.   동생한테 돈을 줘요.
      Gives money to one's younger sibling.

23.   중국사람한테 중국말을 배워요.
      Learns Chinese from a Chinese.

A few processive verbs take an indirect object with the double particle 한테서 (or 에게서) for people and the particle 에서 for things or institutions.

24.   어머니한테서 돈을 받아요.
      Receives money from one's mother.

25.   은행에서 편지를 받아요.
      Gets a letter from the bank.

있어요 and 없어요 cannot take a direct object marked with 을 ~ 를. Any object that may be required for an English translation appears as a subject.

26. 돈이 있어요.
   has money

27. 시간이 없어요.
   has no time

> 주의!
>
> You must never say a sentence like 돈을 있어요.

The copula is a special kind of descriptive verb; it has a number of grammatical peculiarities all its own, which you will learn through the course.

7.11. More on the Particle 도

When you use the particle 도 with a noun, you do not use the particles that would mark that same noun as topic (은 ~ 는), subject (이 ~ 가), or direct object (을 ~ 를); notice how 도 takes the place of those particles.

28. A. 나는 미국사람이에요.
   I'm an American.

   B. 나도 미국사람이에요.
   I'm an American too.

29. A. 담배 있어요?
   Have you a cigarette?

   B. 불도 있어요?
   Have you a light too?

30. 책을 읽어요.
   I read books.

   잡지도 읽어요.
   I read magazines too.

This means that some sentences with 도 are ambiguous out of context: 애기도 봐요 can mean either *The baby sees it* (or *him, her*) *too* or (*She* etc.) *sees the baby too*. You can clear up the ambiguity by adding context: 어머니가 애기도 봐요 *The mother sees the baby too*, or 어머니를 애기도 봐요 *The baby sees the mother too*. You can, however, use 도 after any of the other particles. For example, 학교에서도 means *at school also* or *from school also*. 김 선생님한테도 means *to Mr. Kim too* and so on.

Two occurrences of 도 in the same Korean sentence often correspond to English *both . . . and . . .* or in a negative sentence *(not) either . . . or . . .* (which you will learn how to do in section 8.1.).

31. 아침에도 밤에도 일해요.
    I work both in the morning and at night.

32. 화장실에는 휴지도 수건도 없어요.
    There is neither toilet paper nor a towel in the bathroom.

7.12. Placement of Manner Adverbs

Manner adverbs are adverbs like 잘 *well*; *often*, 많이 *lots, a lot*, and 자주 *often* which tell how you do something. In Korean, such adverbs like to park just in front of the verb. In cases of VERBAL NOUN plus 하-, then, the adverb comes right before 하-:

33. 수진 씨는 공부를 잘 해요. 〔not 잘 공부를 해요.〕
    Sujin studies well.

34. 수진 씨는 일을 많이 해요. 〔not 많이 일을 해요.〕
    Sujin works a lot.

Exercises

Exercise 1: Fill in the Blanks

Fill in the following blanks with the noun-plus-particle expressions indicated below each sentence. Say the complete Korean sentence out loud.

1. 나는 저녁에 _____을~를 읽어요.

   a magazine
   the newspaper
   both a magazine and the newspaper
   a Chinese book
   an English newspaper and a Russian newspaper
   some American magazines

2.   동생이 나한테 _____을~를 줘요.

　　　a radio
　　　some meat
　　　toilet paper and a towel
　　　both cigarettes and matches
　　　a notebook
　　　some money
　　　pencils and paper

3.   나는 오후에 _____을~를 봐요~만나요.

　　　the doctor and his wife
　　　both Manho and Tongho
　　　a movie
　　　both Mrs. Kim and Mrs. Pak
　　　the teacher
　　　my friends
　　　a lot of (many) students

Exercise 2: Building Sentences from Phrases

Here is a list of phrases in Korean. Build a complete Korean sentence around each one. Then practice your sentences aloud.

1.	영화 구경을	2.	의자 옆에
3.	박 박사님한테서	4.	집하고 나무 사이에
5.	집 안에	6.	공원에
7.	극장 오른 쪽에	8.	아버지한테서
9.	요즘	10.	이 방 안에
11.	아침에	12.	왼 쪽에
13.	친구한테	14.	매표소에서
15.	음식점에서	16.	집에

Exercise 3: Verb Phrases

Here are two Korean sentences with blanks in them. Complete the sentences using the verb expressions from the list below—use the same verb in both blanks.

내 친구는 _____. 그리고 나도 _____.

1.	closing windows	2.	looking at a magazine
3.	drinking some water	4.	taking it easy [playing] at home
5.	singing a song	6.	seeing a movie
7.	getting up late	8.	smoking a cigarette
9.	going to school	10.	speaking English
11.	learning Korean	12.	waiting for the doctor
13.	listening to the radio	14.	working

Exercise 4: Korean to English Translation

Translate the following sentences into English.

1. A. 지금 뭘 해요?
   B. 텔레비전을 봐요.
   A. 혼자 봐요?
   B. 아니오. 애기하고 봐요.
2. A. 집에 개 있어요?
   B. 네, 있어요.
   A. 지금은 어디에 있어요?
   B. 모르겠어요.
   A. 개는 잘 놀아요?
   B. 네, 잘 놀아요.
3. 우리 개는 공원에서 놀아요.
4. 우리 애기는 물도 우유도 잘 마셔요.
5. A. 뭐 해요?
   B. 친구를 기다려요.
6. A. 어디에 가요?
   B. 공원에 가요. 우리 개를 찾아요.
7. A. 어디에 가요?
   B. 음식점에 가요.
8. 우리 동생은 은행에서 일해요.
   은행에서는 편지를 많이 받아요.
   그리고 집에서는 편지를 많이 써요.
9. A. 일요일에는 집에 있어요.
   B. 집에서는 뭐 해요? 신문을 읽어요?
   A. 네, 그리고 잡지도 봐요.
10. 동생은 말이 적어요.
11. 호주 대사관이 커요, 작아요?

Exercise 5: English to Korean Translation

Translate the following sentences into Korean. Remember that you do not need to translate literally. The important thing is to convey the ideas that are being expressed.

1. He is a school teacher. He usually teaches English.
2. Saturday morning he reads the newspaper. And Thursday evenings he goes to the cinema.
3. He studies hard (well). He learns a lot.
4. At night I rest.
5. At the library there are lots of books. Nowadays books are expensive.
6. On Friday mornings I get up late. I drink some milk quickly. And then [그리고] I go to school.
7. I'm waiting for Professor Lee.
8. Give me a tissue. Give me a towel too.
9. Our house is little. But it's nice.
10. On Wednesdays I buy bread and milk.
11. The baby is playing by itself.
12. Father sings [songs] well.
13. The mother calls the baby. But the baby is sleeping.
14. My mother lives in Seoul. There are many stores and department stores there.
15. A. Where is the library? Do you know?
    B. Yes, it's between that cafeteria over there and that building.
16. I'm seeing a film this evening.

Exercise 6: Conversation Practice

Make up five conversations based on the following sets of information. First, one asks the other where he is going. Respond appropriately (e.g., by the Korean equivalent of *I'm going to the cafeteria*). The next question is *What do you do/buy/eat/drink there?* (etc., as appropriate), and the response can then be made according to the information supplied. This can be done either as a written or an oral exercise.

1. 식당   비빔밥을 먹-
2. 방   텔레비전을 보-
3. 공원   친구를 만나-
4. 슈퍼마켓   우유를 사-
5. 집   책을 읽-

Exercise 7: Particle Insertion

Copy and translate the following sentences, inserting the correct particles.

1. 텔레비전 ＿＿＿ 봐요.
2. 맛 ＿＿＿ 좋아요.
3. 내일은 우리 동생이 와요. 그리고 동생의 남자친구 ＿＿＿ 와요.
4. 친구 ＿＿＿ 만나요.
5. 책 ＿＿＿ 비싸요.
6. 밥 ＿＿＿ 먹어요.
7. 나는 공원 ＿＿＿ 놀아요.
8. 나 ＿＿＿ 친구 ＿＿＿ 돈 ＿＿＿ 받아요.
9. 우리는 식당 ＿＿＿ 밥 ＿＿＿ 먹어요.
10. 교실 ＿＿＿ 학생 ＿＿＿ 한국말 ＿＿＿ 배워요.
11. 책상 위 ＿＿＿ 신문 ＿＿＿ 있어요.
12. 플랫폼 옆 ＿＿ 기차 ＿＿ 있어요.
13. 매표소 앞 ＿＿＿ 여자 ＿＿ 표 ＿＿ 사요.
14. 주말 ＿＿ 남자친구 ＿＿＿ 영화구경 ＿＿ 해요.

Exercise 8: Vocabulary Drill

1. Express the sentences below in Korean, filling in the blank space with each of the expressions listed beneath the sentence. Say the complete sentence aloud each time. Rearrange or add words if you can make better sentences by doing so.

   나는 아침에 ＿＿＿＿＿＿.

study	play with the dog [use 하고]
take walks	go to the bank
read the paper	come home
go to the park	write letters
go to the movies	sell newspapers
stay home	learn Russian
speak in English	drink milk
listen to the radio	watch films
smoke cigarettes	look for my dog
teach Chinese	drink lots of water
meet [my] friends	work at the library
eat breakfast	open the window

2. 나는 편지를 _____ 써요.

at night	in the morning
Saturdays	fast
on Friday mornings	Tuesday
on Sundays	Thursday
this evening	Wednesday
a lot	in the daytime
in the afternoon	Monday mornings
often	tonight

3. Give the dictionary form, infinitive, and Polite Style for each of the following verbs. Write each one out initially. Then practice them so that you can call them off fluently just by looking at the English. For example, the answer to number (1) will be: 좋다, 좋아, 좋아요.

is good	sleeps
finds	meets
plays	goes
bites	asks
opens it	comes
sits	is hot
is little	receives
lives	looks at
smokes	listens
is large	teaches
knows it	waits
eats	drinks
gives	sells
is fast	buys
calls	is great in number
has	[copula]
closes	puts on [clothes]
gets up	ties
rests	learns
writes	sings

Exercise 9: Dictionary Exercise

In Lesson Three you learned the various alphabetization schemes in use in North and South Korean dictionaries. In this lesson, you have learned the dictionary form in -다 for verbs. Look up the following words and add them to your vocabulary notes.

1.	닮다	2.	�뀌다
3.	굶다	4.	끓다
5.	떠들다	6.	까불다
7.	눋다	8.	무섭다
9.	뺏다	10.	엉터리
11.	쌓이다	12.	시끄럽다
13.	업다	14.	썩다
15.	바뀌다	16.	줍다
17.	파업	18.	직장
19.	호랑이	20.	명함
21.	천사	22.	진짜
23.	가짜	24.	설거지

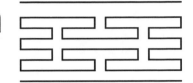

Lesson 8

다른 과목은 안 하세요?

In this lesson you will learn how to talk about your Korean language skills and your university studies, and you will attempt to make a reservation over the telephone. You will learn about verbal nouns, how to negate verbs (*doesn't*, *isn't* and *can't*), how to exalt others by making verbs honorific, and how to use two new particles: instrumental (으)로, and (이)랑 *and*.

Korean Dialogues

Dialogue 1

Miss Lee, Christopher Murphy's secretary, is chatting with Eunice while Eunice waits for Chris at the office.

미스 리	요즘 뭘 하세요?
유니스	한국말을 공부해요.
미스 리	어디서 한국말을 배우세요?
유니스	고려대학교에서 배워요.
미스 리	그래요? 무슨 책으로 배우세요?
유니스	"한국어 회화"를 써요. 책이 괜찮아요.
미스 리	일본말도 아세요?
유니스	아니오, 일본말은 못 해요. 너무 어려워요.
미스 리	그럼 다른 과목은 안 하세요?
유니스	아니오, 경제학이랑 정치학도 배워요.
미스 리	한국말 공부가 잘 되세요?
유니스	아니오, 아주 힘 들어요. 아직 멀었어요.

Notes

. . . 는 잘 돼요?	*Is . . . going well?*
힘(이) 들어요.	*It's tough. I'm having a difficult time. It requires [lots of] effort.*
아직 멀었어요.	[Literally: *It is still distant*, that is, *has a long way to go*.]

Dialogue 2

Eunice and Miss Lee decide to go to the National Theatre together on Sunday. Miss Lee has Eunice dial the National Theatre to reserve seats.

유니스	여보세요?
교환원	네, 국립극장입니다. 말씀하세요.
유니스	예약 좀 부탁합니다.
교환원	네. 성함하고 신용카드 번호를 말씀해 주세요.
유니스	네? 다시 한번 말씀해 주세요! (passing the receiver to Miss Lee)
	아이구, 미스 리. 너무 힘들어요. 못 알아 듣겠어요.
미스 리	그러세요? 그럼 제가 통화할께요.

Notes

. . . (을) 부탁합니다.	(on the telephone) *Please give me so-and-so.* or *I would like so-and-so.*
말씀해 주세요.	*Please say it for me. Please do me the favor of saying.*
못 알아 듣겠어요.	*I can't catch what's being said, I can't make out what* [*you, they,* etc.] *are saying.*
그러세요?	*Really?* (This is the honorific version of 그래요?)
통화할께요.	*I'll get through/speak* (on the telephone). *Let me get through/speak.*

Vocabulary

School and Education

과목	school subject
몇 과목을 들으세요? (들-, 듣다)	How many courses are you taking?
수업	a class, lesson [at school]
경제학	economics
경제	economy
정치학	politics [as a field of study], political science
정치	politics
한국학	Korean studies
. . . (을) 전공(을) 하-	major in something
전공이 뭐에요?	What's your major?
교재	teaching materials; textbook
대학	four-year college

More New Verbs

사랑(을) 하-	love
야구(를) 하-	play baseball
야구	baseball
예약(을) 하-	make a reservation
예약	reservation
통화(를) 하-	get through to/contact somebody by telephone, talk by telephone
수영(을) 하-	swim
수영장	swimming pool
청소(를) 하-	clean up, tidy up
...(을) 좋아하-	like it
나쁘-	be bad
깨끗하-	be clean
깨끗이	neatly, cleanly
같-	be similar; be the same (as something — 하고, (이)랑)
같이 〔가치〕	together
깎-	cut [hair], sharpen [pencil], mow [grass]
연필을 깎아요	(Somebody) sharpens a pencil.

Lesson Eight / 121

머리를 깎아요	(Somebody) gets a haircut. (for males)
머리(를) 자르-	get a haircut (for females)
어려w-	be difficult
쉬w-	be easy
착하-	be good by nature; be a good boy [girl, dog, etc.]
말(을) 들- (듣다)	obey (listen to words)
말을 잘 들어요.	Obeys well.
약(을) 먹-	take (eat) medicine
약	medicine
쓰-	use
싸-	be cheap, inexpensive
힘(이) 드-ㄹ-	be difficult, taxing
힘	strength, energy
오늘은 힘이 없어요.	I have no energy today.
괜찮-	be all right, OK
돼요.	It's OK; It'll do.
안 돼요.	It's not OK; It won't do; One mustn't do it.
잘 돼요.	It's going well. It's turning out well.
잘 안 돼요.	It's not going well.
머-ㄹ-	be distant, far
여기서 멀어요?	Is it far from here?
네, 한 시간 걸려요.	Yes, it takes an hour.
알아 들-	understand [spoken words], catch something said [Literally: hearing after having understood]
부탁(을) 하-	make a request, ask a favor/errand
부탁	a request, favor
PERSON 한테 부탁(을) 하-	ask somebody for a favor
PERSON 한테 부탁(이) 있-	have a favor to ask of somebody
부탁해요.	Please, I beg you. or I'm counting on you. Please do it for me.
만호 씨한테 부탁 하나 있어요.	Manho, I have a favor to ask of you.

Some Honorific Bases

The following verbs have the honorific marker -(으)시- incorporated in their bases.

잡수시-	eat (honorific)
고기 더 잡수세요.	Please eat some more meat. (to a guest, your parents, etc.)

고기 더 먹어요.	Please eat some more meat. (to a friend you usually call 씨)
주무시-	sleep (honorific)
안녕히 주무세요.	Good night (to somebody esteemed, e.g., your parents)
잘 자요.	Good night (to a friend you usually call 씨)
잘 자.	Good night (your parents to you; you to a close friend or younger sibling)
계시-	be, exist, stay (honorific)
교수님 계세요?	Is Professor at home?
만호 씨 있어요?	Is Manho at home?
드시-	eat, drink (honorific)
자, 많이 드세요.	Well then, *bon appetit* [eat up, please eat a lot] (to a guest, your parents, etc.)
자, 많이 먹어요.	Well then, *bon appetit* (to a friend you usually call 씨)
자, 많이 먹어.	Well then, *bon appetit* (your parents to you; you to a close friend or younger sibling)

> **주의:**
> Because these bases already have honorific -(으)시- in them,
> you cannot produce forms like *드시세요, *계시세요, or the like.

Frequency and Quantity

좀	a little; please (to soften a request or command)
늘	always, all the time, continuously
항상	always, at all times, habitually
언제나	always
주로	mainly, for the most part
가끔	sometimes
자주	often
매일	every day
열심히	diligently, very hard
공부를 열심히 해요.	She studies hard/diligently.

More Adverbs

아직	(not) yet, still
먼저	first (of all), before anything else
함께	together
PERSON하고 함께	(together) with a person
참	truly, really
정말(로)	the truth (truly, really)
정말이에요?	Really? Is it true?
정말로 커요.	It is really/truly large.
정열적(으로)	passionate(ly)
천천히	slowly
너무	too much so, too; very [to an excessive degree]
언젠가	sometime or other; at one time; some time ago

Other Nouns

버스, 뻐스	bus
런던	London
전화	telephone
전화(를) 하-	make a telephone call
뉴욕	New York
다른 NOUN	(an)other NOUN(s)
교회	church [Protestant]
교회에 나가세요?	Do you go to church?
나가-	attend, go to (church)
성당	church [Catholic]
신용카드	credit card
성	surname, last name
성씨	[your or his] esteemed surname/last name
이름	name, given name
성함	[someone's esteemed] name (honorific equivalent of 이름)
성함이 어떻게 되세요?	What is your name? (honorific and polite)
머리	head; hair
머리(가) 좋아요.	She is smart.
머리(가) 나빠요.	She is dumb.

회화	conversation
영어회화책	English conversation book
말씀	words, speech (an honorific or humble equivalent of 말)
말씀하세요.	Go ahead. [Literally: Please say what it is you have to say.
한국어	Korean language
국립 NOUN	a national(ly) [established] NOUN
국립대학교	a national university
주	a state, a province
미네소타주	Minnesota; the state of Minnesota
주립 NOUN	a state [-established] NOUN, provincial(ly) [established] NOUN
주립대학교	a state university
사립 NOUN	a private(ly) [established] NOUN
사립대학교	a private university
교환	exchange
교환학생	exchange student
교환교수	exchange professor
교환원	operator (switchboard, telephone exchange-)
쥬스	juice
오렌지 쥬스	orange juice
토마토 쥬스	tomato juice

Lesson Notes

8.1. Verbs: Short Negatives with 안 and 못

The rule for putting a verb into the short negative form is simple: place immediately before the verb one of the two negative words 안 and 못. However, DESCRIPTIVE verbs (translated *is*) cannot take the short negative with 못 in this way; instead you must use the long form that is optional for the other verbs. (The long negative form is discussed later, in Lesson Twelve).

안 is an abbreviation of 아니 *no*; the full form is used before the copula (아니에요 *it isn't*.. It is a simple negative word meaning *not*. 못 basically means *cannot*, but can also be more emphatic than 아니. Its meaning ranges from *not possibly, cannot* to *emphatically (definitely, absolutely) not; not at all*.

Pronunciation of 못

You will never hear the ㅅ written in the word 못, because it never occurs in those environments where the ㅅ can be released—before a particle or the copula -이에요. When 못 precedes a verb beginning with i or y, it is usual for the sequence to be pronounced as **-nni-** or **-nny-**. So when one wants to say 못 읽어요 *can't read; doesn't read at all*, the form is pronounced 몬닐거요, and when one wants to say 못 열어요 *can't open it, doesn't open it at all*, the form is pronounced 몬녀러요. One may occasionally hear versions of these sequences with the final ㅅ retained as unreleased ㄷ: 못 읽어요 as 모딜거요, 못 열어요 as 모뎌러요.

Here are some examples of 안 and 못.

1. 우리 애기는 잘 안 자요.
    My baby doesn't sleep well (or *much*).

2. 요즘은 잘 못 자요.
    Lately I can't sleep well.

3. 나는 술을 못 마셔요.
    I can't drink (alcohol). (Maybe I am allergic to alcohol.)

4. 나는 술을 안 마셔요.
    I don't drink (alcohol). (as a matter of personal policy; it is my conscious decision)

5. A. 비싸요?
    Is it expensive?

    B. 아니오, 안 비싸요. 싸요.
    No, it's not expensive. It's cheap.

6. A. 빵 먹어요?
    Do you eat bread?

    B. 아니오, 안 먹어요.
    No, I don't. (I just don't like it.)

7. A. 빵 먹어요?
    Do you eat bread?

    B. 아니오, 못 먹어요.
    No, I can't. (I'm allergic to wheat-based foods.)

8. A. 학교에 가요?
    Are you going to school?

    B. 아니오, 안 가요.
    No, I'm not. (I've decided to skip class today.)

9. A. 학교에 가요?
    Are you going to school?

    B. 아니오, 못 가요.
    No, I' can't. (I have a doctor's appointment.)

10. A. 야구 좋아해요?
    Do you like baseball?

    B. 아니오, 안 좋아해요. (not *좋아 안 해요)
    No, I don't.

11. A. 한국신문을 읽으세요?
    Do you read Korean newspapers?

    B. 아직 못 읽어요.
    I can't read [them] yet.

12. A. 수영을 해요?
    Do you swim?

    B. 아니오, 못해요.
    No, I can't swim.

13. 만호 씨는 오늘 안 와요.
    Manho doesn't come today.

14. 만호 씨는 오늘 못 와요.
    Manho can't come today.

15. 나는 한국신문을 못 읽어요.
    I can't read Korean newspapers.

16. 나는 한국신문을 안 읽어요.
    I don't read Korean newspapers. (I choose not to.)

8.2. Verbs: Honorifics

8.2.1. The Honorific Marker -(으)시-

When a Korean speaker uses a verb to describe the action of a person he especially esteems (or honors), he makes the verb form honorific. Esteemed (honored) people in Korea include parents and other older relatives; older people in general; high officials; people of education—teachers, doctors, other professional people.

The honorific marker is a two-shape ending attached in the shape -으시- to consonant bases, but -시- to vowel bases. The HONORIFIC BASE of a verb is its base plus this honorific marker. In other words, by adding the honorific marker to a verb base, you are creating a new verb base ending in -시-.

The honorific infinitive consists of the honorific marker -(으)시- plus the infinitive ending -어, with the expected abbreviation of -(으)시어 to -(으)셔, *except*, that is, when followed by 요.

```
주의!

Honorific bases in -(으)시- behave just like the other bases you know
that end in 이-, with the following important exception: honorific present-tense polite
forms end in -(으)세요, the ending introduced in this lesson.
This is the usual pronunciation of what is sometimes written -(으)셔요, the HONORIFIC
INFINITIVE (-(으)시- + -어) plus the polite particle 요.
```

Observe the following forms:

Base		Honorific Base	Honorific Infinitive	Honorific Polite
가-	*go*	가시-	가셔	가세요
오-	*come*	오시-	오셔	오세요
배우-	*learn*	배우시-	배우셔	배우세요
앉-	*sit*	앉으시-	앉으셔	앉으세요
깎-	*cut*	깎으시-	깎으셔	깎으세요
읽-	*read*	읽으시-	읽으셔	읽으세요
빠르-	*be fast*	빠르시-	빠르셔	빠르세요

Base		Honorific Base	Honorific Infinitive	Honorific Polite
노-ㄹ-	*play*	노시-	노셔	노세요
들-	*hear*	들으시-	들으셔	들으세요
더w-	*hot*	더우시-	더우셔	더우세요
나(ㅅ)-	*get better*	나으시-	나으셔	나으세요

The example of 노-ㄹ- *play* shows that when you have an L-extending vowel base, you attach the honorific marker to the unextended base (in this case, 노-). Note also the treatment of ㄹ ~ ㄷ and w ~ ㅂ consonant bases (bases 들- and 더w- above).

> ## 주의!
> The ㅇ or zero consonant sign which gets written before any syllable beginning with a vowel does not count as a consonant for the purposes of our rules.

8.2.2. The Honorific Polite Style: 하세요

We have already mentioned above the sorts of people that might qualify as esteemed, and therefore be worthy of honorification. Often, when questions are asked, the esteemed person is the listener (*you*).

17.　한국말을 무엇으로 배우세요?
What do you learn Korean from [Literally: *with*]*?* (The new particle is explained later this lesson.)

In the following sentence, a parent is spoken of in honorific terms.

18.　아버님은 매일 약을 드세요.
Father takes medicine every day.

Just as important as showing esteem for others is to avoid showing it for yourself.

> ## NEVER use
> ## honorific verb forms
> ## to describe your own actions.

Compare the question and the answer from the conversation of this lesson:

19. 미스 리   요즘 뭘 하세요?
What are you doing lately?

20. 유니스   한국말을 공부해요.
I'm studying Korean.

Ordinarily, a Polite Style verb in 해요 is made Honorific Polite by changing -어요 or -아요 to -으세요 when the verb base ends in a consonant, or just adding -세요 when the verb base ends in a vowel.

If the verb is an L-extending one, then the ㄹ is omitted, and the verb is treated as though it ended simply in a vowel (e.g., 사-ㄹ- *live*, becomes 사세요):

looks for	찾아요	Polite
	찾으세요	Honorific Polite
meets	만나요	Polite
	만나세요	Honorific Polite
lives	살아요	Polite
	사세요	Honorific Polite

A few verbs come in pairs—a neutral and an honorific one; that is, the neutral verb and the honoric verb are completely different and unrelated forms.

자요	*sleeps*	주무세요	*[somebody esteemed] sleeps*
		Base: 주무시-	
있어요	*stays*	계세요	*[somebody esteemed] stays*
		Base: 계시-	
먹어요	*eats*	잡수세요	*[somebody esteemed] eats*
		Base: 잡수시-	

The ending -(으)세요 is sometimes written and sometimes pronounced -(으)셔요, which is the contracted form of honorific -(으)시- plus -어요. However, it is considered more standard to use the forms in -(으)세요.

The ending -(으)세요 is the first two-shape verb ending you have seen. Here is a description of how it behaves with different verbs.

Vowel-final bases attach to the vowel-less (i.e., 으-less) ending of two-shape endings:

가–	가세요?	*Are you going?*
보–	보세요!	*Look at it!*
파–ㄹ–	파세요!	*Please sell it!*

Consonant-final bases attach to the shape with initial –으–.

찾–	찾으세요?	*Are you looking for it?*
받–	받으세요!	*Please take it!*
입–	입으세요!	*Put it on!*
들–	들으세요?	*Are you listening?*
더w–	더우세요?	*Are you hot?*

As the last example shows, the only tricky point to remember here concerns w ~ ㅂ verbs, for which the following rule holds:

$$ \text{W-} \quad + \quad \text{-으} \quad \longrightarrow \quad \text{우} $$

In other words, the final w of a w ~ ㅂ verb base plus the initial –으 of a two-shape verb ending combine to yield the vowel 우.

It is vital that you remember the following point: the honorific part of a verb has no connection whatever with the social style being used. All the verbs in this lesson are in the Polite Style; some of them are honorific, and some are not. Verb forms in any of the Korean social styles can either be made honorific or left as they are, without respect to the suffixes which show the social level on which the speakers are conversing. This means that the honorific marker can be put before the endings of *any* social style, not just the Polite Style, when the speaker uses the verb for the actions of an especially esteemed person.

On the next page is a list of some of the verbs you have learned, in the Polite (해요) Style and the Honorific Polite (하세요) Style.

Gloss	Polite	Honorific Polite
does (IRREG.)	해요	하세요
closes it	닫아요	닫으세요
comes	와요	오세요
drinks	마셔요	마시세요
		드세요
eats	먹어요	잡수세요
		드세요
finds; looks for	찾아요	찾으세요
gets up	일어나요	일어나세요
gives	줘요	주세요
goes	가요	가세요
good	좋아요	좋으세요
has (got)	있어요	있으세요
has not (got)	없어요	없으세요
it is [copula]	–이에요	–이세요
stays	있어요	계세요
(there) is; is (there)	있어요	계세요
(there) isn't; isn't (there)	없어요	안 계세요
learns	배워요	배우세요
is little (in size)	작아요	작으세요
are/has many	많아요	많으세요
sees, looks at, reads	봐요	보세요
sleeps	자요	주무세요
smokes	피워요	피우세요
teaches	가르쳐요	가르치세요
waits for	기다려요	기다리세요
writes	써요	쓰세요
is bad	나빠요	나쁘세요
is big	커요	크세요
opens it	열어요	여세요
lives	살아요	사세요
plays	놀아요	노세요
hears (ㄷ ~ ㄹ: 듣다)	들어요	들으세요
is hot (ㅂ ~ w: 덥다)	더워요	더우세요

8.3. Verbal Nouns: Processive and Descriptive

The verb 해요, as you have observed in this lesson, is a versatile word. First of all, it means *does* or *performs an action*, as in the following sentence.

21.　　요즘 무엇을 해요?
　　　　What are you up to [doing] lately?

Secondly, it means *says*, *speaks*.

22.　　A.　　한국말 잘 하세요?
　　　　　　　Do you speak Korean well?

　　　　B.　　아직 잘 못 해요.
　　　　　　　I can't speak well yet.

8.3.1. Separable Verbal Nouns (Processive)

There is a group of verbal nouns which form phrases with 해요. You have now learned at least five of these:

공부	*study(ing)*
공부(를) 해요	*studies* [Literally: *performs studying*]
산보	*a walk* or *stroll*
산보(를) 해요	*takes* [Literally: *does*] *a walk*
구경	*(sight)seeing, viewing*
구경(을) 해요	*views, watches*
일	*work, job*
일(을) 해요	*works* [Literally: *performs work, does a job*]
청소	*cleaning up*
청소(를) 해요	*cleans up, tidies up*

The verbal noun may be the direct object of the verb 해요 or it may precede it directly, with little difference in meaning.

구경해요	*watches, views*
구경(을) 해요	*does watching/viewing = watches, views*

Even if the verbal noun itself is a direct object (i.e., has the particle 을 ~ 를 after it), there can be another direct object, as you have seen. Ordinarily, most Korean sentences have only one. When the verbal noun is not marked as the direct object of 해요 (e.g., 구경해요), the whole expression as a unit may have a direct object. This means that any of the following combinations is possible.

sees a movie

영화구경을 (pause)해요   *does (pause) movie viewing*

영화를 (pause)구경해요   *watches (pause) a movie*

영화를 (pause) 구경을 (pause)해요   [no English equivalent]

영화 구경해요   [no English equivalent]

studies Korean

한국말을 (pause)공부해요   *studies (pause) Korean*

한국말 공부를 (pause)해요   *does (pause) Korean language studies*

한국말을 (pause) 공부를 (pause)해요   [no English equivalent]

한국말 공부해요   [no English equivalent]

8.3.1.1 Using 안 and 못 with Separable Verbal Nouns (Processive)

As you have just learned, the negative words 안 and 못 are placed immediately before the verb they modify. The situation is no different for processive verbal noun plus 해요 structures. Since 하- is the verb, the negative word goes immediately before it.

sees a movie

영화구경을 (pause) 안 해요   *doesn't do (pause) movie viewing*

영화구경 (pause)안 해요   *doesn't do (pause) movie viewing*

영화를 (pause)구경 안 해요   *doesn't watch (pause) a movie*

studies Korean

한국말 공부를 (pause) 안 해요   *doesn't do (pause) Korean language studies*

한국말 공부 (pause) 안 해요   *doesn't do (pause) Korean language studies*

한국말을 (pause) 공부 안 해요   *doesn't study (pause) Korean*

Of the three possibilities illustrated here, the first and second (which is really the first with the object particle dropped) are most common. The third possibility does not sound elegant in Korean, but you will hear it from time to time. A fourth possibility is to place 안 in front of the verbal noun; you may hear this from time to time, especially from younger speakers, but this is not considered standard, good Korean.

　　　　*영화를　안　구경해요　　　　　*doesn't watch a movie*
　　　　*한국말을　안　공부해요　　　　*doesn't study Korean*

You will learn another way to negate verbs in Lesson Twelve.

8.3.2. Nonseparable Verbal Nouns (Descriptive)

There are also descriptive verbal nouns in which 해요 means *is* rather than *does*: 깨끗해요 *is clean, neat,* 안녕하세요 *is at peace* (*well*, equivalent to 잘 있어요), 미안해요 *is uneasy; sorry.*

Notice that descriptive verbs **never** take the direct object particle 을 ~ 를 because they cannot be separated from the verb 하-. So you can never have something like:

*미안을 해요.

In theory, then, if you wish to negate a nonseparable verbal noun plus 해요 structure, you should be able to put 안 before the entire composite verb (remember that you can't use 못 before descriptive verbs).

　　　　*안 미안해요　　　　*isn't sorry, doesn't feel sorry*
　　　　*안 깨끗해요　　　　*isn't clean, isn't neat*

Again, you may hear such forms spoken in Korean, but these forms are not considered elegant. You will have to wait until Lesson Twelve to learn another way to negate such structures.

8.4. More on Adverbs

Adverbs are words that modify verbs (*fast* in *runs fast*, 빨리 in 빨리 먹어요). Manner adverbs answer the question *how?* or *in what manner?* Time adverbs answer the question *when?* Place adverbs answer the question *where?* Degree adverbs are words like *very, a little,* etc. As you have seen, adverbs like these typically appear just before the verb they modify. They never serve as subjects or objects.

When different types of adverbs co-occur, they tend to follow the order: time, place, degree and manner.

	TIME	PLACE	DEGREE	MANNER	NEG

23.　만호 씨는　요즘　집에서 담배를　아주　　　많이　(안) 피워요.
Lately Manho smokes a lot at home.

Here are some useful adverbs in Korean.

Manner Adverbs

잘	*well; often, a lot*	혼자(서)	*alone, by oneself*
함께	*together*	많이	*lots*
같이	*like; together*	빨리	*fast*
깨끗이	*neatly*	천천히	*slowly*
안녕히	*at peace, in good health*	열심히	*diligently*

Time Adverbs

아직	*still, yet*	일찍	*early*
지금	*now*	먼저	*first (of all)*
늘	*always*	항상	*always*
언제나	*always*	요즘	*nowadays, lately*
보통	*usually, normally*	가끔	*sometimes*

Place Adverbs

We have not learned any place adverbs yet.

Degree Adverbs

참	*very, truly*	좀, 조금	*a little (bit)*
주로	*mainly, for the most part*	너무	*too much so, very*
아주	*very*		

Notice that some of the adverbs listed above end in -이 or -히. It is not always predictable when you can create an adverb like this from a verb base, and you should not attempt to create such adverbs on your own.

Some of the adverbs overlap in meaning: 잘 and 많이 share the meaning *many, much, a lot*, but only 잘 means *well* and *often* (*often* is also expressed by the adverb 자주). The adverb 많이 and the descriptive verb 많아요 should not be confused with each other. The verb means *there is much, there are many* or (someone) *has much/many*; it is equivalent to 많이 있어요. The opposite of 많아요 is 적어요 *there is little, there are few* or (someone) *has little/few.*

24. 교환학생이 많아요. = 교환학생이 많이 있어요.
    There are a lot of exchange students.

25. 수진 씨는 말이 적어요. 그런데 동호 씨는 말이 많아요.
    Sujin doesn't say much. But Tongho talks too much.

26. 교회에는 주로 일요일에 나가요.
    I go to church mostly on Sundays.

27. A. 한국음식을 자주 드세요?
    Do you eat Korean food often?

    B. 가끔 먹어요.
    Sometimes.

28. A. 아직도 수영을 매일 하세요?
    Do you still swim every day?

    B. 아니오. 요즘 너무 바빠요.
    No. Lately I'm too busy.

    A. 보통 혼자 하세요?
    Do you usually do it alone?

    B. 아니오, 친구랑 같이 다녀요.
    No. I go with a friend.

8.5. More New Particles: Instrumental (으)로

When English uses *with* plus the name of an object, *with* is often meant in a special sense, namely *by* or *by means of*. For example, you could take the sentence *I wrote this with a pencil*. This *with* is put into Korean with the particle (으)로. You have also seen (으)로 with the names of languages, to mean *in* (*by means of*) that language—한국말로 *in Korean*, 영어로 *in English*. This is a two-shape particle which is pronounced 으로 after all consonants except ㄹ, but 로 after ㄹ and vowels.

After most Consonants		**After Vowels and** ㄹ	
책으로	*with a book*	종이로	*with paper*
무엇으로	*with what?*	기차로	*by train*
돈으로	*with money*	영어로	*in English*
성냥으로	*with matches*	연필로	*with a pencil*

The particle (으)로 has a variety of meanings which can be set out as follows (there are certain others in addition which you will learn later).

a.   Function: *as, in the capacity of*

29.   교환학생으로 한국에 가요.
I'm going to Korea as an exchange student.

b.   Direction: *toward, to, in the direction of*

30.   오른쪽으로 가세요.
Please go to the right.

31.   이쪽으로 오세요.
Please come this way.

c.   Means: *with, by, by means of*

32.   이 편지를 연필로 써요.
I'm writing this letter with a pencil.

33.   비행기로 가세요?
Are you going by plane?

d.   Manner: *-ly*

34.   정열적으로 노래를 불러요.
He sings passionately.

8.6. More New Particles: (이)랑 *and*

The dialogue of this lesson had the following sentence, which illustrates the use of the next particle.

35.   경제학이랑 정치학도 배워요.
I'm learning Economics and Politics, too.

The two-shape particle (이)랑 has the shape 이랑 after nouns ending in a consonant, and 랑 after nouns ending in a vowel. It has exactly the same function as 하고, i.e., to link two nouns with the meaning *and*. It is somewhat more colloquial than 하고. In Korean, it is also possible to repeat these particles after the last noun enumerated. Here are examples.

36.   A.   런던이랑 뉴욕   *London and New York*
       B.   어제랑 오늘   *yesterday and today*
       C.   고기랑 밥이랑   *meat and cooked rice*
       D.   돈이랑 편지랑 비행기랑   *money, a letter, and an airplane*

8.7. Particle Sequences

A topic in a Korean sentence, i.e., a phrase ending with the particle 은 ~ 는, is most often a noun or noun phrase. But it may also be another particle phrase, i.e., an expression of time, place, manner and so on, such as 아침에 *in the morning,* 학교에서 *from* (or *at*) *school,* 펜으로 *with a pen,* 연필로 *with a pencil,* etc. When such a phrase becomes a topic, the result is a sequence (or string) of particles, the last one being the topic particle 은 ~ 는.

37. 아침에는 커피를 마셔요.
     In the mornings, I drink coffee.   *(compared to what I do the rest of the day)*

38. 학교에서는 야구를 해요.
     At school, we play baseball.   *(talking about what happens at school, we play baseball there)*

39. 자전거로는 못 가요.
     You can't go [there] by bike.   *(talking about going by bike, you can't go there that way)*

40. A. 매일 어머니한테서는 편지를 받아요.
     B. 아버지한테서는 안 받아요?
     A. *I get a letter every day from my mother.*   *(but not from other relatives, by contrast)*
     B. *Don't you get one from your father?*

Particles that do not enter into sequences with 도 or with 은 ~ 는 are 이 ~ 가, the subject particle and 을 ~ 를, the direct-object particle.

41. A.   한국말을 가르쳐요?
            Do you teach Korean?

     B.   아니오, 한국말은 김 선생님이 가르치세요.
            No, its Mr. Kim who teaches Korean.
            (Do you teach Korean? No, if it's Korean, Mr. Kim (is the one who) teaches it.)

42. A.   저녁에는 무엇을 해요?
            What do you do in the evenings?

     B.   노래를 불러요.
            I sing songs.

     A.   편지는 안 써요?
            How about letters: don't you write (any)?

Similarly, 도 appears **instead of** 이 ~ 가 or 을 ~ 를, not in combination with them.

43. A. 개가 있어요?
         Have you a dog?

     B. 네, 있어요.
         Yes, I have.

     A. 고양이도 있어요?
         Have you a cat, too?

44. A. 야구를 좋아해요.
         I like baseball.

     B. 수영도 좋아해요?
         Do you like swimming, too?

This means that some sentences with NOUN은 ~ 는 and NOUN도 are ambiguous, like sentences in which the subject particle 이 ~ 가 or direct object particle 을 ~ 를 is dropped. Ambiguity can usually be cleared up by marking either the subject or the object with what remains understood as the unmarked one, but it is not possible in Korean to specify the subject or object and at the same time mark it with 은 ~ 는 or 도.

Exercises

Exercise 1: Using 안 and 도

Here is a sentence with two blanks in it. Using one of the verb expressions from the list below, fill in the blanks. Use the same verb in both blanks.

선생님은 (_____) 안 _____. 그리고 저도 (_____) 안 _____.

1.	waiting for a train	2.	eating breakfast
3.	giving books to the students	4.	taking medicine
5.	at home	6.	open the door
7.	living with (하고) his parents	8.	taking a walk in the park
9.	meeting a friend	10.	teaching Russian
11.	drinking alcohol	12.	writing letters
13.	watching television	14.	cleaning the room

Exercise 2: Building Sentences from Phrases

Build a complete sentence around each of the following Korean expressions, translating the new sentences into English as you go.

1.	밤에	2.	부모님하고
3.	은행에서	4.	테이블 위에
5.	펜으로	6.	대학교에서
7.	분필로	8.	회사에
9.	공원에서	10.	비행기로
11.	정열적으로	12.	정치학이랑 러시아말
13.	개하고	14.	뉴욕 쪽으로
15.	다른 기차로	16.	무엇으로
17.	영어로	18.	친구하고
19.	오른 쪽으로	20.	오늘하고 내일
21.	그림 밑에	22.	항상

Exercise 3: Practice with 안, 못 and -(으)시-

Convert the following questions to honorific forms, then answer each one negatively in turn (with a full sentence: *No, I don't _____.*) Then say what you **do** do instead.

1.	빵 먹어요?	2.	술 마셔요?
3.	학교에 가요?	4.	야구 좋아해요?
5.	자요?	6.	런던에서 살아요?
7.	텔레비전을 봐요?	8.	연필로 편지를 써요?
9.	노래를 잘 불러요?	10.	교회에 나가요?

Exercise 4: Honorifics in Questions and Answers

For the following sets of information you are required to ask two questions and to give two replies (either positive or negative). Make sure you give full sentences each time. The questions should use the honorific verb forms, the answers should not. For the first set of information, then, you make up Korean sentences corresponding to: *Do you eat rice? Yes, I do eat rice. Do you drink water? No, I don't drink water.*

1.	점심	네	물	아니오
2.	고기	네	술	아니오
3.	담배	네	쥬스	아니오
4.	친구	네	편지	아니오
5.	빵	네	우유	아니오
6.	한국말	네	일본말	아니오
7.	신문	네	잡지	아니오

Exercise 5: Honorific Questions

Each of the following sentences means *I do something*. Change the topic and the verb form so that the meaning is *do you, sir, do something?* Write out the changed sentence and then translate it. Make sure that you practice each one out loud as well. For example, if you are given 나는 학교에 가요 your answer should be 선생님은 학교에 가세요? *Are you going to school?*

1. 나는 은행에서 일해요.
2. 나는 책을 잘 사요.
3. 나는 한국에서 영어를 가르쳐요.
4. 나는 아침에는 빵이랑 우유를 먹어요.
5. 나는 교회에 나가요.
6. 나는 미국사람이에요.
7. 나는 수영을 안 좋아해요.
8. 나는 오늘 저녁에 바빠요.
9. 나는 중국말이 힘들어요.
10. 나는 술을 잘 해요.
11. 나는 많이 못 먹어요.
12. 나는 친구를 기다려요.
13. 나는 담배를 안 피워요.
14. 나는 일찍 자요.

15. 나는 런던대학에서 한국말을 배워요.
16. 나는 여기(서) 살아요.
17. 나는 안 더워요.
18. 나는 항상 약을 먹어요.
19. 나는 다른 교재를 안 써요. (How is this sentence ambiguous?)
20. 나는 라디오를 들어요.
21. 나는 내일 못 떠나요.

Exercise 6: English to Korean Translation

Translate the following sentences into Korean. Where appropriate, put the verb into the honorific form. [Note: it will not always be appropriate.]

1. Are you going to bed now? No, I'm getting up.
2. At the weekends I sometimes take medicine.
3. Mr. Murphy often goes swimming with his wife.
4. Do you smoke? No, I don't.
5. I receive money from my mother. And then I see a movie with my friends.
6. My father studies economics. He studies politics, too.
7. On that student's desk there is a notebook. And he always cleans his room real clean.
8. What subjects are you learning? What's your major?
9. On Sunday, I usually go to church. Sometimes I go on my own.
10. You can't go there by airplane. I know!
11. Come quickly!
12. Please head to the right at that church.
13. I don't have a lot of time.
14. What foreign languages do you know, Mr. Ch'oe [최]? Do you speak English? We learn English from [with] this textbook.

Exercise 7: Korean to English Translation

Translate the following sentences into English.

1. 의사 선생님은 테레비 안 보세요. 애기들도 안 봐요.
2. 우리집 개는 공원에서 안 놀아요. 늘 집에 있어요. 참 착해요.
3. A. 고양이 있으세요? 커요?
    B. 좀 작아요.
    A. 다른 고양이들이랑 같이 자주 놀아요?
    B. 네, 그런데 고기를 많이 먹어요. 그리고 우유도 많이 마셔요.
4. 보통 버스로 다녀요. 빨리는 못 가요.
5. 호텔은 미국 대사관 바로 맞은 편에 있어요. 우리 집 바로 옆에 있어요.
6. 우리 남편은 편지를 잘 안 써요.
7. 여자친구는 집에서 뭘 해요?
8. 오 선생님은 서울에 기차로 가세요. 저녁에는 항상 친구 집에 가요.
9. 저희 아버님은 매일 어머님이랑 같이 산보하세요.
10. 요즘 우리 집에서는 호주 교환학생 한 명이 살아요. 늘 공부해요.
11. 경희 씨는 언제나 일찍 일어나요. 그리고 늦게 자요.
12. 내 방은 보통 깨끗해요. 거기서 가끔은 공부해요. 그렇지만 도서관이 나아요.
13. 박 교수님 사모님하고 배 선생님 부인은 매일 점심을 함께 드세요.
14. 야구는 혼자서 못 해요. 먼저 친구들을 기다려요. 이 근처에서들 살아요.

Lesson 9

주말 재미 있게 보냈어요?

In this lesson you will learn how to exchange pleasanteries and strike up a relationship with a stranger. You will also learn how to talk about something you did in the past (over the weekend). In addition, you will learn two different ways to say *like*, how to express wishes *want to*, a new particle for *and*, and the purposive ending –(으)러.

Korean Dialogues

Dialogue 1

While waiting at Kimp'o Airport on Sunday to meet a colleague flying in from Britain, Chris Murphy is approached by a Korean businessman waiting in the same area. The businessman obviously thinks Chris has just flown in and wants to practice his English.

아저씨	어어 – 하우 두 유 두?
머피	네? 아, 예. 안녕하세요?
아저씨	아이구! 한국말을 하시는군요. 한국에 처음 오셨어요?
머피	네, 그런데 사실은, 작년에 왔어요. 서울에서 살아요.
아저씨	그러세요? 무슨 일로 오셨어요?
머피	사업 때문에 왔어요. 영국회사에서 일해요.
아저씨	그러면 얼마 동안 계세요?
머피	글쎄요. 아직 모르겠어요.
아저씨	미국분이세요?
머피	아닌데요. 영국사람이에요.

아저씨	아, 그러세요? 죄송합니다. 저도 방금 런던에서 도착했어요.
머피	아, 예. 거기서 뭐 하셨어요?
아저씨	저도 사업 때문에 다녀왔어요. 무역 회사에서 일해요. 여기 제 명함 받으세요. 언제 한번 연락하세요.

They exchange namecards and go their separate ways.

Notes

네?	*Excuse me?* or *I beg your pardon?* [Literally: *Yes?* This is how you ask for a repeat in Korean.]
한국말 하시는군요	*Oh, I see you speak Korean!* Forms in –는군요 indicate a sudden, first realization. You will learn more about them in a later lesson.
그러세요?	*Really?* or *Is that so?* This is the polite honorific version of 그래요?
무슨 일로	*on what sort of business?* [Literally: *on account of/by way of what matter?* The whole sentence amounts to: *What brings you to Seoul?*]
얼마 동안?	*[for] how long?* (pronounced: 얼마똥안)
언제 한번	*Some time or other.* [Literally: *some time* 언제 *one time* 한번.]

Dialogue 2

Chris Murphy is talking to his secretary, Miss Lee, at the office.

머피	미스 리, 주말 재미 있게 보냈어요?
미스 리	네, 어제 사모님하고 극장에 갔었어요.
머피	이야기 들었어요. 극장에 사람들이 많았어요?
미스 리	네, 굉장했어요. 남대문시장처럼 사람들이 많았어요.
머피	무슨 영화를 봤어요?
미스 리	한국 영화였어요.
머피	나도 한국영화를 한번 보고 싶어요. 영화 괜찮았어요?
미스 리	별로 재미 없었어요. 그래서 중간에 나왔어요. 그리고 나서 사모님과 같이 차 마시러 다방에 갔어요.

Notes

이야기 들었어요	*I heard [all] about it.* [Literally: *I heard the story.*]
한국 영화였어요	*It was a Korean film.* The past tense of the copula –이었어요 can abbreviate to –였어요 after a noun ending in a vowel.
별로 + NEGATIVE	*not particularly, doesn't particularly*
한번	*one time, once*
그리고 나서	*after that, having done that*

Vocabulary

Places

술집 〔–찝〕	bar, tavern, drinking establishment
여관	small hotel; inn
우체국	post office
사무실	office
댁	house (honorific)
댁이 어디세요?	Where do you live? (not *댁이 어디에 있으세요?)
정원	garden
다방	tearoom, *tabang*

People

사모(님)	prominent man/superior's wife (elegant/honorific) [Literally: *teacher's wife*]
목사(님)	reverend, minister
신부(님)	(Catholic) priest
동생	younger brother or sister
여자동생	younger sister
남자동생	younger brother
영화배우	movie actor
배우	actor or actress
여자배우	actress
남자배우	actor
딸	daughter
아들	son
가족	family

Things You Wear and How To Wear Them

신발	shoes, footwear in general
구두	(dress) shoes
여자구두	women's shoes
구두 한 켤레	a pair of shoes
운동화	sneakers, tennis shoes
부츠	boots
양말	socks
반지	(finger) ring
장갑	gloves
모자	hat
안경	glasses
스카프	scarf
시계 (를) 차–	wear a watch; put on a watch
넥타이 (를) 매–	wear a tie; put on a tie

Nouns you can use with 입– *wear*

옷	clothes
쟈켓	jacket
양복	suit
샤쓰, 와이샤쓰	shirt, dress shirt
바지	trousers
청바지	jeans
코트	coat
치마	skirt
스웨타	sweater, jumper

Examples of 신– *wear (footwear)*

구두를 신어요.	wears shoes, puts on shoes
신발을 신어요.	wears shoes, puts on shoes
양말을 신어요.	wears socks, puts on socks

Examples of 끼– *wear (gloves, ring)*

반지를 껴요.	wears a finger ring, puts on a ring
장갑을 껴요.	wears gloves, puts on gloves

Examples of 쓰– *wear (hat, glasses)*

모자를 써요.	wears a hat
안경을 써요.	wears glasses
스카프를 써요.	wears a scarf

Other New Nouns and Related Expressions

차	tea
뉴스	the news (on radio, TV)
자동차, 차	car, automobile
연구	research
연구(를) 하-	does research
연구실	(professor's) office
중간	middle, midway
중간에	midway, in the middle
사업	business
무역	trade
무역회사	trading company
새 NOUN	new NOUN
새 양복 하나 샀어요.	I've bought a new suit.
값	price
값이 얼마에요?	How much is it [the price]?
명함	namecard, business card
위층	upstairs; the floor above
아래층	downstairs; the floor below
이	tooth, teeth
NOUN 때문에	because of NOUN; on account of NOUN
사업때문에 왔어요.	I'm here [I've come] on business.
애기때문에 못 잤어요.	I couldn't sleep because of the baby.
TIME PERIOD 동안(에)	for TIME PERIOD, during TIME PERIOD
얼마동안? 〔똥안〕	for how long? for what duration?
한 시간 동안	for an hour

Some Adverbial Expressions

더	more
조금 더 주세요.	Please give me a little bit more.
한번 더 하세요.	Please do it one more time.
또	Moreover, What's more; (yet) again
사실	fact; in fact
사실은	In fact; Actually
실은	In fact; Actually
쉽게	easily
아주	very
어제는 아주 더웠어요.	Yesterday was very hot.

방금	just a moment ago, just now
별로 + NEGATIVE	[not] particularly
작년	last year
작년에는	last year
글쎄요.	I don't really know. Let me think.

More New Verbal Expressions

구w-	roast it, broil it
고기를 구워요.	He cooks meat.
재미없-	not interesting, boring; not fun
재미있-	interesting; fun
재미있게	interestingly; in a fun way
	in such a way that it was interesting
영화를 재미있게 보셨어요?	Did you enjoy [watching] the movie?
아니오, 재미없게 봤어요.	No, I didn't find it very interesting.
올라가-	go up
올라오-	come up
오르-	ascend, go up
값이 많이 올랐어요.	The price has gone up a lot.
내려가-	go down
내려오-	come down
내리-	descend; get off/out (bus, taxi)
값이 많이 내렸어요.	The price has come down a lot.
서울역에서 내리세요.	Get off at Seoul Station.
나오-	come out
나가-	go out
굉장하-	be quite something, be impressive
도착(을) 하-	arrive
연락(을) 하-	get in touch, make contact
이야기(를) 하-	talk, chat
이야기, 얘기	story
갔다오-	go (and come back)
어디 갔다왔어요?	Where have you been?
닦-	polish; brush (teeth)
이를 닦아요.	He brushes his teeth.
즐거w-	be enjoyable, pleasant, fun
즐겁게	in an enjoyable way, enjoyably
주말을 즐겁게 보내셨어요?	Did you have a good ['enjoyable'] weekend?

돈(을) 찾-	withdraw money (from/out of the bank)
싶-	want to; it is desired (see Grammar Note 9.6)
전화를 거-ㄹ-	make a phone call
전화를 받-	answer the phone
보내-	spend (time); send
주말을 재미 있게 보내셨어요?	Did you have a fun weekend?
부치-	mail it, post it
생기-	turn out a certain way
잘 생겼어요.	Is handsome/good-looking. [usually said of males]
못 생겼어요.	Is ugly. [said of both males and females]

Lesson Notes

9.1. Verbs: Past Tense

9.1.1. Past Tense, Polite Style

As you know, Korean verb forms are made up of bases with endings on them. The present-tense forms you have learned are all in the Polite Style 해요 and have the particle 요 at the end to mark that style. As you learned in Lesson Seven, when you remove this 요, the part that remains is what we call the infinitive 해. The Korean infinitive is what the past tense is based on. The PAST BASE is made by adding -ㅆ- to the plain infinitive.

Base	Infinitive	Past base	Gloss
하-	해	했-	*did*
앉-	앉아	앉았-	*sat*
자-	자	잤-	*slept*
쓰-	써	썼-	*wrote*
빠르-	빨라	빨랐-	*was fast*
노-ㄹ-	놀아	놀았-	*played*
들- (ㄷ ~ ㄹ: 듣다)	들어	들었-	*listened*
더 w- (ㅂ ~ w: 덥다)	더워	더웠-	*was hot*
구 w- (ㅂ ~ w: 굽다)	구워	구웠-	*broiled it*

To the past base formed in this way you add the infinitive vowel 어 to give the past infinitive. Then you need to add a verb ending. If you are speaking in the Polite Style, which we have been learning up to now, you add the polite particle 요 in the normal way: 앉았어요 *sat*, 잤어요 *went to bed, slept*, 주었어요 *gave*, 왔어요 *came*, 썼어요 *wrote*, 빨랐어요 *was fast*, 놀았어요 *played*. Here are some more examples.

Base	Gloss	Polite Past
하–	*do* (irregular)	했어요
만나–	*meet* (somebody)	만났어요
가르치–	*teach*	가르쳤어요
계시–	*be; exist* (honorific)	계셨어요
오–	*come*	왔어요
배우–	*learn*	배웠어요
쉬–	*rest*	쉬었어요
매–	*ties it*	매었어요
		(pronounced 맸어요)
노–ㄹ–	*play*	놀았어요
주–	*give*	줬어요
서–	*stand*	섰어요
쓰–	*write*	썼어요
나쁘–	*be bad*	나빴어요
모르–	*not to know*	몰랐어요
부르–	*call; sing (a song)*	불렀어요
있–	*be; have; stay*	있었어요
없–	*not exist*	없었어요
읽–	*read*	읽었어요
좋–	*good*	좋았어요
먹–	*eat*	먹었어요
닫–	*close it*	닫았어요
들– (t~l: 듣다)	*listen to; take (a class)*	들었어요
물– (t~l: 묻다)	*ask*	물었어요
더w– (p~w: 덥다)	*is hot*	더웠어요
구w– (p~w: 굽다)	*broils it*	구웠어요
–이–	*it is* (copula)	–이었어요/–였어요

> ### 주의!
>
> The Polite Style past tense of the copula has two shapes. Nouns ending in a consonants take the shape in -이었어요, while nouns ending in a vowel take the shape in -였어요 (a spelling abbreviation):
>
> 양복이었어요. *It was a suit.*
> 구두였어요. *It was a shoe.*

9.1.2. Past and Past-Past

The past tense is usually translated by the English *did (was)* or *had done (had been)*, but for verbs of going and coming a result is implied: 갔어요 means *he went* (and is still gone); *he's gone/left* and 왔어요 means *he came* (and is still here); *he's here*. To say *he went* (but is back now) and *he came* (but left again so he isn't here any more), there is a special PAST-PAST form, like the one you saw in dialogue two of this lesson.

미스 리 네, 어제 사모님하고 극장에 갔었어요.
Yes, yesterday I went to the cinema with your wife (and now I'm back).

You will learn more about Past-Past forms in a later lesson.

Notice that there are two ways to look at English expressions such as *he's here/there*.

a.　　simple location 　　　　　　　　　　　　　　여기/거기에 있어요
b.　　the result of movement from another place 　왔어요/갔어요

When you can paraphrase *he's here* by *he's arrived, here he comes/here he is*, the second rendering is appropriate.

9.1.3. Past Tense, Honorific Polite Style

To make honorific forms past tense, you add the past-tense marker -ㅆ- to the honorific infinitive and complete the form by adding a Polite Style ending.

Honorific Forms

Base	Honorific Base	Infinitive	Past Base	Past Infinitive	Past Polite
가-	가시-	가셔	가셨-	가셨어	가셨어요
오-	오시-	오셔	오셨-	오셨어	오셨어요
앉-	앉으시-	앉으셔	앉으셨-	앉으셨어	앉으셨어요
읽-	읽으시-	읽으셔	읽으셨-	읽으셨어	읽으셨어요
들-	들으시-	들으셔	들으셨-	들으셨어	들으셨어요
구w-	구우시-	구우셔	구우셨-	구우셨어	구우셨어요
노-ㄹ-	노시-	노셔	노셨-	노셨어	노셨어요
나(ㅅ)-	나으시-	나으셔	나으셨-	나으셨어	나으셨어요

Here are some of the verbs you have learned so far, in the polite past and the honorific polite past.

Base	Gloss	Polite Past	Honorific Polite Past
하-	*do*	했어요	하셨어요
계시-	*exist; stay* [**not** *have* !!]	[see 있-, 없-]	계셨어요
기다리-	*wait for*	기다렸어요	기다리셨어요
-이-	*it is*	-이었어요	-이셨어요
주-	*give*	줬어요	주셨어요
가-	*go*	갔어요	가셨어요
크-	*be big*	컸어요	크셨어요
오-	*come*	왔어요	오셨어요
배우-	*learn*	배웠어요	배우셨어요
보-	*look at, see; read*	봤어요	보셨어요
사-	*buy*	샀어요	사셨어요
쉬-	*rest*	쉬었어요	쉬셨어요
노-ㄹ-	*play*	놀았어요	노셨어요
사-ㄹ-	*live*	살았어요	사셨어요
있-	*be, exist; have; stay*	있었어요	있으셨어요 [see also 계시-, 없-]
없-	*not exist*	없었어요	없으셨어요 안 계셨어요

Base	Gloss	Polite Past	Honorific Polite Past
좋-	*good*	좋았어요	좋으셨어요
먹-	*eat*	먹었어요	[잡수셨어요]
닫-	*close it*	닫았어요	닫으셨어요
들-	*listen to; hear*	들었어요	들으셨어요
구w -	*broil*	구웠어요	구우셨어요

9.2. The Particle 과~와 *and*

The two-shape particle 과 ~ 와 means *with* or *and*, just like the more colloquial particles 하고 and (이)랑. 과 ~ 와 is a two-shape particle that is pronounced 과 after consonants and 와 after vowels.

Consonants		**Vowels**	
양말과	*and socks*	전화와	*and the telephone*
그 여관과	*and that inn*	내 코트와	*and my overcoat*
우체국과	*and the post offic*	청바지와	*and the jeans*

Like other particles, 과 ~ 와 is pronounced as though it were part of the word before it. This means that if you are going to pause between nouns linked by 과 ~ 와, you pause after the word for *and*, instead of before it as in English.

종이와(pause) 책과(pause) 연필	*paper* (pause) *and books* (pause) *and a pencil*

Once two or more nouns have been linked with this particle, the group as a whole is followed by whatever particle is necessary to show its relation to the rest of the sentence. For example:

연필과 종이는	*pencil and paper* (as topic)
아버님과 어머님이	*father and mother* (as subject)
상점과 여관을	*the store and the inn* (as object)

Sometimes 과 ~ 와 is added after the last noun before putting on the relational particle: 연필과 종이와는.

9.3. Ways To Say *(together) with*

The adverb 함께 means *together*, and, like 같이, it can follow noun plus 과 ~ 와, noun plus (이)랑, or noun plus 하고 to mean *together with [so-and-so]* or simply *with [so-and-so]*. The noun in these expressions usually denotes a person or other living being. The word 함께 is used in exactly the same way as 같이. [Also see Section 6.4.]

아버님과 같이	or	
아버님하고 같이	or	
아버님이랑 같이	or	*(together) with Father*
아버님과 함께	or	
아버님하고 함께	or	
아버님이랑 함께		
친구와 같이	or	
친구하고 같이	or	
친구랑 같이	or	*(together) with my friend*
친구와 함께	or	
친구하고 함께	or	
친구랑 함께		
같이 갔어요	or	*They went together.*
함께 갔어요		

9.4. Ways To Say *like*

9.4.1. The Particle 처럼

The particle 처럼 means *like* as in *does something like NOUN*. Here are some examples.

1.   나처럼 정치학을 전공했어요.
     He majored in political science like me.

2.   진호 씨는 어머니처럼 착해요.
     Chinho is good-hearted like his mother.

3.   그 여자는 영화배우처럼 예뻐요.
     That woman is pretty, like a movie actor.

4. 우리 신부님은 가수처럼 노래를 잘 부르세요.
    Our priest sings well, like a pop singer.

5. 저 외교관은 영국사람처럼 말해요.
    That diplomat speaks like an Englishman.

The word 같이, in addition to meaning *together*, also means *like*.

나같이	same as	나처럼
선생같이	same as	선생처럼

9.4.2. The Verb 같아요

In order to express *be like NOUN*, you have to use a different pattern: NOUN 같아요. This is illustrated below:.

6. A. 그게 뭐에요?
    What's that?

    B. 약 같아요.
    It looks like medicine. or *It seems to be medicine.*

7. 우리 한국말 선생님은 영화배우 같으세요.
    Our Korean teacher is like a movie actor.

8. A. 저 사람은 누구에요?
    Who's that?

    B. 진영 씨 친구 같아요.
    It looks like Chinyŏng's friend. or *It seems to be Chinyŏng's friend.*

9.5. The Purposive Form -(으)러

The PURPOSIVE form -(으)러 is used to express *going* or *coming for the purpose of. . .* This pattern is typically used with verbs of motion like 가- and 오-. The ending is attached straight on to the base of the verb. L-extending verbs attach the -(으)러 ending to the extended base; for example, 여-ㄹ- *open* becomes 열러.

9. 편지를 쓰러 위층으로 올라갔어요.
    He's gone upstairs to write a letter.

10.   친구를 만나러 역으로 나갔어요.
        He's gone out to the station to meet a friend.

11.   점심을 먹으러 식당에 가요.
        I'm going to the cafeteria to eat lunch.

12.   술을 마시러 우리 집에 왔어요.
        They came to our place to drink (booze).

13.   놀러 오세요.
        Come over sometime (to play, have fun, relax).

주의!

Purposive forms are made only with PROCESSIVE verb bases; there is no -(으)러 form for descriptive verbs, nor for the copula.

9.6. Expressing Wishes with -고 싶어요

This pattern allows you to express that you *wish to do* or *would like to do* something (the action specified by -고). The pattern consists of a processive base plus the one-shape ending -고, followed by the descriptive auxiliary verb 싶어요 (base 싶-). Descriptive verbs cannot appear in this pattern.

The pattern in -고 싶어요 can be used in two meanings: (1) *I* (or *we*) *want* or *would like* and, (2) *Do you want* or *Would you like?* In other words, it is used for first-person statements and second-person questions. To make questions or statements about third persons (*he, she, it, they*), you use -고 싶어해요 (base 싶어하-) instead of -고 싶어요.

Note that the base of the auxiliary verb (싶- or 싶어하-) does all the work with past tense and honorifics: 전화를 걸고 싶었어요 *wanted to make a phone call*, and 새 양복을 입고 싶으세요? *Do you want to wear your new suit?* Here are some more examples.

14.   새 구두를 신고 싶어요.
        I want to wear my new shoes.

15.   새 장갑을 끼고 싶었어요.
        I wanted to wear my new gloves.

16. 공부를 잘하고 싶어요?
    Do you want to study well (Do you want to do well in school?)

17. 이 책을 읽고 싶으세요?
    Would you like to read this book?

18. 새 집에서 살고 싶어요.
    I want to live in a new house.

19. 주말을 재미 있게 보내고 싶었어요.
    I wanted to have fun over the weekend (I wanted to spend the weekend enjoyably).

20. 뉴스를 듣고 싶어요.
    I want to listen to the news.

The 고- form is a one-shape ending: it is always –고, regardless of the kind of base it is attached to. L-extending vowel bases attach the 고- form (and all other one-shape endings that begin with ㅈ, ㄷ, or ㄱ) to the extended shape (with the ㄹ): 여-ㄹ- *open* has the 고- form 열고. In contrast, the consonant bases that end in –ㄹ (ㄷ ~ ㄹ verbs) change this to ㄷ and this is shown in the spelling as well as in the pronunciation, so the 고- form of 들- *listens* is 듣고, pronounced (by automatic change) 듣꼬. Consonant bases that end in -w (ㅂ ~ w verbs) change the -w to ㅂ, so the 고- form of 구w- *broils it* is 굽고, pronounced (by automatic change) 굽꼬.

Statements in –고 싶어요 are ordinarily used only of one's own desires; to state other people's wishes, you use the expression –고 싶어해요. But you can use the simpler form for *you* when asking a question:

21. 나는 가고 싶어요.
    I want to go.

22. 철수 씨, 같이 가고 싶어요?
    Ch'ŏlsu, do you want to go (with us)?

23. 철수 씨는 가고 싶어해요.
    Ch'ŏlsu wants to go.

The particle that follows the object of a transitive verb with –고 싶어요 is usually marked as 을 ~ 를, but this can sometimes be changed to the particle 이 ~ 가, since 싶어요 is an auxiliary descriptive verb meaning *it is desired*. In this case, marking the object with 이 ~ 가 shows that you have a particularly strong feeling or affection for the object.

24. 나는 점심을 먹고 싶어요.
    I want to eat lunch.

25.　　나는 아이스크림이 먹고 싶어요.
　　　I want to eat ice-cream.

Verbal nouns which act as the object of 하- do not normally take 이 ~ 가 here.

　　　*공부가 잘 하고 싶어요.
　　　I want to study well.

Note that the pattern in -고 싶어(해)요 is incompatible with the copula. For *I want to be a doctor* or the like, you have to use the verb 되- *become* (the *thing* you *become* takes the subject marker 이 ~ 가. This is a fact about the verb 되-, not a feature of the pattern -고 싶어(해)요).

26.　　나는 교수가 되고 싶어요.
　　　I want to be a professor (when I grow up).

Here are some more examples of this construction.

27.　　영화를 보러 같이 나가고 싶어요?
　　　Would you like to go out with me to see a movie?

28.　　어머니가 보고 싶어요.
　　　I want to see my mother.

29.　　물을 마시고 싶어요.
　　　I want to drink (some) water.

30.　　여관에 있고 싶어요.
　　　I want to stay in a Korean inn.

31.　　어제도 쉬고 싶었어요.
　　　I wanted to rest yesterday too.

32.　　일본말도 배우고 싶어요.
　　　I want to learn Japanese too.

33.　　김 선생님은 미국에 가고 싶어하세요?
　　　Does Mr. Kim want to go to the US?

34.　　김 선생님도 미국에 가고 싶으세요?
　　　Mr. Kim, do you want to go to the US too?

35.　　친구 만나러 같이 가고 싶어요?
　　　Do you want to go with me to meet my friend?

Finally, notice that it is best to avoid negating this pattern in -고 싶어요 with 안 (negating it with 못 is out of the question, as 싶- is a descriptive verb). The negation pattern with 안 preceding the verb sounds best when 안 is followed by a short and succinct verb, but sounds progressively worse as the verb or verb expression being negated gets longer. You will learn another way to negate verbs by placing a negative element *after* the base in Lesson Twelve.

Exercises

Exercise 1: Past Tense

Each of the following sentences means *someone **does** something*. Change the verb form so that the meaning is *someone **did** something*. Write each one out and translate.

1.   친구를 만나세요?
2.   무슨 영화를 봐요?
3.   어머니는 친구들한테 편지를 많이 쓰세요.
4.   개가 문을 열어요.
5.   아버지는 말이 적으세요.
6.   그렇지만 친구가 많으세요.
7.   실은, 고기를 많이 못 먹어요.
8.   사모님도 그 책을 읽으세요?
9.   그 영화가 좋아요?
10.   사장님이 나한테 돈을 많이 주세요.
11.   나는 공원에서 아이와 같이 놀아요.
12.   사모님은 언제 도착하세요?
13.   나는 우체국에서 와요.
14.   누가 우리를 봐요?
15.   동생은 언제 호주로 떠나요?
16.   그 개는 참 커요.
17.   나는 런던 대학(학)생이에요.
18.   박 교수님은 런던에서 사세요.
19.   내 장갑이 여기 있어요.
20.   김 선생 딸은 참 착해요.
21.   무슨 연구를 하세요?
22.   정원이 예뻐요.

Exercise 2: Using -고 싶어(해)요

Each of the following sentences mean *someone **does** or **did** something*. Change the verb expression in each so that the meaning is *someone **wants** or **wanted to do** something* using the -고 싶어(해)요 pattern.

1.   나는 새 자동차를 사요.
2.   나는 다른 넥타이를 매요.
3.   서울에 같이 올라가세요?
4.   택시를 불러요?
5.   선생님은 학교에 전화를 거세요.
6.   만호 씨는 지난 주일에 부산에 내려갔어요.
7.   나는 한국사람한테 편지를 썼어요.
8.   나는 중국말도 배워요.
9.   수진 씨는 애기와 같이 놀아요.
10.   동호 씨는 청바지를 입어요.
11.   옆집 아들은 영화배우가 됐어요.
12.   나는 명함 하나를 받았어요.
13.   애기는 신발은 안 벗었어요.

Exercise 3: English to Korean Translation

Translate the following sentences into Korean. Remember that the important thing is to get the idea across, not to translate literally.

1.   Where did you go yesterday? I went to the market.
2.   What did you do last night? I slept.
3.   Did you come home late last night? No. I came home early.
4.   What did you buy at the department store yesterday? I bought trousers and an overcoat.
5.   What did you do with your brother? I played in the park.
6.   What did you do in front of the bank? I made a phone call to my mother.
7.   Were there many people on the bus?
8.   Did you find the post office easily?
9.   What did you do in the tabang? I drank juice.
10.   Yesterday I didn't polish my shoes. And I didn't brush my teeth, either.

Exercise 4: Purposives

Translate the following sentences into Korean. Remember that the important thing is to get the idea across, not to translate literally.

1.   He went out to make a phone call.
2.   My daughter went to Korea to research the Korean language.
3.   Mother went to the market on Tuesday to buy new shoes.
4.   My younger brother went to the store on Friday to buy gloves.
5.   I went to the bathroom to brush my teeth.
6.   The student came out to open the door.
7.   Father went to the bank on Monday to get money [use 갔다오-].
8.   Father went to meet a friend.
9.   My friend has gone to Korea to teach English.
10. Last night I went out to drink.

Exercise 5: *Do/Be Like*

Translate the following sentences into Korean. Remember to distinguish between 처럼/같이 and 같아요.

1.   That movie actor speaks English like an English person.
2.   He sings well, like a singer.
3.   Here there are always lots of people, like a market.
4.   A. Who is that person over there?
     B. Gee, I'm, not really sure. It looks like Manho.
5.   Are you busy tomorrow too, like today?
6.   I want to study well like my friend.
7.   She sometimes dresses like a movie actress.
8.   My friends and I are like a family.
9.   Their garden is really big. It's like a park!
10. Today is good. It's like the weekend.
11. In the evenings this room is like a bar.
12. I bought these shoes last year. But they look like new ones.
13. This hat is the same as (is like) that one.

Exercise 6: Fill in and Translate

Copy the following passage and insert the correct particles in the blanks. If there is more than one possibility, then give alternatives too.

월요일에는 수미 씨가 나 ____ 편지를 썼어요.

그래서 나는 화요일에 수미 씨 ____ 전화를 걸었어요.

그리고 어제 만났어요.

수미는 재호 ____ 같이 왔어요.

우리는 공원____ 같이 산보했어요.

재호 씨____ 시간이 별로 없었어요. 그래서 빨리 갔어요.

나는 수미 ____ 같이 극장에 갔어요.

영화 ____ 참 재미 있었어요.

Exercise 7: Korean to English Translation

1. 서울 구경하러 갔다왔어요.
2. 학생들은 다 담배를 피우러 나갔어요.
3. 오늘은 안 나가고 싶어요?
   네. 일찍 자고 싶어요.
4. 오늘 아침에는 아주 더웠어요. 그런데, 저녁에는 별로 안 더웠어요.
5. 영화는 별로 재미 없었어요.
6. 선생님은 좀 쉬러 나가셨어요.
7. 영화 끝났어요?
   아직 안 끝났어요.
8. 친구한테 전화 걸고 싶어요?
9. 아버지는 택시를 부르러 나가셨어요.
10. 공원에 산보하러 나가셨어요.
11. 개가 고양이를 물었어요.
12. 어제 그 새 식당에서 저녁을 먹었어요?
    네. 그런데, 음식은 별로 맛 없었어요.
13. 위층에 술집에 올라가고 싶어요.
14. 대학에서는 경제학 공부를 했어요. 그런데, 별로 재미 없었어요.
15. 어제 연 선생님 댁에 놀러 갔어요.

16. 어디 갔다왔어요?
    방금 우체국에서 왔어요.
17. 영화가 방금 끝났어요.
18. 차를 마시러 다방에 가고 싶어요.
19. 주말에는 좀 쉬고 싶어요.
20. 친구는 무역회사에 다녀요.
21. 이 새 구두 때문에 돈이 많이 나갔어요.
22. 다 왔어요? 아니오, 아직 멀었어요.
23. 사실은 전화를 안 걸었어요.
24. 작년에는 교환학생으로 연대에서 공부했어요.
25. 편지를 부치러 우체국에 방금 갔다왔어요.
26. 아버지는 사업 때문에 유럽에 자주 가세요.
27. 여자친구한테 매일 전화를 걸어요.
28. 돈을 찾으러 은행에 갔다왔어요.

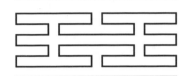 # Lesson 10

REVIEW 1

10.1. Vocabulary Review

Below is a list of most of the major verbs you have learned. Make sure you (1) know the meaning of each base, and (2) know how to make the Polite Style 해요-form for each base.

가-	떠나-	서-	전화 거-ㄹ-	연락(을) 하-
가르치-	마시-	쉬-	전화 받-	일(을) 하-
갔다오-	만나-	신-	좋-	전공(을) 하-
같-	많-	쓰- (x2!)	좋아하-	
걸리-	말(을) 들-	아-ㄹ-	주-	깨끗하-
계시-	맛 없-	앉-	주무시-	미안하-
기다리-	맛(이) 있-	알아 들-	즐거w-	착하-
깎-	매-	어려w-	찾-	
끝나-	머-ㄹ-	없-	치-	
끼-	먹-	여-ㄹ-	크-	
나(ㅅ)-	모르-	오-	파-ㄹ-	
나가-	무-ㄹ-	올라가-	피우-	
나쁘-	물-	-이-	하-	
나오-	바쁘-	일어나-	힘(이) 드-ㄹ-	
내려가-	받-	읽-		
노-ㄹ-	배우-	입-	공부(를) 하-	
노래 부르-	벗-	있-	구경(을) 하-	
다니-	보-	자-	도착(을) 하-	
닦-	보내-	자르-	말(을) 하-	
달-	부르-	작-	부탁(을) 하-	
더w-	비싸-	잡수시-	산보(를) 하-	
되-	빠르-	재미없-	수영(을) 하-	
드시-	사-	재미있-	야구(를) 하-	
들-	사-ㄹ-	적-	연구(를) 하-	

Exercise 1: Find the Misfit

In each of the following sets of six Korean words, five words have meanings which are related to each other, while there is one word which doesn't belong. Read aloud all the words in each group, then name the misfit.

1. 나
   누구
   당신
   아내
   우리
   그 사람

2. 잡지
   책
   종이
   공책
   지금
   신문

3. 친구
   누구
   무슨 일
   무엇
   어디
   어느 것

4. 회사원
   교수
   은행원
   의사
   가수
   남편

5. 여기
   밑에
   오른 편
   사이에
   저기
   문

6. 영어
   한국말
   미국사람
   중국말
   일본말
   러시아말

7. 잡지
   상점
   학생
   신문
   그림
   책상

8. 사모님
   부인
   아버지
   아이
   어머님
   다

9.	배워요	10.	물
	공부해요		속
	산보해요		밖
	써요		위
	가르쳐요		안
	읽어요		앞

11.	집	12.	언제나
	영화관		분필
	여관		좀
	약		매일
	학교		가끔
	대사관		방금

Exercise 2: Related Words

Now, here are some sets of three Korean words each—all of similar meanings. Your task is to supply two or three additional Korean words for each set which match the meanings of the words in the original group.

1.	선생	2.	상점
	교수		은행
	의사		학교

3.	오후	4.	밑
	아침		뒤
	낮		다음

5.	영국	6.	아내
	러시아		애기
	미국		아버지

7.	자요		
	일어나요		
	먹어요		

10.2. Particle Review

Here is a list of the particles you have learned so far in the course.

Particle	Function	Particle	Function
이~가	subject	한테	*to* a person
은~는	topic	한테서	*from* a person
도	*too, also, even*	에게	*to* a person
의	possessive	에게서	*from* a person
에	static location;	(으)로	*with, by means of,* etc.
	direction (*to*)	(이)랑	*and*
하고	*and; with*	과~와	*and*
을~를	object	처럼	*like*
에서	dynamic location;	도 도	*both/and,*
	from a place		*neither/nor*

Exercise 3: Fill in the Blanks

Here are some sentences with all the particles replaced by blank spaces. Say each sentence aloud, putting in the particles that are appropriate for each blank. (Remember that when you pause in your speech to think what particle to use, pause before you say the noun, not between noun and particle.) You will find that some sentences can be completed in more than one appropriate way.

1.　　나 ＿＿＿ 런던 대학 ＿＿＿ 한국말 ＿＿＿ 배워요.
2.　　나 ＿＿＿ 공원 ＿＿＿ 산보해요.
3.　　누(구) ＿＿＿ 선생님이에요? 저 분＿＿＿ 선생님이에요.
4.　　일요일 ＿＿＿ 선생님 ＿＿＿ 일찍 일어나세요?
5.　　저녁 ＿＿＿ 집 ＿＿＿ 무엇 ＿＿＿ 해요? 보통 편지 ＿＿＿ 써요.
6.　　집 ＿＿＿ 무엇 ＿＿＿ 보세요? 신문 ＿＿＿ 잡지 ＿＿＿ 봐요.
7.　　대학 ＿＿＿ 나 ＿＿＿ 정치학 ＿＿＿ 전공했어요.
8.　　알아 들었어요? 아니오, ＿＿＿ 알아 들었어요.
9.　　교회 ＿＿＿ 나가세요?
　　　네. 주로 어머니 ＿＿＿ 함께 다녀요.
10.　남자친구 ＿＿＿ 전화 ＿＿＿ 왔어요.
11.　도서관 ＿＿＿ 어디 ＿＿＿ 있어요?
　　　저기, 저 건물 옆 ＿＿＿ 있어요.

12. 은행 ___ 아버님 ___ 무슨 일 ___ 하세요?
13. 어제 교회 일 때문 ___ 바빴어요. 그래서 연락 ___ ___ 했어요.
14. 이거 혼자서 하셨어요?
    아니오, 친구 ___ 같이 했어요.

Exercise 4: Making Sentences from Phrases

Here is a list of noun-plus-particle phrases. Build a Korean sentence around each phrase, and practice saying your sentence aloud so it comes out smooth and fast. The exercise will do you more good if you write nothing down.

1.	친구와	2.	술집 아주머니가
3.	전화로	4.	러시아사람한테
5.	책상 위에	6.	나무 밑에서
7.	무역회사의	8.	아버지한테서
9.	박 선생님의	10.	교환학생한테서
11.	일요일날에는	12.	사모님과
13.	동생한테도	14.	무엇이
15.	어머님의	16.	딸도 아들도
17.	치마가	18.	이를
19.	일본말로	20.	성냥하고
21.	이 교실에	22.	저 영화배우가
23.	이 종이는	24.	명함을
25.	댁에서	26.	회사에서
27.	그 분은	28.	점심도
29.	그림도 책도	30.	의사선생님한테
31.	그 방에서는	32.	우체국에서
33.	영국사람에게	34.	영화관에서는
35.	약도	36.	시장에서도

10.3. Verb Review

Here is a chart of the major verb endings you have learned so far with some representative bases ("—" means the form is odd or does not exist).

	-어요/-아요	-(으)세요	-(으)러	-고 싶어요
-이-	-이에요	-이세요	—	—
하-	해요	하세요	하러	하고 싶어요
되-	돼요/되어요	되세요	되러	되고 싶어요
만나-	만나요	만나세요	만나러	만나고 싶어요
서-	서요	서세요	—	서고 싶어요
보-	봐요	보세요	보러	보고 싶어요
쉬-	쉬어요	쉬세요	쉬러	쉬고 싶어요
피우-	피워요	피우세요	피우러	피우고 싶어요
쓰-	써요	쓰세요	쓰러	쓰고 싶어요
바쁘-	바빠요	바쁘세요	—	—
다니-	다녀요	다니세요	다니러	다니고 싶어요
모르-	몰라요	모르세요	—	모르고 싶어요
부르-	불러요	부르세요	부르러	부르고 싶어요
힘드-ㄹ-	힘들어요	힘드세요	—	—
드시-	드세요	—	드시러	—
입-	입어요	입으세요	입으러	입고 싶어요
같-	같아요	같으세요	—	—
신-	신어요	신으세요	신으러	신고 싶어요
쉬w-	쉬워요	쉬우세요	—	—
들-	들어요	들으세요	들으러	듣고 싶어요
나(ㅅ)-	나아요	나으세요	—	낫고 싶어요

Exercise 5: Questions and Answers

Express each of the following brief questions aloud in Korean; then answer your own question negatively. The first one, for example, will be the Korean equivalent of: *Is he studying political science?* The answer? *No, he's not studying political science.* (Remember, sentences in Korean do not require you to specify a subject (i.e., *he* in these cases), though you can if you wish, to avoid ambiguity for example).

1. Is s/he studying Political Science?
2. Is s/he waiting for his friend?
3. Is s/he sleeping?
4. Is s/he living alone?
5. Is s/he learning Russian?
6. Are there many Koreans here?
7. Is s/he looking for his socks?
8. Did s/he come on [because of] business?
9. Is s/he at home?
10. Is s/he watching a movie?
11. Is s/he a doctor?
12. Does s/he work in a trading company?
13. Does s/he get many namecards?
14. Is s/he drinking wine?
15. Is s/he speaking Japanese?
16. Is s/he a teacher?
17. Is s/he staying here?
18. Has the price come down a bit?
19. Does s/he go to bars frequently?
20. Does s/he work at the bank now?
21. Does s/he watch TV too much?
22. Did s/he understand [catch] it?
23. Does s/he wear blue jeans often?
24. Does s/he know very much?
25. Is his room clean?
26. When does s/he arrive in Pusan?

Exercise 6: Questions and Answers (Honorific)

Now, ask and answer the following questions aloud in Korean, showing special respect for the person to whom you are referring.

1. 텔레비전을 봐요?
2. 방금 나갔어요?
3. 아이들이랑 같이 자주 놀아요?
4. 부모님과 함께 살아요?
5. 아침 일찍 일어나요?
6. 영화구경을 많이 가요?
7. 지금 사무실에 있어요?
8. 주말을 재미 있게 보냈어요?
9. 한국사람이에요?
10. 대사관에 전화를 걸었어요?
11. 중국말을 배워요?
12. 자동차를 팔았어요?
13. 어디에 갔다왔어요?
14. 가수에요?
15. 보통 늦게 자요?
16. 사립대학교에서 가르쳤어요?
17. 영어를 배워요?
18. 다른 외국어도 해요?
19. 명함을 줬어요?
20. 집에 일찍 들어와요?
21. 그 여자를 공원에서 만나요?
22. 보통 회사에 늦게 가요?

Exercise 7: Negative Honorifics

Repeat the answers to the questions in Exercises Five and Six above, making them mean *No, he doesn't* or *can't do something* whenever possible. Don't copy them. Simply practice asking the question and giving the answer as fluently as possible.

Exercise 8: Opposites

Express the following group of questions aloud in Korean and answer them by using a verb of different or opposite meaning, for example, *Is it large? No, it's small. Is he reading? No, he's writing.*

1.	Is the building large?	2.	Is s/he opening the door?
3.	Are there many students?	4.	Is s/he giving Mrs. Kim some money?
5.	Are you teaching Korean?	6.	Did s/he put on the sweater?
7.	Is s/he getting up?	8.	Did the food taste good?
9.	Did s/he sell the car?	10.	Does s/he obey the teacher('s words)?
11.	Were the gloves expensive?	12.	Does s/he usually stay home?
13.	Is s/he working?	14.	Did s/he just leave?

Exercise 9: Opposites (Honorific)

Now repeat the sentences of Exercise 8 above, both questions and answers, changing them so that they refer to someone highly esteemed.

10.4. Sentence Review

Exercise 10: Korean to English Translation

Here are fifty Korean practices using the vocabulary and constructions you have learned in the first nine lessons. Read each one aloud, then translate it into English. In English, convey the meaning of Korean, but without necessarily making a word-for-word translation.

1.   시간이 다 됐습니다. 시작합시다.

2.   A. 그 사람은 선생이에요?

     B. 아니오, 학생이에요.

3.   A. 지금 무엇을 하세요?

     B. 뉴스를 봐요.

4.   A. 이 반지는 누구의 반지에요?

     B. 내 반지에요. 주세요.

5.   A. 어디서 한국말 공부를 하세요?

     B. 고려대학교에서 해요.

6.   A. 식당에 가세요?

     B. 친구집에 놀러 가요.

7.   A. 저녁에는 공부를 하세요?

     B. 네, 가끔 해요.

8.   못 알아 들었어요. 영어로 하세요.

9.   나는 요즘 참 늦게 일어나요. 그리고 늘 늦게 자요.

10. A. 집을 쉽게 찾으셨어요?

     B. 아니오 – 좀 어려웠어요.

11. A. 전부 다 한국사람이었어요?

     B. 아니오, 외국사람도 왔어요.

12. A. 보통 일찍 주무세요?

     B. 네, 보통 일찍 자요.

13. A. 저는 교환학생으로 왔어요.

B. 그래요? 어느 나라에서 오셨어요?

14. 일본말도 하세요? 저도 일본말 좀 배우고 싶어요.

15. 오후에 안 바쁘세요? 부탁 하나 있어요.

16. A. 여기서 멀어요?

    B. 아니오, 별로 안 멀어요. 같이 가요.

17. A. 저 분이 미국 분이 아니세요?

    B. 네, 영국사람이에요.

18. A. 한국말이 어려워요?

    B. 네, 힘이 들어요.

19. 저 사람이 만호 씨의 여자친구가 아니에요?

20. A. 한국말 가르쳐요?

    B. 아니오, 영어를 가르쳐요.

21. A. 어디서 가르쳐요?

    B. 성당에서 가르쳐요.

22. 우리집 밖에는 나무가 많아요. 정말로 예뻐요.

23. 옆방에서 누가 주무세요?

24. A. 옆 건물은 식당이에요?

    B. 아니오, 술집 같아요.

25. A. 보통 공부를 학교에서 해요, 집에서 해요?

    B. 집에서 해요. 학교에서는 잘 안 돼요.

26. A. 개 있어요?

    B. 네, 있어요. 아주 착해요. 고양이도 있어요.

27. A. 지금 아버님이 댁에 계세요?

    B. 네, 계세요. 조금 기다리세요.

28. A. 아이들은 어디에 있어요?

    B. 집 앞에서 놀아요.

29. 오늘은 영화구경을 못 가요. 미안해요.

30. A. 점심은 보통 학교식당에서 먹어요?

    B. 아니오, 거기는 맛 없어요.

31. A. 차표 샀어요?

  B. 아니오, 아직 못 샀어요. 매표소는 어디에 있어요?

32. 전주행 기차는 언제 떠나요? 그리고 몇 시간 걸려요?

33. A. 어디에 갔다왔어요?

  B. 새 구두를 사러 갔다왔어요.

34. A. 몇 시간 걸려요?

  B. 두 시간 걸려요.

35. A. 러시아말은 어디서 배우셨어요?

  B. 러시아에서 배웠어요.

  A. 그래요? 러시아에는 얼마 동안 계셨어요?

36. A. 외국어를 배우세요?

  B. 네, 외국어를 많이 배우고 싶어요.

37. 이대, 연대와 서강대는 다 신촌에 있어요. 서울대에서는 좀 멀어요.
  고대에서도 좀 멀어요.

38. A. 일요일은 보통 일찍 일어나세요?

  B. 아니오, 일요일은 늦게 일어나요.

39. A. 이 근처에 구두가게 있어요?

  B. 네, 저기 대학 정문 맞은 편에 있어요.

40. 우리 집 차는 언제나 깨끗해요. 그래서 새 것 같아요.

41. A. 누구를 기다리세요?

  B. 아버님하고 어머님을 기다려요.

42. 보통 학교에서 바로 집에 가요.

43. 오후에는 우체국 앞에서 친구를 만나요.

44. A. 실례지만, 부탁 하나 있어요.

  B. 네, 말씀하세요.

45. A. 밥 먹었어요?

  B. 아니오, 아직 안 먹었어요.

46. 천천히 가세요. 시간이 아직 많아요.

47. 시장과 우체국 사이에는 여관이 많이 있어요.

48. A. 저녁에 늦게 집에 들어가세요?

     B. 아니오, 늦게 안 들어가요. 항상 일찍 들어가요.

49. 일요일날 아침에 보통 정원에서 책을 읽어요.

50. A. 나는 술을 못 마셔요. 담배도 못 피워요.

     B. 그래요? 몰랐어요.

Exercise 11: English to Korean Translation

Here are forty-five English practices for you to put into Korean. Write them out and then practice them aloud until you can say each one smoothly. Make sure you use some honorifics.

1.   A. Where's the Korean teacher?
     B. She's in the classroom.
2.   A. Are you American?
     B. I'm afraid not. I'm English.
3.   A. What are you doing here?
     B. I work at an English trading company.
4.   A. Are there Korean newspapers in the library?
     B. Yes, there are.
5.   A. Isn't your wife going to Korea with you?
     B. Yes, she is.
6.   A. Are you learning Japanese?
     B. Yes. I go to Japan often on business.
7.   A. Have you any cigarettes?
     B. Yes, there are both cigarettes and matches on my desk.
8.   It was really fun. The time went quickly.
9.   A. Do you read magazines and books in the evening?
     B. I usually read the newspaper first.
10. A. Who did you hear it from?
     B. It's true. I heard it from my brother.
11. A. Do you live with your parents?
     B. No, I live with a friend near city hall.
12. A. Have you got a pen?
     B. I'm sorry, I haven't either a pen or a pencil.
13. A. What are you doing?
     B. I'm looking for my namecards.
14. Mr. Kim doesn't smoke. He doesn't drink either.

15. I can't go to the movies with you this evening. I'm too busy.

16. I usually stay at home in the evenings. And I go to bed early.

17. A. Are there many gardens and parks in Korea?

  B. Yes, a few. But there are more in England.

18. Mr. Kim taught Korean to diplomats in the United States. But now he lives in Seoul.

19. A. Are you learning Japanese at school?

  B. No, I'm learning Chinese. But I can't speak it well yet.

20. A. Have you got any paper in your briefcase?

  B. Yes, here's some.

21. I haven't got either matches or cigarettes. Have you got (any)?

22. A. Is your house large?

  B. No, it's not particularly large. But it's nice.

23. Yesterday was really enjoyable. I want to go again.

24. A. Have you got a cat?

  B. No, we haven't got either a dog or a cat.

25. I work at a bank daytimes. And at night I work in a hotel. Because of my work I'm always busy.

26. I meet my friend in front of this store in the evenings. Then we go to the movies.

27. A. Do you usually go for walks in the park by yourself?

  B. No, I usually go with a friend of mine. [Literally: my friend]

28. I eat very early (in the morning). Then I go to school.

29. I drink a lot of water. But I don't eat much meat.

30. I'm going to the restaurant to eat lunch.

31. Have you taken your medicine?

32. A. Which one is better?

  B. This one is.

33. I have a little bit of time this evening.

34. I wanted to phone my friend.

35. But he has gone out.

36. Sometimes he works in the garden.

37. Then he can't answer the phone.

38. I want to go straight home now.

39. It was really hot in the theater. So I took off my sweater.

40. I wanted to brush my teeth. However, I didn't have the time.

41. A. Where did you go this morning?

  B. I went to the market to buy some new jeans.

42. A. I want to go by bicycle.

  B. You can't go by bicycle. It's too far.

43.   A. Do you usually eat bread and milk in the morning?
        B. No. I like rice.
44.   I wanted to give my brother some money. But I didn't have any.
45.   I want to get up early tomorrow.

10.5. Korean Conversations

Conversation 1

Practice the following conversation aloud, taking turns with the roles. Speak them as naturally and easily as you can. Try to sound as much like a native Korean speaker as you can. Make sure you know what each sentence means.

선생	안녕하세요?
학생	네. 안녕하세요.
선생	시간이 다 됐습니다. 시작할까요?
학생	그러면, 시작해요.
선생	오늘은 한국말로 하세요.
학생	죄송합니다. 다시 말해 주세요.
선생	오늘은 한국말로 하세요. 알아 들었어요?
학생	네, 알아 들었어요.
성생	이 책이 누구의 책이에요? 대답하세요.
학생	김 선생님의 책이에요.
선생	좋아요. 저 공책도 내 공책이에요?
학생	아니오, 그 공책은 저 학생의 공책이에요.
선생	이 학교 선생들이 어느 나라 사람이에요? 영국사람들이에요?
학생	아니오, 다 한국 분이에요.
선생	좋아요. 시간이 다 됐습니다. 십분만 쉽시다.

Conversation 2

만호	유니스 씨, 어디 가세요?
유니스	학교에 가요.
만호	학교에서 무엇을 해요?
유니스	한국말이랑 다른 과목도 공부해요.
만호	아침에 일찍 일어나세요?
유니스	네, 아침에 아주 일찍 일어나요.
만호	한국말 공부는 오후에도 해요?
유니스	아니오, 오후에는 수업이 없어요. 그래서 친구들이랑 같이 놀아요. 집에는 보통 늦게 가요.
만호	저녁에는 무엇을 해요? 영화구경을 가세요?
유니스	아니오, 보통 집에 있어요. 그리고 잡지를 봐요.

Conversation 3

수진	지금 어디에 가요?
진희	우체국에 가요.
수진	우체국에서 일을 해요?
진희	네, 어제 시작했어요. 오후에는 또 다른 일도 해요.
수진	그래요? 오후에는 무슨 일을 해요?
진희	다방에서 일해요.
수진	그러면, 집에는 늦게 가요?
진희	아니오, 보통 일찍 가요. 집에서는 쉬어요.

LESSON 11

스물한 살이에요. 칠십육년생이에요.

In this lesson, you will learn how to establish age-based hierarchies with your peers and others, and describe the gory details of a party and the food and drink consumed there. In other words, you learn how to manipulate numbers, times, and dates, also how to count and name hours, days, months, years, etc. You also learn how to manipulate telephone numbers and some particles useful for time, numbers and dates. Finally, you learn a new speech style, the FORMAL Style in 합니다.

Korean Dialogues

Dialogue 1

Chris and Eunice's college age son Eric has struck up a new friendship with a Korean student at Korea University.

영철	에릭 씨, 집이 어디에요?
에릭	평창동이에요.
영철	그래요? 부자 동네에서 사는군요! 집에서 학교까지 멀어요?
에릭	한 시간쯤 걸려요.
영철	에릭 씨 나이가 몇 살이에요?
에릭	스물한 살이에요. 칠십육년생이에요.
영철	그래요? 그러면 저하고 동갑이네요! 생일이 언제에요?
에릭	팔월이십사일이에요. 왜요?
영철	하! 그럼 에릭 씨가 형이네요! (jokingly) 형님!
	잘 부탁드립니다. 참, 집 전화번호가 몇번이에요?
에릭	삼오이국의 일공칠삼이에요. 참, 영철 씨, 이번 주말에
	우리 한국어 반에서 파티를 해요. 꼭 와요.

Notes

사는군요!	*Oh, I see you are living* (in a rich neighborhood)*!* Forms in -는군요 indicate a sudden, first realization. You will learn more about them in a later lesson.
동갑이네요!	*Why, we're the same age!* You learn more about mild surprise forms in -네요 later. For now, memorize this as part of the dialogue.
형이네요!	*Why, that makes you my* 형! You learn more about mild surprise forms in -네요 later. For now, memorize this as part of the dialogue.
잘 부탁드립니다.	*Please look out for me. Please take good care of me.* This idiomatic expression is often used by subordinates to those higher ups upon meeting for the first time.

Dialogue 2

Eric meets up again with 영철 again the day after Eric's party.

영철	어제 파티에 몇 사람 왔습니까?
에릭	한 열다섯 사람 왔어요.
영철	그렇습니까? 술을 많이 마셨습니까?
에릭	맥주를 칠십 병쯤 마셨어요.
영철	안주도 많이 먹었습니까?
에릭	오징어 열 마리하고 감자깡 스무 봉지하고 사과 한 상자 먹었습니다.
영철	몇시에 끝났습니까?
에릭	새벽 두시에 끝났습니다. 그런데 왜 안 왔어요?
영철	미안해요, 에릭 씨. 잊어버렸어요. (jokingly) 용서하십시오, 형님!
에릭	알았어요. 괜찮아요. 그런데 지금 몇시에요?
영철	열두시 삼십오분입니다. 벌써 점심 시간이네요. 밥 먹으러 갑시다.

Notes

알았어요.	[Literally: *I've understood.* This idiomatic expression has the effect of *Got it; I see; OK, I get your point.*]

| 그렇습니까? | *Really?* This is the Formal Style version of 그래요? The Formal Style version of the statement is 그렇습니다. |
| 점심시간이네요! | *Why, it's lunchtime!* You learn more about mild surprise forms in -네요 later. For now, memorize this as part of the dialogue. |

Reading Passage

일곱 사람이 음식점에 있습니다.

남자 세 명과 여자 네명이 있습니다.

식탁 위에 맥주가 일곱 병 있습니다. 사람마다 맥주를 한 병씩 시켰습니다.

과일과 안주도 많이 있습니다.

사람들이 맥주를 마십니다. 안주도 먹습니다.

사람들이 밤 늦게까지 재미 있게 이야기합니다.

Vocabulary

Counting and Time Expressions

몇	how many? (some/several)
며칠	how many days? (a few days)
며칠 계십니까?	How many days are you staying?
얼마나	about how much? approximately how much?
번호	number
전화번호	telephone number
전화번호가 어떻게 됩니까?	What's your telephone number?
여러 NOUN	several, various NOUN
여러가지 음식	all kinds of food
여러분	all of you, everybody
한 NUMERAL	about, approximately (NUMERAL)
한 두 시간 걸립니다.	It takes about two hours.
전에	earlier, before
후에	afterwards, later, later on
두 시간 후에 만납시다.	Let's meet in two hours.

나중에	in the future, some time later, later
내년(에)	next year
금년(에)	this year
주중에	during the week, on week days
지난 NOUN	past, last NOUN
지난 번에	last time
-번	a time
한번	once, one time
한번 더	one more time, once more
이번 NOUN	this NOUN
이번 주말	this weekend
생일	birthday
생신	birthday (honorific)
나이	age
나이(가) 많아요.	She is old.
연세	age (of s.b. esteemed)
연세(가) 많으세요.	She is old. (honorific)
-년생(이에요)	is a person born in such-and-such a year (use Sino-Korean numbers)
몇년생이십니까?	What year were you born in?
칠십구년생입니다.	I was born in '79.
-학년(이에요)	is a student in such-and-such a year or grade (at school)
일학년	first-year, Freshman
이학년	second-year, Sophomore
삼학년	third-year, Junior
사학년	fourth-year, Senior
몇학년입니까?	What year are you (in school)?
반	half (as in half hour)
반 시간	half hour
오전	A.M.
오전 아홉시 반	9:30 A.M.
오후	afternoon; P.M.
오후 두시	2 P.M.
새벽	dawn, early morning (1:00 A.M. to 6:00 A.M.)
새벽 두시	2:00 A.M.

Other New Nouns

부자	a rich person
동네	neighborhood, part of town
식탁	dining table, kitchen table
반	a class
파티	party
맥주	beer
안주	food to go with alcoholic beverages
감자	potato(es)
감자깡	crispy fried potatoes, potato chips
오징어	squid
오징어깡	squid chips
새우	shrimp
새우깡	shrimp chips
사과	apple
과일	fruit
동갑	a person of the same age
엉터리	something or someone fake or bogus; rubbish, piece of junk, hogwash
청소를 엉터리로 했어요.	I did a hafl-baked job of cleaning up.
물건	goods
길	road, way, street
끝	the end
처음	the beginning
처음에는	at first, in the beginning
처음부터 끝까지	from beginning to end
방학	school vacation

New Verbs

고생(을) 하–	suffer, endure hardship
용서(를) 하–	forgive
용서하십시오.	Forgive me; I beg your pardon.
태어나–	be born
어디서 태어나셨습니까?	Where were you born?
젊–	be young
고마w–	be grateful, thankful
고맙습니다.	Thank you.

맵w-	spicy, spicy hot
시작(을) 하-	begin
다르-	be different
영어는 한국어하고 달라요.	English is different from Korean.
사람마다 다릅니다.	Everybody is different.
아르바이트(를) 하-	do part-time work as a student
아르바이트	part-time work for students
놓-	put/place it
시키-	order (at a restaurant)
도와주-	help
좀 도와주십시오.	Please help me.
끝나-	it finishes
영화가 언제 끝납니까?	When does the film finish?
끝내-	finishes it
이 일을 빨리 끝내십시오.	Please finish this job quickly.
잊어버리-	forget

Other

왜(요)?	why?
왜냐하면	The reason is, It's because
꼭	without fail, by all means, for sure
꼭 오십시오.	Please be sure to come.

In addition, you are responsible for all the numerals and counters in this lesson.

Lesson Notes

11.1. Numbers and Counting

Korean has two sets of numerals. One of these (일, 이, 삼, etc.) was borrowed from Chinese; the other set is native (하나, 둘, 셋, etc.). Up to 99, both sets are used. For units of 100 and above, only the Chinese set is used; but in compound numbers (like 121) you will hear both (백 이십일 and 백 스물 하나).

In general, the numerals above 10 are combinations of the first ten: 11 is 10 + 1 (열 하나; 십일), 12 is 10 + 2 (열둘; 십이), and so on. The pure Korean (i.e., native Korean as opposed to Chinese) numerals 20, 30, 40, etc., are special words, but in the Chinese system, 20 is 2 x 10 (이십), 30 is 3 x 10 (삼십), etc.

Below are all the numerals you will need to know in Korean. In cases where the actual pronunciation of a numeral differs from the 한글 spelling, we have noted this in square brackets.

Pure Korean Numerals

Sino-Korean Numerals

	Ordinary Pronunciation	Pronunciation before Nouns	
1	하나	한	일
2	둘	두	이
3	셋	세 ~ 석[1]	삼
4	넷	네 ~ 넉[1]	사
5	다섯	same	오
6	여섯	same	육 ~ ‒륙[2]
7	일곱	same	칠
8	여덟 [여덜]	same	팔
9	아홉	same	구
10	열	same	십
11	열하나	열한	십일
12	열둘 [열뚤]	열두 [열뚜]	십이
13	열셋	열세 ~ 석[1]	십삼
14	열넷	열네 ~ 넉[1]	십사
15	열다섯 [열따섯]	same	십오
16	열여섯 [열려섯]	same	십륙 [심뉵][2]
17	열일곱	same	십칠
18	열여덟 [열려덜]	same	십팔
19	열아홉	same	십구
20	스물	스무	이십
21	스물하나	스물한	이십일
22	스물둘 [‒뚤]	스물두 [‒뚜]	이십이
23	스물셋	스물세 ~ 석[1]	이십삼
24	스물넷	스물네 ~ 넉[1]	이십사
30	서른	same	삼십
33	서른셋	서른세 ~ 석[1]	삼십삼
40	마흔	same	사십
44	마흔넷	마흔네 ~ 넉[1]	사십사

	Pure Korean Numerals		**Sino-Korean Numerals**
	Ordinary Pronunciation	Pronunciation before Nouns	
50	쉰	same	오십
55	쉰다섯	same	오십오
60	예순	same	육십
66	예순여섯	same	육십륙 〔육씸뉵〕
70	일흔	same	칠십
77	일흔일곱	same	칠십칠
80	여든	same	팔십
88	여든여덟	same	팔십팔
90	아흔	same	구십
99	아흔아홉	same	구십구
100			백
200			이백
300			삼백
400			사백
500			오백
600			육백
700			칠백
800			팔백
900			구백
1,000			천
10,000			만
60,000			육만
100,000			십만
1,000,000			백만

주의[1]

When the pure Korean numerals for 3 and 4 are used before counters which begin with the sounds ㄷ and ㅈ, they can be pronounced 석 and 넉, respectively.

Each of the Korean numerals from one to four (하나, 둘, 셋, 넷) and twenty (스물) is peculiar in this respect: when used right before the word it is counting, the numeral drops its last sound. Here are some common examples.

하나	one	한 사람	one person
		한 개	one object
		한시	one o'clock
둘	two	두 달	two months
		두 분	two esteemed people
		두 명	people
셋	three	세 병	three bottles
		세 가지	three kinds
		(종이) 세 장	three pieces (of paper)
넷	four	네 마리	four (animals)
		네 살	four years (of age)
		네 시간	four hours
스물	twenty	스무 번	twenty times
		스무 대	twenty vehicles

English allows one to say either *two cows* or *two head of cattle*, but when counting dogs, there is but one choice: *two dogs*. Korean uses both types of construction, but often the latter: 개 두 마리 *two dogs*. The word 마리 is a special kind of COUNTER (also called a CLASSIFIER). It classifies nouns for counting purposes according to some common characteristic. Things counted with 마리 are animals and fishes, things counted with 장 are thin, flat, sheet-like things, and so on.

Other kinds of counters are MEASURES, used to say how much there is of something that can be measured out—by the cupful, the kilogram, pound, the mile (of distance), the dollar or 원 (of money). English has measures, like Korean, and also a few counters (such as *head* for cattle), but Korean has more of these than English has. That is why there is no ready English equivalent for the counters in 책 세 권 *three (volumes of) books*, 집 세 채 *three (buildings of) houses.*

As the lists to follow show, there are some counters which go with the pure Korean numerals and others which require the Sino-Korean numerals. The distinction is sometimes crucial, as in the case of 분.

한 분	*1 esteemed person*	일분	*1 minute*
두 분	*2 esteemed people*	이분	*2 minutes*
세 분	*3 esteemed people*	삼분	*3 minutes*

A NUMERAL EXPRESSION is either a numeral by itself or a numeral plus a counter. When you are using particles with numeral expressions, you enjoy a certain amount of freedom as to where you can put the particle in the sentence. Numeral expressions have the following four usages.

1. Numeral Expressions can modify counters:

    두 사람이 있어요.   *There are two people.*

2. Numeral Expressions can have particles after them:

    | 가게 둘이 있어요. | *There are two shops.* |
    | 책 두 권이 있어요. | *There are two (volumes of) books.* |
    | 책이 두 권 있어요. | *There are two (volumes of) books.* |
    | 책을 두 권 샀어요. | *There are two (volumes of) books.* |
    | 책 두 권을 샀어요. | *There are two (volumes of) books.* |
    | 둘이 있어요. | *There are two.* |
    | 두 권이 있어요. | *There are two (volumes).* |

3. Numeral expressions can be used as adverbs.

책이 둘 있어요.　　　　　　　　*There are two books.*
　　　　　　　　　　　　　　　[Literally: *Books exist to the tune of two or two-wise*]

책이 두 권 있어요.　　　　　　*There are two (volumes of) books.*
　　　　　　　　　　　　　　　[Literally: *Books exist to the tune of two volumes*]

4. Numeral expressions can be used before the copula.

두 시입니다.　　　　　　　　　*It is 2:00 o'clock.*

Here are some examples of numerical expressions in sentences.

1. 이 방 안에는 창문이 일곱 개 있어요.
   There are seven windows in this room.

2. 부산행 기차표 두 장 주세요.
   Please give me two train tickets to Pusan.

3. 나는 우체국 앞에서 자동차 여섯 대를 봤어요.
   I saw six cars in front of the post office.

4. 신문을 세 부 샀어요.
   I bought three newspapers.

5. 그 집에 방이 몇 개 있어요?
   How many rooms are there in that house?

6. 석 달 후에 영국에 가요.
   I'm going to England in [after] three months.

7. 그 서점이 몇 층이에요?
   How many floors is the bookshop? or *Which floor is the bookshop?*

8. 백화점에는 여러 가지 물건을 팔아요.
   They sell many/several/all kinds of goods in department stores.

The following counters are used with pure Korean numerals up to the number twenty, after which Sino-Korean numerals may also be used. Note that some counters can also function as independent nouns. Those counters which cannot function as independent nouns, and are therefore bound, are preceded by a dash: –. Those counters which can function as either a counter or an independent noun are preceded by a dash in parentheses: (-):

Counters used with Pure Korean Numerals

–시	*o'clock*	(–)시간	*hours*
(–)달	*months*	(–)해	*years*
(–)사람	*persons, people*	–군데	*places, institutions*
–명	*persons, people*	–갑	*pack* (of cigarettes)
–분	*esteemed people*	(–)상자	*box; case; chest*
–마리	*animals, fish, birds*	–부	*newspapers; books* (if bought
–살	*years of age* (but not for		in multiple copies)
	esteemed individuals)	–장	*flat objects; pieces of paper*
(–)잔	*cupfuls*	–채	*buildings*
–대	*vehicles, machines*	–개	*items, units, objects*
–가지	*kinds, varieties*	(–)봉지	*paper bag*
(–)병	*bottle*	–권	*bound volumes; books*
–번	*times*		*or magazines*

주의!
The counters above can usually be used with either
pure Korean or Sino-Korean numbers above the number twenty.
Thus, one can say either 이른 병 or 칠십 병 for *seventy bottles*.

Counters used with Sino-Korean Numerals

–분	*minutes*	–초	*seconds*
–일	*days*	–도	*degrees* (temperature)
–년	*years*	–개월	*months* (time or duration)
–층	*floors* (of a building)	–원	*money unit: dollar, wŏn, yen*
–불	*dollars*	–리	*Korean mile (li) = 1/3 U.S. mile*
–달라	*dollars*	–월 (달)	*month names*
–파운드	*pounds* (sterling)		E.g., 이월달 〔이월딸〕 *February*

주의!
In the case of the counters above, note that for the numbers 101-119, one is more
likely to hear 백 + pure Korean number than all Sino-Korean numbers.
For example, 백네 병 is more common than 백사 병 for *104 bottles*.

Counting Days

Counting days in Korean is somewhat awkward since there are two options, at least when counting up to twenty: pure Korean expressions or Sino-Korean expressions. After twenty, only Sino-Korean expressions are used. Furthermore, the pure Korean words used do not follow any immediately obvious pattern and have to be learned separately. Unfortunately there is no substitute for this.

Pure Korean

The following expressions are widely used by Koreans of all generations.

며칠	*how many days?*	하루	*one day*
이틀	*two days*	사흘	*three days*
나흘	*four days*	닷새	*five days*

The following expressions are used rather less by Koreans of younger generations.

엿새	*six days*	이레	*seven days*
여드레	*eight days*	아흐레	*nine days*
열흘	*ten days*		

The following expressions are used primarily by Koreans of older generations.

열하루	*eleven days*	열이틀	*twelve days*
열사흘	*thirteen days*	열나흘	*fourteen days*
열닷새 〔-땃새〕	*fifteen days*	열엿새	*sixteen days*
열이레	*seventeen days*	열여드레	*eighteen days*
열아흐레	*nineteen days*	스무날	*twenty days*

Sino-Korean

Besides the pure Korean expressions above, one can also use Sino-Korean expressions for counting days up to twenty.

일일	*one day*	이일	*two days*
삼일	*three days*	사일	*four days*
오일	*five days*	육일	*six days*

Above twenty, the Sino-Korean numerals are used.

이십 일	*twenty days*
이십일 일	*twenty-one days*, etc.

Less than twenty, the Sino-Korean numerals can also be used for dates, in which case it is common in colloquial Korean to add the word 날 *day* (somewhat redundantly).

오일(날)   *the fifth day of the month*
The 날 here is optional, like the 달 in 이월달 *February*, but is frequent in colloquial usage.

Counting Weeks

Korean has the following words for *week*:

주일   *week*
주간   *week* ['s time]

Weeks are counted with either pure Korean or Sino-Korean numerals, but note in the following list that the Sino-Korean expressions on the right are more common.

Pure Korean		**Sino-Korean**	
한 주일	or	일 주일	*one week*
두 주일	or	이 주일	*two weeks*
세 주일	or	삼 주일	*three weeks*
한 주간	or	일 주간	*one week* ['s time]
두 주간	or	이 주간	*two weeks* ['s time]
세 주간	or	삼 주간	*three weeks* ['s time]

With the Sino-Korean numerals, 주일 *week* can be shortened to 주.

일주   *one week*   이주   *two weeks*

Counting Months

Months are counted with either pure Korean or Sino-Korean numerals.

몇 달	or	몇 개월	*how many months?*
한 달	or	일 개월	*one month*
두 달	or	이 개월	*two months*
석 달, 세 달	or	삼 개월	*three months*
넉 달, 네 달	or	사 개월	*four months*

Talking about Months

무슨 달	or	몇 월 〔며둬ㄹ〕		*what month?*
일월 (달) 〔딸〕	or	정월		*January*
이월 (달) 〔딸〕				*February*
삼월 (달) 〔딸〕				*March*
사월 (달) 〔딸〕				*April*
오월 (달) 〔딸〕				*May*
유월 (달) 〔딸〕				*June* [irregular]
칠월 (달) 〔딸〕				*July*
팔월 (달) 〔딸〕				*August*
구월 (달) 〔딸〕				*September*
시월 (달) 〔딸〕				*October* [irregular]
십일월 (달) 〔딸〕				*November*
십이월 (달) 〔딸〕	or	선달		*December*
지난 달				*last month*
이번 달				*this month*
다음 달 〔optionally pronounced 딸〕				*next month*

Counting Years

As with counting days, Korean has two options for counting years: pure Korean and Sino-Korean. To count years in pure Korean up to 99, one uses a pure Korean numeral with 해 *year*.

몇 해	*how many years?*
한 해	*one year*
두 해	*two years*
세 해	*three years*
네 해	*four years*
여덟 해 〔여덜패〕	*eight years*
스무 해	*twenty years*
아흔 아홉 해	*nintety-nine years*

Starting with 100, one uses Sino-Korean numerals with –년.

백 년	*100 years*

However, it is most common to count and name *all* years (including 1-99) using Sino-Korean, and you will rarely hear Koreans using pure Korean beyond 두 해 *two years*.

몇 년	*what year?* [e.g., *1970*] or *how many years?*
일 년	*one year; Year One*
이 년	*two years; Year Two*
삼 년	*three years; Year Three*
사 년	*four years; Year Four*
팔 년	*eight years; Year Eight*
이십 년	*twenty years; Year Twenty*
구십구 년	*ninety-nine years; Year Ninety-Nine*

11.2. Numerals in Time Expressions

11.2.1. Telling the Time

To tell the time in Korean, you use the pure Korean numerals followed by 시 which is equivalent to *o'clock*.

한 시	*one o'clock*
다섯 시	*five o'clock*
열두 시 〔열뚜시〕	*twelve o'clock*

To say *half past,* you put 반 *and a half* after this expression.

한 시 반	*1:30*
다섯 시 반	*5:30*
열두 시 반	*12:30*

A specific number of minutes after the hour is expressed by the Sino-Korean numerals with –분 *minute* after the expression.

한 시 십 분	*1:10*	[Literally: one o'clock 10 minutes]
다섯 시 십오 분	*5:15*	[Literally: five o'clock 15 minutes]
열두 시 이십삼 분	*12:23*	[Literally: twelve o'clock 23 minutes]

To express the number of minutes before the hour, you use the same expression but add 전 *before* at the end.

| 한 시 십 분 전 | *12:50* |
| | [Literally: one o'clock 10 minutes before] |

다섯 시 십오 분 전   4:45

                                  [Literally: five o'clock 15 minutes before]

For AM and PM, you use 아침 or 오전 *morning*, 오후 *afternoon*, or 밤 *night* at the beginning of the expression.

오전 세 시 (or 아침 세 시)   3:00 A.M.

오후 네 시   4:00 P.M.

밤 아홉 시 반   9:30 P.M.

To say *exactly* such-and-such a time, you put 정각 after the time expression.

한 시 반 정각(에)   *(at) exactly 1:30*

The word 시 means *hour* only in the sense of a point in time, an *o'clock*. For length or duration of time, 시간 *hour* is used (as you know, 시간 also means *time* in general).

9.   A. 몇 시간 일했어요?
          How many hours did you work?

     B. 여섯 시간 일했어요.
         I worked (for) six hours.

10.   날마다 다섯 시간 반씩 공부해요.
       I study for five and a half hours every day.

11.2.2. Dates

11.   오늘은 몇월 며칠이에요?
       What is today's date? [Literally: Today is which month, which day?]

Dates are given in Korean by proceeding from the longest to the shortest time element; English does the opposite. For example:

12.   천구백오십이년, 시월 십일, 금요일, 오후 세 시 십오 분
       3:15 P.M., Friday, 10 October 1952

This breaks down to:

> 천 / 구백 / 오십 / 이년   *1952*
> [Literally: thousand—nine-hundred—fifty—two-year]

> 시월 / 십일   *10 October*
> [Literally: October—ten—day]

> 금요일   *Friday*

> 오후 / 세 시 / 십오 분   *3:15 P.M.*
> [Literally: afternoon—three o'clock—fifteen minutes]

11.2.3. Telephone Numbers

When reading a telephone number in Korean, there is a choice between three closely related patterns. For example, here is how one could read the number 949-1806.

In the full pattern, you spell out everything and round it off with –번 *number*.

A. 949국의 1806   구백사십구국의 천팔백육번
           [Literally: 949-exchange's 1806-number]

However, just as in English one is unlikely to read this number as *nine hundred forty-nine, one thousand eight hundred and six*, in Korean this pattern can also be abbreviated. The first thing is to omit the 국, meaning (telephone) *exchange*, in which case the –번 *number* is optional.

B. 949의 1806   구백사십구의 천팔백육(번)
           [Literally: 949's 1806]

The most usual way to read a number is to omit the 국 and the 번, and just read each number separately:

C. 949의 1806   구사구의 일팔공육
           [Literally: 9—4—9's 1—8—0—6]

11.3. Four New Particles: 마다, 만, 씩, 쯤

11.3.1. 마다 *Each, Every*

13. 아침마다 학교 수영장에서 수영을 합니다.
     I swim in the school swimming pool every morning.

14. 일요일마다 서점들이 문을 닫습니다.
     Every Sunday the bookstores close.

15. 날마다 여덟시부터 열시까지 아르바이트하러 갑니다.
     Every day I go to do my part-time job from 8 o'clock till 10 o'clock.

With time expressions, 마다 is more normally expressed in English by the indefinite article *a(n)*: 날마다 여덟 시간 [literally: every day eight hours] *eight hours a day*. (But to say three days a week 한 주일에 사흘 is more natural than 주일마다 사흘.)

11.3.2. 만 *Only, Just*

The particle 만 restricts the noun expression it follows. It limits the meaning of the noun to no more than what is specified.

16. 이것만 있습니다.
     This is all there is. [Literally: There is only this.]

17. 저만 갑니다.
     I'm the only one who's going. [Literally: Only I am going.]

When 만 follows a noun, the particles 이 ~ 가, 은 ~ 는, and 을 ~ 를 are not normally used with the same expression.

18. 사과만 있습니다.
     There are only apples.

19. 유니스 씨만 압니다.
     Only Eunice knows.

20. 요즘 공부만 합니다.
     Lately all I do is study.

Occasionally you will run across such combinations as 만이, 만을, and 만은. 만 may be used at the end of other noun-plus-particle expressions, as follows.

21. 우체국에만 갑니다.
    I'm going only to the post office.

22. 한국말로만 하십시오.
    Speak only in Korean.

23. 공원에서만 산보를 합니다.
    I only take walks in the park.

24. 에릭 씨한테만 이야기했습니다.
    I only told Eric.

When 만 is used in sentences with numerical expressions, its meaning is to limit the amount to what is specified.

25. 두 시간만 공부했습니다.
    I studied for two hours.
    [만 limits the time to two hours: *Two hours is the length of time I studied. I studied for two hours but not longer.*]

26. 책 열 권만 샀습니다.
    I bought ten books.
    (만 indicates that ten is exactly the number of books bought.)

In this latter sense, 만 represents a shade of meaning which usually goes unexpressed in English; it contrasts in meaning with the particle 쯤, discussed in section 11.3.4 below.

11.3.3. 씩 *Per, Apiece*

The particle 씩 is one which expresses an idea not often made explicit in English. It has a distributive function or expresses the idea of regularity. When English says *I study for three hours **per** night*, Korean says the equivalent of *Every night I study [three hours **per**]*. In other words, the distributive particle goes on the expression of time or quantity, not as in English. Take a look at the following sentence.

27. 하루에 여덟 시간씩 잡니다.
    I sleep 8 hours a day. [Literally: In one day I sleep 8 hours each.]

씩 is used at the end of numerical expressions, but it refers to some other element in the sentence. This may be a subject or object or it may be a time expression generalized with 마

다. It would be on this item of the sentence that *per* would be added in English. You would not use this particle to say *Yesterday I studied for three hours*, since there is no regularity about that (you would use 세 시간 동안 for a duration of 3 hours). But it is used in the following examples in which there is the idea of regularity.

28.　여자친구랑 날마다 세 시간씩 전화로 이야기합니다.
　　　I speak on the phone with my girlfriend three hours every day.

29.　은행에서 날마다 몇 시간씩 일을 하십니까?
　　　How many hours (apiece) *a day do you work at the bank?*

It is also used in a sense more like the English, when the dominant idea is more literal distribution. The next sentence should illustrate this:

30.　학생들한테 책 한 권씩 줬습니다.
　　　I gave the students one book each (apiece).

11.3.4. 쯤 *About, Approximately, By*

The particle 쯤 is used with time expressions. When the time expression refers to a point in time, 쯤 means *at about* [that time].

　　몇시 쯤(에)　　　　　*(at) about what time?*
　　열 시반 쯤(에)　　　　*(at) about 10:30*

With expressions referring to duration of time, 쯤 means *by* (that time) or *for about* (that length of time).

　　네 시간쯤　　　　　　*(for) about four hours*

한 *about, approximately* used at the beginning of a numerical expression has the same meaning as 쯤 at the end of it, as in.

31.　한 열 명 있습니다 same as 열 명쯤 있습니다.
　　　There are about ten people.

Be careful not to confuse this 한, which is always followed by a numerical expression, with 한 the short form of 하나 *one* which is always followed by a noun or a counter. Note also that 한, cannot be used with 언제: *한 언제 vs. the acceptable 언제쯤? *Approximately when?*

한 meaning *about, approximately* is often used in combination with a particle of the same meaning, reinforcing the imprecise character of the expression.

32. 어제 밤 한 이십 명쯤 왔습니다.
     About twenty people were here (came) *last night.*

33. 한 두 시쯤 저희 집에 오십시오.
     Please come to our house about two o'clock.

주의!

Notice that 쯤 cannot combine with the copula in an expression like
두 시쯤이에요. *It is approximately two o'clock.*
Instead, an expression with 되- is preferred:
두 시쯤 됐어요. *It is* [Literally: has become] *approximately two o'clock.*

11.4. The Particles 부터 *from* and 까지 *to*

You have learned ways to say *from* (에서) and *to* (에), and this lesson also introduces the particles 부터 *from* and 까지 *to*.

부터 *from* is usually used with *time* expressions:

다섯 시부터	*from five o'clock*
오늘부터	*from today*

에서 *from* or (happening) *at*, on the other hand, is used *only* in *place* expressions: 집에서 *from home* or (happening) *at home.* 부터 is often used to translate *at* in time expressions with *begin* (though 에 may be used in these expressions, as well): 열 시 부터 시작합니다. *We begin at 10 o'clock.*

Used with both *time* and *place* expressions, 까지 means *to* in the sense of *as far as, up to* or *until.* 에 with time expressions, you recall, means *at* or *in that time* 저녁에 *in the evening*, 밤에 *at night.* With place expressions it means either (being) *in, at* or *on that place*—static location, as in 집에 있습니다 *He's at home*; 의자에 앉습니다 *sits on the chair*; 공원에 있습니다 *it's in the park*—or *to that place*: 학교에 갑니다 *goes to school.*

Here are examples of 부터 and 까지 in sentences.

34. 학교는 내일부터 시작합니다.
    School starts tomorrow.

35. 대사관에서는 아침 아홉시부터 일을 시작합니다.
    I start work at the embassy every morning at nine o'clock.

36. 두시부터 네시까지 사무실에서 잤습니다.
    I slept in the office from two o'clock till four o'clock.

37. 처음부터 끝까지 엉터리였습니다.
    It was rubbish from beginning to end!

38. 아침부터 밤까지 고생을 합니다.
    I suffer from morning till night.

11.5. Formal Style

The Formal Style is used under conditions where formality is called for: in business situations where the relationship between the speakers is official and impersonal, in social situations where the speakers are newly acquainted and the ice is not yet broken, or in any case where reserve seems indicated or desirable. It is also often used in greetings and other conventional expressions (recall some of the basic expressions of Lessons One and Two). This style gives way gradually as the formality of the situation ebbs, i.e., when two speakers have progressed beyond the initial overtures of getting acquainted and feel more at ease, then Formal and Polite Style are often mixed together.

Male speakers are advised to use formal forms occasionally, even when speaking to people with whom one need not be formal: overuse of polite forms in 요 strikes some Koreans as "talking like a woman."

Notice that the keynote to the style that speakers are employing (aside from certain vocabulary items like 저 for 나 *(I)*, rests entirely in the verbs at the end of sentences. All other nonfinal verb forms are neutral in this respect.

Formal statements are made by attaching to the verb at the end of the sentence, an ending which has the shape -습니다 (pronounced -슴니다) after consonants and -ㅂ니다 (pronounced -ㅁ니다) after vowels.

> ## 주의!
>
> If the base is an L-extending vowel base, the ending is added to the unextended base (without the -ㄹ-): 사-ㄹ- → 삽니다 *live*. If the base ends in w, this w changes to ㅂ (remember that w counts as a consonant in our system): 더w- → 덥습니다 *hot*. If the base ends in -ㄹ (i.e., in the case of ㄷ ~ ㄹ verbs), this changes (by our rules) to ㄷ: 들- → 듣습니다 *listen*. Finally, ㅅ-irregular verbs add the ending to the form with ㅅ: 낫습니다 *improve*.

Formal questions are made by replacing the final 다 of the formal statement with 까. In other words add an ending that has the shape -습니까 (pronounced -슴니까) after consonants and the shape -ㅂ니까 (pronounced -ㅁ니까) after vowels. Here are some examples with typical verb bases.

Vowel Bases

Meaning	Base	Formal Statement	Pronounced
go	가-	갑니다	감니다
tie, wear a tie	매-	맵니다	맴니다
see, look at	보-	봅니다	봄니다
give	주-	줍니다	줌니다
write	쓰-	씁니다	씀니다
become	되-	됩니다	됨니다
wait	기다리-	기다립니다	기다림니다
(honorific)	-(으)시-	-(으)십니다	-(으)심니다
know	아-ㄹ-	압니다	암니다
not know	모르-	모릅니다	모름니다

Consonant Bases

Meaning	Base	Formal Statement	Pronounced
wear	입-	입습니다	입씀니다
want to	싶-	싶습니다	십씀니다
receive	받-	받습니다	바씀니다
take off	벗-	벗습니다	버씀니다
seek/find	찾-	찾습니다	차씀니다
eat	먹-	먹습니다	먹씀니다
polish	닦-	닦습니다	닥씀니다
read	읽-	읽습니다	익씀니다
be young	젊-	젊습니다	점씀니다
wear shoes	신-	신습니다	신씀니다
sit down	앉-	앉습니다	안씀니다
put	놓-	놓습니다	노씀니다
much/many	많-	많습니다	만씀니다
be disliked	싫-	싫습니다	실씀니다
exist/have	있-	있습니다	이씀니다
(past)	-었-	-었습니다	어씀니다
lack	없-	없습니다	업씀니다
improve	나(ㅅ)-	낫습니다	나씀니다
hot	더w-(ㅂ ~ w: 덥다)	덥습니다	덥씀니다
listen, hear	들-(ㄷ ~ ㄹ: 듣다)	듣습니다	드씀니다

Note the inclusion of past bases in the list above. The Formal Style endings attach to the Past Base as they would to any other consonant base: -ㅆ습니다 ~ ㅆ습니까. Thus, 했습니다 *did it*, 봤습니까 *Did you see it?*, 들었습니다 *heard it*, etc.

Formal (honorific) commands are made by adding -으(십)시오 to bases that end in consonants and -(십)시오 to bases ending in vowels. -(십)시오 is added to the unextended shape of ㄹ-extending vowel bases (that is, to the shape without the -ㄹ-, e.g., 여십시오 *Open it!*). This ending is often misspelled -(으)(십)시요.

Note that the formal honorific command in -(으)십시오 is much more common than the simply formal command -(으)시오. This latter ending is perceived now as belonging to the authoritative or 하오 style. It tends to be used in controlled fits of anger by indignant individuals displeased with service, etc. It should be used with care or else ironically. You are safe with formal (honorific) commands in -(으)십시오, and here are examples of them:

Consonant Bases		**Vowel Bases**	
입으십시오	*Wear it!*	보십시오	*Look!*
받으십시오	*Receive it!*	가십시오	*Go!*
벗으십시오	*Take it off!*	수십시오	*Give it (to me)!*
찾으십시오	*Look for it!*	쓰십시오	*Write it!*
닦으십시오	*Polish it!*	기다리십시오	*Wait!*
읽으십시오	*Read it!*	파십시오	*Sell it!*
신으십시오	*Put on (shoes)!*	부르십시오	*Call!*
앉으십시오	*Sit down!*	매십시오	*Tie it!*
놓으십시오	*Put it (there)!*		
들으십시오	*Listen!*		
구우십시오	*Broil it!*		

The greetings from Lesson One can also be expressed in the formal honorific style.

안녕히 계십시오! and 안녕히 가십시오!

Inherently honorific verbs which already include -시- in their base add – ㅂ시오 to the honorific base.

Base	**Formal Command**	
계시-	계십시오	*Stay!*
주무시-	주무십시오	*Sleep!*
잡수시-	잡수십시오	*Eat!*

The last verb also appears without –시– (but remains honorific): 잡수– from which is derived 잡수시오 *Eat!*

Formal suggestions (*Let's do it.*) are made by adding the ending –읍시다 to consonant bases and – ㅂ시다 to vowel bases (including the unextended shape of ㄹ– extending vowel bases).

Base	**Formal Suggestion**	
입–	입읍시다	*Let's wear it!*
가–	갑시다	*Let's go!*
받–	받읍시다	*Let's receive it!*
보–	봅시다	*Let's see it!*

Base	Formal Suggestion	
앉-	앉읍시다	*Let's sit down!*
노-ㄹ-	놉시다	*Let's play!*
구w- (ㅂ ~ w: 굽다)	구웁시다	*Let's broil it!*
들- (ㄷ ~ ㄹ: 듣다)	들읍시다	*Let's listen!*

> ### 주의!
> Note that many Korean speakers consider it inappropriate, even rude, for a person of lower status to use a suggestion form in -(으)ㅂ시다 to them. When making a suggestion to somebody with whom you might otherwise use honorifics, you are advised to include the honorific in your suggestion: 가십시다! *Let's go!* or else use a different strategy entirely.

Since the endings -ㅂ니다, -ㅂ니까, -(십)시오 and -ㅂ시다 are added to the unextended shape of ㄹ-extending vowel bases, the resulting forms look as if they might be ordinary vowel bases: thus, from the spelling you can't tell whether 삽니다 means 살아요 (from 사-ㄹ-) *lives* or 사요 (from 사-) *buys*. The context will help you tell.

Exercises

Exercise 1: Numerals and Counters

Count quickly in Korean from one to twelve, putting the following words after each number, in order: one table, two years old, three minutes, and so on. Repeat, from fifteen to twenty-nine; from thirty to forty-four; from forty-five to fifty-nine; from sixty to seventy-four; and so on up to ninety-eight.

1.	양말 ____ 켤레	2.	-살
3.	-분 (minutes)	4.	-불
5.	-명	6.	-주
7.	-년	8.	-잔
9.	고양이 ____ 마리	10.	(-)병
11.	-일	12.	-권
13.	-개월	14.	(-)상자

Exercise 2: Numerals and Counters

Say the following expressions in Korean:

1. 오늘 아침에 ＿＿에 일어났습니다.
   7:00
   8:15 exactly
   7:05
   6:55
   about 6:30

2. 나는 ＿＿ 봤습니다.
   six people
   nine magazines
   three dogs
   eleven buildings
   four cars

3. 나는 보통 ＿＿쯤에 잡니다.
   11:00
   10:45
   11:15
   9:30
   12:00

4. 나는 ＿＿ 있습니다.
   two dollars
   three newspapers
   ten books
   two dogs
   fifteen pieces of paper

5. 나는 사무실에서 ＿＿ 일했습니다.
   two hours
   five days
   fourteen days
   eight and a half hours
   ten minutes

6. 거기서 ＿＿ 있었습니다.
   two days
   ten days
   two weeks
   three months
   six years

7. 나는 ＿＿에 아침을 먹었습니다.
   8:17
   8:47
   7:53
   7:25
   exactly 7:00

Exercise 3: Answer the Questions

Answer these questions in Korean (short answers only and be sure to write out the numbers in 한글).

1. 어제가 무슨 요일이었습니까?

2. 오늘은 며칠이에요?

3. 몇 학년이십니까?

4. 크리스마스는 어느 달에 있어요?

5. 생일이 언제에요?

6. 나는 아침 여덟시 반에 일을 시작 했습니다. 저녁 다섯 시까지

일했습니다. 그러면 몇 시간쯤 일했습니까?

7.   새해가 (New Year) 무슨 달에 시작합니까?

8.   나는 천구백 오십오년에 태어났습니다.

     그러면 몇살입니까?

9.   학교 선생은 해마다 며칠쯤 쉽니까?

10. 은행에서는 몇 시부터 일을 시작합니까?

11. 새벽 한 시부터 열두 시까지는 몇 시간 돼요?

12. 몇 년생이세요?

13. 몇 살이에요?

Exercise 4: Fill in the Missing Particles and Counters

Here are Korean sentences with some of the particles and/or counters missing. Read each sentence aloud and fill in the blanks with appropriate particles you have learned in this lesson.

1.   해____ [every] 며칠 ____ 놉니까? [i.e., have the day off]
2.   학교는 내일 ____ 시작해요.
3.   수요일 ____ [every] 집에서 쉬어요?
4.   그 상 위에는 과일 ____ [only] 있어요.
5.   오늘 새벽 두시 ____ 세시 반 ____ 애기 때문에 고생을 많이 했어요.
6.   보통 몇 시간 ____ 주무세요?
7.   사무실에서 아홉 시 반 ____ 네 시 반 ____ 일을 해요.
8.   아침 ____ 몇 시 ____ 일어나요?
9.   아침 뉴스는 아홉 시 ____ 시작해요.
10. 시장에서 오징어 열 ____ 하고 사과 두 ____ 하고 맥주
     스무 ____ 샀습니다.

Exercise 5: Formal Style

Each of the following sentences is a simple statement in the Polite Style. Change each one so that it is four different expressions in the Formal Style: (1) a simple statement; (2) a question; (3) an honorific command; and, (4) a suggestion. Watch out for trick questions!

Part One: Easier Verbs

1. 여기 앉아요.
2. 늦게 떠나요.
3. 거기 있어요
4. 친구를 기다려요.
5. 애기한테 음식을 줘요.
6. 빨리 시작해요.
7. 술집에 가요.
8. 편지를 써요.
9. 교회에 나가요.
10. 전화를 받아요.
11. 십분만 쉬어요.

Part Two: Trickier Verbs

1. 라디오를 들어요.
2. 택시를 불러요.
3. 사장님한테 전화를 걸어요.
4. 고기를 구워요.
5. 즐거워요.
6. 오늘은 참 더워요.
7. 나는 이 사람을 잘 알아요.
8. 한국 음식은 아주 매워요.
9. 밖이 좀 추워요.
10. 내 동생은 서울에서 살아요.

Exercise 6: English to Korean Translation

Translate each of the following sentences into Korean, using the Formal Style.

1. I brush my teeth three times a day.
2. I am very busy from today.
3. Until when will you stay?
4. Let's go out for a walk.
5. Everybody is different [every person].
6. When do you wish to meet?
7. I've come to look for part-time work.
8. Every student likes that teacher.
9. I stayed in that inn until Saturday.

10. Why are you late?
    Please forgive me.
11. About what time are you going?
12. This year I forgot my wife's birthday.
13. Please give them 10,000 wǒn each.
14. Let's start from nine o'clock.
15. About when are you leaving for Seoul?

Exercise 7: Vocabulary Drill

This is a rapid-fire drill. Call off the Korean for each group below. Use numeral and counter, and, if appropriate, a noun.

1. One person, one building, one o'clock.
2. Two months, two years, two days.
3. Three honored people, three o'clock, three years old.
4. Four dollars, four dogs, four newspapers.
5. Five li, five days, five houses.
6. Six pounds, six floors, six years old.
7. Seven months, seven books, seven years.
8. Eight hours, eight cars, eight minutes.
9. Nine times, nine days, nine cats.
10. Ten cents, ten people, ten o'clock.
11. One o'clock, two o'clock, three o'clock.
12. Two years old, three years old, four years old.
13. Three years, four years, five years.
14. Four people, five people, six people.
15. Five days, six days, seven days.
16. Six sheets of paper, seven sheets of paper, eight sheets of paper.
17. Seven magazines, eight magazines, nine magazines.
18. Eight days, nine days, ten days.
19. Nine floors, ten floors, eleven floors.
20. Ten times, eleven times, twelve times.
21. Eleven pounds, twelve pounds, thirteen pounds.
22. Twelve cats, thirteen cats, fourteen cats.
23. Thirteen days, fourteen days, fifteen days.
24. Fourteen years old, fifteen years old, sixteen years old.
25. Fifteen months, sixteen months, seventeen months.

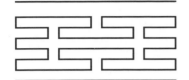 

Lesson 12

연극은 좋아하지만, 음악은 별로 좋아하지 않아요.

This lesson introduces how to make suggestions to go and do things. It also covers how to suggest *not* to do things. Further points covered are how to express likes and dislikes, how to say one *feels like* doing something or not, and how to ask someone for a date. Finally, we introduce a new way to link two sentences with *but*, a new way to make sentences negative, and the new particle (이)나.

Korean Dialogues

Dialogue 1

Chris and Eunice's college-age daughter, Sandy, has recently struck up a relationship with a Korean boy, 석만. They have met at a 커피숍 near campus.

석만	뭐 마실래요?
샌디	아무거나 좋아요. 커피나 한 잔 할까요?
석만	(to 아가씨) 아가씨! 여기 커피 두 잔만 주세요.
	(to Sandy) 그런데 심심하지 않아요? 오늘 우리 뭐 할까요?
샌디	글쎄요. 음악회에 갈까요? 아니면 연극 보러 갈까요?
석만	음악회에는 가지 맙시다. 나는 연극은 좋아하지만, 음악은 별로 좋아하지 않아요.
샌디	그럼, 연극을 보러 갑시다. 나도 연극을 좋아해요.
석만	그런데 나는 한국 연극이 보고 싶어요. 샌디 씨는 어때요?
샌디	글쎄요. 아직 한번도 못 봤어요. 한번 봅시다!

Notes

아무거나   *anything at all.* See section 12.6.2.

샌디 씨는 어때요?   [Literally: As for Sandy, how is it?] 어때요? *How is it? What is it like?*
can be used to elicit opinions like this: *What do* ***you*** *think?*, etc.

글쎄요.   *I don't really know; Let me think about it a moment; I'm not really sure.*
This is a useful idiomatic expression.

Dialogue 2

Eric is hitting the 커피숍 scene, too. While waiting for 영철 at their favorite hangout, Eric tries his luck with one of the 아가씨 working there.

에릭	아가씨, 저하고 같이 차나 한 잔 하실까요?
아가씨	지금은 좀 바쁜데요.
에릭	그럼, 저녁에는 시간 있으세요? 어디 좀 놀러 가실래요?
아가씨	저녁에도 바쁜데요.
에릭	아, 그래요? 알겠습니다. 실례했습니다. (Eric backs off)
아가씨	잠깐만요! 내일은 바쁘지 않아요.

Notes

바쁜데요.   *I'm afraid I'm busy.* The ending is treated in detail in a later lesson.

Reading Passage

우리는 어제 저녁에 한국식당에 갔습니다.
식당에 사람들이 아주 많았습니다.
저는 냉면을 주문했지만 제 친구는 비빔밥을 시켰습니다.
한국음식은 맛이 좋지만 별로 비싸지 않습니다. 그리고 건강에도 좋습니다.
저도 언젠가 한국요리를 배우고 싶습니다.

Vocabulary

New Nouns: Food and Drink

커피	coffee
냉커피	ice coffee
냉수	ice water
냉면	cold noodle dish
콜라	cola
얼음	ice
요리	cooking, cuisine
중국요리	Chinese cuisine
이태리요리	Italian cuisine
아이스크림	ice cream
소주	Korean rice vodka, *soju*
양주	whiskey; western spirits
설탕	sugar
설탕을 타–	add/put in sugar
설탕을 타세요?	Do you take sugar?
설탕을 넣–	add/put in sugar
크림	cream
생크림	fresh cream
프리마	nondairy creamer
홍차	black tea, English tea
생맥주	draft beer
피자	pizza
사이다	a Korean soft drink like Seven-up™
빙수	shaved ice/ice slush, usually with fruit toppings
샌드위치	sandwich
햄버거	hamburger
핫도그	hotdog

Other New Nouns

까페	café (more upscale than a tabang)
양담배	western cigarettes; non-Korean cigarettes
미인	a beautiful woman
아주 미인입니다.	She's a real beauty.
미남	a handsome man
풀	starch; glue
풀(을) 먹이-	starch something [feed it starch]
때	time [when]
아무때나 오세요.	Come any time.
그 때에는	At that time
잠깐	a moment
잠깐만 기다리십시오.	Please wait a moment.
만화	comics, cartoons (both the written variety and the TV variety)
꽃	flower(s)
꽃이 피-	flowers bloom, blossom
꽃들이 다 폈어요.	All the flowers have bloomed.
음악	music
음악회	concert
째즈	jazz
째즈음악	jazz music
연극	play, drama
산	mountain
시골	countryside, the country
바다	the ocean, the sea
비치	the beach
도시	city
교외	suburb(s)
복도	hallway, corridor
손님	customer; guest
마음	mind, heart

마음(이) 좋아요	has a good heart, is good natured
지하철	subway, underground, metro
형제	brothers (for males); brothers and sisters
형제가 몇명이에요?	How many brothers and sisters do you have?
오빠	elder brother (for females)
언니	elder sister (for females)

New Verbs and Related Expressions

똑똑하-	be bright, intelligent
결혼(을) 하-	marry
결혼하셨어요?	Are you married?
약혼(을) 하-	get engaged
약혼했어요.	I'm engaged.
약혼자	fiancé(e)
세탁(을) 하-	launder it, do laundry
세탁소	a laundry, laundromat, cleaners
은퇴(를) 하-	retire
타-	ride in, ride on
자전거를 타-	ride a bike
택시를 타-	take a taxi
스키를 타-	ski, go skiing
스케이트를 타-	skate, go skating
걸- (ㄷ ~ ㄹ: 걷다)	walk
우리 애기는 아직 걷지 못 해요.	Our baby can't walk yet.
걸어가-	walk, go on foot
걸어갑시다.	Let's go on foot. Let's walk.
심심하-	be/feel bored
피곤하-	be tired
넣-	put in, insert
설탕을 넣으세요?	Do you put sugar in [your coffee]?
테니스(를) 치-	play tennis
피아노(를) 치-	play the piano

무거w-	be heavy
가벼w-	be light [in weight]
마치-	finish it
배(가) 부르-	[stomach] be full
배 불러요.	I'm full.
돌아가-	goes back, returns there
돌아오-	comes back, returns here
춤(을) 추-	dances (a dance)
어때요?	how is it? how about it?
서울은 어때요?	How do you like Seoul?
서울은 어떻습니까?	[same as above, but Formal Style]
들어오-	come in, enter; return home
어제 늦게 들어왔어요.	I got in late last night.
들어가-	go in, enters
좋-	be good; be liked
나는 서울이 좋아요.	I like Seoul.
좋아하-	like it
나는 서울을 좋아해요.	I like Seoul.
싫-	be disliked, distasteful
싫어하-	dislike it
주문(을) 하-	order [at a restaurant]
건강하-	be healthy
건강	health

New Adverbs

어떻게?	how? in what way?
별로 + NEGATIVE	(not) particularly
갑자기	suddenly
벌써	already
인제, 이제	now (finally)
아니면	Or (sentence-initially)
NOUN A 아니면 NOUN B?	NOUN A or NOUN B?

How to Get the Attention of Service Personnel

저기요!	Hey there! [a bit brusque, or even rude]
저기!	[same as above, but even less cultured]
여보세요!	Hello! Excuse me!
여기 좀 봐요!	Say there! Excuse me!
학생!	[if the server looks to be a student]

If the Server is Female:

언니!	older sister [usually used by young women to other women, but also used, in jest, by some cheeky men]
아가씨!	Girl! Usually used by men to (presumably) unmarried women, but some women take offense now.
누나!	older sister [usually used by young men to older women, especially if it looks like they might be offended by either 아가씨! or 아주머니!]
아주머니!	Ma'am' [used about or to any woman who looks married]
아줌마!	[same as above but more familiar]

If the Server is Male:

아저씨!	Mister [used about or to any man who looks married]

Lesson Notes

12.1. Verbs: Suspective Form -지

Korean verbs with the suffix -지 attached to them are in the SUSPECTIVE form. L-extending vowel bases attach -지 to the extended shape: 여-ㄹ- *open* has the suspective form 열지. The consonant bases that end in -ㄹ (i.e., ㄷ ~ ㄹ bases) change this to ㄷ, so the suspective form of 들- *listens* is 듣지 pronounced (by automatic change) [듣찌]. See the examples for -고 싶어요 in Lesson Nine.

The suffix -지 is a one-shape ending: it is always -지, regardless of the kind of base it is attached to. In pronouncing the resulting form you have to follow the usual rules of sound change, as is the case for the -고 form.

Here is a list of the -지 forms for some representative verbs you have learned with the pronunciation (when different) shown between square brackets:

Base	Gloss	Suspective	Past Suspective	Pronunciation
하-	*do*	하지	했지	해찌
-이-	*be...*	이지	이었지	이어찌
자-	*sleep*	자지	잤지	자찌
주-	*give*	주지	줬지	줘찌
배우-	*learn*	배우지	배웠지	배워찌
기다리-	*wait*	기다리지	기다렸지	기다려찌
오-	*come*	오지	왔지	와찌
보-	*look at*	보지	봤지	봐찌
쉬-	*rest*	쉬지	쉬었지	쉬어찌
쓰-	*write*	쓰지	썼지	써찌
크-	*big*	크지	컸지	커찌
모르-	*not know*	모르지	몰랐지	몰라찌
사-ㄹ-	*live*	살지	살았지	사라찌
앉-	*sit*	앉지 〔안찌〕	앉았지	안자찌
먹-	*eat*	먹지 〔먹찌〕	먹었지	머거찌
좋-	*good*	좋지 〔조치〕	좋았지	조아찌
많-	*many*	많지 〔만치〕	많았지	마나찌
싫-	*be disliked*	싫지 〔실치〕	싫었지	시러찌

Lesson Twelve /219

Base	Gloss	Suspective	Past Suspective	Pronunciation
없–	*lack*	없지 〔업찌〕	없었지	업써찌
있–	*be; stay*	있지 〔이찌〕	있었지	이써찌
닫–	*close it*	닫지 〔닫찌〕	닫았지	다다찌
들–	*listen*	듣지 〔듣찌〕	들었지	드러찌
구w–	*broil*	굽지 〔굽찌〕	구웠지	구워찌
더w–	*be hot*	덥지 〔덥찌〕	더웠지	더워찌

12.2. Uses of the Suspective -지

12.2.1: Any Base + -지만 *but*

1.   A. 형제 있으세요?
        Do you have brothers and sisters?

     B. 언니는 있지만 동생은 없어요.
        I have an older sister, but no younger siblings.

2.   A. 그 집 애들이 공부를 잘 해요?
        Are the children in that family good students?

     B. 딸은 똑똑하지만, 아들은 공부를 못 해요.
        The daughter is bright, but the son isn't much of a student.

3.   날이 좀 덥지만, 테니스나 칠까요?
     The day is a bit hot, but shall we play some tennis or something?

4.   A. 아버님이 뭐 하세요?
        What does your father do?

     B. 대학 교수이셨지만, 이제는 은퇴하셨어요.
        [He] used to be a college professor, but now he's retired.

5.   A. 저분은 연세가 많으세요?
        Is that person old?

     B. 나이는 많지만, 마음은 젊어요.
        He is old in years, but his heart is young.

Phrases consisting of a verb base plus –지만 mean *(such-and-such)* **but . . .** English can retain the Korean phrasing by using *though, although*: *Although I have an older sister. . ., Though the daughter is bright . . .* The translation *but*, of course, is much more natural and conveys the Korean more realistically.

The special phrase 그렇지만 [Literally: *It is so, but . . .*] is used at the beginning of sentences in the same way English uses *however* or *on the other hand, on the contrary*. The expression –지만, then, is a device to put together two sentences that could be said separately, with the second introduced by 그렇지만.

12.2.2: Long Negatives in –지 않아요, –지 못해요

In addition to the short negative forms that you have learned to make by prefixing verbs and adjectives with 안 and 못, there is a more complex type of negative made with:

plain base plus –지 않아요   or   plain base plus –지 못해요

6.   A. 언니는 요즘 뭐 해요?
   What's your older sister up to these days?

       B. 인제는 우리하고 같이 살지 않아요.
   She doesn't live with us anymore.

7.   A. 저집 딸이 똑똑합니까?
   Is the daughter in that family bright?

       B. 딸은 똑똑하지만, 아들은 똑똑하지 못합니다.
   The daughter is bright, but the son isn't bright at all.

8.   A. 샌디 씨, 오빠가 결혼했습니까?
   Sandy, is your older brother married?

       B. 아니오, 오빠는 아직 결혼하지 않았습니다.
   No, he isn't (hasn't) married yet.

9.   A. 피아노를 치세요?
   Do you play the piano?

       B. 아니오. 피아노를 치지 못 합니다.
   No, I don't know how.

The long negative is a phrase which consists of a plain base plus -지 followed by a negative element. The -지 form names the verb. The element following it carries the other meanings for the phrase—negativeness and tense, as well as the meaning carried in its ending (e.g., Polite Style).

The element 않- following the -지 suspective form in long negative phrases is, in origin, a negative form of the auxiliary base 하-, that is, a form of 안 하- shortened to 않아요 It is, in effect, a new verb with the base form 않-, which behaves in the same way as the base 많- *(there are) many*.

The past tense of a long negative is made by putting 않- into the past tense. The -지 suspective form remains unchanged.

가지 않았습니다	*didn't go*
듣지 않았습니다	*didn't listen*
앉지 않았습니다	*didn't sit down*

The long negative differs from the short negative (the one you have been using up until now) only in that it is a phrase rather than a single word; the meaning of each corresponding form is the same. Here is a group of representative examples. Every verb has both forms except for the copula, which has only the form 아니에요.

Present Tense

Base	English	Short Negative	Long Negative
앉-	*sit*	안 앉아요	앉지 않아요
자-	*sleep*	안 자요	자지 않아요
좋-	*be good*	안 좋아요	좋지 않아요
읽-	*read*	안 읽어요	읽지 않아요
많-	*much/many*	안 많아요	많지 않아요
먹-	*eat*	안 먹어요	먹지 않아요
오-	*come*	안 와요	오지 않아요
쓰-	*write*	안 써요	쓰지 않아요
사-ㄹ-	*live*	안 살아요	살지 않아요
들-	*listen*	안 들어요	듣지 않아요
구w-	*broil*	안 구워요	굽지 않아요

Past Tense

Base	English	Short Negative	Long Negative
앉-	*sit*	안 앉았어요	앉지 않았어요
자-	*sleep*	안 잤어요	자지 않았어요
좋-	*be good*	안 좋았어요	좋지 않았어요
읽-	*read*	안 읽었어요	읽지 않았어요
많-	*much/many*	안 많았어요	많지 않았어요
먹-	*eat*	안 먹었어요	먹지 않았어요
오-	*come*	안 왔어요	오지 않았어요
사-르-	*live*	안 살았어요	살지 않았어요
쓰-	*write*	안 썼어요	쓰지 않았어요
들-	*listen*	안 들었어요	듣지 않았어요
구w⁻	*broil*	안 구웠어요	굽지 않았어요

Long negatives with the STRONG NEGATIVE 못 *cannot, emphatically not* rather than 안 *not* are made in the same way.

Base		Short Strong Negative	Long Strong Negative	Meaning
앉-	*sit*	못 앉아요	앉지 못해요	*can't sit*
		못 앉았어요	앉지 못했어요	*couldn't sit*
좋-	*good*	[impossible]	좋지 못해요	*is no good*
		[impossible]	좋지 못했어요	*was no good*
먹-	*eat*	못 먹어요	먹지 못해요	*can't eat*
		못 먹었어요	먹지 못했어요	*couldn't eat*
쓰-	*write*	못 써요	쓰지 못해요	*can't write*
		못 썼어요	쓰지 못했어요	*couldn't write*
들-	*hear*	못 들어요	듣지 못해요	*can't hear*
		못 들었어요	듣지 못했어요	*couldn't hear*
구w-	*broil*	못 구워요	굽지 못해요	*can't broil*
		못 구웠어요	굽지 못했어요	*couldn't broil*

Notice with descriptive verbs, long strong negatives have the added nuance of dissatisfaction on the part of the speaker or a sense that the situation was not up to expectation.

Lesson Twelve / 223

```
┌─────────────────────────────────────────────────────────────────┐
│                            주의!                                  │
│                                                                   │
│    The short negative with 안 occurs for processive verbs (안 가요 doesn't go),│
│  less commonly for adjectives (안 작아요 is not small), and in a slightly different│
│  form for the copula (책[이] 아니에요  it is not a book). The short negative with│
│  못 occurs only for processive verbs (못 가요 can't go; definitely doesn't go).│
│  There is no corresponding form for descriptive verbs or the copula, so that you will│
│            never hear 못 좋아요 or 책이 못이에요.                     │
│                                                                   │
│       There are long negatives with 못 for both processive verbs   │
│      (가지 못해요 can't go; definitely doesn't go) and descriptive verbs│
│  (작지 못해요 definitely isn't small), though not for the copula. There are no long│
│              negatives for the copula at all.                     │
└─────────────────────────────────────────────────────────────────┘
```

In the examples above the long negatives have the Polite Style endings. Other endings are also possible, when you want to put the negative into some larger sentence, for example, you can put a negative sentence into the construction with -지만 *but* discussed above.

앉지 않지만	[same as 안 앉지만]	*doesn't sit but*
앉지 않았지만	[same as 안 앉았지만]	*didn't sit but*
좋지 못하지만		*is no good but*

Finally, note also that the long negatives are more appropriate for longer verbs (i.e., bases with three or more syllables) and complex verb expressions (e.g., -고 싶어요) that sound awkward or marginal (hence the ?)preceded by 안:

Base	English	Short Negative	Long Negative
심심하-	*feel bored*	?안 심심해요	심심하지 않아요
먹고 싶-	*want to eat*	?안 먹고 싶어요	먹고 싶지 않아요

12.2.3. Negative Commands and Suggestions in -지 마- ㄹ -

You have noticed that the polite forms in 요 can be used as a statement (가요 *I'm going*), a question (가세요? *Are you going?*), a command (가세요! *Please go!*), and occasionally even a suggestion (가요! *Let's go!*).

The negative forms of these can be used as statements (안 가요 or 가지 않아요 *I'm not going.* 못가요 or 가지 못해요 *I can't go*) and as questions (안 가세요? or 가지 않으세요? *Aren't you going?* 못가세요? or 가지 못하세요? *Can't you go?*), but not as commands or suggestions.

| *앉지 않아요! | for | *Don't sit!* |
| *보지 않아요! | for | *Don't look!* |

Negative Commands

Instead, you make negative commands (prohibitions) and negative suggestions (dissuasions) with another auxiliary verb 마-르- *avoid* (an L-extending base) added to the suspective -지.

10. Base 들- *listen* 듣지 마세요!
                        듣지 말아요!   *Don't listen!*
                        듣지 마십시오!

11. Base 앉- *sit*   앉지 마세요!
                        앉지 말아요!   *Don't sit down!*
                        앉지 마십시오!

12. Base 보- *see; look* 보지 마세요!
                          보지 말아요!   *Don't look!*
                          보지 마십시오!

Negative Suggestions

You have learned the ending for suggestions in the Formal Style, with the shape -(으)ㅂ시다 as in 시작합시다! *Let's begin!* To make negative suggestions you add this ending to the unextended base of 마-르- and produce the form 맙시다 to use after the suspective -지.

13. 책을 보지 맙시다!
     Let's not look at our books!

14. 오늘은 걸어가지 맙시다! 시간이 없어요.
     Let's not go on foot today; there's no time.

15.   A. 뭘 마실까요? 양주로 할까요?
      What shall we drink? Shall we have some whiskey?

      B. 오늘은 술을 하지 맙시다.
      Let's not do any drinking today.

12.2.4. Negative Honorifics

In speaking about an esteemed person, you can add the honorific element to the long negative in any of several ways.

a.   You can make the verb honorific (가요 → 가세요) and then build the negative on this: 가시지 않아요. This is the most common.

b.   You can make the verb negative (가요 → 가지 않아요), then build the honorific on that: 가지 않으세요. This is also common.

c.   You can make the verb honorific (가요 → 가세요), build a negative on this (가세 요 → 가시지 않아요) and build a further honorific on that: 가시지 않으세요. Usually such double honorifics are overdoing things so you would do well to avoid them.

The 못 negative behaves in the same way: 가시지 못해요, 가지 못하세요, and 가시지 못하세요 are all *somebody* (esteemed) *can't/won't go*.

12.3. The Particle 도: Noun Agreement

Observe the following sentences:

16.   A. 샌디 씨, 다른 반 애들이랑 같이 비치에 안 가요?
      Sandy, aren't you going to the beach with the kids in the other class?

      B. 못 가요. 돈도 시간도 없습니다.
      I can't go; I have neither the time nor the money.

17.   오빠는 술집에도, 다방에도 안 다닙니다.
      My brother doesn't frequent either bars or tabangs.

As you know, the particle 도 often occurs twice in a sentence, showing a kind of tandem agreement between noun phrases (*both A and B do; neither A nor B does*). In affirmative sentences, the 도 mean *both . . . and*. When the verb is negative, they mean *neither . . . nor*.

The literal wordings *both . . . and* and *neither. . . nor* are actually somewhat formal in English. In conversational style some other phraseology is more usual.

Notice that the phrases with 도 must agree with each other; that is, you are saying the same thing about both of them. To say different things about two noun expressions, you do not use 도.

18.　　딸은 똑똑하지만 아들은 똑똑하지 못 합니다.
　　　　The daughter is bright, but the son isn't bright at all.

12.4. Suggestions and Tentative Questions with -(으)ㄹ까(요)?

Observe the following sentences:

19.　　A. 맥주를 한잔 할까요?
　　　　　How about a beer? [Literally: Shall we do a beer?]

　　　　B. 네, 그럽시다.
　　　　　Sure, let's do it.

20.　　A. 걸어 갈까요?
　　　　　How about walking (there)?

　　　　B. 아니오, 택시로 갑시다.
　　　　　No, let's take a taxi.

21.　　A. 테니스를 칠까요?
　　　　　How about playing tennis?

　　　　B. 네, 언제 칠래요?
　　　　　Sure. When would you like to play?

22.　　설탕을 넣을까요? 말까요?
　　　　Shall I put sugar in or not?

The ending -(으)ㄹ까요 is a two-shape verb ending, the third you have seen (the others were honorific polite -(으)세요 and purposive -(으)러). The -(으)ㄹ preceding the 까 is the prospective modifier, about which you will learn more in Lesson Twenty-three. The little word 까 is a post-modifier—a noun that always has a modifier in front of it—with the meaning *[it's a] question [of]* (it is related to the 까 of Formal Style questions in 합니까).

Let us review how verb bases attach to two-shape endings. Vowel-final bases attach to the vowel-less ending of two-shape endings.

가-	갈까요?	*Shall we go?*
보-	볼까요?	*Shall we look at it?*

With L-extending verbs, the ending attaches to the unextended base, but note that this is somewhat camouflaged.

사-ㄹ-	살까요?	*Shall we live?*

That is, this form is 사- + -ㄹ까요, and not 사-ㄹ- + 까요. Contrast this with ㄷ ~ ㄹ verbs.

23. A. 음악이나 들을까요?
Shall we listen to some music or something?

  B. 네, 어떤 음악을 좋아해요?
  Sure. What kind of music do you like?

Consonant-final bases attach to the shape with initial -으-.

찾-	찾을까요?	*Shall I look for it?*
받-	받을까요?	*Shall I receive it?*
입-	입을까요?	*Shall I put it on?*
들-	들을까요?	*Shall I listen to it?*
구w-	구울까요?	*Shall I broil it?*

The only tricky point to remember here concerns w - ㅂ verbs, for which you learned the following rule (repeated from section 8.2.2.).

$$ \text{W-} \quad + \quad \text{-으} \quad \longrightarrow \quad \text{우} $$

In other words, the final w of a w ~ ㅂ verb base plus the initial -으 of a two-shape verb ending combine to yield the vowel 우. Another example:

더w- + -을까요? → 더울까요?
Do you suppose it will be hot?

The 할까요? pattern makes future or tentative questions and has two distinct usages.

a. In the examples above, the questions are usually directed to the first person *I/we*. *Shall we do thus-and-so? Shall I do such-and-such?* or *How about doing thus-and-so?* These mean about the same thing as suggesting *let's do thus-and-so*. Sometimes these questions are rhetorical (not expecting an answer). You can only use processive bases with this meaning.

b. The second usage refers to third-persons (he, she, it, they), and translates as *Do you suppose?* or *I wonder: does/is?* For this, you can use either a processive or a descriptive base.

24. 상자가 너무 무거울까요?
     Do you suppose the box is too heavy?

25. 박 선생님이 지금 교실에 계실까요?
     Do you suppose Dr. Pak is in the classroom now?

In this second usage, the pattern can also be used on the past base, as follows.

26. A. 벌써 왔을까요?
        Do you suppose he's already come?

     B. 네. 방금 복도에서 봤어요.
        Yes. I saw him just a moment ago in the corridor.

Here are some more examples of how ㅂ ~ w verbs attach to this two-shape ending.

27. 그게 너무 어려울까요? (어려w-)
     Do you suppose that is too difficult?

28. 내일 더울까요? (더w-)
     Do you suppose tomorrow will be hot?

29. 어머니: 불고기를 좀 더 구울까요? (구w-)
             Shall I broil some more pulgogi?

     아버지: 됐어요. 배 불러요.
             It's OK. I'm full.

12.5. *Thinking of Doing. . .* with -(으)ㄹ까 해요.

Another construction involving 까 is -(으)ㄹ까 해요, which means *is thinking of [do]ing thus-and-so*, as follows.

30.　　A.　내일 뭐 합니까?
　　　　　What are you doing tomorrow?

　　　　B.　테니스를 칠까 합니다.
　　　　　I'm thinking of playing tennis.

31.　　A.　음악회에는 어떻게 가요?
　　　　　How are you getting to the concert?

　　　　B.　지하철로 갈까 해요.
　　　　　I'm thinking of going by subway.

32.　　A.　요즘 피곤해요?
　　　　　Are you tired lately?

　　　　B.　네. 시골에 좀 쉬러 갈까 해요.
　　　　　Yes. I'm thinking of going to the countryside for a rest.

We see that the verb 해요 besides meaning *does* and sometimes (as an auxiliary) *is*, also means *thinks*. This construction can be regarded as the equivalent of *I'm thinking, shall I VERB?* Here are some more examples.

33.　　A.　점심은 언제 먹어요?
　　　　　When are you eating lunch?

　　　　B.　두 시쯤에 먹을까 해요.
　　　　　I'm thinking of eating at around two o'clock.

34.　　A.　애들 학교가 괜찮습니까?
　　　　　Is the kids' school OK?

　　　　B.　나쁘지는 않지만, 다른 학교에 보낼까 합니다.
　　　　　It's not bad, but I'm thinking of sending them to another school.

12.6. The Adverb 또, Particle 도, and Pseudo-particle (이)나

12.6.1. Adverb 또 Versus Particle 도

The adverb 또 has the same general type of meaning as the particle 도 *and, again, too*. However, since 또 is an adverb it is independent and does not have to be attached to a noun expression, unlike the particle 도. The adverb 또 at the beginning of a sentence means *and also* or *and further(more)*. You have also had 그리고 in this meaning, and you can start a sentence with both of them: 그리고 또 *And moreover*. Notice the similarity between 도 the particle and 또 the adverb in such sentences as the following.

35.　여기에 종이도 있습니다.
　　　There's some paper here, too.

　　　저기에 종이(는) 또 있습니다.
　　　There's still some more paper over there.

An occasional accident of sound change may even make 도 and 또 sound the same in some environments (책또 here).

36.　여기에 책도 있습니다.
　　　There are books here, too.

　　　책 (pause) 또 있어요.
　　　There are some/yet more books over there.

12.6.2. The Particle (이)나

The particle (이)나, like the copula, has two shapes. After nouns ending in a consonant, it has the shape 이나. After nouns ending in a vowel it loses the 이 and has the shape 나. The particle (이)나 has several meanings, grouped into three headings.

1.　*about/approximately*
2.　generalizer
3.　*or*

1. -(이)나: *about/approximately*

Korean is often less precise about numbers than English is. Thus, such words as (이)나 (usually written 나 after vowels) are often used with numerical expressions (especially in questions) to make them sound more vague and hence less abrupt.

37. A. 몇 시간이나 걸립니까?
      About how many hours does it take?

     B. 한 세 시간 반 걸립니다.
      It takes about three and a half hours.

38. A. 몇 개나 살까요?
      About how many should we buy?

     B. 스무 개쯤 삽시다.
      Let's buy about twenty.

Note in (38 A) above that (이)나 replaces the object particle; i.e., one cannot say *몇 개를 이나 or *몇 개나를. In this respect, (이)나 behaves like 도.

2. Question word + (이)나: Generalizer *any/every*

When used after certain question words, (이)나 removes the interrogative meaning and generalizes the scope of the word.

누구	*who?*	누구나	*anyone; everyone*
무엇	*what?*	무엇이나	*anything; everything*
언제	*when?*	언제나	*any time; all the time; always*
어디	*where?*	어디나	*anywhere; everywhere*
어디서	*where?*	어디서나	*[happening] anywhere; everywhere*
어느 것	*which. . . ?*	어느 것이나	*anything; either [thing]*

39. A. 누구를 부를까요?
      Whom shall we invite?

     B. 누구나 좋아요.
      Anybody is fine.

40. A. 주말에 어디에 갈까요?
Where shall we go (this) weekend?

B. 어디나 좋아요.
Anywhere is fine.

41. 우리 오빠는 언제나 어디서나 노래를 불러요.
My older brother is always singing wherever he goes.

42. A. 어느 것을 살까요?
Which one shall we buy?

B. 어느 것이나 좋아요.
Either one is fine.

A similar meaning can be obtained with the word 아무, which by itself means *anyone, anybody*, but in front of another noun means *any, any old*.

아무나	*anyone, anybody*
아무 것이나	*anything*
아무 때나	*any time*
아무 데나	*any place*
아무 데서나	*[happening at] any place; from any place*
아무 책이나	*any book [at all]*

43. 저기는 아무나 못 가요.
Not just anybody can go over there.

44. A. 뭘 드릴까요?
What can I get for you?

B. 아무거나 주세요.
Give me any old thing (anything at all).

45. A. 언제 놀러 갈까요?
When shall we come over? (When would you like us to come [to play]?)

B. 아무 때나 오세요 – 별로 바쁘지 않아요.
Come any time. I'm not particularly busy.

46. 아무 데서나 담배 피우지 마세요!
Don't just smoke anywhere you please!

47.　　A.　어떤 꽃을 살까요?
　　　　　What kind of flowers should we buy?

　　　　B.　아무 꽃이나 좋아요! 빨리 사세요!
　　　　　Any old flowers are OK! Hurry up and buy some!

The only way to make a negative version of this type of expression is with the 아무 pattern followed by 도 instead of (이)나. Note that the verb must be in the negative.

아무도	*nobody; nobody at all*
아무 것도	*nothing; nothing at all*
아무 데도	*nowhere; not any place*
아무 데서도	*nowhere, not from anywhere;*
	not [happening at] *any place*

48.　　A.　파티에는 사람 많이 왔어요?
　　　　　Did a lot of people come to the party?

　　　　B.　아무도 안 왔어요.
　　　　　Nobody came.

49.　　A.　주말에는 뭐 했어요?
　　　　　What did you do over the weekend?

　　　　B.　아무 것도 안 했어요.
　　　　　Nothing at all.

50.　　애기 때문에, 주말에는 아무 데도 못 갑니다.
　　　　Because of the baby, we can't go anywhere on weekends.

51.　　그 책은 아무 데에서도 안 팝니다.
　　　　They don't sell that book anywhere.

3. (이)나 meaning *or:* Two Related Patterns

Sub-pattern 1: Noun₁(이)나 Noun₂ meaning *Noun₁ or Noun₂*

The particles 도 and (이)나 are alike in some ways. You have just seen (이)나 in its meaning *about, approximately* and as a generalizer of questions words (누구나 *anybody at all*). Like 도, (이)나 can be used twice in a sentence to show tandem agreement, but (이)나 shows freedom or indifference of choice.

52.　　노트도, 연필도 안 돼요.
　　　　Neither notebooks nor pencils will do.

53.   노트나, 연필이나 다 돼요.
       Either notebooks or pencils will do.

Whereas 도 is definite, (이)나 is vague or unspecific.

54.   이것도 저것도 다 좋습니다.
       Both this one and that one are OK.

55.   이것이나 저것이나 다 좋습니다.
       Either this one or that one is OK.

The particle (이)나, then, when it is used after each of two (or more) comparable noun expressions, means *(either). . . or (. . .or yet somethingelse).*

Sub-pattern 2: NOUN(이)나 meaning *NOUN or something, NOUN or the like*

When (이)나 follows just a single noun, it still retains the sense of indifference to choice (even slightly denigrating the choice), but is best translated in English as *or something*.

56.   A. 영화나 볼까요?
           Shall we see a movie or something?

       B. 네, 그럽시다.
           Yes, let's do that.

57.   A. 술이나 마실까요?
           Shall we have something [alcoholic] *to drink* [or something]*?*

       B. 아니오, 아이스크림이나 먹읍시다.
           No, let's eat some ice-cream or something.

12.7. More Ways To Say *or*

The phrase 또는 means *or (else)* between plain noun expressions.

58.   커피 또는 홍차
       coffee or (else) black tea

Another way to do the same thing is to link two words with the word 아니면 *or.*

59.   커피 아니면 홍차
       coffee or (else) black tea

At the beginning of a sentence, the phrase 또는 also has this contrastive idea, as in the following sentence.

60. 또는 음악회에도 가지 않았어요.
    Nor (on the other hand) have I been to any concerts either [and I **do** like concerts].
    [Background: I haven't been to a single movie this fall, hating them as I do.]

The word 아니면 can also begin a sentence, but has the meaning of *Or else*.

61. 지하철로 갈까요? 아니면, 택시로 갈까요?
    Shall we take the subway? Or (else) shall we take a taxi?

또는, (이)나, and 아니면 thus all translate as *or*. (이)나 and 아니면 accept either choice indifferently where 또는 excludes one of the choices, by contrasting it with the accepted choice.

12.8. The *wanna* Form in -(으)ㄹ래(요)

Observe the following exchange:

62. A. 뭘 마실래요?
       What do you feel like drinking?

    B. 나는 커피를 마실래요.
       I think I'd like a coffee.

A plain processive base followed by -(으)ㄹ래요 means something like *I feel like VERBing, I wanna VERB, I've a mind to VERB, I'd prefer to VERB (if I had a choice), I'd like to VERB*. L-extending bases attach the full ending -ㄹ래요 onto the unextended form, so that we get 안 알래요, *I'd rather not know* (about it) [base 아- plus -ㄹ래요]. The pattern expresses a weak intention, inclination, and/or desire. It is used only in first person statements and second person questions, as in the exchange above. This is a highly colloquial form, though not quite as informal as English *wanna* (we have glossed the pattern this way because, like English *wanna*, the Korean form is a contraction in origin.)

63. A. 소주로 할래요, 양주로 할래요?
       Would you prefer soju or whiskey?

    B. 맥주 마실래요.
       I think I'd prefer beer.

64.   A. 춤을 출래요?
         Would you like to dance?

       B. 아니오, 춤을 추지 못해요.
         No, I can't dance.

In general, the form in -(으)ㄹ래요 has the force of a gentle suggestion and implies a choice. You should use this form rather than -고 싶어요 in questions, since the latter forces the other person into a yes or no answer.

12.9. Meanings for 좋아요 and Related Words

The descriptive verb 좋아요 means (1) *is good* or *fine* or *all right* and, (2) *is liked*. In the first meaning, only one noun phrase is involved, but in the second meaning, it often has two subjects, or else a topic and a subject.

65.   이것이 좋아요.
       This is good.

66.   나는 이것이 좋아요.
       I like this. [Literally: As for me, this is liked.]

The processive verb phrase 좋아해요 means *finds it good* or *likes it* and takes direct objects.

67.   나는 이것을 좋아해요.
       I like this.

This phrase also has the emotional connotation [someone] *is happy* (*glad*) which is commonly used in speaking of someone else, but sometimes for special emphasis to mean *I am happy/glad.* Notice the negative forms of each of these.

68.   좋지 않아요
       [something] *isn't good* or *isn't liked*

69.   좋아하지 않아요
       [someone] *doesn't like* [something]

The opposites are comparable expressions.

좋아요	*is liked*	싫어요	*is disliked* [base 싫-]
좋아해요	*likes it*	싫어해요	*dislikes it*

70.   나는 중국요리가 싫어요.
       I don't like Chinese cuisine.
       [Literally: As for me Chinese cuisine is disliked, hence the thing disliked is the subject]

71.   우리 남편은 빙수를 싫어해요.
       My husband dislikes shaved ice.
       [The thing disliked is the direct object]

72.   나는 뉴욕을 싫어해요.
       I don't like New York.

73.   나는 뉴욕이 싫어요.
       I don't like New York.

Notice that in English the meanings of the negative phrase 좋아하지 않아요 *doesn't like* and the affirmative phrase 싫어해요 *dislikes* usually fall together as the phrase *do(es)n't like*. The Korean 좋아하지 않아요 implies simple absence of fondness, without actual aversion. 싫어해요, on the other hand, implies an active or positive dislike. You can, of course, make a negative out of the dislike phrases too: 싫지 않아요 *I don't dislike it*, 싫어 하지 않아요 *he doesn't dislike it.*

Exercises

Exercise 1: Manipulating -지만

Here is a series of sentence pairs. The first sentence ends in -어요 and the second begins with 그렇지만. Put the sentences together into one so that the first clause ends with -지만 *but* . . . Then translate the new sentence. For example, the first will be 택시를 불렀지만 아직 안 왔어요. *I called a taxi, but it hasn't come yet.*

1.   택시를 불렀어요. 그렇지만 아직 안 왔어요.
2.   아기는 자요. 그렇지만 어머니는 안 주무세요.
3.   음악회는 가지 않아요. 그렇지만 연극은 가요.
4.   내 나이는 여든살이에요. 그렇지만 오십년 더 살고 싶어요.
5.   점심때까지 일을 마치고 싶었어요. 그렇지만 손님이 갑자기 오셨어요.
6.   맥주는 좋아요. 그렇지만 소주는 싫어요.
7.   지금 잡지를 보고 싶지 않아요.
      그렇지만 만화는 보고 싶어요.

8. 양주는 비싸요. 그렇지만, 소주는 싸요.
9. 우리 오빠는 결혼했어요. 그렇지만 아직도 대학에 다녀요.
10. 선생님을 만나고 싶어요. 그렇지만 시간이 없어요.
11. 돈은 있어요. 그렇지만 사고 싶지 않아요.
12. 나는 영화구경을 가끔 가요.
    그렇지만 동생은 잘 가지 않아요.
13. 나는 돈이 적어요. 그렇지만 친구는 많아요.
14. 김 사장은 아들이 없어요. 그렇지만 딸은 둘이 있어요.
15. 오빠는 일찍 왔어요. 그렇지만 동생은 늦게 왔어요.
16. 그 분의 아버님은 우체국에서 일을 하세요. 그렇지만 편지를 많이 안
    쓰세요.
17. 나는 전에는 학생이었어요. 그렇지만 지금은 선생이에요.
18. 내 약혼자는 나한테 꽃을 줬어요. 그렇지만 나는 꽃을 좋아하지 않아요.
19. 어머니는 부산에 사세요. 그렇지만 가끔 서울에 한 번씩 오세요.
20. 우리집은 크지 않아요. 그렇지만 좋아요.
21. 아침마다 수영을 해요. 그렇지만, 건강하지 못합니다.
22. 학생들은 많아요. 그렇지만 학교는 작아요.

Exercise 2: Suggestions and Tentative Questions

Here are a series of sentences that end in　-어요. Change each sentence to the suggestion/ tentative question pattern in - (으) ㄹ까요 and then translate each resulting sentence. Some will translate as *Shall we?* and others as *Do you suppose?* For example, the first will be 집 에 돌아갈까요? *Shall we go home?*

1. 집에 돌아가요?
2. 그 책을 읽어요?
3. 춤을 춰요?
4. 길에서 코트를 벗어요.
5. 걸어가요.
6. 음악회에 같이 가요?
7. 소주를 시켜요? 아니면 생맥주를 시켜요?
8. 언니가 그 남자와 결혼해요.
9. 그 이야기를 다시 한번 들어요?
10. 어머니가 백화점에서 어떤 옷을 사요?
11. 김 선생님은 여자 친구하고 같이 오세요?
12. 한국 옷을 입어요?

13. 다른 집에서 살아요.
14. 택시를 불러요?
15. 크림을 넣어요? 아니면 프리마를 넣어요?

Exercise 3: The *wanna* Form

Here is a series of sentences that end in -어요. Change each sentence to the *Do you wanna. . .?* question form with -(으)ㄹ래요? and then translate each resulting sentence. For example, the first will be 술 마실래요? *Do you feel like drinking?*

1. 술 마셔요.
2. 테니스 쳐요.
3. 내일 극장에 가요.
4. 한국 신문을 읽어요.
5. 우리 집에 가요.
6. 한국 노래를 들어요.
7. 햄버거나 빨리 먹어요.
8. 한국 담배를 피워요? 양담배를 피워요?
9. 학교 식당에서 나를 기다려요.
10. 토요일에 은행 앞에서 만나요.
11. 이게 힘이 들어요. 좀 도와줘요.
12. 내일 떠나요? 아니면 모레 떠나요?

Exercise 4: Long Negatives

Each of the following Korean sentences means *(someone) does something*. Change the verb expression so that the meaning is *(someone) doesn't do something*, using the longer way of saying *does not do*. Then translate the sentence. For example, the first will be 그 여자의 언니는 학교에서 공부를 하지 않았어요. *Her sister did not study at school.*

1. 그 여자의 언니는 학교에서 공부를 했어요.
2. 이 상자는 여자에게는 너무 무거워요?
3. 애들 때문에 피곤하세요?
4. 나는 일본서 왔어요.
5. 저를 많이 기다렸어요?
6. 언니는 담배를 피워요.
7. 나는 한국말을 한국에서 배웠어요.

8. 저 아저씨는 부자 동네에서 살아요.
9. 아들은 춤을 췄어요.
10. 아이들은 날마다 학교에 가요.
11. 그 여자는 그 남자와 약혼하고 싶어해요.
12. 수미 씨는 오빠와 같이 라디오를 들어요.
13. 일요일에 나는 성당에 나가요.
14. 커피에 설탕이랑 크림을 타요?

Exercise 5: Negative Commands

Here are a series of honorific polite commands in -(으)세요. Convert them to negative commands and translate the resulting sentences.

1. 책을 보세요.
2. 여자 친구를 만나세요.
3. 술을 많이 마시세요.
4. 담배를 피우세요.
5. 그 의자에 앉으세요.
6. 얼음을 넣으세요.
7. 설탕을 타세요.
8. 늦게 들어오세요.
9. 날마다 술집에 다니세요.
10. 그 남자랑 춤을 추세요.
11. 모레 떠나세요.
12. 걸어가세요.
13. 혼자 다니세요.
14. 내년에는 은퇴하세요.
15. 그 사람한테 전화번호를 주세요.
16. 이 샤쓰에 풀을 먹이세요.
17. 이 바지를 세탁하세요.

Exercise 6: English to Korean Translation

Translate the following sentences into Korean. Use long negatives wherever possible.

1. Don't go to either *tabangs* or pubs.
2. I didn't want to eat an ice cream, but my brother gave me one.
3. Is it already 7 o'clock (PM)? Then don't stay here; go home.
4. I went back to Korea last year, but I didn't like it.
5. Please put some sugar in this coffee.
6. Do you feel like a whisky or *soju*?
7. I don't drink alcohol. Don't you drink, either!
8. A. Let's play baseball.
   B. I don't feel like it (wanna). I feel like resting upstairs.

9.   My older brother doesn't come home early nowadays.
10.   Neither my son nor my daughter are very bright.

Exercise 7: Korean to English Translation

Translate the following sentences into English.

1.   남 선생님은 음악을 좋아하지 않으세요. 저희 집사람도 안 좋아해요.
2.   저 공원에서 산보나 할까 합니다.
3.   이 물건들은 아주 무거워요. 좀 도와주실래요?
4.   집에는 언제 들어왔어요?
5.   불고기를 맛이 있게 구웠지만, 아무도 먹지 않았어요.
6.   어제 우리집 개가 아버지를 갑자기 물었어요.
7.   이 크림은 비싸지만, 맛은 하나도 없어요. 먹지 말아요!
8.   김 선생님은 배우같이 예쁘세요.
9.   A.콜라 마실래요? 아니면 냉수 마실래요?
      B.둘 다 싫어요. 맥주 한병 주실래요?
10.   오늘 저녁에 부산에 갈까 해요. 같이 갈래요?
11.   전화를 여러번 걸었지만, 아무도 받지 않았어요.
12.   A.뭐 살래요?
      B.아무것도 사고 싶지 않아요.
13.   한국말 잘 하십니다. 몇 년이나 배우셨어요?
14.   심심해요. 다방에나 갈까요?
15.   A. 양주나 소주는 건강에 나쁠까요?
      B.글쎄요. 마시지 맙시다.

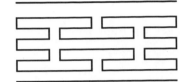 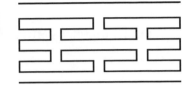

Lesson 13

아까 전화하니까, 아무도 받지를 않아요.

This lesson centers on families and kinship relations. We introduce new patterns meaning *since/because* and *as soon as*, two new honorific particles, PROBABLE FUTURES in -(으)ㄹ 거에요, the *is doing* pattern with -고 있어요 and RHETORICAL RETORTS in -잖아요.

Korean Dialogues

Dialogue 1

Eric and 미스 곽, the waitress from the 커피 숍, have met at a tabang for their '데이트'.

에릭	어디 다른데로 갈까요? 아니면 여기 그냥 있을까요?
미스 곽	밖이 추우니까 여기 그냥 있어요.
에릭	미스 곽, 형제가 많으세요?
미스 곽	오빠 한 명하고 언니 한 명 있어요.
에릭	둘 다 결혼하셨어요?
미스 곽	오빠만 결혼했어요. 아들도 하나 있어요. 언니는 아직 미혼이지만, 대학을 졸업하자 마자 결혼할 거에요. 에릭 씨는 가족이 어떻게 돼요?
에릭	나는 어머니랑 아버지랑 여동생이 하나 있습니다. 동생 이름은 샌디에요.
미스 곽	실례지만, 아버지께서는 뭘 하세요?
에릭	무역회사에 다니고 계세요.
미스 곽	아버지께서 연세가 많으십니까?
에릭	네, 이번 구월에 쉰 살이 되세요.
미스 곽	아이, 아직 젊으시잖아요?!

Dialogue 2

Back at Chris Murphy's office, Chris has asked Miss Lee to get Mr. Nam, a colleague, on the phone.

크리스	남 사장하고 통화했어요?
미스 리	아까 전화하니까, 아무도 받지를 않아요.
크리스	아, 맞아요. 오늘은 안 계실 거에요. 금요일이니까, 골프를 치고 계실 거에요.

Reading Passage

오늘은 일요일입니다.

그래서 가족들이 모두 집에 있습니다.

할아버지께서는 보통 공원에서 운동을 하시지만, 오늘은 비가 쏟아지고
　　　있으니까 못 나가십니다.

아버지께서는 마루에서 무슨 스포츠 프로를 보고 계십니다.

　　　일요일에는 일어나시자 마자 테레비를 보고 싶어 하십니다.

어머니께서는 부엌에서 설겆이를 하십니다.

나는 내 방에서 친구 전화를 기다리고 있습니다. 전화가 오자 마자
　　　친구를 만나러 나갈 겁니다.

Vocabulary

Family and Relatives

식구	members of the family
식구가 몇 명이세요?	How many people in your family?
사촌	cousin
사촌누나(누님)	cousin (boy's older female cousin)
사촌형(님)	cousin (boy's older male cousin)
사촌언니	cousin (girl's older female cousin)
사촌동생	cousin (boy or girl's younger cousin)
삼촌	uncle (on father's side)
외삼촌	uncle (on mother's side)
큰아버지	uncle (father's elder brother)
작은아버지	uncle (father's younger brother)
이모	aunt (mother's sister)
이모부	uncle (mother's sister's husband)
고모	aunt (father's sister)
고모부	uncle (father's sister's husband)
아드님	son (honorific)
따님	daughter (honorific)
아저씨	uncle (generic); mister
아주머니	aunt (generic); ma'am
아줌마	auntie (casual for 아주머니)

Brothers and Sisters

형(님)	elder brother (for males)
남매	brother and sister
저 두 사람은 남매예요.	Those two are brother and sister.
자매	sisters
누나	elder sister (for males)
남동생	younger brother
여동생	younger sister

In-laws

장인	father-in-law (for males)
장인어른	father-in-law (elegant)
장모	mother-in-law (for males)

시아버지	father-in-law (for females)
시어머니	mother-in-law (for females)
시부모	parents-in law (for females)
시댁	esteemed house/home of the parents-in law (for females)
장인장모	parents-in-law (for males)
사위	son-in-law
며느리	daughter-in-law

Other

조부모	grandparents
할아버지	grandfather
외할아버지	grandfather (on mother's side, if you need to specify this)
할머니	grandmother
외할머니	grandmother (on mother's side, if you need to specify this)
손주	grandchild(ren)
손자	grandson
손녀	granddaughter
손녀딸	(same)
조카	nephew
조카 딸	niece
자녀분	children (honorific)
자녀분이 있으세요?	Do you have children?
자제분	children (honorific, interchangeable with 자녀분)
친척	relative

Verbal Expressions

드리–	give (to somebody esteemed)
설겆이	dirty dishes
설겆이(를) 하–	wash the dishes, do the dishes
걱정	a worry; worries
걱정(을) 하–	worry
데이트	a date
데이트(를) 하–	go on a date

흐리-	become/get cloudy
날씨가 흐렸어요.	The weather has become cloudy/clouded over.
비(가) 오-	rain comes (it rains)
비가 쏟아지고 있어요.	It is pouring down/It is raining buckets.
눈(이) 오-	snow comes (it snows)
운동	sports; exercise
운동(을) 하-	do sports; exercise
운동장	sports stadium
골프	golf
골프(를) 치-	play golf
미혼(이에요)	(is) unmarried
말씀(을) 하시-	(somebody esteemed) says; humbly say
말씀(을) 드리-	humbly say, say to somebody esteemed
사장님께 말씀 드릴까요?	Shall I tell the boss?
늦-	be late
이상하-	be strange, odd
통하-	go through; (a language/message) is understood, gets across
추w-	be cold
가까w-	be close, nearby
어리-	(a child) be young; be childish
맞-	be right, correct; hit the mark
네, 맞습니다.	Yes, that's right.
이혼(을) 하-	get divorced
이혼했어요.	is divorced
졸업(을) 하-	graduate
런던대학을 졸업했어요.	I graduated from the University of London. (not with 에서)
넥타이(를) 매-	put on/wear a tie
콘택트렌즈(를) 끼-	wear contact lenses
버리-	throw it away

Nouns

숙제	homework
-데	a place
스포츠	sports (especially in the newspaper or on TV)
프로	pro (sports); TV program
프로 야구	professional baseball

코메디 프로	a television comedy show
날씨	weather
마루	the living area in a Korean-style apartment/house; wooden floor
진지	cooked rice (honorific equivalent of 밥)
할아버지 – 진지 잡수세요.	Grandfather, the meal is served.
장마	Korea's rainy season, Korea's seasonal rains
장마(가) 지-	the rainy season sets in
한국은 여름에 장마가 집니다.	The rainy season in Korea comes in the summer.
봄	spring
여름	summer
가을	autumn, fall
겨울	winter
군인	soldier, serviceman
선교사	missionary
둘 다	both, both of them [Literally: all two]
부엌	kitchen

Adverbs

아까	a short while ago; just a moment ago
모두	all, everyone
그냥	just (as one/it is), without doing anything; just
맛 없지만 그냥 먹읍시다.	It doesn't taste like much, but let's eat (it as it is).
만호: (What should I bring to the potluck?)	
수진: 그냥 오세요.	Just come anyway (as you are, without anything).
이렇게	in this way, like this
그렇게	in that way, like that; so
그렇게 어렵지는 않아요.	It's not so difficult.
저렇게	in that way
멀리	far
멀리 가지 마세요.	Don't go far.
멀리서	from a distance
그러니까	So, what I mean to say is; So, what you're saying is
아마	maybe, probably (often used with -(으)ㄹ 거에요 and -겠어요)
아마도	maybe, probably (but a bit more tentative than just 아마)

Lesson Notes

13.1. Verbs: the Sequential Form -(으)니(까)

Verbs have a sequential form, which is made by attaching the ending -(으)니까 to them: -으니까 after consonants, -니까 after vowels. The ending may also be attached to past bases to make past-tense forms (-었으니까), and to the probable future in -(으)ㄹ 거에요: -(으)ㄹ 거니까 (see section 13.4 in this lesson for more on the probable future). For example:

하니까	*as/since* [he] *does*	먹으니까	*as/since* [he] *eats*
했으니까	*as/since* [he] *did*	먹었으니까	*as/since* [he] *ate*
할 거니까	*as/since* [he] *will do*	먹을 거니까	*as/since* [he] *will eat*

The sequential form in -(으)니까 is called the extended sequential and is widely used in colloquial speech. It can also be heard as -(으)니깐 or -(으)니까는 with the particle 은/는 or its abbreviation.

There is also a short sequential form, which is obtained by dropping the -까 (-까는, -깐), i.e., -(으)니. This short sequential form is bookish or literary/poetic, and does not occur much in colloquial Korean.

13.1.1. -(으)니(까) *As, Since, Because*

The sequential ending -(으)니(까) can mean *as* or *since* or *because* or *in view of the fact that*. In this usage, the second clause often contains a suggestion or a command. Here are some examples.

1. 시간이 늦었으니까 빨리 갑시다.
    It has become late, so let's hurry.

2. 너무 작으니까 버립시다.
    It's too small; let's throw it away.

3. 오늘은 좀 바쁘니까 그 일은 내일 합시다.
    I'm rather busy today, so let's take care of that matter tomorrow.

4. 오늘 저녁은 박 선생님 댁에서 먹을 거니까 많이 잡수시지 마세요.
    We're going to eat at Mr. Pak's house tonight, so don't eat much (now).

5. 버스에 사람이 많으니까, 걸어갑시다.
   There are too many people on the bus, so let's walk.

6. 일이 끝났으니까, 맥주나 한 잔 할까요?
   Since the work is finished, shall we have a beer or something?

7. 시간이 다 됐으니까, 빨리 끝냅시다.
   Time is up, so let's finish quickly.

8. 한국말을 잘 모르니까, 천천히 말씀하세요.
   I don't know Korean very well, so please speak slowly.

13.1.2. -(으)니(까) *When . . . , [I realized or discovered . . .]*

Both sequential forms, but particularly the extended sequential, also have the meaning *when* in the past [something happened], *then* [I found/realized/discovered], indicating a close sequence of actions. In this usage, the sequential ending cannot appear on a past base. In addition, the subject of the -(으)니까 clause is usually the speaker (I), and the subject of the following clause is something or someone different. Here are some examples.

9. 전화를 하니까, 받지 않았어요.
   When I telephoned, they didn't answer [literally: receive it].

10. 내가 가니까 그 사람이 신문을 보고 있었어요.
    When I went [to see him], he was reading the newspaper.

11. 멀리서 보니깐 학교 같습니다.
    When I look at it from a distance, it looks like a school.

12. 방에 들어 가니까, 장인어른이 신문을 보고 계셨어요.
    When I entered the room, [I found that] my father-in-law was reading the newspaper.

13. 한국말을 공부하니까, 너무 재미 있어요.
    Now that I study Korean, I find it is incredibly fun.

14. 한국사람을 사랑하니까, 한국음식도 맛이 있어요.
    Now that I [am in] love [with] a Korean, Korean food tastes good, too.

15. 영국에 오니까, 날씨가 너무 안 좋아요.
    Now that I'm here in England, I find that the weather is really not very good.

13.2. Honorifics: Nouns and Particles

When you are talking in Korean about someone who has relatively high social status—a government official, a foreign guest, a minister, a teacher—you use some special forms called honorifics. Remember that when you are talking to someone of high status, you use either the Polite Style or the Formal Style, depending on which endings you put on the verbs at the end of sentences. Honorifics are also used frequently to refer to the second person. This is a way of honoring your listener, as well as showing that you mean *you* without actually using a pronoun. There are several kinds of honorifics.

13.2.1. Nouns

Some English nouns are translated by two different Korean nouns, one neutral and the other honorific:

집	*house, home*	댁	*esteemed house or home*
나이	*(years of) age*	연세	*age of someone esteemed*
사람	*person*	분	*an esteemed person*
밥	*cooked rice*	진지	*same, for an esteemed person*
아이	*children*	자녀분	*same, for an esteemed person*
		자제분	*same, for an esteemed person*

Some kinship terms also have separate honorific forms; see section 13.3 below.

13.2.2. Particles

The Particle 께: Honorific 에게/한테

The particle 께 is honorific; it means the same thing as 에게 and 한테, *to* [a person], but is used only after nouns denoting a specially honored person.

아버님께   *to* [esteemed] *father*

The Particle 께서(는): Honorific 이/가

The combination 께서 marks as subject an esteemed person and is the honorific equivalent to the two-shape subject particle 이/가.

16. 선생님께서 오셨어요.

    The [esteemed] *teacher came.*

The honorific subject marker 께서 can be used either alone or followed by the topic particle 는:

17. 아버님께서는 무엇을 하세요?

    What does your father do?

The honorific particle 께서 is used only for persons. Here are some examples of 께 and 께서(는).

18. 할머님께 편지를 썼습니다.
    I wrote Grandmother a letter.

19. 교수님께서 저한테 부탁하셨어요.
    My professor asked a favor of me.

20. 할아버지께서 자동차가 없으세요?
    Doesn't your grandfather have a car?

21. 아버님께서 댁에 안 계세요?
    Isn't your father at home?

22. 사장님께 연락했습니까?
    Did you get in touch with the company president?

13.3. Kinship Terms

The Korean words for relatives can be divided into two types: those for which some of the words differ according to the gender of the person (that is, whether you are speaking about a man's brother or a woman's brother), and those for which the words are the same regardless of the gender of the person related. You will have noticed also that Korean does not allow its speakers to refer to brothers and sisters (or cousins, who are regarded as extended siblings) without specifying whether that person is older or younger than the person related.

The words for *grandfather* 할아버지 and *grandmother* 할머니 are also used to mean *old man* and *old woman*. Similarly, the words for *uncle* 아저씨 and *aunt* 아주머니, 아줌마 are used to mean *(older) man* and *(older) lady*, particularly in expressions used by children, or in speaking to children, such as *Say hello to the man, dear* or *the lady who lives next door.*

The word 집 (댁) *house* may also used in the way English uses the word *family*: 우리집이 커요 *Our house* [family] *is large.* 식구 [Literally: mouths to feed] means *members of the family.* To ask or tell how many people there are in someone's family, you can use a form of either 있- *(there) are* or 이- (the copula).

23. 식구가 몇명이세요?
     Your family members are how many (people)?

24. 식구가 몇명이 있어요?
     Your family members, how many of them are there?

You may have noticed that Korean often prefers the plural *we/us* where English would require *I/me*: 우리 개 *my dog.* [This is extended even to cases where the explanation given earlier (belonging to our family) is not so convincing.] 우리 남편 is the usual way of saying *my husband* and 우리 아내 *my wife.*

Kinship Terms

In the following lists, honorific kinship terms are in AppleGothic Bold (고딕).

a. Relatives for which the terms differ according to the sex of the person related.

A male's	A female's	English
장인, 장인어른	시아버지, 시아버님	*father-in-law*
장모, 장모님	시어머니, 시어머님	*mother-in-law*
아내 (부인)	남편	*spouse*
형제	(오빠들과 남동생들)	*brothers*
형(님)	오빠	*older brother*
누나, 누님	언니	*older sister*

b. Relatives for which the terms do not differ according to the gender of the person related.

조부모, 조부모님	*grandparents*
할아버지, 할아버님	*grandfather*
할머니, 할머님	*grandmother*
부모, 부모님	*parents*
아버지, 아버님	*father*

어머니, 어머님	*mother*
아이, 애	*child(ren)*
아들, 아드님	*son*
딸, 따님	*daughter*
손주, 손주아이	*grandchild(ren)*
손자	*grandson*
손녀〔-딸〕	*granddaughter*
사위	*son-in-law*
며느리	*daughter-in-law*
사촌	*cousin*
아저씨	*uncle*
아주머니	*aunt*
조카	*nephew*
조카 딸	*niece*
동생	*younger sibling*

13.4. Probable Futures with -(으)ㄹ 거에요

13.4.1. Probable Futures in -(으)ㄹ 거에요 on Plain Bases

Dialogue One from this lesson contained the following sentence.

25.　　네, 이번 구월에 쉰 살이 되실 거에요.
Yes. He's going to be (become) fifty this September.

The usual way to make a future tense in Korean is to add -(으)ㄹ 거에요 to the plain or honorific base of any verb, processive or descriptive. It can also be added to the past base to mean *probably VERBed, must have VERBed.* We will look at this probable past usage of -(으)ㄹ 거에요 later on in the section. First, here is the construction on a plain base.

먹을 거에요	*is going to eat, will probably eat*
있을 거에요	*is going to have, probably will have*
넥타이를 맬 거에요	*is going to wear a tie, will probably wear a tie*
추울 거에요	*is going to be cold, will probably be cold*
들을 거에요	*is going to listen, will probably listen*
살 거에요	*is going to live, will probably live*
바쁠 거에요	*is going to be busy, will probably be busy*
빠를 거에요	*is going to be quick, will probably be quick*

As can be seen from the examples above, ㄷ ~ ㄹ verbs like *listen* retain the ㄹ as the base-final consonant, as is always the case when the base is followed by a two-shape ending. The w ~ ㅂ verb base 추w- *cold* also ends in a consonant (*w*), but the *w* + 으 of the ending combine to give 우, so w ~ ㅂ verb bases when combined with two-shape endings always change to 우. L-extending bases attach this ending in their unextended shape: 사-ㄹ- *live* → 사- + -ㄹ 거에요 → 살 거에요.

주의!

Note that all verb endings that attach to a plain base of a verb can also be attached to the plain base with the honorific ending -(으)시- attached. From now on, therefore, when we refer to an ending being attached to a plain base, we mean one either with or without the honorific form included in it.

You will also see the spelling -을 거예요 for this form, because the 예요 portion is actually the copula (-이에요, squished to -예요), but people pronounce -을 거에요.

주의!
Remember to tense up the ㄱ of -거에요:
-을꺼에요 in pronunciation.

In origin, this ending is complex, built on the prospective modifier -(으)ㄹ plus 것 *thing; fact* plus the copula. For now, you need not worry about the prospective modifier (wait until Lesson Twenty-three). Simply keep in mind that it is the -(으)ㄹ here which lends the future or forward-looking meaning to the construction (and which tenses up the ㄱ of 거 ← 것). What you are really saying is *it is a prospective case/matter of VERBing*. Since the last element is just the copula, you can change this to other styles or put other endings on.

먹을 겁니다   *is going to eat, will probably eat* (formal)

You can also undo the rather colloquial contraction of 것 to 거.

먹을 것입니다   *is going to eat, will probably eat* (formal)
먹을 것이에요   *is going to eat, will probably eat* (polite)

Note, however, that if you wish to use an honorific, this must appear on the verb base, not on the copula involved in the probable future ending.

넥타이를 매실 거에요   *is going to wear a tie, will probably wear a tie*
    [not *맬거세요!]

Often, especially with the copula, forms in -(으)ㄹ 거에요 can mean a probable present.

26.   그 미국사람이 군인일 거에요.
        That American must be a soldier.

27.   그것이 크리스 씨의 집이 아닐 거에요.
        That surely wouldn't be Chris' house.

Here are more examples of the probable future.

28.   내일은 [아마] 비가 올 거에요.
        It will [probably] *rain tomorrow.*

29.   내년에 [아마] 졸업을 할 거에요.
        He will [probably] *graduate next year.*

30.   밤에 [아마] 추울 거에요.
        It will [probably] *be cold at night .*

31.   박 선생님은 [아마] 부산에서 살고 계실 거에요.
        Mr. Pak is [probably] *living in Pusan.*

13.4.2. Probable Futures in -(으)ㄹ 거에요 on Past Bases

The following examples show the way in which you can add the -(으)ㄹ 거에요 form to a past base to make a probable future perfect (*likely will have done*) or a probable past (*must have done*).

32.   영국으로 떠났을 거에요.
        He must have departed for England.

33.   아마 한국에서 영어를 좀 배우셨을 거에요.
        He probably studied some English in Korea.

13.5. Rhetorical Retorts in -잖아요

Recall the following exchange from this lesson's conversation.

34.   B.   네, 이번 구월에 쉰 살이 되실 거예요.
            Yes. He'll be fifty years old this September.

       A.   아직 젊으시잖아요?!
            Oh, go on. He's still young [don't you think?].

In origin, this verb ending is a squished (contracted) long-form negative. Thus, the example above is obtained from the sentence below by adding a rhetorical twist to your intonation:

       젊-으시-지 않아요?
       Is he not young? [stupid question—of course he is!]

The squish process went like this: -지 않아요 → -잖아요 → -잖아요. We regard this squished negative as a new and separate verb ending because it behaves differently from the negatives in -지. Like -지, this is a one-shape ending, and ㄹ-extending bases keep their ㄹ: 팔잖아요! But whereas negatives in -지 attach only to plain (and honorific) bases, the ending -잖아요 can attach to *any* base.

-잖아요 **on Plain Bases**

35.   A. 빨리 와요!
          Hurry up!

       B. 그런데 이게 무겁잖아요!
          But this thing is (so) heavy! [isn't it/can't you see?]

36.   A. 왜 이렇게 늦을까요?
          Why do you suppose he's so late?

       B. 비가 오잖아요!
          But it's raining! [isn't it/can't you see?]

37.   A. 이 음식이 왜 이렇게 맛없을까요?
          Why do you suppose this food is so tasteless?

       B. 영국음식이잖아요!
          But it's English food! [isn't it/can't you see?]

38.   에릭   외국사람이 처음이세요?
                  Is this your first time with a foreigner?

       미스 곽   네, 그래서 좀 이상해요.
                  Yes, so it's a bit strange.

에릭   아이, 뭐가 이상해요? 나도 사람이잖아요?
Go on, what's so strange about it? Aren't I a person, too?

-잖아요 on Past Bases

39.   A. 오늘 박 선생님을 만날 거에요.
        I'll probably meet Mr. Pak today.

        B. 그런데, 벌써 떠나셨잖아요!
        But he's already left! [hasn't he/didn't you know?]

40.   A. 오늘이 우리 한국말 시험이에요?
        Is today our Korean language exam?

        B. 어제였잖아요!
        It was yesterday! [wasn't it/didn't you know?]

13.6. *Is doing* with -고 있어요

A phrase consisting of a –고 form and a form of 있– *is; stays* corresponds to English verb phrases like *is writing, is eating, is buying*, as opposed to simple forms like *writes, eats, buys.*

41.   어머니는 아침을 아직 잡수시고 계세요.
    Mother is still eating breakfast.

42.   고모가 밖에서 기다리고 있으니까, 빨리 해요.
    Auntie (father's sister) is waiting [for you] outside, so hurry up.

43.   동생이 아직 자고 있어요.
    My little brother (or little sister) is still asleep.

44.   시어머니께서 새 옷을 입고 계셨어요.
    The mother-in-law was wearing [or had on] a new dress.

This correspondence is by no means 100 percent, however; English says *is going* where Korean uses the single verb 가요. For most cases of -고 있어요 you can substitute a simple verb, so that 먹어요 *eats* covers about the same ground as 먹고 있어요 *is eating.* This does not work in the other direction, though. You may not automatically substitute a –고 있어요 phrase for every simple verb form.

The -고 of this pattern behaves in the same way as the -고 of -고 싶어요. In other words, it keeps the ㄹ of ㄹ-extending verbs: 살고 있어요 *is living.* Insofar as this pattern emphasizes that a particular action or process is in progress, it can only be used with processive bases.

Note that, with verbs of donning (verbs related to the putting on and wearing of clothes) this pattern creates an ambiguity.

45.　나는 넥타이를 매고 있어요.
　　　I am wearing a necktie. or *I am putting on my tie.*

46.　모자를 쓰고 있습니다.
　　　I am wearing a hat. or *He is putting on his hat.*

To show tense, you change the verb 있어요: 쓰고 있어요 *is writing* becomes 쓰고 있었어요 *was writing.* For other sentence types you also make the change on the last verb, as you can see in 쓰고 있지만 *is writing, but.*

For honorific expressions you substitute 계세요 for 있어요, so that 쓰고 있어요 becomes 쓰고 계세요 (or 쓰시고 계세요) to mean *(someone esteemed) is writing.*

The negative can be made either on the underlying verb or on the expression as a whole, with slightly different meanings. If you merely want to deny an assertion you can say 쓰고 있지 않아요 *is not writing,* but if you want to imply that the subject goes along nicely without the activity, you say 쓰지 않고 있어요 *is not writing* [for the time being, these days, etc.] or *gets along (manages to get by) without writing* or *keeps away from one's typewriter.* Both kinds of negative can be put into the various other sentence types, so that for the meaning *isn't writing, but,* you will hear both 쓰고 있지 않지만 or 쓰고 있지 못하지만, usually as a denial of an assertion, and 쓰지 않고 있지만 or 쓰지 못하고 있지만. Here are some more examples.

47.　큰아버지는 요즘도 술을 드시지 않고 계십니다.
　　　My uncle is keeping off the booze lately (still/too).

48.　이모는 아직 콘택트렌즈를 찾지 못하고 있어요.
　　　Auntie (mother's sister) still can't find her contact lens.

13.7. *As soon as* with -자 마자

The pattern for *as soon as* is made by attaching the one-shape ending -자 to verb bases. The pattern is usually intensified in spoken language with 마자: 오자 or 오자 마자 *as soon as* [someone] *comes/came*. Note that even if the event in the second clause is past, the verb with the -자 마자 ending still attaches to a plain base—the verb at the end of the whole sentence does all the work of showing the tense. Here are some more examples.

49.　내가 서울역에 도착하자마자, 기차가 떠났어요.
The train left as soon as I arrived at Seoul station.

50.　수업이 끝나자 마자 점심을 먹으러 갈 겁니다.
We're going to go eat lunch as soon as class finishes.

51.　숙제를 마치자마자, 집에 돌아갔어요.
He went home as soon as he finished his homework.

52.　밥을 먹자 마자 손님이 왔어요.
I had no sooner eaten than someone came.

53.　부산에서 내리자마자 사촌동생을 만났어요.
I saw (or met) my cousin as soon as I got off at Pusan.

54.　방학이 되자 마자 시골에 쉬러 가고 싶습니다.
As soon as vacation comes, I want to go to the countryside to take a rest.

55.　버스에서 내리자 마자 비가 쏟아졌어요.
As soon as I got off the bus, it poured.

Exercises

Exercise 1: Sequentials in -(으)니까

Join each of the sentences below using the sequential pattern in -(으)니까 and translate the resulting sentence into English.

1. 밤에 눈이 왔습니다. 골프를 못 칠 거에요.

2. 저희 어머니가 항상 집에 계십니다. 걱정 마세요.

3. 한국말이 너무 어렵습니다. 다른 외국어를 배울래요.

4. 오늘 좀 바쁩니다. 내일 만날까요?

5. 나는 중국사람이 아닙니다. 중국말은 못 가르칩니다.

6. 극장 앞으로 나갔습니다. 친구가 벌써 기다리고 있었어요.

7. 방 안으로 들어갔습니다. 아무도 없었어요.

8. 밖에 나갔습니다. 눈이 오고 있었어요.

9. 연구실에서 편지를 쓰고 있었습니다. 일본에서 전화가 왔어요.

10. 서울역에 도착했습니다. 벌써 밤이었습니다.

Exercise 2: -(으)ㄹ 거에요 as Probable Future

Each of the following sentences means *someone does/is something*. Make each one mean *someone probably will do/be something*. Then translate the sentence. For example, the first will be 동생은 교회에 갈 거에요. *My brother is going to go to church.*

1. 동생은 교회에 가요.
2. 시아버지는 일주일동안 계세요.
3. 선생님은 넥타이를 매세요.
4. 할아버지는 모자를 쓰세요.
5. 내일 숙제가 많아요.
6. 내일 비가 와요.
7. 오늘 밤에 조카가 와요.
8. 나는 한국에서 영어를 가르쳐요.
9. 아저씨는 이번 겨울에 가족을 만나요.

10. 형은 군인이 돼요.
11. 내일 아침부터 눈이 와요.
12. 나는 이번 가을에는 일본에 가요.
13. 조카한테 뭘 줘요?
14. 김 선생님이 내년에 결혼해요.
15. 내 약혼자는 이번 가을에 졸업해요.

Exercise 3: -(으)ㄹ 거에요 as Probable Present

Each of the following sentences means *someone does/is something*. Make each one mean *someone probably does/is something*. Then translate the sentence. For example, the first will be: 외삼촌은 중국에 살고 계실 거에요. *My uncle is probably living in China.*

1. 외삼촌은 중국에 살고 계세요.
2. 장인어른은 지금 주무세요.
3. 밖이 추워요.
4. 영국은 날씨가 별로 안 좋아요.
5. 우리 시어머니는 교회에 나가세요.
6. 그 아이가 아직 어려요.
7. 그 부모님들이 젊지 않으세요.
8. 그 상점이 가까워요.
9. 극장은 너무 멀어요.
10. 우리 시아버지는 돈이 많으세요.
11. 우리 며느리는 영어를 잘해요.
12. 선생님의 약혼자는 꽃을 좋아 하세요.
13. 내 사위가 미국사람이지만 한국말을 좀 해요.
14. 아저씨는 남동생 집에서 사세요.
15. 선생님의 아드님이 졸업했어요.
16. 오빠가 운동하고 있어요.
17. 고모부가 그걸 모르세요.
18. 할아버지가 일찍 주무셨어요.
19. 영화가 인제 끝났어요.
20. 조카가 그 편지를 이틀 전에 받았어요.

Exercise 4: Kinship terms and Honorifics

Here are some English sentences. Express each one in Korean twice: the first time insert *my younger brother* as the subject, and the second time use *my father* as the subject (and use honorifics).

1. In the spring he plays golf, but in the summer he plays tennis.
2. He went to bed early last night, but he didn't get up early this morning.
3. He doesn't eat much meat, and he doesn't drink much water, either.
4. He's old, but his heart is young.
5. He doesn't like his daughter-in-law, but he likes his son-in-law.
6. He wasn't home yesterday afternoon, but he's home now.
7. He works hard in the daytime. At night, he rests.
8. He taught English at the University last year, but he doesn't teach there now.
9. He waited at the hotel for an hour, but his friend didn't come.
10. He gave my little sister some money yesterday.
11. He listened to the radio for two hours last night.

Exercise 5: English to Korean Translation

Translate the following sentences into Korean.

1. A. My family [house] is big. There are many members [literally: members are many].

   B. How many siblings do you have, Ho-ch'ŏl? (호철 씨, male)

   A. I have four younger brothers and one younger sister.

   B. You don't have any older brothers or sisters?

   A. That's right, I haven't. I have neither older brothers nor older sisters.

   B. Do you have children, Ho-ch'ŏl?

   A. Yes, we now have a son and a daughter.

2. A. What are you doing here?

   B. I'm waiting for my girlfriend.

3. A. Whats the baby doing now?

   B. He's sleeping.

4. The teacher is wearing a tie.

5. My uncle is putting on his shoes.

6. As soon as I graduate, I want to go to Japan.

7. As soon as the film ended, we went to a tabang.

8. As soon as my uncle returned from Canada, it snowed.

Lesson Thirteen / 263

9.	As soon as we arrived at Pusan, we called home.
10.	As soon as I found the telephone number, I called.
11.	As soon as the price went up a bit, I sold the car.

Exercise 6. Korean-to-English Translation

Translate the following sentences into English.

1.	그 아저씨는 군인이었을 거에요.
2.	내일은 서울에서 구경을 좀 할 거에요.
3.	A. 오늘 저녁에 이 선생님 만나실 겁니까?
	B. 그런데, 벌써 서울로 떠났잖아요?
4.	어제 밤에 눈이 왔을 거에요.
5.	저희 조부모들은 대구에서 살고 계십니다.
6.	저는 이번 봄에 졸업할 겁니다.
7.	A. 아드님은 몇살입니까?
	B. 스물네살입니다.
8.	그 아주머니는 이혼했을 겁니다.
9.	A. 저는 경제학을 전공했습니다.
	B. 그러세요? 어렵잖아요?!
10.	A. 운동 좀 하러 운동장에 나갈까요?
	B. 그런데, 비가 오잖아요?!
11.	우리 누나는 책을 쓰고 있어요.
12.	우리 손녀딸은 언제나 모자를 쓰고 있어요.
13.	우리 집은 식구가 많습니다. 남동생 다섯명이랑 언니 두명이 있습니다.
14.	A. 수잔 씨는 인제 한국말을 잘해요.
	B. 언제나 공부를 열심히 하잖아요?!
15.	A. 이 식당은 언제나 손님이 많아요.
	B. 음식이 맛이 있잖아요?!
16.	추우니까, 나가지 맙시다.
17.	이 프로는 재미 없으니까, 보지 맙시다.
18.	밖에 나가니까, 아주 추웠어요.
19.	아까 전화하니까, 아무도 받지 않았어요.
20.	영화가 지금 끝났을 거에요.

Exercise 7: More Practice with Sequentials

Each of the items below contains two sentences. Reconstruct them as one sentence connected by the sequential ending –(으)니까 and then translate into English. Note that the first ten sentences are of the discovery-when type (and thus have "I" as their subject). Be sure to delete the past tense ending before attaching –(으)니까.

1. 집에 돌아갔어요. 아무도 없었어요.
2. 밖에 나갔어요. 아주 더웠어요.
3. 산에 올라갔어요. 참 추웠어요.
4. 다시 한번 봤어요. 외삼촌이었어요.
5. 누님한테 전화 걸었어요. 받지 않았어요.
6. 양복을 입었어요. 다른 사람 같아요.
7. 은퇴를 했어요. 아주 심심해요.
8. 맥주 한잔 마셨어요. 노래를 부르고 싶어요.
9. 그 여자랑 데이트 했어요. 부모님이 싫어하셨어요.
10. 택시 탔어요. 아저씨가 [i.e. the driver] 영어를 잘 했어요.
11. 좀 피곤해요. 오늘은 나가지 맙시다.
12. 한국은 겨울에 추워요. 봄에 갑시다.
13. 선교사에요. 한국말을 잘 할 거에요.
14. 나이가 많아요. 너무 빨리 걷지 말아요.
15. 내일 눈이 올 거에요. 다음 주일에 합시다.
16. 사장님께 말씀드렸습니다. 걱정하지 마십시오.
17. 장마가 졌습니다. 비가 많이 올 겁니다.
18. 한국사람이에요. 김치를 좋아해요.
19. 커피가 없어요. 홍차로 할까요?
20. 댁에 혼자 계세요. 심심하실 겁니다.
21. 부자동네에 살아요. 돈이 많을 거에요.

Exercise 8: Practice with -고 있어요

Each of the following sentences or exchanges contains a phrase which means *someone does something*. Make each one mean *someone is* [in the process of] *doing something* using the -고 있어요 pattern. Then translate the sentence. For example, the first will be 동생은 넥타이를 매고 있어요. *My brother is putting on/wearing a tie.*

1.   동생은 넥타이를 매요.
2.   A. 뭐 해요?
    B. 냉커피 마셔요.
3.   순희 씨는 째즈 음악을 들어요.
4.   사장님은 손님하고 이야기를 하세요.
5.   A. 아까 그 학생이 뭘 했어요?
    B. 복도에서 기다렸어요.
6.   A. 아직도 시청 근처에 사세요?
    B. 아니오, 인제는 친척 집에서 살아요.
7.   내 노트를 찾아요.
8.   언니하고 오빠는 지금 테니스를 쳐요.
9.   〔디스코에서〕
    A. 언니는 뭘 해요?
    B. 저기서 춤을 추잖아요?
10.   요즘 왜 안경을 안 써요?

Exercise 9: Vocabulary Drill

Say each of the following sentences in Korean five different times, each time inserting one of the expressions listed below in the blank space.

1.   ____한테 편지를 받았습니다.

2.   우리 ____(가/이/께서) 돈을 좀 주셨습니다.

spouse	father
older brother	aunt
nephew	older sister
grandmother	parents
mother-in-law	grandfather

3.   제 친구가 _____ 옆에 앉았습니다. 4. 제 친구는 _____하고 같이 삽니다.

younger brother   parents
older brother   father-in-law
father-in-law   grandchildren
nephew   aunt
spouse   older brother

5.   우리 여동생은 공원에서 ____과/와 산보를 하고 있습니다.

her husband
her father
my daughter
my daughter-in-law
our mother's sister

 # Lesson 14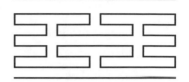

아무래도 동대문 시장이 제일 좋겠지요?

In this lesson we follow Eunice Murphy and Mrs. Kim as they head out for a day's shopping, then observe Chris Murphy at work being introduced to a new Korean business colleague and then greeting a caller at his office. The lesson shows how to introduce friends and order food at a restaurant. It provides a taste of verbal niceties in an office environment. We introduce two new types of future tense, the Korean equivalent of tag questions in English (Isn't that right? Isn't that so?), and more on also, going, and coming.

Korean Dialogues

Dialogue 1

Mrs. Kim (진영이 엄마) has dropped in to see Eunice one morning in December.

유니스	오늘 시내에 가실거에요?
진영이 엄마	네, 오늘 쇼핑 좀 할까 해요.
	같이 가시지 않겠어요?
유니스	네, 좋지요! 그런데, 뭘 사시겠어요?
진영이 엄마	크리스마스까지 시간이 조금 밖에 안 남았으니까, –
	크리스마스 선물 좀 사고 싶어요. 어디가 제일 좋을까요?
	아무래도 동대문 시장이 제일 좋겠지요?
유니스	그렇겠지요. 저도 거기 여러번 갔었어요.
	물건 값이 아주 싸지요?
진영이 엄마	네, 아주 싸요. 자, 슬슬 가볼까요?

As they're on the way out the door

유니스	잠시만요. 화장실에 갔다올께요.
진영이 엄마	빨리 갔다오세요. 엘리베이터 앞에서 기다리고 있을께요.

Downstairs on the street

유니스	자, 갈까요? 지하철을 타고 갈까요? 택시를 타고 갈까요?
진영이 엄마	편히 가고 싶으니까, 택시를 타고 갑시다.
	제가 돈을 내지요.

Notes

아무래도	*most likely; I'd venture to say; probably*
그렇겠지요.	*That is probably the case, That must be the case.* This is the future presumptive -겠- form of 그래요 *it is so*, followed by *don't you think?* -지요.
슬슬 가볼까요?	슬슬 is an adverb meaning something like *in a slow, leisurely fashion.* The entire expression is a useful way to say, *It's time we start moving.*

Dialogue 2

Chris has arranged a dinner meeting with Mr. Kang, who will introduce a new friend.

강	제 친구를 소개하겠습니다. 이 친구는 남주형입니다.
크리스	처음 뵙겠습니다. 크리스 머피입니다.
남	처음 뵙겠습니다. 남주형입니다.
강	자, 앉으시지요.

They sit down

크리스 (to 남)	이 집에 처음 오십니까?
남	아닙니다. 전에도 몇번 왔었습니다.
여종업원	뭐 하시겠어요?
강	(여종업원에게) 잠시만요. (남 씨에게) 뭐 시킬까요?
남	아무거나 좋지만, 저는 갈비로 하지요, 뭐.
크리스	그럼, 나도 갈비 하겠어요.

Lesson Fourteen /269

여종업원 (to 강)	아저씨는요?
강	나는 불고기 하겠어요.
여종업원	네, 알겠습니다. 갈비 이인분하고 불고기 일인분요.
	음료수는요?
크리스 (to others)	술 좀 하시겠어요?
강, 남	좋지요!
크리스	그러면, 우선 맥주 세병만 갖다 주세요.

Dialogue 3

Mr. Nam has come to see Chris at the office.

남 (to Miss Lee)	수고하십니다. 머피 사장님 계십니까?
미스 리	네, 계신데요. 어떻게 오셨어요?
남	네?
미스 리	성함이 어떻게 되시지요?
남	남주형입니다.
미스 리	잠깐만 기다리세요.

Miss Lee ushers Mr. Nam into Chris Murphy's office

크리스	아이구, 반갑습니다. 들어오십시오. 여기 앉으시지요.
	미스 리, 여기 커피 두잔만 갖다 주세요.
남	그동안 어떻게 지내셨어요?
크리스	덕분에 별 일 없습니다.
	자, 그런데 무슨 용무로 오셨어요?

Notes

어떻게 오셨어요?	[Literally: *How have you come?*] *What brings you here?*
계신데요	*He is in.* The -ㄴ데요 here is softer and politer than just 계십니다 or 계세요, but you will learn the ending formally at a later stage.
그동안	*in the meantime; during the interval* [that we weren't in touch]

덕분에	*Thanks to* [you]. You can also say *so-and-so* 덕분에: *Thanks to so-and-so.*
별 일 없습니다.	[Literally: There are no particular matters (to report)]. Also: 별 일 없으세요? *Are you getting along well?* or 별 일 없으셨어요? *Have you been getting along well?*

Vocabulary

Verbal Expressions

돈(이) 드-르-	cost money [Literally: money enters]
이건 돈이 많이 들었어요.	This cost a lot of money.
빗-	comb
머리를 빗어요.	I comb my hair.
(돈을) 내-	pay
제가 낼께요.	I'll pay.
아프-	hurt, be painful
예쁘-	be pretty, cute
드-르-	lift; hold
이것 잠깐 들고 있을래요?	Would you mind holding this for a moment?
죽-	die
돌아가시-	die , pass away (honorific)
다치-	be wounded, get hurt, get injured
머리를 다쳤어요.	He injured his head.
타고가-	go (riding something)
타고오-	come (riding something)
푸-르-	solve it; undo it
초대(를) 하-	invite someone
초대(를) 받-	be/get invited
소개(를) 하-	introduce someone/something
소개(를) 받-	be/get introduced (to someone)
만호 씨한테서 수진 씨를 소개 받았어요.	I was introduced to Sujin by Manho.
갖다주-	bring it, fetch it
누w-	lie down
취하-	get drunk
취했어요.	I'm drunk.

지내-	get along (e.g., How are you getting along?)
요즘 어떻게 지내십니까?	How are you doing these days?
끊-	hang up (the telephone); quit (smoking/drinking)
끊어요.	Good-bye. (on the telephone) [Literally: 'I'm hanging up now.]
담배를 끊었어요.	I've quit smoking.
개학(을) 하-	start term/school
어제 개학했어요.	We started the new term yesterday.
개학은 언제에요?	When is the beginning of term?
편하-	be comfortable; be convenient
불편하-	be uncomfortable; be inconvenient
갈아입-	change (clothes)
바꾸-	change; exchange
수업시간을 바꿨어요.	We changed our class time.
이 양말을 다른 걸로 바꿔 주세요.	Please exchange these socks for a different pair.

Adverbs

물론	of course
물론이에요.	[It is a matter] of course.
굉장히	very, very much
그저께	day before yesterday
모레	day after tomorrow
내일모레	day after tomorrow (same)
우선	first of all, before everything, before anything else
우선 선생님께 연락 드립시다.	Let's contact the teacher first.
편히	comfortably, in comfort
편히 앉으세요.	Please make [seat] yourself comfortable.
잠시	a short while
잠시만 기다리세요.	[Please wait] Just a moment.
제일	the most; the first, number one
수영이 건강에 제일이에요.	Swimming is the best thing for your health.
지하철이 제일 빨라요.	The subway is fastest.
가장	the most
이 집 반찬이 가장 맛이 있어요.	This place [restaurant] has the tastiest side dishes.

Nouns

| 반찬 | side dishes to go with rice |

엘리베이터	elevator, lift
시내	downtown, city center
용무	business, a matter to be taken care of
무슨 용무로 오셨어요?	What business brings you here?
자료	material(s) [of a written nature], data
-인분	[-many] portions, servings [used in ordering at restaurants]
몇인분 드릴까요?	How many portions would you like?
삼인분	three portions [this word takes Sino-Korean numerals]
음료수	a beverage, something to drink
계산서	the bill, the check (in a restaurant)
계산서 좀 갖다 주세요.	Please bring me the check.
정류장	bus stop
다음 정류장에서 내리세요?	Are you getting off at the next stop?
정거장	(train) station/stop
시험	examination
시험(을) 보-	take an exam
선물	present, gift
기분	feelings, mood
기분이 좋아요.	I'm in a good mood.
기분이 나빠요.	I'm in a bad mood.
쇼핑	shopping
학기	term, semester
문제	problem
졸업반	graduating class

Some Body Parts

머리	head; hair
머리(가) 좋아요.	She is bright/intelligent.
머리(가) 예뻐요.	She has pretty hair.
팔	arm
다리	leg
손	hand
손가락 〔-까락〕	finger
눈	eye
코	nose

발	foot
발가락 〔-까락〕	toe
무릎	knee
등	upper back; spine
허리	lower back, waist
귀	ear

Lesson Notes

14.1. Ways to Say *only*: 만 plus AFFIRMATIVE, 밖에 plus NEGATIVE

Observe the following sentences.

1.   돈 만원만 주세요.
    Let me have [just, exactly] *10,000 wŏn, please.*

2.   이천오백원 밖에는 안 들어요.
    It will only cost 2500 wŏn.

The particle 만 plus an affirmative verb means *only, just, to the extent of.* The quasi-particle 밖에 (derived from the place noun 밖 *outside* plus the particle 에) plus a negative verb arrives at the same meaning by a more circuitous route. Here is another example.

3.   만원 밖에 없어요.
    I have only ten thousand wŏn.
    [Literally: Except for or outside of ten thousand won, I haven't (anything) or
    I haven't (anything) but ten thousand wŏn.]

The pattern in 밖에 plus negative implies that the amount in question is less than, or not quite up to, one's expectations. Thus, in (3) above, the implication is that the speaker had rather hoped or expected to have more than 10,000 wŏn. Here are some more examples of the 밖에 plus negative pattern.

4.   나는 아이 한명 밖에 없습니다.
    I have only one child.

5.   연필 밖에 없습니다.
    I have nothing but a pencil. All I have is a pencil.

6. 어제 밤 극장에 저 밖에 가지 않았어요.
   I was the only one who went to the movies last night.

7. 고기 밖에 못 먹었어요.
   I could only eat meat.

8. 만원 밖에 들지 않았습니다.
   It only cost 10,000 wŏn.

Remember that with numerical expressions 만 *only* or *just* has no English equivalent. It means *no more*, *no less* or *exactly* [the number specified].

9. 만원만 주실래요?
   Would you mind giving me 10,000 wŏn?

14.2. Another Use of (이)나 *as many as*

Observe the following examples.

10. 일찍 떠났지만, 그래도 사십분이나 늦었습니다.
    He departed early, but nonetheless he was (as much as) 40 minutes late.

11. 어제 파티에 백명이나 왔어요.
    (As many as) a hundred people came to the party yesterday.

In sentences like the above, the particle (이)나 attached to a number or numeral expression implies that the speaker believes the amount to be a high one, or at least, he or she finds that amount higher than expected. Thus, in number (10) above, the speaker is implying that he or she thinks being late by 40 minutes is quite a lot. Likewise, in sentence (11), the speaker implies that, for her, three letters is a lot. Here are some more examples.

12. 어제는 열시간이나 잤어요.
    Yesterday I slept for (as much as) ten hours.

13. 사장님은 하루에 커피를 열 잔이나 드세요.
    The boss drinks (as many as) ten cups of coffee a day.

14. 맥주를 열병이나 마셨어요.
    I drank (as many as) ten bottles of beer.

15. 두시간이나 늦게 도착했습니다.
    I arrived (as many as) two hours late.

14.3. Expressions for *Going* and *Coming*

Observe the following examples.

16. 지하철로 가요
     goes by subway, goes on a subway

17. 기차로 왔어요
     came by train, came on the train

18. 택시로 학교에 가요
     goes by taxi to school

The particle (으)로 *with, by (means of)* is used with vehicles when the verb is 가요 *goes* or 와요 *comes*. On the other hand, the verb 타요 *gets on* (a vehicle, a horse), *rides*, takes a direct object.

19. 기차를 타요
     rides [on] a train

20. 기차를 타고오지 않아요
     doesn't come (riding) [on] the train

주의!

The pattern for these constructions with 타- is:

[destination] plus vehicle을 ~ 를 타고 plus [destination] plus *go/come*

That is, the destination can come either before or after the vehicle plus (을 ~ 를) plus 타고. For example:

21. 택시를 타고 학교에 가요
     rides/takes a taxi to school

22. 쇼핑하러 지하철을 타고 갔습니다
     rode the subway to go shopping

The ㄷ ~ ㄹ verb 걸어요 (걷다) *walks* resembles 타요 *rides* in that it is not used alone in sentences implying purposeful direction. It, too, joins in phrases with 가요 *goes* or 와요 *comes,* but in its infinitive (걸어) form.

23.   걸어 갔어요
      went walking, walked (there)

24.   걸어 오지 않아요
      doesn't come walking, doesn't walk (here)

14.4. Verbs: Future-Presumptives in -겠-

14.4.1. How to Attach -겠-

This lesson contains a number of verbs in the FUTURE-PRESUMPTIVE form (called future for short, but see the explanations below). The marker for the future is -겠-. It is a one-shape ending. Here are some examples showing how this form attaches to bases.

Base	Gloss	Future Base
가-	*go*	가겠-
기다리-	*wait*	기다리겠-
주-	*give*	주겠-
보-	*see*	보겠-
드-ㄹ-	*lift; cost*	들겠-
쓰-	*write; use*	쓰겠-
부르-	*call*	부르겠-
입-	*wear*	입겠-
받-	*get*	받겠-
찾-	*look for; find*	찾겠-
빗-	*comb*	빗겠-
있-	*stay, have*	있겠-
먹-	*eat*	먹겠-
닦-	*polish*	닦겠-
없-	*be lacking*	없겠-
읽-	*read*	읽겠-
젊-	*be young*	젊겠-
신-	*wear (shoes)*	신겠-
앉-	*sit down*	앉겠-
많-	*be much/many*	많겠-
좋-	*be good*	좋겠-
누w- (ㅂ ~ w: 눕다)	*lie down*	눕겠-
들- (ㄷ ~ ㄹ: 듣다)	*hear*	듣겠-

To make honorific future forms, you simply add -겠- to the honorific base.

가-	*go*	→	가시-	→	가시겠-
받-	*get*	→	받으시-	→	받으시겠-

A future base, like any base, is not a complete word by itself: it needs an ending. To make it Polite Style, you add -어요.

가-	*go*	→	가(시)겠어요	*will go*
받-	*get*	→	받(으시)겠어요	*will get*

For long negatives in the future, you use a plain -지 form and make the auxiliary 않- future.

가-	*go*	→	가지 않겠어요	*won't go*
받-	*get*	→	받지 않겠어요	*won't get*

As usual, the -지 form merely says what action is performed, while the negative word 않- carries the other meanings of the phrase. Also, as usual, either word (or both) may be honorific if the phrase refers to someone esteemed.

가-	*go*	가지	않으시겠어요
		가시지	않겠어요
		가시지	않으시겠어요

14.4.2. Meaning and Usage of -겠-

Although most textbooks of Korean refer to the -겠- form as a future, when it comes to meaning, the -겠- form has a variety of corresponding English expressions, none of which really corresponds fully to an English future.

The meanings of -겠- can be grouped into two: Inferential *I'll bet* and Intentional *I shall*.

a.   Inferential -겠-: *I'll bet*

Inferential -겠- usually occurs with verbs in the second- and third-person (*you, he, she, it, they*). The verb marked with -겠- carries the following sorts of connotations: *I'll bet that, I would wager that, I have good reasons to infer that, Judging by my evidence, it is highly likely that.*

25.   내일은 덥겠어요.
      Tomorrow will likely be hot. [I know, because I always get a funny twitch in my elbow the day before it turns hot.]

26.   오후에 비가 오겠습니다.
      It is going to rain in the afternoon. [I've just seen the weather map.]

27.   그 영화는 재미 있겠어요.
      I'll bet that film is probably interesting. [I saw lots of people standing in line for it downtown the other day.]

28.   아프겠어요.
      Ooh, that must hurt. [you have just seen somebody trip and fall prostrate onto the pavement]

29.   어제 기분이 굉장히 좋으셨겠습니다.
      You must have been in a super mood yesterday. [since you just heard that your son was accepted at Seoul National University]

30.   부산에 벌써 도착했겠어요.
      She must already have arrived in Pusan. [I know, because her train was due to arrive there at 5:30 PM, and it is now past 6:00 P.M.]

b.   Intentional -겠-: *I have a firm intention to; Do you intend to?*

Intentional -겠- usually occurs in first-person statements and second-person questions. In statements, it has the effect of a strong declaration of intent, and often has a somewhat ceremonial touch, as if one were making a solemn pronouncement. In questions, it is a polite way of getting somebody to do something.

31.   인제 시험을 시작하겠습니다.
      I'm going to start the exam now. [teacher standing in front of the examination hall]

32.   다방 앞에서 기다리겠습니다.
      I'll wait for you in front the of the tabang.

33.   내일 모레 다시 오겠습니다.
      I'll come again the day after tomorrow.

34. 그러면, 제가 하겠습니다.
   In that case, I shall do it.

35. A. 뭘 드시겠습니까?
   Would you like something to drink?

   B. 네, 커피 한잔 주십시오.
   Yes, a cup of coffee, please.

36. A. 여기 앉으시겠어요?
   Why don't you sit here?

   B. 예, 감사합니다.
   Yes, thank you.

37. 내일 다시 찾아오겠습니다.
   I'll come again tomorrow.

Here are some more examples with verbs in -겠-.

38. 편지는 쓰겠지만, 전화는 안 하겠어요.
   I'll write a letter, but I won't telephone.

39. 이 책이 서점에 아직도 있겠지요?
   This book is still probably at the bookshop, right?

40. 일은 하겠지만, 돈은 안 받겠어요.
   I'll do the job, but I won't accept [Literally: receive] any money (for it).

41. 이 자료를 김 선생님께 드리겠어요?
   Will you give (would you mind giving) these materials to Mr. Kim?

42. 사장님은 지금쯤 비행기를 타셨겠어요.
   The company president must be on the plane by now.

43. 어머니도 가끔 영화구경을 가고 싶으시겠어요.
   I imagine Mother must sometimes want to go see movies too.

44. 밖이 춥겠어요.
   It must be cold outside.

45. 내일 동대문 시장에 같이 가지 않겠습니까?
   How about going to Tongdaemun Market tomorrow?

46. 우리 집에 놀러 오지 않으시겠습니까?
   How about coming round to our place to visit?

14.5. Verbs: Past-Future and Past-Past.

As you have just seen, there is a PAST-FUTURE verb form which is made by attaching the future marker –겠– to the past base of any verb (either the plain past base or the honorific past base) like this.

Base	Gloss	Past Base	Past-Future Base
가–	*go*	갔–	갔겠–
가시–		가셨–	가셨겠–
받–	*get*	받았–	받았겠–
받으시–		받으셨–	받으셨겠–

Here are some examples in full sentences.

47. 아마 벌써 했겠어요.
     They have probably (will have) already done it.

48. 돈이 많이 들었겠어요.
     It must have cost a lot.

49. 머리가 굉장히 아팠겠어요.
     You must have had a really bad headache.

The past marker gives to the form the same meaning as the English auxiliary verb *has* or *have*, while the future marker gives it the meaning of *probably*.

When you are listening to Korean, your only clue to the difference between a future verb form and a past-future verb form is very small. Sometimes only the difference between ㄱ and ㄲ.

가겠어요	〔가게써요〕	*will go*
갔겠어요	〔갇께써요 → 가께써요〕	*will have gone, must have gone*

Another problem in fine distinctions comes in past-past verb forms, which are made by attaching the past tense marker –었– to the past base of any verb, either honorific or plain, forming in effect a double past base.

	Plain Base	Past Base	Past-Past Base
do	하–	했–	했었–
	하시–	하셨–	하셨었–

The form is made complete by adding an appropriate ending. The past-past, then, is distinguished from the past by being longer.

Past	했어요	*did*
Past-past	했었어요	*did (earlier)*

Before a one-shape ending, this is a little more difficult to detect.

Past	했지만	*did, but*	〔해찌만〕
Past-past	했었지만	*did (earlier), but*	〔해써찌만〕

Here are some examples of the past-past.

50.　나는 경제학을 공부했었어요. 그런데 정치학으로 바꿨어요.
　　　I used to study Economics, but I changed to Political Science.

51.　A. 어디 갔었어요?
　　　　Where have you been?

　　　B. 친구를 만나러 시내에 갔었어요.
　　　　I went downtown to meet a friend.

52.　나도 거기 한 번 갔었어요.
　　　I've been there once, too.

53.　그 분이 우리 학교에 한 번 오셨었어요.
　　　He came to our school once.

These forms do not correspond to any single English word. In general, they mean about the same thing as regular past-tense forms, except that they have the feeling of a more definitely completed action or a comparatively *remote* past action.

There is one area of meaning where a real difference exists: if an action has come full circle, you use the past-past. For a similar action which has not yet come full circle, you use the plain past. This distinction is common in verbs meaning *come* and *go* and is illustrated by the sentences just above. Compare these sentences.

54.　만호 씨는 서울에 왔어요.
　　　Manho came to Seoul [and is still here].

55.　만호 씨는 서울에 한 번 왔었어요.
　　　Manho came to Seoul once [but is no longer here].

Come and *go* in the past-past may be literally translated as *come and return* and *go and come back*, respectively. In the past they mean *(came and) is here* and *(went and) is gone*, respectively.

14.6. Immediate Futures in -(으)ㄹ께요

The dialogue in this lesson illustrates the next pattern.

유니스   잠시만요. 화장실에 갔다올께요.
                    Do you mind waiting a minute? I'll just pop into the bathroom.

진영이 엄마   그래요. 에레베이터 앞에서 기다리고 있을께요.
                    Sure. I'll be waiting in front of the elevator.

The IMMEDIATE FUTURE in -(으)ㄹ께요 attaches to processive plain bases only, is almost always first-person (I or we), and conveys to the hearer a reassuring, usually beneficial, and promise-like future which is immediate in the sense that the action to be performed is within the direct control of the speaker who has every intention of seeing that the action is carried through.

The -(으)ㄹ of this ending is the same prospective modifier which goes into suggestions in -(으)ㄹ까요 and the probable future in -(으)ㄹ거에요. You will learn more about it in the sequel volume to this course.

56.   A: (Struggling with a heavy bag)
        B: 내가 들고 있을께요.
           Let me hold it for you. or *Here, I'll hold it for you.*

57.   A (on the phone): 오늘 올래요?
           Would you like to come over today?

        B: 내일 갈께요.
           I'll come [go] tomorrow.

58.   A: 이 숙제를 모레까지 마치세요.
           Please finish this homework by the day after tomorrow.

        B: 네, 할께요.
           Sure, I will.

14.7. Synopsis: Types of Bases and Types of Future

14.7.1. Types of Base

Now you have learned all three verbal base forms in Korean: plain, past and future-presumptive.

Base Type	Processive	Descriptive
Plain	찾-	높-
Honorific	찾으시-	높으시-
Past	찾았-	높았-
Honorific	찾으셨-	높으셨-
Future	찾겠-	높겠-
Honorific	찾으시겠-	높으시겠-

Sometimes it is convenient to speak of honorific bases, but really the honorific marker -(으)시- is just an extension of the plain base, which can then be further converted to past or future. Whenever you learn a new ending or pattern, you need to learn which bases the ending is compatible with [see section 14.8 for a recap of how -겠- works with the various endings you already know].

14.7.2. Types of Future

Now you have learned several different kinds of future verb form in Korean. None of them corresponds exactly to a future as we might conceive of it English, and each has different nuances.

PROBABLE FUTURE	-(으)ㄹ거에요
	-(으)ㄹ겁니다

The probable future is the most common way to refer to future events in Korean. It can be used in all persons with both processive and descriptive verbs.

On a plain base, it means *(probably) will do / happen / be*. On past bases it means *must have done / been / happened*. For example:

59.　철민 씨가 벌써 왔을거에요.
　　　Ch'ŏlmin must have arrived already.

This usage is equivalent to, but increasingly more common than, the past-future 왔겠어요.

IMMEDIATE FUTURE　　　　　　-(으)ㄹ께요

The immediate future is used only on plain processive bases. It is always first person (I, we), and the action referred to is usually beneficial to the hearer.

60.　점심은 내가 낼께요.
　　　Let me pay for lunch or Why don't I pay for lunch.

FUTURE-PRESUMPTIVE BASE　　　-겠-

Although is is often called a future in most textbooks, the future-presumptive is more of:

a) a matter-of-fact statement of personal intention in first-person declaratives and second-
　　　person questions
b) a supposition in third-person sentences.

Here are some example sentences.

61.　A. 내일 오시겠습니까?
　　　　Will you (do you intend to) come tomorrow?

　　　B. 네, 내일 가겠습니다.
　　　　Yes, I will (do).

62.　A. 그 책이 도서관에 있을까요?
　　　　Do you suppose that book will be in the library?

　　　B. 있겠지요.
　　　　Sure (I'll bet it would be).

63.　(a little child falls on his face on the pavement)
　　　야, 아프겠다!
　　　Ooh, that must hurt! [ignore the 다 for now; you will learn it in the sequel volume]

On past bases, the future-presumptive –겠–has only the meaning of supposition (*must have; I'll bet that*).

64. 아마 기차로 갔겠지요.
I'll bet he must have gone by train.

In order to understand the various Korean futures fully, it may be helpful to have a careful look at the meanings of certain English words used for future-like purposes.

a.   *Will, is going to*
Simple future action is expressed in English by *will* and *is going to*. These have slightly different connotations, but both are covered by the Korean futures.

읽겠어요   *I will read, am going to read*
(strong statement of intention)

읽을거에요   *will read, am/is going to read*
(probable future; less certain than 읽겠어요)

읽을께요   *I'll read it, I promise*
(more immediate, with a hint of promise, assurance, or even reassurance)

b.   *Would*
Korean often prefers to construe verbs of knowing in the future-presumptive: one often hears 알겠어요 *I know* or *I understand* where one would expect 알아요; 모르 겠어요 *I wouldn't know* or *I don't understand* where one would expect 몰라요. The present forms are also used, but the –겠– form has a suggestion of tentativeness (English *I wouldn't know*) and perhaps for that reason it seems more polite, especially in second-person questions: 아시겠어요 *Do you know?* or *Do you understand?* (English *Would you happen to know?*)

c.   *Is willing to, wants to*
In both English and Korean, a future verb form may mean *will* in the sense *is willing to* or *wants to* [do so-and-so]. In this sense, one usually uses –겠–.

65. 산보하시겠어요?
Would you like to take a walk?
or *Are you willing to take a walk?* or *Will you take a walk?* or *Are you going to take a walk?*

Sometimes a verb in this form is made negative, and the result is a polite suggestion. We had an example of this in Dialogue One of this lesson.

66. 같이 가시지 않겠어요?
Wouldn't you like to go with me?

You cannot make questions or suggestions like this with immediate futures in -(으)ㄹ께요, or probable futures in -(을)거에요. Thus, the probable future form of sentences (65) and (66) above is just a matter-of-fact question.

67. 산보하실거에요?
     Are you going to take a walk?

68. 같이 가지 않으실거에요?
     You're not going to go with us?

d.   *Probably, must* (Conjecture)

      The words *probably* and *must* are alike in adding the same flavor to English sentences in a certain usage. In this connection, it is necessary first to distinguish between the two kinds of English *must*. One *must* expresses obligation:

           I simply must get my work finished.

      This obligational *must* is expressed by the Korean construction -어야 해요, a pattern introduced in the sequel volume to this course.

      The other *must* expresses probability or likelihood.

           That girl with Bill must be his fiancée.
           It's raining—it must be getting cooler.

      It is this probability kind of *must* which is sometimes conveyed by both the Korean -겠- and -(으)ㄹ거에요 forms. [In British English, the future is sometimes used in this Korean way.] In sentences with a future form, there often appears the adverb 아마 or 아마도, which means *probably* or *likely* and strengthens the connotation of the future verb form.

14.7.3. A Reminder about First-, Second- and Third-Person with -겠-

In first-person statements, the meaning will most frequently be on the lines of uses (a) *will, is going to* and (b) *would* above. In second-person questions, the meaning will usually be along the lines of (b) *would* or (c) *is willing, wants to*. However, when the sentence is in the third-person, the meaning will more commonly correspond to usage (d) *probably, must*. This is because Korean does not readily allow its speakers to express the intentions of others with any certainty. When speakers want to refer to what others will do, they are more likely to use the probable future with -(으)ㄹ거에요. The difference is that -겠어요 expresses a definite future intention or a probable/likely present, while -(으)ㄹ거에요 represents a greater degree of uncertainty.

14.8. Suppositives in –지요

This lesson offers a number of sentences ending in –지요. The one-shape SUPPOSITIVE ending –지 carries the basic meaning *supposedly* and can attach to any base: plain 하지요, past 했지요, future-presumptive 하겠지요. Notice how it combines with probable futures in –(으)ㄹ거에요: 할거지요.

Suppositive verb forms in –지요 correspond to a number of English meanings, depending on whether they occur in statements, yes-no questions, question-word questions, or suggestions and imperatives.

In statements, the basic meaning of –지요 is *I suppose*. In this usage, the –지 is particularly compatible with –겠–. In a particularly emphatic or assertive intonation (e.g., in response to a dumb question), –지요 means something like *Of course!* or *You bet!*

69.　　아마 언니가 하겠지요.
　　　I suppose my big sister will probably do it.

70.　　A. 그 사람이 한국사람이에요?
　　　　Is that person Korean?

　　　B. 물론이지요!
　　　　Of course she is!

71.　　교수님이 주무시겠지요.
　　　I suppose Professor is sleeping.

In yes-no questions (with the rising intonation of English yes-or-no questions, such as *Is it raining?* or *Are you coming with me?*), –지요 makes tag–questions with the effect of *Isn't that right? Isn't that so? Right? N'est-ce pas? Nicht wahr? Eh?*

72.　　미국서 돌아오셨지요?
　　　She came back from America, didn't she?

73.　　값이 비싸지요?
　　　I suppose the price is expensive? or *It's pricey, isn't it?*

74.　　꽃을 좋아하시지요?
　　　I imagine you like flowers, don't you?

75. 김 선생님 부인이시지요? (on the telephone)
It's Mrs. Kim, isn't it?

76. 갔지요?
He's gone, hasn't he?

In question-word questions, –지요 carries the nuance of *I wonder* or *What, where, why—did you say it is/was?*

77. 이것은 얼마지요?
How much is this (I wonder)? or *How much did you say this was?* or
How much is this again?

78. 내 안경 어디 갔지요?
Now where have my glasses gone (I wonder)?

Korean suppositives in –지요 can also convey mild or casual suggestions or commands with the force of *how about?* or *Why don't you?* In the command usage, the –지요 is often accompanied by the honorific, giving –(으)시지요.

79. 인제 라디오를 좀 듣지요.
How about [us] *listening to the radio now?*

80. 자, 드시지요.
Well then, [why don't you] *drink up.*

81. 여기 앉으시지요.
Please sit here!

82. 제가 (돈을) 내지요!
I'll pay! or *Why don't I pay?* or *Let me pay!*

주의!

You usually do not answer questions about yourself with –지요; instead, use the regular Polite Style. In pronouncing the ending –지요, be careful not to pronounce it too slowly; these two short syllables are often run together as –죠.

14.9. Synopsis: Compatibility of -겠- with Endings Previously Learned

The ending –겠– can combine with the following endings from previous lessons.

Ending	Ending with -겠-	Example with 하-
-(으)시-	-으시겠-	하시겠어요
-(스)ㅂ니다	-겠습니다	하겠습니다
-(스)ㅂ니까?	-겠습니까?	하겠습니까?
-지만	-겠지만	하겠지만
-잖아요	-겠잖아요	하겠잖아요
-(으)니까	-겠으니까	하겠으니까
-지요	-겠지요	하겠지요

Exercises

Exercise 1: Future-Presumptives in -겠-

Each of the following sentences means *I/you do something*. Make each one mean *I will do something* or *will you do something?* Then translate the sentence. For example, the first will be 나는 우체국까지 가겠어요 *I will go to the post office*.

1. 나는 우체국까지 가요.
2. 나는 서울대학교에서 공부해요.
3. 선생님은 무엇을 하세요?
4. 내일까지 집에 돌아와요.
5. 지하철을 타고 시내에 가요.
6. 나는 한국에서 영어를 가르쳐요.
7. 점심 값을 내가 내요.
8. 김 선생님이 자동차를 파세요?
9. 다방 앞에서 기다려요.
10. 나는 이번 가을에 일본에 가요.

Exercise 2: Suppositives in -지요

Each of the following sentences is in the polite style in -어요. Change each one to the suppositive -지요. Then translate the sentence. For example, the first will be 선생님이 매일 술값을 내지요 *Our teacher pays for drinks every day, you know.*

1. 선생님이 매일 술값을 내요.
2. 복동 씨의 할아버님은 연세가 많으세요?
3. 할머님은 벌써 삼년 전에 돌아가셨어요.
4. 언니는 우리와 같이 살지 않아요.
5. 일본에 돌아가고 싶어요?
6. 그 사람은 지금 쉬고 있겠어요.
7. 동생 옷이 예뻐요.
8. 조금 더 걸어가요.
9. 그 사람을 매일 만나요.
10. 화장실에 내 우산이 없었어요?
11. 머리가 아파요?

Exercise 3: English to Korean Translation

Put the following sentences into Korean (you need not translate literally).

1. A. You like concerts, don't you?
    B. Yes; I don't like films, but I like concerts.
2. A. Then how about going to a concert with me tonight?
    B. Fine.
3. A. I wonder what time it is.
    B. I don't know.
4. The weather is nice today, isn't it? Suppose we take a walk in the park.
5. A. How did you learn that song?
    B. I heard it on the radio.
6. It snowed a lot last night, didn't it?
7. A. Did you buy that CD at the bookshop?
    B. No! They don't sell CDs at the bookshop!
8. A. Will the train arrive by three o'clock, I wonder?
    B. Of course it will!
9. I guess he's probably watching TV, right?
10. I have [as many as] four brothers (two ways).

11.   Mr. Kim appeared [Literally: came out] on the TV, didn't he?

12.   Didn't you live in Seoul last year?

13.   I'll come by car [immediate future].

14.   A. I'll bet it will cost about $15.

         B. It costs (as much as) $15?

15.   He has probably already written the letter, don't you think?

16.   He went to Korea (and is still there).

17.   That old man (grandfather) must already have passed away, don't you think?

18.   I'll wait here for you a moment [immediate future].

19.   We came up in the elevator.

20.   Shall we meet at Great East Gate?

21.   A. Did you have any money in your bag?

         B. Yes, but all I have is 20,000 won.

22.   The day before yesterday I did lots of work, but I wasn't paid [Literally: couldn't get any money].

Exercise 4: Practice with -겠지요

Each of the following sentences means *someone does/is something*. Make each one mean *(I'll bet) someone probably does/is something*. Then translate the sentence. For example, the first will be 장 선생님은 공부하고 계시겠지요. *Mr. Chang is probably/must be studying.*

1.   장 선생님은 공부하고 계세요.
2.   밖이 추워요.
3.   오빠가 기분이 좋아요.
4.   학생들이 일찍 학교에 와요.
5.   그 아이가 어려요.
6.   부모님들이 젊으세요.
7.   그 상점은 굉장히 비싸요.
8.   영화관은 너무 멀어요.
9.   시험이 어려워요.
10.   선생님의 약혼자는 꽃을 좋아하세요.
11.   선생님의 따님이 예뻐요.
12.   내일 아침부터 눈이 와요.

Exercise 5: *only*

Change the following Korean 만 sentences to the pattern with 밖에 plus negative.

1. 저희 학교에는 여자는 많지만, 남자는 한 명만 있어요.
2. 지금은 방학이에요. 학교에는 학생 몇 명만 있어요.
3. 어제 두 사람만 왔습니다.
4. 맥주 몇 병 사셨어요?
   한 병만 샀어요.
5. 돈 얼마나 있으세요?
   조금만 있어요.
6. 어제 밤에는 네 시간만 잤어요. 그래서 굉장히 피곤하지요.
7. 지난 달에는 영화구경을 두 번만 갔어요.
8. 크리스마스에는 선물을 많이 받으셨어요?
   아니오, 몇 개만 받았어요.
9. 이건 빨리 합시다. 시간이 조금만 있어요.
10. 한국말을 잘 하세요?
    아니오, 한 학기만 배웠어요.

Exercise 6: Korean-to-English Translation

Put the following sentences into English (you need not translate literally).

1. A. 진호 씨, 담배 안 피워요?
   B. 전에는 피웠었지만, 끊었어요.
2. A. 지난 파티에 누구누구 왔었지요?
   B. 우리 기숙사 친구들이랑 교회 친구들도 왔었어요.
3. A. 수진 씨는 요즘 수영을 배우러 수영장에 다녀요.
   B. 그래요? 나도 전에 거기에 다녔었어요.
4. A. 에릭 씨는 한국말 잘 하지요?
   B. 네. 일년 전에는 하나도 못 했었지만, 이젠 아주 잘 해요.
5. A. 진호 씨 요즘도 그 여자와 데이트하세요?
   B. 아니오, 한 달 전까지는 자주 만났었지만, 인제는 다른 여자하고 데이트를 하고 있어요.
6. A. 날씨가 덥지요?
   B. 네, 정말 더워요.
7. A. 불고기를 좋아하시지요?
   B. 네, 몇 인분 시킬까요?

8.   A. 이 구두가 나한테 너무 커요.

        B. 그럼 나한테 주세요. 내가 신을께요.

9.   A. 양복으로 갈아입을거지요?

        B. 네. 빨리 갈아입을께요.

10.   A. 인제 술 끊을거지요?

        B. 네. 담배도 끊을께요.

Lesson 15

REVIEW 2

Review of Lesson Notes

15.1. Verb Forms: Summary.

Any Korean verb form used in a Korean sentence has two parts to it: a base and an ending. A base is not complete, ready for use, until it is finished off with an ending. Obviously, an ending must be attached to something before it can be put into a sentence (just as you don't use the English endings *ing* or *ed* in midair). In summarizing verb forms, then, it is convenient to split the discussion into the two large categories: bases and endings.

15.1.1. Verb Bases

Each verb has a simple base that is the source of all its changes. Some simple bases end with vowels, others with consonants. Some of the vowel-base verbs are L-extending: they add an – ㄹ – before certain markers and endings. A few of the vowel-base verbs end in –르– which changes to –ㄹㄹ– before adding the infinitive ending –어～-아. The infinitive of a verb is its base plus an infinitive ending. The infinitive ending has so many shapes, however, that it is perhaps harder to learn rules for adding the ending than it is to memorize the form for each verb.

Here is a comprehensive list of all the verb bases that have appeared so far in these lessons, classified according to type (vowel base, consonant base). Alternative, nonstandard, but nonetheless frequently heard pronunciations for certain infinitive forms are recorded in square brackets next to the standard infinitive. Subsequent lists in this section are representative of the following complete list in that they contain a base of each type to act as a pattern for all the others of that type.

BASE	GLOSS	INFINITIVE
Vowel-base verbs		
가-	*go*	가
갔다오-	*go* [and come back]	갔다와
갖다주-	*bring*	갖다줘
걸리-	*take* [time]; *catch* [cold]	걸려
가르치-	*teach*	가르쳐
걸어가-	*go on foot*	걸어가
걸어오-	*come on foot*	걸어와
기다리-	*wait for*	기다려
끝나-	*end*	끝나
끝내-	*finish it*	끝내
끼-	*put on* [gloves]; *wear* [lenses]	껴
나가-	*go out; attend* [church]	나가
나쁘-	*be bad*	나빠 〔나뻐〕
나오-	*come out*	나와
내-	*pay*	내
내려가-	*go down*	내려가
내려오-	*come down*	내려와
내리-	*descend; get off*	내려
다니-	*attend, go on a regular basis*	다녀
다치-	*get hurt, injure oneself*	다쳐
돌아가-	*go back, return*	돌아가
돌아가시-	*die (honorific)*	돌아가셔
도와주-	*help*	도와줘
되-	*become; be OK*	되어 ~ 돼
드리-	*give* [to someone esteemed]	드려
드시-	*eat, drink (honorific)*	드셔
들어가-	*go in, enter*	들어가
들어오-	*come in, enter*	들어와
떠나-	*leave, depart*	떠나
마시-	*drink*	마셔
마치-	*finish* [it]	마쳐

BASE	GLOSS	INFINITIVE
만나–	*meet*	만나
매–	*tie; wear a tie*	매
바쁘–	*be busy*	바빠 〔바뻐〕
배우–	*learn*	배워
버리–	*throw away*	버려
보–	*look at, see*	봐
보내–	*spend (time); send*	보내
부치–	*send*	부쳐
비싸–	*be expensive*	비싸
사–	*buy*	사
서–	*stand*	서
쉬–	*rest*	쉬어
시키–	*order*	시켜
싸–	*be inexpensive*	싸
쏟아지–	*pour* [rain]	쏟아져
쓰–	*write; wear* [on head]; *use*	써
아프–	*it hurts*	아파 〔아퍼〕
어리–	*be young*	어려
예쁘–	*be cute, lovable*	예뻐
오–	*come*	와
올라가–	*go up*	올라가
올라오–	*come up*	올라와
–이–	*be* [copula]	–이어 ~ 여
일어나–	*get up*	일어나
자–	*go to bed; sleep*	자
잡수시–	*eat*	잡수셔
주–	*give*	줘
주무시–	*sleep (honorific)*	주무셔
추–	*dance*	춰
치–	*beat, strike; play* [golf]	쳐
크–	*be large*	커
타–	*ride; put in* [e.g., sugar]	타
타고가–	*go* [riding in]	타고가
타고오–	*come* [riding in]	타고와
태어나–	*be born*	태어나

BASE	GLOSS	INFINITIVE
피-	*bloom, blossom*	펴
피우-	*smoke*	피워
하-	*do*	해

L-doubling vowel-base verbs

다르-	*be different*	달라 〔달러〕
모르-	*don't know or understand*	몰라
부르-	*sing (a song); be full*	불러
빠르-	*be fast*	빨라 〔빨러〕
오르-	*rise, ascend, go up*	올라

L-extending vowel-base verbs

거-ㄹ-	*make* [a phonecall]	걸어
노-ㄹ-	*have fun, play*	놀아
드-ㄹ-	*cost (money); lift, hold*	들어
머-ㄹ-	*be far, distant*	멀어
무-ㄹ-	*bite*	물어
사-ㄹ-	*live*	살아 〔살어〕
아-ㄹ-	*know, understand*	알아 〔알어〕
여-ㄹ-	*open it*	열어
〔-지〕 마-ㄹ-	*avoid; don't!*	말아 〔말어〕
파-ㄹ-	*sell*	팔아 〔팔어〕
푸-ㄹ-	*undo it; solve it*	풀어

Consonant-base verbs

같-	*be the same/like*	같아 〔같애〕
괜찮-	*OK, all right*	괜찮아 〔괜찮어〕
깎-	*cut; sharpen*	깎아 〔깎어〕
끊-	*hang up; quit* [e.g., smoking]	끊어
넣-	*put in, insert*	넣어
놓	*put, place*	놓아
늦-	*be late*	늦어
닦-	*shine, polish*	닦아 〔닦어〕

BASE	GLOSS	INFINITIVE
닫-	*close it*	닫아 〔닫어〕
많-	*be much/many*	많아 〔많어〕
맞-	*be right, correct*	맞아 〔맞어〕
먹-	*eat*	먹어
받-	*receive, get*	받아 〔받어〕
벗-	*remove, take off*	벗어
빗-	*comb*	빗어
신-	*wear* [on feet]	신어
싫-	*be disliked*	싫어
싶-	*want to*	싶어
앉-	*sit*	앉아 〔앉어〕
않-	*doesn't, isn't*	않아 〔않어〕
없-	*be lacking*	없어
읽-	*read*	읽어
입-	*wear*	입어
있-	*exist; stay; have*	있어
잊어먹-	*forget*	잊어먹어
작-	*be small*	작아 〔작어〕
적-	*be little/few*	적어
젊-	*be young*	젊어
좋-	*be good*	좋아
죽-	*die*	죽어
찾-	*look for, find; get [money]*	찾아 〔찾어〕

ㅂ ~ W Verbs

가까 w -	*be near(by)*	가까워
가벼 w -	*be light*	가벼워
고마 w -	*be thankful*	고마워
구 w -	*broil*	구워
누 w -	*lie down*	누워
더 w -	*be hot, warm*	더워
매 w -	*be hot, spicy*	매워
무거 w -	*be heavy*	무거워
쉬 w -	*be easy*	쉬워
어려 w -	*be difficult*	어려워
즐거 w -	*be enjoyable, pleasant*	즐거워

BASE	GLOSS	INFINITIVE
추 w -	*be cold*	추워

ㄷ ~ ㄹ Verbs

걸- (걷다)	*walk*	걸어
들- (듣다)	*listen (to), hear*	들어
물- (묻다)	*ask*	물어
알아들- (듣다)	*understand, catch*	알아들어

ㅅ ~ Ø Verbs

나 (ㅅ)-	*get/be better*	나아

The plain base of a verb, then, is the verb reduced to its minimum form: nothing can easily be taken away from the simple base, because it has only one part. But a variety of things can be added to it, still without making it a complete verb form—without putting on an ending. A simple base with further base-forming things attached to it is a complex base. One kind of complex base is an honorific base—the plain base plus the honorific marker.

BASE	GLOSS	HONORIFIC BASE
걸-	*walk*	걸으시-
기다리-	*wait for*	기다리시-
닫-	*close*	닫으시-
더 w-	*hot*	더우시-
만나-	*meet*	만나시-
모르-	*do not know*	모르시-
배우-	*learn*	배우시-
벗-	*remove*	벗으시-
보-	*look at*	보시-
서-	*stand*	서시-
신-	*wear [on feet]*	신으시-
아-ㄹ-	*know*	아시-
앉-	*sit*	앉으시-
없-	*(there) isn't*	없으시-
입-	*wear*	입으시-
젊-	*be young*	젊으시-
좋-	*be good*	좋으시-
하-	*do*	하시-

Nearly every Korean verb form is subject to the dichotomy of plain and honorific, so that when we speak of any form of a verb, we should keep in mind the fact that each form comes in two varieties: (1) the general variety; and, (2) the variety that we must not use for ourselves or younger members of our family.

Here are the other kinds of complex bases you have learned, illustrated by 하- *do*, first shown with its infinitives.

INFINITIVES (base plus infinitive ending)
해   하셔

PAST BASES (infinitive plus the past marker - ㅆ -)
했-   하셨-

FUTURE BASES (base plus the future-presumptive marker -겠-)
하겠-   하시겠-

PAST-PAST BASES (past base plus the past marker -었-)
했었-   하셨었-

PAST-FUTURE BASES (past base plus future-presumptive marker -겠-)
했겠-   하셨겠-

However many ingredients may go into them, all complex bases share this feature with one another and with simple bases: none are complete until they are finished off with an ending.

15.1.2. Verb Endings

Endings added to bases make the verb form complete. In addition to this function, they often perform another job at the same time: they tell whether or not you have come to the end of a sentence.

Any form of a verb ends a clause in Korean. Some clauses are final: the verb at the end completes a sentence. Some are nonfinal: the verb form does not complete a sentence. In this category are the infinitive -어 ~ 아, the suspective -지, the -고 form, the *as-soon-as* form in -자 마자, and the sequential -(으)니(까) ending. (In the Intimate Style, which you will learn in the sequel volume to this course, the infinitive and the suppositive can end a sentence.)

The most important final endings you have learned so far are these.

> a. the Polite Style ending –어요 which consists of the infinitive –어 ~ 아, etc.) plus the polite particle 요

> b. the Formal Style endings in –(스)ㅂ니다 (declaratives), –(스)ㅂ니까 (questions), –(으)ㅂ시다 (suggestions), and –(으)십시오 (commands)

The Polite Style ending typically finishes a sentence, whether it is a present-tense form (attached to a base), a past-tense form (attached to a past base), or a future-presumptive form (attached to a future base).

Plain		Honorific	
해요	*does*	하세요	[someone esteemed] *does*
했어요	*did*	하셨어요	[someone esteemed] *did*
하겠어요	*will do*	하시겠어요	[someone esteemed] *will do*

When you use this ending at the end of your sentence, it implies that you are on informal, though dignified, terms with the person to whom you are talking.

One-shape Endings and Two-shape Endings

Endings are either one-shape endings or two-shape endings. One-shape endings are much the same, regardless whether they are attached to a vowel base or a consonant base. Two-shape endings have one shape which attaches to vowel bases and another which attaches to consonant bases. For purposes of attaching endings, the group of vowel bases includes not only simple bases (like 가-, 서-, 기다리-, 보-) but also *all* honorific bases since each ends in –(으)시– regardless of the plain base on which it is built.

Base		Honorific base
가-	*go*	가시-
받-	*get*	받으시-

Similarly, all past bases and future bases are consonant bases, regardless of what sort of base you began with.

Base		Past base	Future base
가-	*go*	가(셔)ㅆ-	가(시)겠-
받-	*get*	받(으시)었-	받(으시)겠-

Lesson Fifteen / 302

Here are all the endings you have learned, grouped according to whether they are one-shape or two-shape.

ONE-SHAPE ENDINGS	
past marker	–ㅆ–
suspective	–지
suppositive	–지요
but	–지만
future-presumptive	–겠–
rhetor. retort	–잖아요
고–form	–고 (싶–, 있–)
dictionary form	–다
as soon as	–자 마자

TWO-SHAPE ENDINGS	After vowel	After consonant
honorific	–시–	–으시–
honorific polite	–세요	–으세요
sequential	–니 (까)	–으니 (까)
purposive	–러	–으러
formal decl.	–ㅂ니다	–습니다
formal imper.	–십시오	–으십시오
formal propos.	–ㅂ시다	–읍시다
formal interrog.	–ㅂ니까	–습니까
suggestions	–ㄹ까요	–을까요
consider doing	–ㄹ까 하–	–을까 하–
wanna	–ㄹ래요	–을래요
prob. future	–ㄹ거에요	–을거에요
immed. future	–ㄹ께요	–을께요

One special feature about two-shape endings is that some of them, like the purposive ending –(으)러 (and other endings you will learn in the sequel volume), are attached to the extended base of L-extending bases.

노–ㄹ–   *play*   놀러

Several peculiarities, however, must be mentioned about one-shape endings. The past marker –ㅆ– is omitted here because it is attached to infinitives rather than directly to other bases and so does not follow the same rules.

1. The base 잡수시– *eat* can abbreviate to 잡숫– before one-shape endings.

잡수시지만   →   잡숫지만   [someone esteemed] *eats, but*
잡수시겠어요   →   잡숫겠어요   [someone esteemed] *will eat*

2. One-shape endings are attached to the extended bases of L-extending verbs.

아-ㄹ-　　　*know*　　　　　알지만　　　*knows, but*

　　　　　　　　　　　　　　　알겠어요　　*knows* or *will know*

3. When a one-shape ending that begins with ㄷ, ㅈ, or ㄱ is attached to a consonant base that ends in ㅎ , the strings ㅎ.ㄷ, ㅎ.ㅈ, and ㅎ.ㄱ are pronounced ㅌ, ㅊ, and ㅋ.

좋-　　　　　*be good*　　　　　좋지　　　〔조치〕

　　　　　　　　　　　　　　　좋겠-　　〔조케ㅆ-〕

This is true also of ㄶ and ㅀ :

많-　　　　　*be much/many*　　많지　　　〔만치〕

　　　　　　　　　　　　　　　많겠-　　〔만케ㅆ-〕

싫-　　　　　*be disliked*　　　싫지　　　〔실치〕

　　　　　　　　　　　　　　　싫겠-　　〔실케ㅆ-〕

4. When a one-shape ending is attached to a consonant base that ends in w, the w changes to ㅂ.

더w-　　　　*hot*　　　　　　덥지　　　〔덥찌〕

　　　　　　　　　　　　　　　덥겠-　　〔덥께ㅆ-〕

Were it not for the other forms (더워, 더우시-) we would not know that such bases are different from the usual bases ending in ㅂ like 입- *wear*: 입지, 입고, 입겠-; 입어, 입으시-. In traditional Korean grammar, the ㅂ ~ w verbs are called "irregular ㅂ- verbs."

5. When a one-shape ending is attached to a consonant base that ends in ㄹ (ㄷ ~ ㄹ verbs) the ㄹ changes to ㄷ.

들-　　　*hear*　　　　　　　　듣지　　　〔드찌〕

　　　　　　　　　　　　　　　듣고　　　〔드꼬〕

　　　　　　　　　　　　　　　듣겠-　　〔드께ㅆ-〕

Notice the difference between the behavior of these bases and the L-extending vowel bases: 드-ㄹ- *lift; cost* has the forms 들지, 들고, 들겠-. The infinitives are the same. Both 드-ㄹ- and 들- come out as 들어.

6. The usual automatic sound changes take place when a base ending in a consonant attaches an ending shape that begins with a consonant. First, if the base ends in a consonant or cluster other than ㅂ, ㄷ, ㄱ, ㅁ, ㄴ, ㄹ, in pronouncing the resulting form you reduce the consonant or cluster to one of those: ㅄ and ㅍ are treated like ㅂ; ㄲ and usually ㄺ are treated like ㄱ; ㄻ is treated like ㅁ; ㄵ is treated like ㄴ; ㅅ, ㅆ, ㅈ, and ㅊ are all treated like ㄷ.

Next, there are a number of automatic adjustments between the syllable-final consonant at the end of the base and the syllable-beginning consonant at the start of the ending.

A. Voiceless consonants are doubled (reinforced) after a voiceless consonant, so that

-ㅂㄷ-	is pronounced	ㅂㄸ
-ㅂㅈ-	is pronounced	ㅂㅉ
-ㅂㅅ-	is pronounced	ㅂㅆ
-ㅂㄱ-	is pronounced	ㅂㄲ
-ㄱㄷ-	is pronounced	ㄱㄸ
-ㄱㅈ-	is pronounced	ㄱㅉ
-ㄱㅅ-	is pronounced	ㄱㅆ

However, -ㄱ.ㄱ- comes out just ㄲ (since you don't get the same consonant repeated more than once).

Note that sequences like -ㄷㄱ- and -ㄷㅈ- can sound like ㄲ and ㅉ, e.g. 받고 싶어요 〔바꼬 시퍼요〕 *wants to receive* and 받지요 〔바찌요〕 *Of course I receive it!*

B. After verb-base final ㅁ or ㄴ (or an ㄹ that is reduced from a cluster—simple ㄹ changes to ㄷ), you reinforce (double) a ㄷ, ㅈ, ㅅ, or ㄱ that begins an ending. Since the Korean spelling does not show this doubling, you should be especially mindful of this.

신-	*wears* [on feet]	신지 〔신찌〕
		신고 〔신꼬〕
		신겠- 〔신께써-〕

Below is a chart of the major verb endings you have learned so far with some representative bases (----- means the form is odd or does not exist).

Representative Bases and Endings

	-(스)ㅂ니다	-지요	-(으)ㄹ래요	-(으)니까
-이-	-입니다	-이지요	-----	-이니까
하-	합니다	하지요	할래요	하니까
되-	됩니다	되지요	될래요	되니까
피-	핍니다	피지요	-----	피니까
젊-	젊습니다	젊지요	-----	젊으니까
다르-	다릅니다	다르지요	-----	다르니까
놓-	놓습니다	놓지요	놓을래요	놓으니까
끝내-	끝냅니다	끝내지요	끝낼래요	끝내니까
왔-	왔습니다	왔지요	-----	왔으니까
걸-	걷습니다	걷지요	걸을래요	걸으니까
오겠-	오겠습니다	오겠지요	-----	오겠으니까
싫-	싫습니다	싫지요	-----	싫으니까
추-	춥니다	추지요	출래요	추니까
맞-	맞습니다	맞지요	-----	맞으니까
어리-	어립니다	어리지요	-----	어리니까
빗-	빗습니다	빗지요	빗을래요	빗으니까
아프-	아픕니다	아프지요	-----	아프니까
예쁘-	예쁩니다	예쁘지요	-----	예쁘니까
무거w-	무겁습니다	무겁지요	-----	무거우니까
누w-	눕습니다	눕지요	누울래요	누우니까
나(ㅅ)-	낫습니다	낫지요	나을래요	나으니까

REVIEW EXERCISES

Vocabulary Review

Exercise 1: Matching Synonyms

Here are two columns of Korean expressions. For each expression in the first column, there appears in the second column an expression of similar meaning. Call out each word in the first column, then find its matching word in the second column. Now translate and explain any difference between the words (by example, if possible). You may want to say 같아요 *They are exactly alike* or 좀 달라요 *They are a little different.* Your tutor may want to ask 어떻게 달라요? *How are they different?*

1.	좋아요	학교
2.	줘요	일주일
3.	한 주간	괜찮아요
4.	일년	매일
5.	읽어요	열두 달
6.	교수	배워요
7.	거기	봐요
8.	세 명	세 사람
9.	날마다	상점
10.	백화점	드려요
11.	대학	그 곳
12.	공부해요	선생

Exercise 2: Matching Opposites

Now, here are two more columns of Korean expressions. This time, you are to pick from the first column the expression of opposite meaning to match each of the expressions in the second column. Use the two expressions in sentences; if possible, put them both into one sentence.

1.	전에		앉아요
2.	추워요		아들
3.	여름		어제
4.	일해요		할머니
5.	딸		쉬어요
6.	일어나요		후에
7.	가을		오후
8.	손자		겨울
9.	이야기해요		마쳐요
10.	내일		낮
11.	할아버지		남동생
12.	싸요		더워요
13.	오전		누워요
14.	밤		팔아요
15.	사요		비싸요
16.	서요		봄
17.	시작해요		손녀
18.	여동생		들어요

Exercise 3: Picking the Misfits

Here are six sets of Korean expressions—four to a set. Three expressions in each set have meanings that are grouped around the same subject matter; one does not. You are to pick the misfit. Then speaking Korean, try to show why it is a misfit.

1. 개가 나와요
   추워요
   눈이 와요
   비가 와요

2. 장갑
   구두
   교회
   넥타이

3. 자동차로 가요
   걸어가요
   기차를 타요
   전화를 걸어요

4. 자매
   시내
   사위
   손주

5. 입어요
   심어요
   신어요
   써요

6. 모자를 써요
   머리가 아파요
   옷을 입어요
   머리를 빗어요

Particle Review

Exercise 4: Particle Manipulation

The new particles, and new uses for old particles, that you have learned about in Lessons Eleven through Fourteen are listed here, together with the sections where they were discussed.

쯤	*about, approximately* (see 11.3.)
(이)나	*about, approximately* (12.6.)
	either. . . or. . . (12.6.)
까지	*to, up to, as far as; until* (11.4.)
께	*to* or *for* [someone esteemed] (13.1.)
께서	subject [someone esteemed] (13.1.)
	(honorific equivalent of 이 / 가)
만	*only, just* (11.3.)
마다	*every* (11.3.)

밖에	outside of, except for; only (14.1.)
부터	from (11.4.)
씩	each, apiece (11.3.)
도	also, too; both . . . and, neither . . . nor (12.3.)
(으)로	by [a vehicle] (14.2.)

Express the English sentences in Korean. Make sure you use in each at least one of the particles in the list. Notice the multiple Korean translations for the English word *get*: 받- (*receive*), 가- (*go*), 사 - (*buy*), 있- (*have got*).

1. I want to get married by next year.
2. Shall we go on the train?
3. Either the train or the subway is all right.
4. I haven't any clothes except these.
5. It'll be expensive, but I'll buy some new clothes.
6. I bought both hat and shoes.
7. Approximately ten people came to the party.
8. I read the paper every morning.
9. How long does it take to get [go] from Seoul to Pusan on the train?
10. I ride the subway about once a day.
11. Its raining today, but I'm going downtown in order to see a movie.
12. How much time have we got? Only about ten minutes.
13. I've eaten nothing but meat today.
14. I telephoned the teacher twice, but he wasn't home.
15. How many times a year do you go to concerts?
16. I worked from 8 A.M. till 10 P.M. today.
17. It didn't snow yesterday. And it didn't rain, either.

To reinforce your hold on these particles, repeat the list and make up a Korean sentence using each of them.

Honorifics

Exercise 5: Tell a Story

Here is the bare outline of a story in English. Elaborating on this outline and changing details as you wish to, you must tell the story in Korean twice. The first time, use as the central character (he) your younger brother or sister, or a close friend, or some other person for whom it is not normal to use honorifics. In the second telling, construct your story around a highly esteemed person, your parents, a teacher who is very old, some other elderly relative. Practice your story aloud ahead of time so that you can tell it smoothly, with a minimum of pausing for thought.

> He's very old. He's __ years old. He lives in Seoul. His house is not large, but it's very nice. He usually eats his meals and sleeps at home, but sometimes he goes to town and stays there for several days. He gets up early every day and works hard. On Sundays, he rests. He goes to the cinema or to the park, or he stays home and reads. He owns a great many books. He smokes and reads the newspaper every evening. He doesn't like radio music so he doesn't listen much, but he often goes to concerts. I telephone him several times a week. I often get letters from him. Sometimes he gives me books or clothes. He likes his family. There are six people in his family. He lives with his wife and children, and he often takes walks with them and plays with them.

Autobiographical Sketch

Exercise 6

You are now in a position to compose a fairly detailed autobiographical sketch. Include some dates, your birthday, other significant events, and ages of close relatives and friends. You can also tell about the sort of things you do all day on typical days, what you like and why, and what you have done and will do.

Plan a five-minute talk in Korean along the lines of this scanty outline. Get firm enough control of it so that your speech will be smooth talk, very little silence. Don't write out every word you are going to say. Just jot down an outline and reminders of the expressions you will need. At home, practice making up the right sort of sentences to express what you want to say. Instead of memorizing the sentences, make them up again, with spontaneous variations, when you deliver it orally.

The Formal Style

Exercise 7: Change to Formal Style

Each of the following items is a statement or question in the Polite Style. Change them to Formal Style. (Remember that the formal equivalent of 나 *I* is 저, and of 우리 *we* is 저희 or 저희들). Translate each sentence.

1. 영국분이세요?
2. 나는 영국사람이 아니에요.
3. 그럼, 어디서 오셨어요?
4. 미국서 왔어요.
5. 미국은 한국서 멀어요?
6. 가깝지 않아요. 대단히 멀어요.
7. 미국에서는 무슨 일을 하셨어요?
8. 학교에서 경제학을 가르쳤어요.
9. 지금 우리 학교를 좀 구경하시겠어요?
10. 네, 학생들을 만나고 싶어요.
11. 우리 학교는 작지만, 학생은 많아요.
12. 담배를 하나 피우시겠어요?
13. 고맙습니다. 나는 담배를 너무 좋아해요, 늘 피워요.
14. 학생들이 어디서 점심을 먹어요?
15. 학생들의 집이 다 가까워요. 그래서, 집에서 점심을 먹지요.
16. 선생들은 좋아요?
17. 여기가 우리 교실이에요.
18. 교실이 참 커요.
19. 교실이 크지만, 책이 많지 않아요.
20. 우리 학교는 돈이 없어요. 그래서, 책을 많이 못 사요.

Review of Numbers

Exercise 8: Numerals and Counters

Here are eight brief sentences, each with something missing. Say each sentence aloud in Korean five times, inserting one after another of the number expressions listed below it. (Watch out for changes in meaning that might call for a shift in one of the basic words of the sentence.)

1. 나는 어제 _____ 일했습니다.

    for six hours
    from ten A.M. until four P.M.
    for only forty minutes
    from quarter to seven until quarter
        after one
    for three hours

2. 지난 주에 서울에서 ____ 봤습니다.

    three friends
    four movie theaters [use 개]
    ten American doctors
    five pop singers
    about 10,000 people
    eighteen buildings

3. 교실 안에 ____ 있습니다.

    three newspapers
    about fifty books
    forty students
    three teachers
    six windows and two doors

4. 나는 중국말을 _____ 배웠습니다.

    for three years
    for only five weeks
    for several months
    in 1987
    from February till June

5. 우리 동생은 ____입니다.

    two years old
    one year old
    four years old
    forty years old
    twenty years old

6. 우체국 앞에는 _____ 있습니다.

    two bicycles
    twelve cars
    four dogs
    five doctors

7. 나는 _____ 태어났습니다.

    twenty-one years ago
    on April 1, 1940
    on September 30, 1966
    on May 27, 1928
    on January 14, 1945

8. 기차는 _____ 떠납니다.

    at 6:18 P.M.
    at 4:42 A.M.
    at 7:37 P.M.
    at 5:05 P.M.
    at 1:19 A.M.

Korean to English Translation

Exercise 9: Translate into English

1. 그 영화가 너무 재미 없었어요. 중간에 나오고 싶었어요.
2. 육년 전에는 안경을 썼지만, 요즘은 콘택트렌즈를 끼고 다니지요.
3. 그 책을 어제 책상 위에 놓았어요. 누가 읽고 있을거에요.
4. 어제까지는 일본에 가고 싶었지만, 오늘은 한국에 가고 싶어요.
5. A. 이를 닦으셨어요?
   B. 지금 닦고 있잖아요?!
6. 문제를 세 개씩 줄께요. 그런데, 풀겠어요?
7. 저는 대학교에서 정치학만 공부하고 있어요. 가끔 하루에 여섯
   시간씩 숙제를 하지요. 그리고 그 다음에는 쉬어요.
8. 오늘 아침에 누구를 안 만났어요? 아니오. 아직 나가지 않았잖아요?
9. 내일은 개학입니다. 금년에는 열심히 공부할겁니다.
10. 나는 열심히 하겠지만 형은 아마 주로 놀거에요.
11. 나는 나가지 않을래요. 집에서 커피를 마실래요.
12. 이 음식은 별로 맛이 없어요. 다른 거 먹을까요?
13. 그 책이 얼마에요? 은행에서 돈을 찾을께요.
14. 어제 내가 우리 고양이를 찾으러 나갔지만 못 찾았어요.
15. 사장님 덕분에 잘 지내고 있습니다.
16. A. 이 문제를 못 풀겠어요.
    B. 그럼 제가 할께요.
17. 빨리 자요! 늦었잖아요!
18. 내일 추울까요? 모르겠어요.
19. 학교에 갈까요? 오늘은 일요일이잖아요!
20. 그 샤쓰가 내 거지요? 빨리 주세요!
21. 목요일날은 커피 마시러 다방에 갑시다.
22. 오층에서는 구두랑 장갑을 팔아요.
23. 테니스 칠래요?
24. 나는 한 달에 두 번씩 교회에 나가요.
25. 커피를 다 마셨지만, 맛은 없었어요.
26. 사장님이 벌써 오셨어요? 그럼 맥주 한잔 드리지요.
27. 어느 나라에서 오셨어요? 러시아에서 왔지만, 십년 전이었지요.
28. 이 책들은 다 달라요. 그리고 또 재미 있어요.
    어느 서점에서 사셨어요?
29. 우리 딸은 똑똑하지만, 공부를 열심히 안 해요.
30. 그 이야기는 싫어요. 다른 거 하지요.

31. 오늘은 날씨가 나쁘지만, 기분이 좋아요.

32. 그 빵을 먹지 말아요!

33. 이 일을 다음 주일까지 마칠까 해요.

34. 우리하고 같이 살지 않지만, 같이 살고 싶어하지요.

35. 잔디밭에 앉을까요?

36. 여자 친구를 찾고 있지만, 아직 결혼하고 싶지 않아요.

37. 런던에서는 지하철도 버스도 문제가 많아요.

38. 이번 학기에는 정치학이랑, 경제학이랑, 한국말을 공부하고 있어요.

39. 식구가 몇 명이에요?

40. 저희 아버지는 교회에 다니시지만, 동생은 안 다녀요.

41. 요즘 책을 읽지 못 하고 있어요.

42. 교수님이 지난 여름에 우리 집에 오셨어요.

43. 우리 조카는 아직 미혼이지만, 언젠가 결혼하겠지요.

44. 할아버지가 돈을 많이 주세요?

45. 오늘 저녁은 시내에서 연극을 볼까 해요.

46. 서점에서 꽃을 팔아요? 물론 안 팔지요.

47. 우리 사촌 동생은 미국에서 군인이에요.

48. 형제가 몇 명이시지요?

49. 커피 드실거에요? 아니오, 일찍 자고 싶어요.

50. 미국에서 러시아말 좀 배웠을거에요.

English to Korean Translation

Exercise 10: Translate into Korean

1. He's probably already come (three ways).

2. That student is waiting for Mr. Brown.

3. I've only 3000 wŏn. So I can't buy all these goods.

4. Do you often ride that bike?

5. I'm going to study for just fifteen minutes.

6. He won't get the money from his father this week, I bet.

7. Is Mr. Pak's nephew going to graduate next year?

8. Would you happen to know the time?

9. Would you like to take a walk in the park together?

10. That girl must be my brother's fiancée.

11. Excuse me, but I'll just pop upstairs a moment.

12. The day after tomorrow I'll meet Mr. Chang's sister.

13. Would you like to (do you wanna) try these clothes on now?

14. Are you in a good mood?

15. My head aches terribly.

16. In the summer I'll have lots of exams.

17. Where is the bus stop?

18. I saw it yesterday, but I don't know.

19. Comb your hair!

20. Do you suppose he is at home? Of course he must be!

KOREAN to
ENGLISH
VOCABULARY

가–	go (7)
가게	a shop; store (6)
가까w–	be close, near (13)
가끔	sometimes (8)
가르치–	teach (7)
가방	bag, briefcase (6)
가벼w–	be light (12)
가수	pop singer (5)
가을	autumn, fall (13)
가족	family (9)
가장	the most (14)
가지	kinds, varieties (counter) (11)
갈아입–	change (clothes) (14)
감자	potato(es) (11)
감자깡	crispy fried potatoes, potato chips (11)
갑	pack (cigarettes) (11)
갑자기	suddenly (12)
값	price (9)
갔다오–	go (and come back) (9)
갖다주–	bring (14)
같–	be similar; be the same
같이	together (8)
개	dog (7)
개	items, units, objects (counter) (11)

개월	months (time or duration) (counter) (11)
개학(을) 하–	start term/school (14)
거기	there (6)
걱정	a worry (13)
걱정(을) 하–	worry (13)
건강	health (12)
건강하–	be healthy (12)
건너편	across/opposite from (6)
건물	building (6)
걸–	walk (12)
걸리–	take (time) (7)
걸어가–	walk, go on foot (12)
걸어오–	walk, come on foot (12)
겨울	winter (13)
결혼(을) 하–	marry (12)
경제	economy (8)
경제학	economics (8)
계산서	bill, check (14)
계시–	be, exist, stay (honorific) (8)
고기	meat (7)
고대	Korea University (6)
고마w–	be/feel thankful (11)
고모	aunt (father's sister) (13)
고모부	uncle (father's sister's husband) (13)
고양이	cat (7)

골프	golf (13)	그냥	just, just (as one is), without doing anything (13)
골프(를) 치-	play golf (13)	그래도	Even so; Nevertheless (6)
-곳	place (5)	그래서	And so; And then; Therefore (6)
공부(를) 하-	study (7)		
공원	park (6)	그러니까	So, what I mean to say is; So, what you're saying is (13)
공책	notebook (5)		
과목	school subject (8)		
과일	fruit (11)	그러면	Then, In that case, If so (5)
광화문	Kwanghwamun, Kwanghwa Gate (6)	그런데	But. And then; By the way (6)
괜찮-	be OK, be alright (8)	그럼	In that case; Then (5)
		그렇게	in that way, like that; so (13)
굉장하-	be quite something, be impressive (9)		
		그렇지만	But (5)
굉장히	very, very much (14)	그리고	And also; And then (6)
교수	professor (5)	그림	picture (6)
교실	classroom (6)	그저께	day before yesterday (14)
교외	suburb(s) (12)		
교재	teaching materials; textbook (8)	극장	theatre; cinema (7)
교환	exchange (8)	근처	the area near, the vicinity (6)
교환원	switchboard, telephone, exchange operator (8)	글쎄요	I don't really know. Let me think. (9)
		금년	this year (11)
교환학생	exchange student (8)	금요일	Friday (7)
교회	church (Protestant) (8)	기다리-	wait (7)
구경(을) 하-	do viewing or sightsee (7)	기분	feelings, mood (14)
		기분(이) 나쁘-	be in a bad mood (14)
구경(을) 가-	go viewing/sightseeing (7)	기분(이) 좋-	be in a good mood (14)
구두	shoes (9)	기숙사	dormitory (6)
국립	national (-ly) established (8)	기차	train (7)
국립대학교	a national university (8)	길	road, way, street (11)
군데	places, institutions (counter) (11)	까페	café (12)
군인	soldier, serviceman (13)	깎-	cut (hair), sharpen (pencil), mow (grass) (8)
권	bound volumes (counter) (11)		
귀	ear (14)	깨끗이	neatly, cleanly (8)
그 NOUN	that NOUN (5)	깨끗하-	be clean (8)

꼭	without fail; be sure to (11)	내일	tomorrow (7)
꽃	flower(s) (12)	냉면	cold noodle dish (12)
끊–	quit (smoking, drinking) (14)	냉수	ice water (12)
		냉커피	ice coffee (12)
끝	the end; the tip (11)	너무	too much so, too; very, to an excessive degree (8)
끝나–	it stops, ends, finishes (7)		
끝내–	finishes it (11)	넣–	put in, insert (12)
끼–	wear (gloves, ring) (9)	넥타이	tie, necktie (9)
끼–	wear (lenses) (13)	–년생 (이에요)	is a person born in such-and-such a year (11)

ㄴ

		노–ㄹ–	play (7)
		노래	song (7)
나	I (5)	노래방	noraebang; Korean karaoke box (7)
나(ㅅ)–	get/be better (7)		
나가–	attend (church) (8); go out (9)	노트	notebook (6)
		놓–	put/place it (11)
나라	country, nation (5)	누w–	lie down (14)
나무	tree (6)	누가	who? (as subject) (5)
나쁘–	be bad (8)	누구	who? (non-subject) (5)
나오–	come out (9)	누나	(boy's) older sister (13)
나이	age (11)	누님	(boy's) older sister
나중에	in the future, some time later, later (11)		(honorific) (13)
		눈	snow (13)
날	day (7)	눈	eye (14)
날씨	weather (13)	뉴스	the news (9)
남대문	Great South Gate (6)	뉴욕	New York (8)
남동생	younger brother (13)	늘	always (8)
남매	brother and sister (13)	늦–	be late (13)
남자	man (6)	늦게	late (adv) (7)
남자친구	boyfriend (6)		
남편	husband (5)		

ㄷ

낮	daytime; noon (7)		
내–	pay (14)	다	all, everything (5)
내년	next year (11)	다니–	attend, go on a regular basis (7)
내려가–	go down (9)		
내려오–	come down (9)	다르–	be different (11)
내리–	descend (9)	다른 NOUN	(an)other NOUN(s) (8)

다리	leg (14)	돌아오-	comes back, returns here (12)
다방	tea room, tabang (9)	동네	neighborhood (11)
다음	after; adjacent, next to (6)	동대문	Great East Gate (6)
다치-	get hurt, injure oneself (14)	동생	younger brother or sister (9)
닦-	polish; brush (teeth) (9)	동안	for the duration of, during, for (a week) (13)
닫-	close it (7)		
달	months (counter) (11)	돼요	It's OK; It'll do; It's acceptable; It works (8)
달라	dollar (counter) (11)		
담배	cigarette(s) (5)	되-	become (7)
대	vehicles, machines (counter) (11)	둘 다	both, both of them (13)
		뒤	at the back; behind (6)
대사관	embassy (6)	드-ㄹ-	costs (money) (14)
대학	four-year college (8)	드-ㄹ-	lift; hold (14)
대학교	university (6)	드라이크리닝	dry cleaning (12)
댁	house (honorific) (9)	드리-	give (honorific) (13)
더	more (9)	드시-	eat, drink (honorific) (8)
덕분에	Thanks to NOUN; Thanks to you (14)	들-	listen to; hear (7); take (courses) (8)
더 w-	be hot (7)	들어가-	go in, enters (12)
데	place (13)	들어오-	come in, enter; return home (12)
데이트	a date (13)		
데이트(를) 하-	have a date (13)	등	back, spine (14)
도	degree of temperature (11)	따님	daughter (hon.) (13)
		딸	daughter (9)
도서관	library (7)	때	time (when) (12)
도시	city (12)	때문에	because of, on account of (9)
도와주-	help (11)		
도착(을) 하-	arrive (9)	떠나-	leave, depart (7)
독어	German language (5)	또	Moreover, What's more; (yet) again (9)
독일	Germany (5)		
독일말	German language (5)	똑똑하-	be bright, intelligent (12)
독일사람	a German (5)		
돈	money (6)		
돈(이) 드-ㄹ-	costs money (14)		
돌아가-	goes back, returns there (12)		
돌아가시-	die, pass away (honorific) (14)		

ㄹ

라이타	lighter (6)
러시아	Russia (5)
러시아말	Russian language (5)
러시아사람	Russian person (5)
런던	London (8)
레스토랑	restaurant (7)
리	Korean mile (li) = 1/3 U.S. mile) (counter) (11)

ㅁ

마루	the living room (in an apartment) (13)
마리	animals, fish, birds (counter) (11)
마시-	drink (7)
마음	one's mind, spiritual center, heart (12)
마치-	finish it (12)
만나-	meet (7)
만화	comics, cartoons (12)
많-	be much/many (7)
많이	a lot (adverb) (7)
말	language; words (5)
말(을) 들-	obey (listens to words) (8)
말씀	words, speech (humble or honorific equivalent of 말) (8)
말씀하-	say (humble), say (humble) (13)
말씀하세요.	Go ahead; Please say what you have to say. (8)
말(을) 하-	speak, talk (7)
맛	taste (7)
맛 없-	taste bad, not taste good (7)
맛(이) 있-	be tasty, delicious (7)

맞-	be right, correct; hit the mark (13)
맞은편	across/opposite from (6)
매-	put on/wear (a tie) (9)
매-	tie (7)
매w-	be spicy (11)
매일	every day (8)
매표소	ticket counter (7)
맥주	beer (11)
머	what? (5)
머-르-	be distant, far (8)
머리	head; hair (8)
머리(가) 나쁘-	be dumb (8)
머리(가) 좋-	be bright/intelligent (8)
먹-	eat (7)
먹이- (w/ 풀)	starch it (12)
먼저	first (of all), before anything else (8)
멀리	far (13)
멀리서	from a distance (13)
며느리	daughter-in-law (13)
명	persons, people (counter) (11)
명함	namecard, business card (9)
몇	how many? (7)
몇	how many? some/several (11)
몇년생이세요?	What year were you born in? (11)
몇학년이세요?	What year are you (in school)? (11)
모두	all, everyone (13)
모레	day after tomorrow (14)
모르-	not know (7)
모자	hat (9)
목요일	Thursday (7)
잘 생겼-	be ugly (9)
무-르-	bite (7)
무거w-	be heavy (12)
무릎	knee (14)
무슨	which/what kind of? (5)
무엇	what? (5)
무역	trade (9)

무역회사	trading company (9)	배	stomach (12)
문	door, gate (6)	배(가) 부르-	(stomach) be full, sated (12)
문제	problem (14)	배우-	learn (7)
물	water (7)	백화점	department store (6)
물-	ask (7)	버리-	throw it away (13)
물건	goods (11)	버스	bus (8)
물론	of course (14)	번	times (counter) (11)
물론이에요.	Of course. (14)	번호	number (11)
뭐	what? (5)	벌써	already (12)
미국	America, USA (5)	벗-	take off (clothes) (7)
미국사람	person from USA, American (5)	별로 + negative	(not) particularly (9)
		병	bottle (counter) (11)
미안하-	be sorry, feel sorry (7)	보-	look at, see (7)
미혼(이에요)	(is) unmarried (13)	보내-	spend (time); send (9)
밑	at the bottom, below under(neath) (6)	보통	usually, normally (7)
		복도	corridor, hallway (12)
		볼펜	ballpoint pen (5)

ㅂ

		봄	spring (13)
		봉지	paper bag (counter) (11)
바꾸-	exchange, change (14)	부르-	sing (a song) (7)
바다	ocean, sea (12)	부르-	be full (stomach) (12)
바로	just (below, above); straight (6)	부모(들)	parents (6)
		부엌	kitchen (13)
바쁘-	be busy (7)	부인	your/his wife (5)
바지	trousers (9)	부자	rich person (11)
박사	Dr., Ph.D. (5)	부츠	boots (9)
밖	outside (6)	부치-	post it, mail it (9)
반	half (11)	부탁(을) 하-	make a request, ask a favor/errand (8)
반	one's class, homeroom (14)	-분	esteemed people (counter) (11)
반지	(finger)ring (9)	-분	minutes (counter) (11)
반찬	side dishes (14)	-분	person (honorific) (5)
받-	receive, get (7)	분필	chalk (5)
발	foot (14)	불	fire; light; a light (7)
발가락	toe (14)	불	U.S. dollars (counter) (11)
밤	night (7)		
밥	cooked rice (7)	불고기	*pulgogi* (7)
방	room (6)	불어	French language (5)
방금	just a moment ago, just now (9)	불편하-	be uncomfortable, inconvenient (14)
		비	rain (13)
방학	vacation (11)	비빔밥	*pibimpap* (7)

비싸-	be expensive (7)	사촌형	cousin (boy's older male cousin) (13)
비치	beach (12)	산	mountain (12)
비행기	airplane (7)	산보(를) 하-	stroll, take a walk (7)
빌딩	building (6)	살	years of age (counter) (11)
빗-	comb (14)	삼촌	uncle (on father's side) (13)
빙수	shaved ice, ice slush (12)	삼학년(생)	third-year student (14)
빠르-	be fast (7)	상	table (6)
빨리	quickly (7)	상자	box, case, chest (counter) (11)
빵	bread (7)	새	new (9)
뻐스	bus (8)	새벽	dawn (11)

ㅅ

		새우	shrimp (11)
사-	buy (7)	새우깡	shrimp chips (11)
사-ㄹ-	live (7)	샌드위치	sandwich (12)
사과	apple (11)	생맥주	draft beer (12)
사람	people (counter) (11)	생신	birthday [honorific] (11)
사람	person (5)	생일	birthday (11)
사랑(을) 하-	love (8)	생기-	turn out a certain way (9)
사립	private (-ly established) (8)	생크림	fresh cream (12)
사립대학교	a private university (8)	샤쓰	shirt, dress-shirt (9)
사모님	your wife; somebody else's wife (elegant/ honorific) (9)	서-	stand (7)
		서강대	Sogang University (6)
사무실	office (9)	서울대	Seoul National University (6)
사실	fact; in fact (9)	서점	bookstore (6)
사실은	In fact (9)	선교사	missionary (13)
사업	business (9)	선물	present, gift (14)
사위	son-in-law (13)	선생	teacher (5)
사이	between (6)	설겆이	dirty dishes (13)
사이다	a Korean soft drink like Seven-up™ (12)	설겆이(를) 하-	wash the dishes (13)
사장	company president (5)	설탕	sugar (12)
사촌	cousin (13)	성	surname (8)
사촌누나	cousin (boy's older female cousin) (13)	성씨	[your or his] esteemed surname (8)
사촌동생	cousin (boy or girl's younger cousin (either gender) (13)	성함	surname (honorific) (8)
		성냥	match(es) (5)
사촌언니	cousin (girl's older female cousin) (13)	성당	church [Catholic] (8)

세탁	laundry (12)	시내	downtown, city center (14)
세탁(을) 하-	do laundry, launder (12)	시댁	esteemed house/home of the parents-in law (for females) (13)
세탁소	laundromat, cleaners (12)		
스웨타	sweater, jumper (9)		
소개(를) 하-	introduce (14)	시부모	parents-in-law (for females) (13)
소개(를) 받-	be/get introduccd (14)		
소주	Korean rice vodka, soju (12)	시아버님	father-in-law (woman's) (honorific) (13)
속	inside (6)	시아버지	father-in-law (woman's) (13)
손	hand (14)		
손가락	finger (14)	시어머니	mother-in-law (woman's) (13)
손녀(딸)	granddaughter (13)		
손님	guest; customer (12)	시어머님	mother-in-law wo-man's, honorific) (13)
손자	grandson (13)		
손주[아이]	grandchild(ren) (13)		
쇼핑	shopping (14)	시작(을) 하-	begin (11)
수건	towel (7)	시장	market (6)
수업	class, lesson (8)	시청	city hall (6)
수영(을) 하-	swim (8)	시키-	order (11)
수영장	swimming pool (8)	시험	examination (14)
수요일	Wednesday (7)	식구	family members (13)
수입품	imported goods (5)	식당	dining room, restaurant, cafeteria, refectory (7)
슈퍼마켓	supermarket (7)		
숙제	homework, assignment (13)	식탁	dining table, kitchen table (11)
술	any alcoholic drink (5)	신-	wear (footwear) (9)
술집	bar, tavern, drinking establishment (9)	신문	newspaper (5)
		신용카드	credit card (8)
쉬-	rest (7)	신발	shoes, footwear in general (9)
쉬w-	be easy (8)		
쉽게	easily (9)	실은	In fact (9)
스카프	scarf (9)	싫-	be disliked, distasteful (12)
스케이트	skate(s) (12)		
스케이트(를) 타-	skate (12)	싫어하-	dislike it (12)
스키	ski(s) (12)	심심하-	be bored (12)
스키(를) 타-	ski (12)	싶-	want to (9)
스포츠	sports (13)	싸-	cheap, inexpensive (8)
시	o'clock (counter) (11)	쏟아지-	pours (rain) (13)
시간	hours (counter); time (7, 11)	쓰-	wear (glasses) (13)
		쓰-	wear (a hat) (13)
시계	watch (9)	쓰-	use it (8)
시골	countryside, the country (12)	쓰-	write (7)
		-씨	polite title for name (5)

아-ㄹ-	know it (7)
아가씨	young lady; form of address for unmarried women (6)
아기	baby (6)
아까	a short while ago, just a moment ago (13)
아내	my wife (5)
아니면	Or (sentence-initial), or (between nouns) (12)
아니에요	No; It is not (5)
아드님	son (honorific) (13)
아들	son (9)
아래	below, lower, down, downstairs (6)
아래층	downstairs; the floor below (9)
아르바이트	part-time work for students (11)
—(를) 하-	do part-time work for students (11)
아마	maybe, probably (13)
아마도	maybe, probably (more tentative) (13)
아무거나	anything, anything at all (14)
아버님	father (honorific) (7)
아버지	father (6)
아이	child (6)
아이스크림	ice cream (12)
아저씨	mister (any man old enough to be married) (13)
아저씨	mister; form of address (6)
아주	very (7)
아주머니	ma'am (any woman old enough to be married) (13)
아줌마	ma'am (casual for 아주머니) (13)

아직	(not) yet, still (8)
아침	morning; breakfast (7)
아프-	hurt, be painful (14)
안	inside (6)
안경	glasses (9)
안녕히 주무세요.	Good night (honorific) (8)
안 돼요	It's no good; It won't do; It's not acceptable; It doesn't work. (8)
안주	snacks to go with alcohol (11)
앉-	sits (7)
알아 들-	understand, catch (something said) (8)
앞	in front (6)
애	child (6)
애기	baby (6)
야구	baseball (8)
야구(를) 하-	play baseball (8)
약	medicine (8)
약(을) 먹-	take (eat) medicine (8)
약혼(을) 하-	get engaged (12)
약혼자	fiancé(e) (12)
양담배	foreign cigarettes (12)
양말	socks (9)
양복	a suit (9)
양주	whiskey; western spirits (12)
얘기	talk, chat, story (9)
어느	which? what kind of? (5)
어디	where? (6)
어때요?	How is it? How about it? (12)
어떻게?	how? in what way? (12)
어려w-	be difficult (8)
어리-	be young (a child) (13)
어머니	mother (6)
어머님	mother (honorific) (7)

어제	yesterday (7)	연필	pencil (5)
언니	older sister (girl's) (12)	열심히	diligently (8)
언제	when? (7)	영국	England (5)
언제나	always (8)	영국사람	English person (5)
언젠가	sometime or other, at one time; some time ago (7)	영사관	consulate (6)
		영어	English language (5)
		영화	movie, film (7)
얼마	how many? how much? (6)	영화구경 (을) 하-	see a film (7)
얼마나	about how much? approximately how much? (11)	영화배우	movie actor (9)
		옆	next to, beside (6)
		예쁘-	pretty, cute (14)
얼음	ice (12)	예약	reservation (8)
없-	be nonexistent, not exist, not have (7)	예약 (을) 하-	make a reservation (8)
		오-	come (7)
없어요	does not exist, there is not, aren't (6)	오늘	today (7)
엉터리	rubbish, junk; something or someone cheap and shabby (11)	오렌지 쥬스	orange juice (8)
		오르-	ascend, rise (9)
		오른쪽	on the right (6)
엘리베이터	elevator, lift (14)	오른편	on the right (6)
여-르-	open it (7)	오빠	older brother (girl's) (12)
여관	small hotel, inn (9)		
여기	here (6)	오전	morning, A.M. (11)
여기 좀 봐요!	Say there! Excuse me! (12)	오징어	squid (11)
		오징어깡	squid chips (11)
여동생	younger sister (13)	오후	afternoon (7)
여러	several, various (11)	오후	P.M. (11)
여름	summer (13)	올라가-	go up (9)
여보세요!	Hello! Excuse me! (12)	올라오-	come up (9)
여자	woman (6)	옷	clothes (9)
여자친구	girlfriend (6)	와이샤쓰	shirt, dress shirt (9)
역	train station (6)	와인	wine (5)
-연/-년	years (counter) (11)	왜 (요)?	why? (11)
연구	research (9)	왜냐하면	The reason is; Because (11)
연구(를) 하-	do research (9)		
연구실	(professor's) office (9)	외교관	diplomat (5)
연극	play, drama (12)	외국	foreign country (5)
연대	Yonsei University (6)	외국사람	a foreigner (5)
연락(을) 하-	get in touch, make contact (9)	외국어	foreign language (5)
		외삼촌	uncle (on mother's side) (13)
연세	age (honorific) (11)		

외할머니	grandmother (on mother's side) (13)
외할아버지	grandfather (on mother's side) (13)
왼쪽	on the left (6)
왼편	on the left (6)
요리	cooking, cuisine (12)
요리(를) 하-	cook (12)
요즘	nowadays, these days (7)
용무	business, matter to take care of (14)
용서(를) 하-	forgive (11)
우리	we, our (5)
우산	umbrella (5)
우선	first of all, before anything else (14)
우유	milk (7)
우체국	post office (9)
운동	sports (13)
운동(을) 하-	do sports; exercise (13)
운동장	sports stadium (13)
운동화	sneakers, tennis shoes (13)
-원	Korean monetary unit (6)
월(달)	month names (counter) (11)
월요일	Monday (7)
위	above, over, on (top); upstairs (6)
위스키	whisky (5)
위층	upstairs, the floor above (9)
은퇴(를) 하-	retire (12)
은행	bank (5)
은행원	banker (5)
음료수	beverage, something to drink (14)
음식	food (7)
음식점	restaurant (7)
음악	music (12)
음악회	concert (12)
의사	doctor, physician (5)

의자	chair (6)
이	tooth, teeth (9)
이	this (5)
-이-	be (the same as, equal to) (copula) (7)
이대	Ewha Women's University (6)
이따가	in a while, a while later (7)
이렇게	in this way, like this (13)
이름	(given) name (8)
이모	aunt (mother's sister) (13)
이모부	uncle (mother's sister's husband) (13)
이번 NOUN	this NOUN (week, month) (11)
이상하-	be strange, odd (13)
이야기	talk, chat, story (9)
이야기(를) 하-	talk, chat (9)
이제	now (finally) (12)
이학년(생)	second-year student (14)
이혼(을) 하-	get divorced (13)
-인분	portion (of food) (14)
인삼	ginseng (5)
인삼주	ginseng wine (5)
인제	now (finally) (12)
일	matter, business (7)
일	days (counter) (11)
일(을) 하-	work, do work (7)
일본	Japan (5)
일본말	Japanese language (5)
일본사람	person from Japan (5)
일어	Japanese language (5)
일어나-	get up; stand up (7)
일요일	Sunday (7)
일찍	early (adv) (7)
일학년(생)	first-year student (14)
읽-	read (7)
입-	wear; put on (7)

있-	be, exist; stay; have (7)	장모	mother-in-law (man's) (13)
있어요	it exists, there is/are (6)	장인	father-in-law (man's) (13)
잊어버리-	forget (11)	장인어른	father-in-law (man's) (elegant) (13)
		장인장모	parents-in-law (man's) (13)

ㅈ

자-	sleep (7)	쟈켓	jacket (9)
자녀분	children (honorific) (13)	재미 없-	be not interesting, boring (9)
자동차	car, automobile (9)	재미 있-	be interesting (9)
자료	materials (written) (14)	재미있게	interestingly, in such a way that it is interesting (9)
자르-	cut (8)		
자매	sisters (13)	저	yon, that (over there) (5)
자전거	bicycle (7)		
자제분	children (honorific) (13)	저기	over there (6)
자주	often (8)	저기요!	Hey there! (a bit brusque or even rude) (12)
작-	be little (7)		
작년	last year (9)	저녁	evening; supper (7)
작은아버지	uncle (father's younger brother) (13)	저렇게	in that way (13)
		적-	are few (7)
잔	cupfuls (counter) (11)	전공	one's major, specialization (8)
잘	well; often (7)	전공(을) 하-	major in something (8)
잘 돼요.	It's going well. It's turning out well. (8)	전부	the whole thing, total (5)
잘 생겼-	be good-looking, handsome (9)	전부 다	everything, all of it (5)
잘 안 돼요.	It's not going well. (8)	전에	earlier, before (11)
잘 자요!	Good night. (polite, but not honorific) (8)	전화	telephone (8)
잘하-	do well, do (it) well (7)	전화(를) 하-	make a phone call (8)
잠깐	a short while, a moment (12)	전화(를) 거-ㄹ-	make a phone call (9)
		전화(를) 받-	answer the phone (9)
잠시	a short while (14)	전화번호	telephone number (11)
잡수시-	eat (honorific) (8)	젊-	be young (but past puberty) (11)
잡지	magazine (5)		
장	flat objects (counter) (11)	점심	lunch (7)
장(을) 보-	do grocery shopping (7)	정각(에)	exactly at (a time) (11)
장갑	gloves (9)	정거장	station/stop (train) (14)
장마	rainy season, seasonal rains (13)	정류장	bus stop (14)
장마(가) 지-	rainy season sets in (13)	정말(로)	truly, really (8)

정말이에요?	Really? Is it true? (8)	중간에	midway, in the middle (9)
정문	main gate (of a university) (6)	중국	China (5)
정열적(으로)	passionate(ly) (8)	중국말	Chinese language (5)
정원	garden (9)	중국사람	person from China (5)
정치	politics (8)	쥬스	juice (8)
정치학	political science (8)	즐거w-	be enjoyable, pleasant, fun (9)
제일	the most; number one (14)		
제품	manufactured good(s) (5)	즐겁게	enjoyably (9)
조금	a little (7)	지금	now (7)
조부모	grandparents (13)	지난	past, last (11)
조카	nephew (13)	지내-	get along (14)
조카 딸	niece (13)	지하철	subway, underground, metro (12)
졸업(을) 하-	graduate (13)		
좀	a little; please (8)	진지	rice, meal (honorific) (13)
종이	paper (5)		
좋-	be good; be liked (12)	집	house, home (5)
좋-	be good (7)	집사람	my wife (5)
좋아하-	like it (8, 12)	째즈	jazz (12)
주	a state, a province (8)	쪽	side, direction (6)
주-	give (7)		
주간	week (counter) (11)		

ᄎ

주로	mainly, mostly, for the most part (8)
주립	state (-established), provincial (-ly established] (8)

주립대학교	a state university (8)	차	car, vehicle (7)
주말	weekend (7)	차	tea (9)
주무시-	sleep (honorific) (8)	차-	wear (a watch) (9)
주문(을) 하-	order (at restaurant) (12)	차표	ticket (train, bus) (7)
		착하-	be good by nature; be a good boy (girl, dog) (8)
주세요	Please give. (6)	참	truly, really (8)
주일	week (counter) (11)	창문	window (6)
주중에	during the week, on week days (11)	찾-	look for; find (7)
		찾-	withdraw (money) from; fetch (money) (9)
죽-	die (14)	채	buildings (counter) (11)
중간	middle, midway (9)	책	book (5)
		책상	desk (6)
		처음	the beginning (11)

천	thousand (6)
천천히	slowly (8)
첫	first (7)
청바지	jeans (9)
청소(를) 하-	clean up (8)
초대(를) 하-	invite someone (14)
초대(를) 받-	be/get invited (14)
-초	(a) second (11) (counter)
추w-	be cold (13)
춤(을) 추-	dances (a dance) (12)
취하-	get tipsy/drunk (14)
-층	floors (of a building)) (counter) (11)
치-	strike, hit (7)
치-	play (tennis, golf) (12)
치마	skirt (9)
친구	friend (5)
친척	relative (13)
칠판	blackboard (5)

캐나다	Canada (5)
캐나다 사람	a Canadian (5)
캠퍼스	campus (6)
커피	coffee (12)
켤레	pair [of shoes, etc.] (9)
코	nose (14)
코메디	comedy (13)
코트	coat (9)
콘택트렌즈	contact lenses (13)
콜라	cola (12)
크-	be large (7)
크림	cream (12)
큰아버지	uncle (father's elder brother) (13)

타-	add/put in (sugar) (12)
타-	ride in, ride on (12)
타고가-	go (riding) (14)
타고오-	come (riding) (14)
타올	towel (7)
태어나-	be born (11)
테니스	tennis (12)
테니스(를) 치-	play tennis (12)
테이블	table (6)
텔레비전	television (6)
토마토 쥬스	tomato juice (8)
토요일	Saturday (7)
통하-	get through to, make contact with (13)
통화(를) 하-	get through to, make contact with on phone (8)

ㅍ

파-ㄹ-	sell it (7)
파운드	pounds (sterling) (counter) (11)
파티	party (11)
팔	arm (14)
펜	ballpoint pen (5)
편	side, direction (6)
편지	letter (7)
편하-	be comfortable; convenient (14)
편히	comfortably; conveniently (14)
표	ticket (7)
푸-ㄹ-	solve it; undo it (14)
풀	starch, glue (12)
풀(을) 먹이-	starch it (12)
프랑스	France (5)
프랑스말	French language (5)

프랑스사람	person from France (5)	햄버거	hamburger (12)
프로	program (TV); pro (sports) (13)	-행	bound for (a place) (7)
프리마	nondairy creamer (12)	허리	waist, lower back (14)
플랫폼	platform (7)	형	older brother (boy's) (13)
피-	bloom, blossom (12)		
피곤하-	be tired (12)	형제	brothers (for males); brothers and sisters (12)
피아노	piano (5)	호주	Australia (5)
피아노(를) 치-	play piano (12)	호주사람	an Australian (5)
피우-	smoke (7)	호텔	hotel (6)
피자	pizza (12)	혼자〔서〕	alone, on one's own, by oneself (7)

ㅎ

		홍차	black/English tea (12)
		홍콩	Hong Kong (5)
하-	do (7)	홍콩사람	person from Hong Kong (5)
학교	school (6)		
학기	term, semester (14)	화요일	Tuesday (7)
-학년(이에요)	is a student in such-and-such a year or grade (at school) (11)	화장실	toilet, restroom, bathroom, washroom (6)
학생	student (5)	회사	company (5)
학생회관	student union (building) (6)	회사원	company employee (5)
		회화	conversation (8)
한	about, approximately (11)	후에	after, later (11)
		휴지	tissue paper; toilet tissue, Kleenex™ (7)
한국	Korea (5)		
한국말	Korean language (5)	흐리-	be cloudy, overcast (13)
한국사람	a Korean (5)	흐리-	become/get cloudy (13)
한국어	Korean language (8)	힘	strength, energy (8)
한국학	Korean Studies (8)	힘(이) 드-ㄹ-	be difficult, taxing (strength enters) (8)
할머니	grandmother (13)		
할머님	grandmother (honorific) (13)		
할아버님	grandfather (honorific) (13)		
할아버지	grandfather (13)		
함께	together (8)		
핫도그	hot dog (12)		
항상	always (8)		
해	years (counter) (11)		

ENGLISH to KOREAN VOCABULARY

a lot (adverb)	많이 (7)
a while later	이따가 (7)
a worry	걱정 (13)
about (numeral)	한 plus numeral (11)
above	위 (6)
across from	맞은편, 건너편 (6)
actor	배우 (9)
add (sugar)	타- (12)
adjacent to	다음 (6)
after	다음 (6); 후에 (11)
afternoon	오후 (7; 11)
again	또 (9)
age	나이 (11)
age (honorific)	연세 (11)
airplane	비행기 (7)
alcoholic drink	술 (5)
all	다 (5)
all	모두 (13)
all of it	전부 다 (5)
allright	괜찮- (8)
alone	혼자[서] (7)
already	벌써 (12)
always	항상 (8)
always	언제나 (8)
always	늘 (8)
A.M.	오전 (11)
America	미국 (5)
American	미국사람 (5)
And also	그리고 (6)

And so	그래서 (6)
And then	그래서 (6)
And then	그런데 (6)
And then	그리고 (6)
animal (counter)	마리 (11)
another	다른 (8)
answer (he phone)	받- (9)
anything (at all)	아무거나 (14)
apple	사과 (11)
approximately	한 (plus numeral) (11)
area near	근처 (6)
arm	팔 (14)
arrive	도착(을) 하- (9)
ascend	오르- (9)
ask	물- (7)
assignment	숙제 (13)
attend	다니- (7)
attend (church)	나가- (8
aunt (father's sister)	고모 (13)
aunt (mother's sister)	이모 (13)
Australia	호주 (5)
Australian	호주사람 (5)
automobile	자동차, 차 (9)
autumn	가을 (13)

baby	아기 (6)
baby	애기 (6)
back	뒤 (6)
back	등 (14)

bad	나쁘- (8)	black tea	홍차 (12)	
bad mood	기분(이) 나쁘- (14)	bloom	피- (12)	
		blossom	피- (12)	
bag	가방 (6)	book	책 (5)	
ballpoint pen	볼펜 (5)	bookstore	서점 (6)	
bank	은행 (5)	boots	부츠 (9)	
banker	은행원 (5)	bored	심심하- (12)	
bar	술집 (9)	boring	재미 없- (9)	
baseball	야구 (8)	born	태어나- (11)	
bathroom	화장실 (6)	both	둘 다 (13)	
be	있- (7)	bottle	병 (11)	
be (honorific)	계시- (8)	bottom	밑 (6)	
be better	나(ㅅ)- (7)	bound for	-행 (7)	
be introduced	소개(를) 받- (14)	bound volumes (counter)	권 (11)	
be invited	초대(를) 받- (14)	box	상자 (11)	
be sure to	꼭 (11)	boyfriend	남자친구 (6)	
be (same as, equal to)	-이- (7)	bread	빵 (7)	
beach	비치 (12)	breakfast	아침 (7)	
Because (sentence-initially)	왜냐하면 (11)	briefcase	가방 (6)	
because of	때문에 (9)	bright	똑똑하- (12)	
		bright	머리(가) 좋- (8)	
become	되- (7)	bring	갖다주- (14)	
beer	맥주 (11)	Briton	영국사람 (5)	
before	전에 (11)	brother (boy's older)	형 (13)	
before anything else	우선 (14)	brother (girl's older)	오빠 (12)	
before anything else	먼저 (8)	brothers (for males)	형제 (12)	
begin	시작(을) 하- (11)	brother and sister	남매 (13)	
beginning	처음 (11)	brothers and sisters	형제 (12)	
behind	뒤 (6)	brush (teeth)	닦- (9)	
below	아래 (6)	building	건물, 빌딩 (6)	
below	밑 (6)	buildings (counter)	채 (11)	
beside	옆 (6)	bus	버스 (8)	
between	사이 (6)	bus	뻐스 (8)	
beverage	음료수 (14)	bus stop	정류장 (14)	
bicycle	자전거 (7)	business	일 (7)	
bill (in a restaurant)	계산서 (14)	business	사업 (9)	
bird (counter)	마리 (11)	business	용무 (14)	
birthday	생일 (11), 생신 (honorific) (11)	business card	명함 (9)	
bite	무-ㄹ- (7)	busy	바쁘- (7)	
blackboard	칠판 (5)			

But (sentence-initially)	그런데 (6)	cigarette(s)	담배 (5)
But (sentence-initially)	그렇지만 (5)	cinema	극장 (7)
buy	사- (7)	city	도시 (12)
by oneself	혼자[서] (7)	city center	시내 (14)
By the way	그런데 (6)	City Hall	시청 (6)
		class	반 (14)
		class	수업 (8)

C

		classroom	교실 (6)
		clean	깨끗하- (8)
cafe	까페 (12)	cleaners	세탁소 (12)
cafeteria	식당 (7)	clean up	청소(를) 하- (12)
campus	캠퍼스 (6)	cleanly	깨끗이 (8)
Canada	캐나다 (5)	close	가까w- (13)
Canadian person	캐나다사람 (5)	close it	닫- (7)
car	자동차, 차 (9)	clothes	옷 (9)
car	차 (7)	coat	코트 (9)
cartoon	만화 (12)	coffee	커피 (12)
case	상자 (11)	cola	콜라 (12)
cat	고양이 (7)	cold	추w- (13)
catch (something said)	알아들- (8)	college	대학 (8)
chair	의자 (6)	comb	빗- (14)
chalk	분필 (5)	come	오- (7)
change (clothes)	갈아입- (14)	come (riding)	타고오- (14)
change, exchange	바꾸- (14)	come back	돌아오- (12)
chat	얘기, 이야기 (9)	come down	내려오- (9)
chat	이야기(를) 하- (9)	come in	들어오- (12)
cheap	싸- (8)	come on foot	걸어오- (12)
check (in a restaurant)	계산서 (14)	come out	나오- (9)
chest	상자 (11)	come up	올라오- (9)
child	아이 (6)	comedy	코메디 (13)
child	애 (6)	comfortable	편하- (14)
children (honorific)	자녀분, 자제분 (13)	comfortably	편히 (14)
China	중국 (5)	comic	만화 (12)
Chinese language	중국말 (5)	company	회사 (5)
Chinese person	중국사람 (5)	company employee	회사원 (5)
church (Catholic)	성당 (8)	company president	사장 (5)
church (Protestant)	교회 (8)	concert	음악회 (12)

consulate	영사관 (6)	daughter-in-law	며느리 (13)
contact	연락(을) 하- (9)	dawn	새벽 (11)
contact	통하- (13)	day	날 (7)
contact lenses	렌즈 (13)	day after tomorrow	모레 (14)
convenient	편하- (14)	day before yesterday	그저께 (14)
conveniently	편히 (14)	days (counter)	일 (11)
conversation	회화 (8)	daytime	낮 (7)
cook	요리(를) 하- (12)	degree of temperature	도 (11)
cooking	요리 (12)	delicious	맛(이) 있- (7)
copula	-이- (7)	depart	떠나- (7)
correct	맞- (13)	department store	백화점 (6)
corridor	복도 (12)	descend	내리- (9)
cost	값 (9)	desk	책상 (6)
cost money	돈(이) 드-ㄹ- (14)	die	죽- (14)
country	나라 (5)	die (honorific)	돌아가시- (14)
countryside	시골 (12)	different	다르- (11)
cousin	사촌 (13)	difficult	힘(이) 드-ㄹ- (8)
cousin (boy or girl's younger cousin)	사촌동생 (13)	difficult	어려w- (8)
cousin (boy's older female cousin)	사촌누나 (13)	diligently	열심히 (8)
cousin (boy's older male cousin)	사촌형 (13)	dining room	식당 (7)
cousin (girl's older female cousin)	사촌언니 (13)	diplomat	외교관 (5)
		direction	쪽 (6)
cream	크림 (12)	direction	편 (6)
cream (fresh)	생크림 (12)	dirty dishes	설겆이 (13)
creamer (nondairy)	프리마 (12)	dislike it	싫어하- (12)
credit card	신용카드 (8)	disliked	싫- (12)
cuisine	요리 (12)	distant	머-ㄹ- (8)
cupfuls (counter)	잔 (11)	distasteful	싫- (12)
customer	손님 (12)	divorce	이혼(을) 하- (13)
cut	자르- (8)		
cut (hair)	깎- (8)	do	하- (7)
cute	예쁘- (14)	do (it) well	잘하- (7)
		do laundry	세탁(을) 하- (12)
D		do the dishes	설겆이(를) 하- (13)
		doctor	의사 (5)
dance	춤(을) 추- (12)	dog	개 (7)
date	데이트 (13)	dollar	달라 (11)
daughter	딸 (9)	dollar (counter)	불 (11)
daughter (honorific)	따님 (13)	door	문 (6)
		dormitory	기숙사 (6)

down	아래 (6)
downstairs	아래 (6)
downstairs	아래층 (9)
downtown	시내 (14)
Dr., Ph.D.	박사 (5)
draft beer	생맥주 (12)
drama	연극 (12)
dress shirt	와이샤쓰, 샤쓰 (9)
drink	마시- (7)
drink	음료수 (14)
drink (honorific)	드시- (8)
drinking establishment	술집 (9)
dry cleaning	드라이크리닝 (12)
dumb	머리(가) 나쁘- (8)
during	동안 (13)
during the week	주중에 (11)

ear	귀 (14)
earlier	전에 (11)
early (adv)	일찍 (7)
early morning	새벽 (11)
easily	쉽게 (9)
easy	쉬w- (8)
eat	먹- (7)
eat (honorific)	잡수시- (8)
eat (honorific)	드시- (8)
economics	경제학 (8)
economy	경제 (8)
elevator	엘리베이터 (14)
embassy	대사관 (6)
end	끝 (11)
end	끝나- (7)
energy	힘 (8)
engaged	약혼(을) 하- (12)
England	영국 (5)
English language	영어 (5)

English tea	홍차 (12)
Englishman	영국사람 (5)
enjoyable	즐거w- (9)
enjoyably	즐겁게 (9)
enter	들어오- (12)
enter	들어가- (12)
errand	부탁(을) 하- (8)
esteemed people (counter)	-분 (11)
Even so (sentence-initially)	그래도 (6)
evening	저녁 (7)
every day	매일 (8)
everyone	모두 (13)
everything	다 (5)
everything	전부 다 (5)
Ewha Women's University	이대 (6)
exactly at (a time)	정각(에) (11)
examination	시험 (14)
exchange	교환 (8)
exchange, change	바꾸- (14)
exchange student	교환학생 (8)
Excuse me!	여기 좀 봐요! (12)
exercise	운동 (13)
exist	있- (7)
exist (honorific)	계시- (8)
expensive	비싸- (7)
eye	눈 (14)

fact	사실 (9)
fall	가을 (13)
family	가족 (9)
family members	식구 (13)
far	머-ㄹ- (8)
far (adverb)	멀리 (13)
fast	빠르- (7)
father	아버지 (6)
father (honorific)	아버님 (7)

father-in-law (man's)	장인 (13)
father-in-law (man's) (elegant)	장인어른 (13)
father-in-law (woman's, honorific)	시아버님 (13)
father-in-law (woman's)	시아버지 (13)
favor	부탁(을) 하- (8)
feel sorry	미안하- (7)
feelings	기분 (14)
fetch (money)	찾- (9)
few	적- (7)
fiancé(e)	약혼자 (12)
film	영화 (7)
find	찾- (7)
finger	손가락 (14)
finish	끝나- (7)
finish it	끝내- (11)
finish it	마치- (12)
fire	불 (7)
first (of all)	먼저 (8)
first	첫 (7)
first of all	우선 (14)
first-year student	일학년(생) (14)
fish (counter)	마리 (11)
flat objects (counter)	장 (11)
floor above	위층 (9)
floor below	아래층 (9)
floor, story (counter)	층 (11)
flower	꽃 (12)
food	음식 (7)
foot	발 (14)
footgear	신발 (9)
for the duration of	동안 (13)
for the most part	주로 (8)
for (a week, etc.)	동안 (13)
foreign cigarettes	양담배 (12)
foreign country	외국 (5)
foreign language	외국어 (5)
foreigner	외국사람 (5)
forget	잊어버리- (11)

forgive	용서(를) 하- (11)
France	프랑스 (5)
French language	프랑스말; 불어 (5)
French person	프랑스사람 (5)
fresh cream	생크림 (12)
Friday	금요일 (7)
friend	친구 (5)
from a distance	멀리서 (13)
front	앞 (6)
fruit	과일 (11)
full	배(가) 부르- (12)
full (stomach)	부르- (7)
fun	즐거w- (9)

G

garden	정원 (9)
gate	문 (6)
German	독일사람 (5)
German language	독일말; 독어 (5)
Germany	독일 (5)
get	받- (7)
get a haircut	머리(를) 자르- (females), 머리(를) 깎- (males) (8)
get across (message)	통하- (13)
get along	지내- (7)
get (money) from	찾- (9)
get better	나(ㅅ)- (7)
get drunk	취하- (14)
get engaged	약혼(을) 하- (12)
get hurt	다치- (14)
get in touch	연락(을) 하- (9)
get introduced	소개(를) 받- (14)
get invited	초대(를) 받- (14)
get tipsy	취하- (14)
get up	일어나- (7)
gift	선물 (14)
ginseng	인삼 (5)
ginseng wine	인삼주 (5)

girlfriend	여자친구 (6)
give	주- (7)
give (honorific)	드리- (13)
given name	이름 (8)
glasscs	안경 (9)
gloves	장갑 (9)
glue	풀 (12)
go	가- (7)
go (riding)	타고가- (14)
go (and come back)	갔다오- (9)
go back	돌아가- (12)
go down	내려가- (9)
go in	들어가- (12)
go on a regular basis	다니- (7)
go on foot	걸어가- (12)
go out	나가- (9)
go sight-seeing	구경 (을) 가- (7)
go up	올라가- (9)
go viewing	구경 (을) 가- (7)
golf	골프 (13)
good	좋- (7)
good by nature, good	착하- (8)
good-looking	잘 생겼- (9)
good mood	기분 (이) 좋- (14)
Good night. (polite, but not honorific)	잘 자요. (8)
good(s)	제품 (5)
goods	물건 (11)
graduate	졸업 (을) 하- (13)
grandchild(ren)	손주 (아이) (13)
granddaughter	손녀 (딸) (13)
grandfather	할아버지 (13)
grandfather (honorific)	할아버님 (13)
grandfather (mother's side)	외할아버지 (13)
grandmother	할머니 (13)
grandmother (honorific)	할머님 (13)
grandmother (mother's side	외할머니 (13)
grandparents	조부모 (13)

grandson	손자 (13)
Great East Gate	동대문 (6)
Great South Gate	남대문 (6)
grocery shopping	장 (을) 보- (7)
guest	손님 (12)

 H

hair	머리 (8)
half	반 (11)
hallway	복도 (12)
hamburger	햄버거 (12)
hand	손 (14)
handsome	잘 생겼- (9)
hat	모자 (9)
have	있- (7)
head	머리 (8)
health	건강 (12)
healthy	건강하- (12)
hear	들- (7)
heart	마음 (12)
heavy	무거w- (12)
Hello!	여보세요! (12)
help	도와주- (11)
here	여기 (6)
Hey there!	저기요! (12)
his wife	부인 (5)
hit	치- (7)
hit the mark	맞- (13)
hold	드-ㄹ- (14)
home	집 (5)
homework	숙제 (13)
Hong Kong	홍콩 (5)
hot	더 w- (7)
hot dog	핫도그 (12)
hotel	호텔 (6)
hotel	여관 (9)
hours (counter)	시간 (11)
house	집 (5)
house (honorific)	댁 (9)

how about it?	어때요? (12)	inside	안 (6)
how is it?	어때요? (12)	inside	속 (6)
how many?	얼마 (6)	institution (counter)	군데 (11)
how many?	몇 (7)	intelligent	똑똑하- (12)
how much (about)?	얼마나 (11)	intelligent	머리(가) 좋- (14)
how much?	얼마 (6)	interesting	재미 있- (9)
how?	어떻게? (12)	interestingly	재미있게 (9)
hurt	아프- (14)	introduce	소개(를) 하- (14)
husband	남편 (5)	invite someone	초대(를) 하- (14)

I

		Is it true?	정말이에요? (8)
		It doesn't work.	안 돼요. (8)
		It won't do.	안 돼요. (8)
I	나 (5)	It works.	돼요. (8)
I don't really know, Let me think.	글쎄요 (9)	It'll do.	돼요. (8)
ice	얼음 (12)	It's acceptable.	돼요. (8)
ice coffee	냉커피 (12)	It's going well.	잘 돼요. (8)
ice cream	아이스크림 (12)	It's no good.	안 돼요. (8)
ice slush	빙수 (12)	It's not acceptable.	안 돼요. (8)
ice water	냉수 (12)	It's not going well.	잘 안 돼요. (8)
If so (sentence-initially)	그러면 (5)	It's OK.	돼요. (8)
imported goods	수입품 (5)	It's turning out well.	잘 돼요. (8)
impressive	굉장하- (9)	item (counter)	개 (11)
in a while	이따가 (7)		

J

in fact	사실 (9)		
in fact	실은 (9)		
In fact (sentence-initially)	사실은 (9)	Japan	일본 (5)
In that case (sentence-initially)	그러면 (5)	Japanese language	일본말; 일어 (5)
In that case (sentence-initially)	그럼 (5)	Japanese person	일본사람 (5)
in that way	그렇게 (13)	jacket	쟈켓 (9)
in what way?	어떻게? (12)	jazz	째즈 (12)
inconvenient	불편하- (14)	jeans	청바지 (9)
in-law's home (honor-fic, for females)	시댁 (13)	juice	쥬스 (8)
inexpensive	싸- (8)	jumper (sweater)	세타 (9)
injure oneself	다치- (14)	junk	엉터리 (11)
inn	여관 (9)	just (as one is)	그냥 (13)
insert	넣- (12)	just (below, above)	바로 (6)
		just a moment ago	방금 (9)
		just a moment ago	아까 (13)
		just now	방금 (9)

K

karaoke box	노래방 (7)
kind (counter)	가지 (11)
kitchen	부엌 (13)
Kleenex™	휴지 (7)
knee	무릎 (14)
know it	아-ㄹ- (7)
Korea	한국 (5)
Korea University	고대 (6)
Korean language	한국말 (5)
Korean language	한국어 (8)
Korean mile (counter)	리 (11)
Korean monetary unit	-원 (6)
Korean person	한국사람 (5)
Kwanghwa Gate	광화문 (6)

L

language	말 (5)
large	크- (7)
last	지난 (11)
last year	작년 (9)
late	늦- (13)
late (adverb)	늦게 (7)
later	후에 (11) 나중에 (11)
launder	세탁(을) 하- (12)
laundromat	세탁소 (12)
laundry	세탁 (12)
learn	배우- (7)
leave	떠나- (7)
left side	왼쪽 (6)
left side	왼편 (6)
leg	다리 (14)
lesson	수업 (8)
letter	편지 (7)
library	도서관 (7)
lie down	누w- (14)
lift	엘리베이터 (14)

lift	드-ㄹ- (14)
light	가벼w- (12)
light	불 (7)
lighter	라이타 (6)
like it	좋아하- (8, 12)
like that	그렇게 (13)
like that	저렇게 (13)
like this	이렇게 (13)
liked	좋- (12)
listen to	들- (7)
little	작- (7)
little	조금 (7), 좀 (8)
live	사-ㄹ- (7)
living room	마루 (13)
London	런던 (8)
look at	보- (7)
look for	찾- (7)
love	사랑 (8)
love	사랑(을) 하- (8)
lower	아래 (6)
lower back	허리 (14)
lunch	점심 (7)

M

ma'am (any woman old enough to be married)	아주머니 (13)
ma'am (casual)	아줌마 (13)
machine (counter)	대 (11)
magazine	잡지 (5)
mail it	부치- (9)
main gate	정문 (6)
mainly	주로 (8)
major	전공
major in something	전공(을) 하- (8)
make contact	연락(을) 하- (9)
make a reservation	예약(을) 하- (8)
man	남자 (6)
manufactured good(s)	제품 (5)
many	많- (7)
many (adverb)	많이 (7)

market	시장 (6)
marry	결혼(을) 하- (12)
match(es)	성냥 (5)
materials (written)	자료 (14)
matter	일 (7)
matter to take care of	용무 (14)
maybe	아마 (13)
maybe (more tentative)	아마도 (13)
meal (honorific)	진지 (13)
meat	고기 (7)
medicine	약 (8)
meet	만나- (7)
members of the family	식구 (13)
metro	지하철 (12)
midway	중간, 중간에 (9)
middle	중간 (9)
milk	우유 (7)
mind	마음 (12)
minutes (counter)	분 (11)
missionary	선교사 (13)
mister (any man old enough to be married)	아저씨 (13)
moment	잠깐 (12)
Monday	월요일 (7)
money	돈 (6)
month	달 (11)
month (counter)	개월 (11)
month names	월 (달) (11)
mood	기분 (14)
more	더 (9)
Moreover (sentence-initially)	또 (9)
morning	아침 (7)
most	가장, 제일 (14)
mostly	주로 (8)
mother	어머니 (6)
mother (honorific)	어머님 (7)
mother-in-law (man's)	장모 (13)

mother-in-law (woman's, honorific)	시어머님 (13)
mother-in-law (woman's)	시어머니 (13)
mountain	산 (12)
movie	영화 (7)
movie actor	영화배우 (9)
movie theatre	극장 (7)
mow (grass)	깎- (8)
much	많- (7)
music	음악 (12)

name	이름 (8)
namecard	명함 (9)
nation	나라 (5)
national	국립 (8)
national university	국립대학교 (8)
near	가까w- (13)
neatly	깨끗이 (8)
necktie	넥타이 (13)
neighborhood	동네 (11)
nephew	조카 (13)
Nevertheless (sentence-initially)	그래도 (6)
new	새 (9)
New York	뉴욕 (8)
news (radio/TV)	뉴스
newspaper	신문 (5)
next to	다음 (6)
next to	옆 (6)
next year	내년 (11)
nice	좋- (7)
niece	조카 딸 (13)
night	밤 (7)
nondairy creamer	프리마 (12)
nonexistent	없- (7)
noon	낮 (7)
normally	보통 (7)

nose	코 (14)		opposite	맞은편, 건너편 (6)
not exist	없- (7)		or	아니면
not have	없- (7)		orange juice	오렌지 쥬스 (8)
not interesting	재미 없- (9)		order	시키- (11)
not know	모르- (7)		order (at restaurant)	주문(을) 하- (12)
not particularly	별로 + negative (9)		other	다른 (8)
not yet	아직 (8)		our	우리 (5)
notebook	공책 (5), 노트 (5)		outside	밖 (6)
now	지금 (7)		over	위 (6)
now (finally)	이제 (12)		over there	저기 (6)
now (finally)	인제 (12)			
nowadays	요즘 (7)			
number	번호 (11)			
number one	제일 (14)			

o'clock (counter)	시 (11)
obey	말(을) 들- (8)
object (counter)	개 (11)
ocean	바다 (12)
odd	이상하- (13)
Of course.	물론이에요. (14)
of course	물론 (14)
office	사무실 (9)
office (professor's)	연구실 (9)
often	자주 (8)
often	잘 (7)
OK	괜찮- (8)
older sister (boy's)	누나 (13)
older sister (boy's) (honorific)	누님 (13)
older sister (girl's)	언니 (12)
on account of	때문에 (9)
on one's own	혼자[서] (7)
one time	언젠가 (7)
open it	여-ㄹ- (7)
operator	교환원 (8)

pack (of cigarettes)	갑 (11)
painful	아프- (14)
pair [of shoes, etc.]	켤레 (9)
paper	종이 (5)
paper bag	봉지 (11)
parents	부모(들) (6)
parents-in-law (man's)	장인장모 (13)
parents-in-law (for females)	시부모 (13)
parents-in-law's home for females, honorific)	시댁 (13)
park	공원 (6)
(not) particularly	별로 + negative (9)
part-time student work	아르바이트 (11)
party	파티 (11)
pass away	돌아가시- (14)
passionate(ly)	정열적(으로) (8)
past	지난 (11)
pay	내- (14)
pen	펜 (5)
pen (ballpoint)	볼펜 (5)
pencil	연필 (5)
people (counter)	사람 (11)
people (counter)	명 (11)
people (honorific counter)	-분 (11)
person	사람 (5)

person (counter)	명 (11)	probably	아마 (13)
person (honorific)	-분 (5)	probably (more tentative)	아마도 (13)
person born in such-and-such a year	-년생 (이에요) (11)	problem	문제 (14)
Ph.D. (Dr.)	박사 (5)	professor	교수 (5)
physician	의사 (5)	program on TV	프로 (13)
piano	피아노 (5)	province	주 (8)
pibimpap	비빔밥 (7)	provincial(-ly estab-lished)	주립 (8)
picture	그림 (6)	*pulgogi*	불고기 (7)
pizza	피자 (12)	put in	넣- (12)
place	-곳 (5), 데 (13)	put in (sugar)	타- (12)
place (counter)	군데 (11)	put it	놓- (11)
place it	놓- (11)	put on	입- (7)
platform	플랫폼 (7)	put on (a tie)	매- (9)
play	연극 (12)		
play	노-ㄹ- (7)		
play baseball	야구(를) 하- (8)	**Q**	
play golf	골프(를) 치- (13)		
play piano	치- (12)	quick	빠르- (7)
play tennis	테니스(를) 치- (12)	quickly	빨리 (7)
pleasant	즐거w- (9)	quit (smoking, drinking)	끊- (14)
please (to soften a request)	좀 (8)	quite something	굉장하- (9)
P.M.	오후 (11)		
polish	닦- (9)	**R**	
political science	정치학 (8)		
politics	정치 (8)	rain	비 (13)
popsinger	가수 (5)	rainy season	장마 (13)
portion (of food)	-인분 (14)	rainy season sets in	장마(가) 지- (13)
post it	부치- (9)	read	읽- (7)
post office	우체국 (9)	read	보- (7)
potato chips	감자깡 (11)	Really?	정말이에요? (8)
potato(es)	감자 (11)	really	정말(로) (8)
pounds (sterling))	파운드 (11)	really	참 (8)
pour (rain)	쏟아지- (13)	receive	받- (7)
present	선물 (14)	refectory	식당 (7)
pretty	예쁘- (14)	relative	친척 (13)
price	값 (9)	request	부탁(을) 하- (8)
private university	사립대학교 (8)	research	연구 (9)
private(-ly established)	사립 (8)	reservation	예약 (8)

residence hall	기숙사 (6)	see	보- (7)
rest	쉬- (7)	see a film	영화구경(을) 하- (7)
restaurant	식당, 음식점, 레스토랑 (7)	sell it	파-ㄹ- (7)
		semester	학기 (14)
restroom	화장실 (6)	Seoul National University	서울대 (6)
retire	은퇴(를) 하- (12)		
return here	돌아오- (12)	set in (rainy season)	장마(가) 지- (13)
return home	들어오- (12)	several	몇 (11)
return there	돌아가- (12)	several	여러 (11)
rice (honorific)	진지 (13)	sharpen (pencil)	깎- (8)
rice (cooked)	밥 (7)	shaved ice	빙수 (12)
rich person	부자 (11)	shirt	와이샤쓰 (9)
		shirt	샤쓰 (9)
ride in/on	타- (12)	shoes	구두, 신발 (9)
right	맞- (13)		
right side	오른편, 오른쪽 (6)	shop	가게 (6)
ring	반지 (9)	shop	상점 (7)
rise	오르- (9)	shopping	쇼핑 (14)
road	길 (11)	short while	잠깐 (12)
room	방 (6)	short while	잠시 (14)
rubbish	엉터리 (11)	short while ago	아까 (13)
Russia	러시아 (5)	shrimp	새우 (11)
Russian language	러시아말 (5)	shrimp chips	새우깡 (11)
Russian person	러시아사람 (5)	side	쪽 (6)
		side	편 (6)
		side dishes	반찬 (14)
		sightsee	구경(을) 하- (7)

S

		similar	같-
same	같-	sing (a song)	부르- (7)
sandwich	샌드위치 (12)	single (unmarried)	미혼(이에요) (13)
Saturday	토요일 (7)	sister (older, girl's)	언니 (12)
Say there!	여기 좀 봐요! (12)	sister (younger)	여동생 (13)
says (honorific)	말씀(을) 하시- (13)	sisters	자매 (13)
says (humble)	말씀(을) 드리- (13)	sits	앉- (7)
scarf	스카프 (9)	skate(s)	스케이트 (12)
school	학교 (6)	skate	스케이트(를) 타- (12)
school subject	과목 (8)		
seasonal rains	장마 (13)	skirt	치마 (9)
second (time)	초 (11)	ski(s)	스키 (12)
second-year student	이학년(생) (14)	ski	스키(를) 타- (12)
sea	바다 (12)	skirt	치마 (9)

sleep	자- (7)	starch it	풀(을) 먹이- (12)
sleep (honorific)	주무시- (8)	start term/school	개학(을) 하- (14)
slowly	천천히 (8)	state	주 (8)
smart	머리(가) 좋- (8)	state university	주립대학교 (8)
smoke	피우- (7)	state (-established)	주립 (8)
snacks to go with alcohol	안주 (11)	station	정거장 (14)
		stay	있- (7)
sneakers	운동화 (9)	stay (honorific)	계시- (8)
snow	눈 (13)	still	아직 (8)
so	그렇게 (13)	stomach	배 (12)
So, what I mean to say is	그러니까 (13)	stop	끝나- (7)
		stop	정거장 (14)
socks	양말 (9)	stop (bus)	정류장 (14)
soldier	군인 (13)	store	상점 (7)
solve it	푸-ㄹ- (14)	story	얘기, 이야기 (9)
some	몇 (11)	straight	바로 (6)
some time ago	언젠가 (7)	strange	이상하- (13)
sometime or other	언젠가 (7)	street	길 (11)
sometimes	가끔 (8)	strength	힘 (8)
son	아들 (9)	strike	치- (7)
son (honorific)	아드님 (13)	stroll	산보(를) 하- (7)
son-in-law	사위 (13)	student	학생 (5)
song	노래 (7)	student union (building)	학생회관 (6)
sorry	미안하- (7)	study	공부(를) 하- (7)
speak	말(을) 하- (7)	subject	과목 (8)
specialization	전공	suburb(s)	교외 (12)
speech (honorific or humble)	말씀 (8)	subway	지하철 (12)
		suddenly	갑자기 (12)
spend (time)	보내- (9)	sugar	설탕 (12)
spicy	매w- (11)	suit	양복 (9)
spine	등 (14)	summer	여름 (13)
spiritual center	마음 (12)	Sunday	일요일 (7)
sports	운동 (13)	supermarket	슈퍼마켓 (7)
sports	스포츠 (13)	supper	저녁 (7)
sports stadium	운동장 (13)	surname	성 (8)
spring	봄 (13)	surname (honorific)	성함, 성씨 (8)
squid	오징어 (11)	sweater	세타 (9)
squid chips	오징어깡 (11)	swim	수영(을) 하- (8)
stand	서- (7)	swimming pool	수영장 (8)
starch	풀 (12)		

T

tabang	다방 (9)
table	상, 테이블 (6)
take (courses)	들- (듣다) (8)
take (time)	걸리- (7)
take medicine	약(을) 먹- (8)
take off (clothes)	벗- (7)
talk	얘기, 이야기 (9)
talk	말(을) 하- (7), 이야기(를) 하- (11)
taste	맛 (7)
taste bad	맛 없- (7)
tasty	맛(이) 있- (7)
tavern	술집 (9)
taxing	힘(이) 드-ㄹ- (8)
tea	차 (9)
tea (black/Indian)	홍차 (12)
tea room	다방 (9)
teach	가르치- (7)
teacher	선생 (5)
teaching materials	교재 (8)
teeth	이 (9)
telephone	전화 (8)
telephone	전화(를) 하- (8); 전화(를) 거-ㄹ- (9)
telephone number	전화번호 (11)
television	텔레비전 (6)
tennis	테니스 (12)
tennis shoes	운동화 (9)
term	학기 (14)
textbook	교재 (8)
thankful	고마w- (11)
thanks to	덕분에 (14)
that	그 (5)
that way	저렇게 (13)
The reason is (sentence-initially)	왜냐하면 (11)
theatre	극장 (7)
Then (sentence-initially)	그럼 (5)
Then (sentence-initially)	그러면 (5)
there	거기 (6)
Therefore (sentence-initially)	그래서 (6)
these days	요즘 (7)
third-year student	삼학년(생) (14)
this	이 (5)
this (week,)	이번 (11)
this way	이렇게 (13)
this year	금년 (11)
thousand	천 (6)
throw it away	버리- (13)
Thursday	목요일 (7)
ticket	표 (7)
ticket (for train or bus)	차표 (7)
ticket counter	매표소 (7)
tie	넥타이 (13)
tie	매- (7)
time	시간 (7)
time (when)	때 (12)
times (counter)	번 (11)
tip	끝 (11)
tired	피곤하- (12)
tissue paper	휴지 (7)
today	오늘 (7)
toe	발가락 (14)
together	같이 〔가치〕 (8)
together	함께 (8)
toilet	화장실 (6)
toilet tissue	휴지 (7)
tomato juice	토마토 쥬스 (8)
tomorrow	내일 (7)
too	너무 (8)
too much so	너무 (8)
tooth	이 (9)
top	위 (6)
total	전부 (5)
towel	수건, 타올 (7)

trade	무역 (9)
trading company	무역회사 (9)
train	기차 (7)
train station	역 (6)
tree	나무 (6)
trousers	바지 (9)
truly	정말(로) (8)
truly	참 (8)
Tuesday	화요일 (7)
turn out a certain way	생기- (9)

ugly	못 생겼- (9)
umbrella	우산 (5)
uncle (father's elder brother)	큰아버지 (13)
uncle (father's sister's husband)	고모부 (13)
uncle (father's younger brother)	작은 아버지 (13)
uncle (mother's sister's husband)	이모부 (13)
uncle (father's side)	삼촌 (13)
uncle (mother's side)	외삼촌 (13)
uncomfortable	불편하- (14)
underneath	밑 (6)
underground	지하철 (12)
understand something said	알아들- (8)
undo it	푸-ㄹ- (14)
unit (counter)	개 (11)
university	대학교 (6)
unmarried	미혼(이에요) (13)
upstairs	위 (6)
upstairs	위층 (9)
USA	미국 (5)
use it	쓰- (8)
usually	보통 (7)

vacation	방학 (11)
variety (counter)	가지 (11)
various	여러 (11)
vehicle	차 (7)
vehicle (counter)	대 (11)
very	아주 (7)
very	굉장히 (14)
very	너무 (8)
very much	굉장히 (14)
vicinity	근처 (6)
view	구경 (을) 하- (7)

waist	허리 (14)
wait	기다리- (7)
walk	걸- (12)
walk	걸어오- (12)
walk	걸어가- (12)
walk	산보(를) 하- (7)
want to	싶- (9)
wash the dishes	설겆이(를) 하- (13)
washroom	화장실 (6)
watch	시계 (9)
water	물 (7)
way	길 (11)
we	우리 (5)
wear	입- (7)
wear (a tie)	매- (9)
wear (a watch)	차- (9)
wear (glasses)	쓰- (13)
wear (a hat)	쓰- (13)
wear (footwear)	신- (9)
wear (gloves, ring)	끼- (9)
wear (lenses)	끼- (13)
weather	날씨 (13)

Wednesday	수요일 (7)		
week	주일 (11)		

Wednesday	수요일 (7)
week	주일 (11)
week (counter)	주간 (11)
weekend	주말 (7)
well	잘 (7)
western spirits	양주 (12)
what kind of?	무슨? (5)
what NOUN?	어느 NOUN? (5)
What's more (sentence-initially)	또 (9)
what?	무엇, 뭐 (5)
when?	언제 (7)
where?	어디 (6)
which?	어느 NOUN? 무슨 NOUN? (5)
while (in a while, a while later)	이따가 (7)
whiskey	양주 (12); 위스키 (5)
who? (as subject)	누가 (5)
who? (nonsubject)	누구 (5)
whole thing	전부 (5)
why	왜 (요)? (11)
wife (my)	아내, 집사람 (5)
wife (elegant/honorific)	사모님 (9)
wife (his/your)	부인 (5)
window	창문 (6)
wine	와인 (5)
winter	겨울 (13)
withdraw (money)	찾- (9)
without doing anything	그냥 (13)
without fail	꼭 (11)
woman	여자 (6)
words	말 (5)
words (honorific or humble)	말씀 (8)
work	일 (을) 하- (7)
worry	걱정 (을) 하- (13)
write	쓰- (7)

Y

year	해 (11)
year or grade (at school)	-학년 (이에요) (11)
years of age	살 (11)
yesterday	어제 (7)
yet again	또 (9)
yon	저 (5)
Yonsei University	연대 (6)
young (a child)	어리- (13)
young (but past puberty)	젊- (11)
young lady	아가씨 (6)
younger brother	남동생 (13)
younger brother or sister; younger cousin (either gender)	동생 (9)
younger sister or brother	동생 (9)
your wife	부인 (5)

KOREAN to ENGLISH
PATTERN GLOSSARY

<u>Korean Pattern</u>	<u>English Gloss</u>	<u>Section</u>
ㄱ		
가 ~ 이	subject/focus particle	5.2
같아요	be like something	9.4
같이	like; together	9.4
-겠-	future-presumptive base; inferential or intentional (*I shall, I will, I'll bet*)	14.4
-고 싶어요	want to, wish to, would like to	9.6
-고 있어요	progressive (*is doing*)	13.6
과 ~ 와	and	9.2
과 ~ 와 같이	(together) with	9.3
과 ~ 와 함께	(together) with	9.3
까지	as far as; by; until; up to	11.4
께	honorific 에게 ~ 한테	13.2
께서 (는)	honorific 이 ~ 가	13.2
ㄴ		
나 ~ 이나	generalizer (*any/every*); about,; approximately; or, or something;	12.6.2
	as many as, as much as	14.2
는 ~ 은	topic/contrast Particle	5.2, 6.6
-니 (까) ~ -으니 (까)	sequential ending (*as, because, since; when* [I realized])	13.1

ㄷ

ㄷ ~ ㄹ	special consonant base	7.4
-다	dictionary form	7.3
도	also, even, too, [not] either	5.4, 7.11, 12.3, 12.6
들	plural marker	6.8
또	again, and, moreover; then again; what's more (adverb)	12.6

ㄹ

-ㄹ (← 을)	(direct) object particle	7.6
ㄹ ~ ㄷ	special consonant base	7.4
ㄹ- doubling	special vowel base	7.5
ㄹ- extending	special vowel base	7.5
-ㄹ 거에요 ~ -을 거에요	probable future (*is going to, will probably*)	13.4
-ㄹ까 해요 ~ -을까해요	thinking of doing	12.5
-ㄹ까요 ~ -을까요	suggestions/tentative questions (*do you suppose? how about? I wonder: do(es)? Shall I/we?*)	12.4
-ㄹ께요 ~ -을께요	immediate future (*Let me*)	14.6
-ㄹ래요 ~ -을래요	wanna form (*feel like, have a mind to, would like to*)	12.8
랑 ~ 이랑	and	8.6
랑 ~ 이랑 같이	(together) with	9.3
랑 ~ 이랑 함께	(together) with	9.3
-러 ~ -으러	purposive ending (*for the purpose of, intending to, with the intention to*)	9.5
로 ~ 으로	instrumental particle	8.5
를 ~ 을	(direct) object particle	7.6

마다	each; every	11.3
만	just; only	11.3
못	negative marker (*cannot, not*)	8.1

ㅂ ~ w	special consonant base	7.4
-ㅂ니까 ~ -습니까	formal question	11.5
-ㅂ니다 ~ -습니다	formal statement	11.5
-ㅂ시다 ~ -읍시다	formal suggestion	11.5
밖에 + negative	only	14.1
부터	from	11.4

ㅅ- irregular verbs	special consonant base	7.4
-ㅆ-	past base	9.1
-ㅆ겠-	past-future (*must have done/been*)	14.5
-ㅆ어-	past infinitive	9.1
-ㅆ어요	past tense, Polite Style	9.1
-ㅆ었-	past-past	14.5
서 ← 에서	dynamic location (*at/in*); from (places)	7.8
-세요 ~ -으세요	honorific Polite Style	8.2.1
-습니까 ~ -ㅂ니까	formal question	11.5
-습니다 ~ -ㅂ니다	formal statement	11.5
-시- ~ -으시-	honorific marker	8.2.2
-시오 ~ -으시오	formal command	11.5
-시지요 ~ -으시지요	Please do it.	14.8
싫어요 ~ 싫어해요	dislike it	12.9
-십시오 ~ -으십시오	formal (honorific) command	11.5
씩	distributive (*apiece, per*)	11.3

-아 ~ -어	infinitive ending	7.1
아니다	negative copula	5.3
아니면	or	12.7
아니에요	negative copula	5.3
아닙니다	negative copula	5.3
안	negative marker (*doesn't, not*)	8.1
-았-	past base	9.1
-았어-	past infinitive	9.1
-았어요	past tense, Polite Style	9.1
-어 ~ -아	infinitive ending	7.1
없어요 ~ 있어요	existence; location; possession (*not be/be, not have/have*)	6.2
-었-	past base	9.1
-었어-	past infinitive	9.1
-었어요	past tense, Polite Style	9.1
에	Static Location (*at*), Direction Particle (*to*)	7.8
에게	Direction Particle (*to* [people])	7.7
에게서	Direction Particle (*from* [people])	7.7
-에요 ~ -이에요	copula	5.3
와 ~ 과	and	9.2.
와 ~ 과 같이	(together) with	9.3
와 ~ 과 함께	(together) with	9.3
요	Polite Style particle	7.1
-으니(까) ~ -니(까)	sequential ending (*as, because, since; When* [I realized])	13.1
-으러 ~ -러	purposive ending (*for the purpose of, intending to, with the intention to*)	9.5
으로 ~ 로	instrumental particle	8.5
-으세요 ~ -세요	honorific Polite Style	8.2.1
-으시- ~ -시-	honorific marker	8.2.2
-으시오 ~ -시오	formal command	11.5
-으시지요 ~ -시지요	Please do it.	14.8
-으십시오 ~ -십시오	formal (honorific) command	11.5
은 ~ 는	topic/contrast particle	5.2., 6.6
을 ~ 를	(direct) object particle	7.6

쯤	about; approximately; by	11.3

처럼	like	9.4

하고	and; with	6.4
하고 같이	(together) with	9.3
하고 함께	(together) with	9.3
한테	direction particle (*to* [people])	7.7
한테서	direction particle (*from* [people])	7.7

ENGLISH to KOREAN
PATTERN GLOSSARY

English Gloss	Korean Pattern	Section

A

about	(이)나	12.6.2
	쯤	11.3
adverbs		8.4
again (adverb)	또	12.6
also	도	5.4, 7.11, 12.3, 12.6
although	-지만	12.2.1
am	-이다, -이에요, -입니다	5.3
and	하고	6.4
	와 ~ 과	9.2
	(이)랑	8.6
and (adverb)	또	12.6
any/every	(이)나	12.6.2
apiece	씩	11.3
approximately	(이)나	12.6.2
	쯤	11.3
are	-이다, -이에요, -입니다	5.3
as	-(으)니(까)	13.1
as far as	까지	11.4
as many as	(이)나	14.2
as much as	(이)나	14.2
as soon as	-자 마자	13.7
at (dynamic location)	에서, 서	7.8
at (static location)	에	7.8

B

C

D

each	마다	11.3
equals	-이다, -이에요, -입니다	5.3
even	도	5.4, 7.11, 12.3, 12.6
every	마다	11.3
existence	없어요~있어요	6.1

feel like	-(으)ㄹ래요	12.8
for the purpose of	-(으)러	9.5
formal (honorific) command -	(으)십시오	11.5
formal command	-(으)시오	11.5
formal question	-ㅂ니까~-습니까	11.5
formal statement	-ㅂ니다~-습니다	11.5
formal suggestion	-ㅂ시다~-읍시다	11.5
from	부터	11.4
from (people)	한테서~에게서	7.7
from (places)	에서, 서	7.7
future-presumptive base	-겠-	14.4

generalizer	(이)나	12.6.2
going and coming		14.3
guess	-지요	14.8

have	없어요~있어요	6.2
have a mind to	-(으)ㄹ래요	12.8
honorific marker	-(으)시-	8.2.2

L

l ~ t (ㄹ ~ ㄷ) verbs	special consonant base	7.4
L-doubling verbs	special vowel base	7.5
L-extending verbs	special vowel base	7.5
Let me	-(으)ㄹ께요	14.6
Let's not	-지 맙시다	12.2.3
like	같이	9.4
	처럼	9.4
like it	좋아요~좋아해요	12.9
location	있어요~없어요	6.1
long negative	-지 않아요	12.2.2
long negative	-지 못 해요	12.2.2
long negatives		12.2.2

M

manner adverbs		7.12
moreover (adverb)	또	12.6
must have done/been	-ㅆ겠-	14.5

N

n'est-ce pas?	-지요	14.8
negative commands	-지 마-ㄹ-	12.2.3
negative copula	아닙니다, 아니에요, 아니다	5.3
negative honorifics		12.2.4
negative marker	안; 못	8.1
neither, nor	도, 도	7.11, 12.3
nicht wahr?	-지요	14.8
no sooner than	-자 마자	13.7
not (negative marker)	안; 못	8.1
not either	도	5.4, 7.11, 12.3, 12.6

object particle	-ㄹ, 를~을	7.6
only	만 plus affirmative	11.3
	밖에 plus negative	14.1
or	아니면	12.7
	또는	12.7
	(이)나	12.6.2
or something	(이)나	12.6.2

p ~ w (ㅂ ~ w) verbs	special consonant base	7.4
past base	-ㅆ-, -았-/-었-	9.1
past future	-ㅆ겠-	14.5
past infinitive	-았어-/-었어-, -ㅆ어-	9.1
past tense, Polite Style	-았어요/-었어요, -ㅆ어요	9.1
past-past	-ㅆ었-	14.5
per	씩	11.3
Please do it.	-(으)시지요	14.8
plural marker	들	6.8
Polite Style particle	요	7.1
possession	있어요~없어요	6.2
possessive particle	의	5.5
presume	-지요	14.8
	-겠-	14.4
probable future	-(으)ㄹ 거에요	13.4
progressive	-고 있어요	13.6
promise-like future	-(으)ㄹ께요	14.6
pronouns		5.1
purposive ending	-(으)러	9.5

R

S

T

until	까지	11.4
up to	까지	11.4

verbal nouns (descriptive)		8.3
verbal nouns (processive)		8.3

w - ㅂ verbs	special consonant base	7.4
wanna	-(으)ㄹ래요	12.8
want to	-고 싶어요	9.6
what's more (adverb)	또	12.6
When, [I realized]	-(으)니(까)	13.1
will	-겠-	14.4
will probably	-(으)ㄹ 거에요	13.4
wish to	-고 싶어요	9.6
with	하고,	6.4
	와~과,	9.2
	(이)랑	8.6
with the intention to	-(으)러	9.5
would like to	-(으)ㄹ래요	12.8
	-고 싶어요	9.6

you know	-지요	14.8

English Equivalents
to the
Korean Dialogues

Lesson Five
Dialogue 1

Chris	*Uh, excuse me.*
Kim	*Oh, Mr. Murphy. Long time no see.*
Chris	*Mr. Kim, this is my wife.*
Eunice	*I'm Eunice. How do you do?*
Kim	*I'm Kim Ch'anggi. How do you do?*
Chris	*Mr. Kim is my Korean teacher.*
Eunice	*Oh, I see. Pleased to meet you.*

Dialogue 2

Chris	*My wife is a piano teacher.*
Kim	*Oh, really? You're (an) English (person), aren't you, Mr. Murphy?*
Chris	*Yes.*
Kim	*Is your wife also English?*
Chris	*No, she isn't English. She's from Australia (she's an Australia person).*

Dialogue 3

Chris	*Is this your umbrella, Mr. Kim?*
Kim	*Yes, it's mine. Thank you.*
Eunice	*Is this newspaper yours, too?*
Kim	*No, that's not mine.*

Dialogue 4

Kim	*Where is that wine from? (As for that thing, what country's wine is it?)*
Eunice	*(Do you mean) This one? This one is French wine.*
Kim	*Well then, what is that (thing over there)?*
Eunice	*Ah, that is an English alcoholic beverage.*
Kim	*What kind of drink is it?*
Eunice	*It's whiskey.*
Kim	*It's all imported stuff, isn't it?*
Chris	*No. That ginseng wine is a Korean product.*

Lesson Six
Dialogue 1

Store Clerk	*Welcome! What can I get for you?*
Chris	*Do you have cigarettes?*
Store Clerk	*Yes, we do.*
Chris	*Do you have matches, too?*
Store Clerk .	*No, we don't. We have lighters.*
Chris	*In that case, please give me some cigarettes and a lighter.*
Store Clerk	*Shall I give you the American cigarettes?*
Chris	*No, please give me those Korean cigarettes.*
Store Clerk	*Yes, all right. Here you are.*
Chris	*How much is it altogether?*
Store Clerk	*1000 wŏn.*

Dialogue 2

Eunice	*Excuse me, Miss, but where's the Plaza Hotel?*
Young Lady	*The Plaza Hotel? Over there—across from City Hall.*
Eunice	*Oh, right. In that case, what about the British Embassy?*
Young Lady	*The British Embassy? It's just behind this building.*
Eunice	*Thanks.*

Lesson Seven
Dialogue 1

Eunice	*Hello.*
Halmŏni	*Good morning. Where are you going?*
Eunice	*I'm off to school.*
Halmŏni	*You're going to school these days?*
Eunice	*Yes. On Mondays and Wednesdays I go to Korea University. I'm learning Korean at Korea University.*
Halmŏni	*Really? Hurry home!*

Dialogue 2

Eunice	*Hi, I'm back.*
Halmŏni	*Where do you eat lunch usually?*
Eunice	*I eat at the school cafeteria.*
Halmŏni	*Do they make good food, there?*
Eunice	*Yes. They do a good job on the pulgogi and pibimpap. It's very tasty.*
Halmŏni	*Do they sell alcohol, too?*
Eunice	*Go on, halmŏni — since when do they sell alcohol at a school cafeteria?*

Dialogue 3

Chris	*Excuse me. Where do they sell tickets for trains to Taejŏn?*
ajŏssi	*The ticket counter is over there.*
Chris	*Thanks.*
Chris	*From what platform does the train to Taejŏn leave?*
agassi	*It leaves from the first platform.*
Chris	*How many hours does it take?*
agassi	*It takes two hours.*
Chris	*What are you looking for?*
agassi	*My pen.*
Chris	*Oh, here it is! Sorry.*

Lesson Eight

Dialogue 1

Miss Lee	*What are you doing lately?*
Eunice	*I'm studying Korean.*
Miss Lee	*Where are you studying Korean?*
Eunice	*At Korea University.*
Miss Lee	*Really? What book are you learning from?*
Eunice	*We're using Korean Conversation. The book's OK.*
Miss Lee	*Do you also know Japanese?*
Eunice	*No! I can't speak Japanese. It's too difficult.*
Miss Lee	*So, you're not doing any other subjects?*
Eunice	*No. I'm also learning economics and political science.*
Miss Lee	*Are your Korean language studies going well?*
Eunice	*No, it's really hard. I have a long way to go.*

Dialogue 2

Eunice	*Hello?*
Operator	*Yes, this is the National Theatre. Go ahead.*
Eunice	*I'd like to make a reservation, please.*
Operator	*Yes, Ma'am. Please tell me your name and credit card number.*
Eunice	*Excuse me? One more time, please! Oh, Miss Lee! This is too difficult. I can't catch what they're saying.*
Miss Lee	*Really? In that case, I'll talk to them.*

Lesson Nine
Dialogue 1

ajŏssi	*Uh, how do you do?*
Murphy	*What? Oh—right, hello.*
ajŏssi	*Oh! You speak Korean! Is this your first time in Korea?*
Murphy	*Yes. Well, in fact, I came last year. I live in Seoul.*
ajŏssi	*Really? What brought you here?*
Murphy	*I'm here on business. I work in an English company.*
ajŏssi	*So, how long are you here?*
Murphy	*Well, I don't really know yet.*
ajŏssi	*Are you American?*
Murphy	*No, I'm English.*
ajŏssi	*Oh, really? My apologies. I've just arrived from London, too.*
Murphy	*Really? What were you doing there?*
ajŏssi	*I've also been on business. I work in a trading company. Here, please take my namecard. Get in touch sometime.*

Dialogue 2

Murphy	*Did you have a fun weekend, Miss Lee?*
Miss Lee	*Yes. I went to the cinema yesterday with your wife.*
Murphy	*So I heard. Were there lots of people at the theatre?*
Miss Lee	*Yes, it was quite something. There were lots of people, like Namdaemun Market.*
Murphy	*What film did you see?*
Miss Lee	*It was a Korean film.*
Murphy	*I'd like to see a Korean film sometime (once) too. Was the film OK?*
Miss Lee	*It wasn't particularly interesting. So we came out in the middle. After that we went to a tabang to drink tea.*

Lesson Eleven
Dialogue 1

Yŏngch'ŏl	*Eric, where do you live? (Where's your house?)*
Eric	*In P'yŏngch'ang-dong.*
Yŏngch'ŏl	*Really? My, you live in quite a rich neighborhood! Does it take a long time from home to school?*
Eric	*It takes about an hour.*
Yŏngch'ŏl	*How old are you, Eric?*
Eric	*I'm 21. I was born in 1976.*
Yŏngch'ŏl	*Really? That makes us the same age! When's your birthday?*
Eric	*August 24. Why?*
Yŏngch'ŏl	*Ha! Then that makes you my older brother! (jokingly) Older brother, please take good care of me! Say, what's your telephone number at home?*
Eric	*352-1073. By the way, Yŏngch'ŏl, our Korean class is having a party this weekend. Be sure to come.*

Dialogue 2

Yŏngch'ŏl	*How many people came to the party yesterday?*
Eric	*About fifteen.*
Yŏngch'ŏl	*Really? Did you drink a lot?*
Eric	*We drank about seventy bottles of beer.*
Yŏngch'ŏl	*Did you consume a lot of snacks, too?*
Eric	*Ten squid, twenty packs of potato chips, and a box of apples.*
Yŏngch'ŏl	*What time did it finish?*
Eric	*At 2 o'clock in the morning. Say, why didn't you come?*
Yŏngch'ŏl	*I'm sorry. I forgot. Please forgive me, older brother!*
Eric	*OK, OK. No problem. Say, what time is it now?*
Yŏngch'ŏl	*It's 12:35 P.M. It's already lunchtime! Let's go eat.*

Lesson Twelve

Dialogue 1

Sŏngman	*What would you like to drink?*
Sandy	*Anything is fine. Shall we have a cup of coffee or something?*
Sŏngman	(to waitress) *Excuse me! Two cups of coffee here, please.*
	(to Sandy) *So, aren't you bored? What should we do today?*
Sandy	*Hmm, I don't know. Shall we go to a concert?*
	Or shall we go see a play?
Sŏngman	*Let's not go to a concert. I like plays, but I don't particularly like music.*
Sandy	*In that case, let's go see a play. I like plays, too.*
Sŏngman	*But I want to see a Korean play. What do you think, Sandy?*
Sandy	*I don't really know. I've never seen one yet (even once). Let's see one once!*

Dialogue 2

Eric	*Miss, won't you join me for a cup of tea or something?*
Waitress	*I'm afraid I'm a bit busy.*
Eric	*In that case, do you have any time this evening? Would you like to go somewhere and have a good time?* [without any of the tacky connotations of the English phrase]
Waitress	*I'm afraid I'm busy in the evening, too.*
Eric	*Really? I see. My apologies.* (Eric backs off)
Waitress	*Just a minute! I'm not busy tomorrow.*

Lesson Thirteen
Dialogue 1

Eric	*Shall we go someplace else? Or shall we just stay here?*
Miss Kwak	*It's cold outside, so let's just stay here.*
Eric	*Miss Kwak, do you have many brothers and sisters?*
Miss Kwak	*I have one older brother and one older sister.*
Eric	*Are they both married?*
Miss Kwak	*Just my older brother. They have a son too. My older sister is still single, but as soon as she graduates from college, she's getting married. What's your family like, Eric?*
Eric	*There's just my mother, my father, and my sister. My sister's name is Sandy.*
Miss Kwak	*I hope you don't mind my asking, but what does your father do?*
Eric	*He's with a trading company.*
Miss Kwak	*Is your father old?*
Eric	*Yes, he'll be fifty this September.*
Miss Kwak	*Oh, go on—he's still young!*

Dialogue 2

Chris	*Did you get through to Mr. Nam?*
Miss Lee	*When I called just a moment ago, nobody answers.*
Chris	*Oh, that's right. He probably isn't there today. It's Friday, so he's probably playing golf.*

Lesson Fourteen
Dialogue 1

Eunice	*Are you going to go downtown today?*
Mrs. Kim	*Yes. I'm thinking of doing some shopping today. Won't you go with me?*
Eunice	*Yes, fine. So what are you going to buy?*
Mrs. Kim	*There's not much time left until Christmas, so I want to buy some Christmas presents. Where do you suppose would be best? Probably Tongdaemun Market would be the best, right?*
Eunice	*Yes, that's probably the case. I've been there several times, too. The prices of things (there) are very cheap, aren't they?*
Mrs. Kim	*Yes, it's very cheap. Well then, shall we get moving?*
Eunice	*Just a moment. I'll just go to the restroom.*
Mrs. Kim	*Hurry up. I'll be waiting in front of the elevator.*
Eunice	*So, shall we go? Shall we ride the subway? Or shall we take a taxi?*
Mrs. Kim	*I want to go in comfort, so let's take a taxi. I'll pay.*

Dialogue 2

Kang	*Let me introduce a friend to you. This is Nam Chu-hyŏng.*
Chris	*How do you do? I'm Chris Murphy.*
Nam	*How do you do? I'm Nam Chu-hyŏng.*
Kang	*Well then, let's sit down, shall we?*
Chris	*Is this your first time here (in this establishment)?*
Nam	*No, I've been here a few times before.*
Waitress	*What would you like?*
Kang	(to waitress) *Just a moment.* (to Nam) *What shall we order?*
Nam	*Anything at all is fine, but I think I'll have kalbi.*
Chris	*In that case, I'll have kalbi, too.*
Waitress	*And you, sir?*
Nam	*I'll have pulgogi.*
Waitress	*Right then. Two servings of kalbi and one serving of pulgogi. How about beverages?*
Chris	*Would you like to imbibe a bit?*
Kang, Nam	*Sure!*
Chris	*In that case, why don't you start off by bringing us three bottles of beer.*

Dialogue 3

Nam	*Hello. Is Chris Murphy in?*
Miss Lee	*Yes he is. What shall I say it is about?*
Nam	*Beg your pardon?*
Miss Lee	*May I have your name please?*
Nam	*It's Nam Chu-hyŏng.*
Miss Lee	*Just a moment please.*
Chris	*Well, well, well! How good to see you! Do come in. Please sit down.* *Miss Lee — would you mind bringing us two cups of coffee?*
Nam	*How have you been keeping all this time?*
Chris	*Thank you. Nothing special to report. Well then, so what business brings you here?*

Answer Key to Written Exercises

Lesson One

Exercise (1): English Equivalents

(1) Is that so? Really?

(2) Thank you.

(3) See you later (Formal).

(4) How are you, Mr. Kim?

(5) Hello (to someone working).

(6) Please come in.

(7) Hello (on the phone).

(8) Excuse me (for what I did).

(9) Pleased to make your acquaintance.

(10) Please come in.

Exercise (2): Korean Equivalents

(1) 만나서 반갑습니다.

(2) 수고 하셨어요.

(3) 안녕하세요, 이 선생님.

(4) 어서 오세요.

(5) 천만에요.

(6) 시간이 다 됐습니다.

(7) 또 뵙겠습니다. or 또 봐요.

(8) 실례하겠습니다.

(9) 안녕히 계세요.

(10) 수고하세요.

Exercise (3): How do you Respond?

(1) 죄송합니다. or 실례했습니다.

(2) 여보세요.

(3) 처음 뵙겠습니다.

(4) 만나서 반갑습니다.

(5) 그래요?

(6) 안녕하세요.

(7) 들어오세요. 앉으세요.

(8) 선생님, 시간이 다 됐습니다.

(9) 실례합니다.

(10) 감사합니다. or 고맙습니다.

(11) 네 or 예/아니오.

(12) 실례했습니다.

(13) 또 봐요.

(14) 안녕히 가세요.

(15) 또 뵙겠습니다.

Lesson Two

Exercise (1): Practicing Responses

(1) a (2) b (3) c (4) b (5) a/b/c (6) a/b (7) a/b (8) a (9) b (10) b

Exercise (2): Match the Appropriate Response

(1) d (2) h (3) b (4) c (5) i/g (6) f (7) a (8) c (9) c

Exercise (3): Remember the Korean Equivalent

(1) 시작할까요?

(2) 실례합니다.

(3) 네, 시작합시다.

(4) 다 같이. 한국말로 하세요.

(5) 질문 있어요?

(6) 책을 보지 마세요.

(7) 다시 말해 주세요.

(8) 크게 말해 주세요.

(9) 대답하세요. 알겠어요?

(10) 다음 페이지를 보세요.

(11) 천천히 말해 주세요.

(12) 모르겠어요.

(13) 네, 알겠어요.

(14) 그래요?

(15) 십분만 쉽시다.

(16) 영어로 하지 마세요.

(17) 하나, 둘, 셋, 넷, 다섯, 여섯, 일곱, 여덟, 아홉, 열

(18) (다시) 십분만 쉽시다.

(19) 듣기만 하세요.

(20) 늦어서 미안합니다.

(21) 첫 페이지를 보세요.

(22) 따라 하세요.

(23) 감사합니다. or 고맙습니다.

(24) 안녕히 가세요. or 안녕히 계세요.

Exercise (4): Practice with Korean Names

(1) 김정호 male,

(2) 이석헌 male,

(3) 박은미 female,

(4) 최홍석 male,

(5) 장혜경 female,

(6) 남경자 female,

(7) 홍진호 male,

(8) 허미선 female,

(9) 서지선 male,

(10) 배경희 female,

(11) 조철민 male,

(12) 노호철 male,

(13) 정재훈 male,

(14) 임석준 male,

(15) 오경애 female,

(16) 강승자 female,

(17) 안철호 male,

(18) 한수미 female,

(19) 심진회 female,

(20) 윤철수 male

Lesson Three

Exercise (2): Recognizing Country Names

(1) Kenya

(2) France

(3) Pakistan

(4) Mexico

(5) Laos

(6) Greece

(7) Iraq

(8) Finland

(9) New Zealand

(10) Singapore

(11) Denmark

(12) Netherlands

(13) Thailand

(14) Poland

(15) Chile

(16) Sweden

(17) Libya

(18) Brazil

(19) Indonesia

(20) Canada

(21) Malaysia   (22) Nicaragua   (23) Cuba   (24) Vietnam

(25) Lichtenstein   (26) Lebanon

Exercise (3): Recognizing Loans from English

(1) radio   (2) bus   (3) taxi   (4) piano

(5) kangaroo   (6) toast   (7) tennis   (8) banana

(9) camera   (10) sausage   (11) lemon   (12) cheese

(13) cake   (14) ice cream   (15) cassette   (16) interview

(17) hotel   (18) golf   (19) tomato   (20) nightclub

(21) television   (22) tire   (23) computer   (24) hamburger

(25) truck   (26) sandwich

Lesson Five

Exercise (2): Complete the Sentence

(1) 일본사람

(2) 한국가수

(3) 은행원

(4) 러시아 학생

(5) 미국 의사

(6) 회사원

(7) 김 교수님 사모님

(8) 내 친구 or 제 친구

(9) 제 집사람 or 아내 ; 저희 집사람
    or 아내 ; 우리 집사람 or 아내

(10) 내 남편 or 제 남편 ; 우리 남편
     or 저희 남편

(11) 중국 외교관

(12) 영어 선생님

Exercise (3): Complete the Sentences

(1) 칠판   (2) 잡지   (3) 분필   (4) 성냥

(5) 중국말 신문   (6) 신문   (7) 담배   (8) 종이

(9) 볼펜   (10) 연필   (11) 일본말 잡지   (12) 러시아말 책

Exercise (4): Complete the Sentence

(1) 박 박사님(의)

(2) 김복동씨(의)

(3) 그 사람(의)

(4) 박 박사님(의) 부인(의)

(5) 제

(6) 만호씨(의) 부인(의)

(7) 제 친구(의)

(8) 수진씨(의)

(9) 남편(의)

(10) 집사람(의) or 아내(의)

Exercise (5): Translation into Korean

(1) 그 것은 박 선생님의 공책이에요? or 그 공책은 박 선생님 것이에요?
(2) 아니오. 박 선생님 것이 아니에요.
(3) 이 우산은 누구(의) 것이에요?
(4) 가수(의) 것이에요.
(5) 장 선생님의 부인은 학생이에요?
(6) 아니오. 학생이 아니에요. 한국말 선생님이에요.
(7) 그 외국학생은 미국사람이에요?
(8) 아니오. 미국사람(이) 아니에요. 호주사람이에요.
(9) 이 성냥은 만호씨(의) 것이에요?
(10) 이 공책은 어느 나라(의) 제품이에요?
(11) 저 사람은 중국외교관이에요.
(12) 이 것은 중국외교관의 한국말책이에요.
(13) 어떤 것이 러시아신문이에요?
(14) 모르겠어요. 그 것이에요?
(15) 모가미 박사님은 일본분이에요.
(16) 부인이 러시아분이에요? 아니오, 러시아사람(이) 아니에요.
　　　프랑스사람이에요.
(17) 그 사람은 누구에요? 장교수님이에요.
(18) 그 잡지는 어떤 잡지에요? 모르겠어요.

Exercise (6): Vocabulary Drill

(1) 신문　　　(2) 은행　　　(3) 영어　　　(4) 책
(5) 한국　　　(6) 회사원　　　(7) 성냥　　　(8) 칠판

Lesson Six

Exercise (1): Fill in the Blanks

(1)　　a. 안에　　　b. 밖에 c. 앞에 d. 옆에　　　e. 뒤에
(2)　　a. 위에　　　b. 속에 c. 옆에 d. 아래(에)/밑에　　e. 오른쪽/편에
(3)　　a. 에　　　　b. 뒤에 c. 옆에 d. 앞에　　　　　e. 근처에

Exercise (2): Sentence Construction

(1) 방 안에 책상이 있어요 ~ 없어요.
(2) 집에 텔레비전이 있어요 ~ 없어요.
(3) 교실에 선생님이 있어요 ~ 없어요.

(4) 방 안에 의자가 있어요~없어요.

(5) 학교에 화장실이 있어요~없어요.

(6) 가방 속에 책이 있어요~없어요.

(7) 대사관 안에 교실이 있어요~없어요.

(8) 호텔 안에 가게가 있어요~없어요.

(9) 백화점 안에 커피숍이 있어요.~없어요.

(10) 대학교에 은행이 있어요~없어요.

Exercise (3): Naming Locations

(1) 김선생님은_____옆에, 왼편/쪽에, 맞은편에, (___하고___) 사이에,
　　오른편/쪽에 있어요.

(2) 제 책은_____ 위에, 밑에, 옆에, (___하고___) 사이에, 안에/속에
　　있어요.

(3) 은행은_____ 옆에, 맞은편에, 뒤에, 왼편/쪽에, 밖에 있어요.

(4) 공원이 _____ (___) 근처에, 앞에, (___하고___) 사이에, 맞은편에,
　　뒤에 있어요.

Exercise (4): English to Korean Translation

(1) 제 담배가 어디 있어요?

(2) 만호씨의 가방 속에 있어요?

(3) (제) 가방 속에는 책하고 종이하고 라이타가 있어요.

(4) 그런데 담배는 없어요.

(5) 여기 담배가 있어요. 성냥이 있어요?

(6) 성냥은 책상 위에 있어요.

(7) 미안합니다. 성냥은 책상 위에 없어요.

(8) 텔레비전 위에 있어요?

(9) 없어요. 그렇지만 옆방에는 있어요. 실례합니다.

(10) 여기 성냥이 있어요. 한국성냥이에요.

(11) 만호씨의 담배는 한국담배에요?

(12) 아니오. 미국 것이에요.

(13) 박교수님의 부인이 만호씨하고 수진씨 사이에 있어요.

(14) 만호씨는 제 친구에요. 한국 학생이에요.

(15) 수진씨가 누구에요? 수진씨도 학생이에요? 회사원이에요?

Exercise (5): Korean to English Translation

(1) There is a tree in front of the school.

(2) What is under the tree? Is it a baby? I don't know.

(3) Yongjin and his parents are here. Manho is in the next room.

(4) There is a picture beside the desk. What is inside the picture?

(5) How much money does Mr. Ch'oe have?

(6) How much is it? Please give me one thousand won.

(7) There is a newspaper and a magazine on the desk. (There are newspapers and magazines on the desk.)

(8) Where is my notebook? I'm sorry. Please say it again. And please speak slowly.

(9) What buildings are there in the vicinity of the embassy? On the left there is a hotel. And opposite there is City Hall.

Exercise (6): Possession and Plurals

(1) 저는 책들하고 잡지들이 있어요.
(2) 저 성냥들을 주세요. 저는 없어요.
(3) 그런데, 한국신문들이 없어요?
(4) 이 선생님은 펜들이 없어요.
(5) 이 방 안에는 의사들이 있어요?
(6) 라이타들은 없어요. 그렇지만 성냥들은 있어요.
(7) 종이가 없어요? 아니오, 있어요.
(8) 만호씨의 친구는 책들이 없어요? 네, 없어요.
(9) 방 안에 그림들이 있어요? 아니오, 그렇지만 부모님들의 방에는 있어요.

Exercise (7): Vocabulary Drill

(1) 책상 옆에 ＿＿＿＿＿ 이 ~ 가 있어요?

펜	가방	라이타
공책	아이	텔레비전
연필	그림 (들)	책상
문	책	애기
의자	칠판	
천원	성냥	

(2) 만호씨 집 근처에 ＿＿＿＿＿ 은 ~ 는 없어요?

학교	대사관	은행
공원	백화점	호텔
회사	대학교	가게

Lesson Seven

Exercise (1): Fill in the Blanks

(1) 잡지를, 신문을, 잡지도 신문도, 중국책을, 영국신문하고 러시아신문을,
　　미국잡지들을
(2) 라디오를, 고기를, 휴지하고 수건을, 담배도 성냥도, 공책을, 돈을,
　　연필(들)하고 종이를
(3) 영화관도 공원도, 의사 선생님하고 의사 선생님의 부인을, 영화를, 김
　　선생님 부인도 박 선생님 부인도, 선생님을, 제 친구들을, 학생을
　　많이

Exercise (2): Building Sentences from Phrases

(1) 영화관에　　　　　　(2) 의자 옆에
(3) 박 박사님한테서　　　(4) 집하고 나무사이에
(5) 집에서　　　　　　　(6) 공원에
(7) 영화관 오른편/쪽에　 (8) 아버지한테서
(9) 요즘에　　　　　　　(10) 이 방에서
(11) 아침에　　　　　　 (12) 왼쪽/편에
(13) 제 친구에게(한테)　 (14) 매표소에서
(15) 음식점에서　　　　 (16) 집에서

Exercise (3): Verb Phrases

(1) 창문을 닫아요.　　　 (2) 잡지를 봐요
(3) 물을 마셔요.　　　　 (4) 방에서 놀아요.
(5) 노래를 불러요.　　　 (6) 영화구경을 해요.
(7) 늦게 일어나요.　　　 (8) 담배를 피워요.
(9) 학교에 가요.　　　　 (10) 한국말을 말해요.
(11) 영어를 배워요.　　　(12) 의사를 기다려요.
(13) 라디오를 들어요.　　(14) 일해요.

Exercise (4): Korean to English Translation

(1) What are you doing now? I am watching television. Are you watching alone?
　　No, the baby is watching, too.
(2) Do you have a dog at home? Yes, we do. Where is it now? I don't know. Does
　　the dog play well? Yes, it plays well.
(3) Our dog plays in the park.

(4) Our baby drinks both water and milk well.

(5) What are you doing? I am waiting for my friend.

(6) Where are you going? I am going to the park. I am looking for our dog.

(7) Where are you going? I am going to the restaurant.

(8) Our/ my father works in a bank. He receives a lot of letters at the bank. And he writes a lot of letters at home.

(9) I stay at home on Sundays. What do you do at home? Do you read the newspaper? Yes, and I read magazines, too.

(10) My younger sibling doesn't talk much.

(11) Is the Australian embassy big or small?

Exercise (5): English to Korean Translation

(1) 학교 선생님이에요. 보통 영어를 가르쳐요.

(2) 토요일 아침에는 신문을 읽어요. 그리고 목요일 저녁에는 극장에 가요.

(3) 공부(를) 잘 해요. 많이 배워요.

(4) 밤에는 쉬어요.

(5) 도서관에는 책이 많아요. 요즘에는 책이 비싸요.

(6) 금요일 아침에는 늦게 일어나요. 우유를 빨리 마셔요. 그리고 학교에 가요.

(7) 이 교수님을 기다려요.

(8) 휴지를 주세요. 수건도 주세요.

(9) 우리 집은 작아요. 그렇지만 좋아요.

(10) 수요일에는 빵하고 우유를 사요.

(11) 애기는 혼자(서) 놀아요.

(12) 아버지는 노래를 잘 불러요.

(13) 어머니가 애기를 불러요. 그렇지만 애기는 자요.

(14) 우리 어머니는 서울에서 살아요. 거기에는 상점하고 백화점이 많이 있어요.

(15) 도서관이 어디에요? 알아요? 네, 저기 식당하고 저 건물 사이에 있어요.

(16) 오늘 저녁에 영화를 봐요.

Exercise (7): Particle Insertion

(1) I watch TV. 을

(2) It tastes good. 이

(3) The baby is coming. 가

(4) I meet a friend. 를

(5) Books are expensive. 이

(6) We eat [rice/a meal]. 을

(7) I play in the park. 에서

(8) I get money from my friend. 는/한테서/을

(9) We eat [a meal] at the restaurant. 에서/을

(10) Students learn Korean in the classroom. 에서/이/을

(11) There is a newspaper on top of the desk. 에/이

(12) There is a train beside the platform. 에/가

(13) A woman is buying a ticket in front of the ticket counter. 에서/가/를

(14) On the weekend I see movies with my boyfriend. 에/하고/을

Exercise (8): Vocabulary Drill

(1) 나는 아침에 _____.

공부(를) 해요, 개하고 놀아요, 산보(를) 해요, 은행에 가요, 신문을 읽어요, 집에 와요, 공원에 가요, 편지를 써요, 영화구경을 가요, 신문을 팔아요, 집에 있어요, 러시아말을 배워요, 영어로 말해요, 우유를 마셔요, 라디오를 들어요, 영화구경(을) 해요, 담배를 피워요, 개를 찾아요, 중국말을 가르쳐요, 물을 많이 마셔요, 친구를 만나요, 도서관에서 일(을) 해요, 아침을 먹어요, 창문을 열어요.

(2) 나는 _____ 편지를 써요.

밤에, 아침에, 토요일에, 빨리, 금요일 아침에, 화요일에, 일요일에, 목요일에, 오늘 저녁에, 수요일에, 많이, 낮에, 오후에, 월요일 아침에, 자주, 오늘 밤에

Lesson Eight

Exercise (1): Using 안 and 도

(1) 기차를 안 기다리세요./안 기다려요. (2) 아침을 안 잡수세요./안 먹어요. (3) 학생에게 책을 안 주세요./안 줘요. (4) 약을 안 잡수세요./안 먹어요. (5) 댁에 안 계세요./집에 없어요. (6) 문을 여세요/열어요. (7) 부모님하고 안 사세요./안 살아요. (8) 공원에서 산책을 안 하세요./안 해요. (9) 친구를 안 만나세요./안 만나요. (10) 러시아말을 안 가르치세요./안 가르쳐요. (11) 술을 안 마시세요./안 마셔요. (12) 편지를 안 쓰세요./안 써요. (13) 텔레비전을 안 보세요./안 봐요. (14) 청소를 안 하세요./청소를 안 해요.

Exercise (2): Building Sentences from Phrases

(1) 밤에 (2) 부모님하고 (3) 은행에서 (4) 책상 위에 (5) 펜으로 (6) 대학교에서 (7) 분필로 (8) 회사에 (9) 공원에서 (10) 비행기로 (11) 정열적으로 (12) 정치학하고 러시아말 (13) 개하고 (14) 뉴우 요크로 (15) 다른 기차로 (16) 무엇으로 (17) 영어로 (18) 내 친구하고 (19) 오른편으로 (20) 오늘하고 내일 (21) 그림 아래에 (22) 항상

Exercise (3): Practice with 안, 못 and -(으)시-

(1) 안 먹어요./못 먹어요. (2) 안 마셔요./못 마셔요. (3) 안 가요./못 가요. (4) 안 좋아해요. (5) 안 자요./못 자요. (6) 안 살아요. (7) 안 봐요./ 못 봐요. (8) 안 써요./못 써요. (9) 잘 안 불러요./잘 못 불러요. (10) 안 나가요./못 나가요. (11) 없어요.

Now repeat the exercise.

(1) 빵 잡수세요? (2) 술 마시세요? (3) 학교에 가세요? (4) 야구 좋아하세요? (5) 주무세요? (6) 런던에서 사세요? (7) 텔레비전을 보세요? (8) 분필로 편지를 쓰세요? (9) 노래를 잘 부르세요? (10) 교회에 나가세요? (11) 오후에도 수업 있으세요?

Exercise (5): Honorific Questions

(1) 선생님은 은행에서 일하세요?
(2) 선생님은 펜을 잘 사세요?
(3) 선생님은 한국에서 영어를 가르치세요?
(4) 선생님은 아침에 빵이랑 우유를 잡수세요?
(5) 선생님은 교회에 나가세요?
(6) 선생님은 미국사람이세요?
(7) 선생님은 수영을 안 좋아하세요?
(8) 선생님은 오늘 저녁에 바쁘세요?
(9) 선생님은 중국말이 힘드세요?
(10) 선생님은 술을 잘 하세요?
(11) 선생님은 많이 못 잡수세요?
(12) 선생님은 친구를 기다리세요?
(13) 선생님은 담배를 안 피우세요?
(14) 선생님은 밤에 일찍 주무세요?
(15) 선생님은 런던대학교에서 한국말을 배우세요?
(16) 선생님은 여기(서) 사세요?

(17) 선생님은 안 더우세요?

(18) 선생님은 항상 약을 잡수세요?

(19) 선생님은 다른 교재를 안 쓰세요? (use/write)

(20) 선생님은 라디오를 들으세요?

(21) 선생님은 내일 못 떠나세요?

Exercise (6): English to Korean Translation

(1) 지금 주무세요? 아니오, 일어나요.

(2) 주말에는 가끔 약을 먹어요.

(3) 머피씨는 부인이랑 수영을 자주 하세요.

(4) 담배를 피우세요? 아니오, 안 피워요.

(5) 어머니한테서 돈을 받아요. 그리고 친구랑 영화를 봐요.

(6) 우리 아버지는 경제학을 공부하세요. 정치학도 공부하세요.

(7) 그 학생의 책상 위에는 공책이 있어요. 그리고 방도 항상 깨끗이 청소
(를) 해요.

(8) 무슨 과목을 배우세요? 전공이 무엇이에요?

(9) 일요일에는 보통 교회에 가요. 가끔 혼자서 가요.

(10) 비행기로는 못 가세요. 알아요!

(11) 빨리 오세요!

(12) 그 교회에서 오른편으로 가세요.

(13) 시간이 많이 없어요.

(14) 최 선생님, 어떤 외국어를 아세요? 영어를 말하세요? 우리는 이 교과
서로 영어를 배워요.

Exercise (7): Korean to English Translation

(1) The doctor doesn't watch television. The children don't watch television, either.

(2) Our dog doesn't play in the park. He is always in the house. He is a really good dog.

(3) Do you have a cat? Is it big? She is rather small. Does she often play with other cats? Yes, and she also eats a lot of meat. And drinks a lot of milk.

(4) Usually I go by bus. It doesn't [Literally: can't] go very fast.

(5) The hotel is directly across from the American embassy. It is right next to our house.

(6) My husband doesn't write letters very often (or well).

(7) What does your girlfriend do at home?

(8) Mr. Oh goes to Seoul by train. He always goes to is friend's house in the evening.

(9) My father goes for a walk every day with my mother.

(10) These days we have an Australian exchange student living at our house. She is always studying.

(11) Kyonghee always gets up early. And she goes to bed late.

(12) My room is usually clean. I sometimes study there. But the library is preferable.

(13) Professor Pak's wife and Mr. Pae's wife eat lunch together every day.

(14) I can't play baseball alone. First I wait for my friends. They live in this neighborhood.

Lesson Nine

Exercise (1): Past Tense

(1) 친구를 만나셨어요? *Did you meet your friend?*

(2) 무슨 영화를 봤어요? *Which movie did you see?*

(3) 어머니는 친구들한테 편지를 많이 쓰셨어요. *My mother wrote a lot of letters to her friend.*

(4) 개가 문을 열었어요. *The dog opened the door.*

(5) 아버지는 말이 적으셨어요. *My father didn't say much.*

(6) 그렇지만 친구가 많으셨어요. *But he had a lot of friends.*

(7) 실은, 고기를 많이 못 먹었어요. *Actually, I wasn't able to eat a lot of meat.*

(8) 사모님도 그 책을 읽으셨어요? *Did your wife read that book, too?*

(9) 그 영화가 좋았어요? *Was the movie good?*

(10) 사장님이 나한테 돈을 많이 주셨어요. *The company president gave me a lot of money.*

(11) 나는 공원에서 아이와 같이 놀았어요. *I played in the park with the child.*

(12) 사모님은 언제 도착하셨어요? *When did your wife arrive?*

(13) 나는 우체국에서 왔어요. *I came from the post office.*

(14) 누가 우리를 봤어요? *Who saw us?*

(15) 동생은 언제 호주로 떠났어요? *When did your younger sibling leave for Australia?*

(16) 그 개는 참 컸어요. *That dog was very big.*

(17) 나는 런던 대학생이었어요. *I was a student at the University of London.*

(18) 박 교수님은 런던에서 사셨어요. *Professor Pak lived in London.*

(19) 내 장갑이 여기 있었어요. *My gloves were here.*

(20) 그 집 딸은 참 착했어요. *Mr. Kim's daughter was a really nice girl.*

(21) 무슨 연구를 하셨어요? *What kind of research did you do?*

(22) 정원이 예뻤어요. *The garden was pretty.*

Exercise (2): Using –고 싶어(해)요

(1) 나는 새 자동차를 사고 싶어요.
(2) 나는 다른 넥타이를 매고 싶어요.
(3) 서울에 같이 올라가고 싶으세요?
(4) 택시를 부르고 싶어요?
(5) 선생님은 학교에 전화를 걸고 싶어하세요?
(6) 지난 주일에 부산에 내려가고 싶었어요.
(7) 나는 한국사람한테 편지를 쓰고 싶었어요.
(8) 나는 중국말도 배우고 싶어요.
(9) 애기와 같이 놀고 싶어요?
(10) 청바지를 입고 싶어요.
(11) 옆집 아들은 영화배우가 되고 싶어했어요.
(12) 나는 명함 하나를 받고 싶었어요.
(13) 신발은 안 벗고 싶었어요.

Exercise (3): English to Korean Translation

(1) 어제 어디 가셨어요? 시장에 갔었어요.
(2) 어제 밤에 뭘 했어요 or 하셨어요? 잤어요.
(3) 어제 밤에 늦게 왔어요? or 오셨어요? 아니오. 일찍 왔어요.
(4) 어제 백화점에서 무엇을 샀어요? or 사셨어요? 바지하고 외투를
      샀어요.
(5) 남동생하고 뭘 했어요? or 하셨어요? 공원에서 놀았어요.
(6) 은행 앞에서 뭘 했어요? or 하셨어요? 어머니한테 전화를 걸었어요.
(7) 버스에 사람이 많이 있었어요?
(8) 우체국을 쉽게 찾았어요?
(9) 다방에서 뭘 했어요? or 하셨어요? 쥬스를 마셨어요.
(10) 어제 신발을 안 닦았어요. 그리고 이도 안 닦았어요.

Exercise (4): Purposives

(1) 전화를 걸러 나갔어요.
(2) 우리 딸은 한국어 연구를 하러 한국에 갔어요.
(3) 화요일에 우리 어머니는 신발을 사러 시장에 가셨어요.
(4) 남동생이 토요일에 장갑을 사러 백화점에 갔어요.
(5) 이를 닦으러 화장실에 갔어요.
(6) 학생이 문을 열러 나왔어요.

(7) 아버지는 월요일에 돈을 찾으러 은행에 갔다오셨어요.

(8) 아버지가 친구를 만나러 가셨어요.

(9) 제 친구가 영어를 가르치러 한국에 갔어요.

(10) 어제 밤에 술 마시러 나갔어요.

Exercise (5): Do/Be Like

(1) 그 영화배우는 영국사람처럼 영어를 말해요.

(2) 가수처럼 노래를 잘 불러요.

(3) 여기는 시장처럼 사람이 늘 많이 있어요.

(4) 저 사람이 누구에요? 글쎄요, 모르겠어요. 만호씨 같아요.

(5) 오늘처럼 내일도 바빠요?

(6) 내 친구처럼 공부를 잘 하고 싶어요.

(7) 가끔 영화배우처럼 옷을 입어요.

(8) 나하고 내 친구는 가족 같아요.

(9) 그 분들의 정원은 아주 커요. 공원 같아요!

(10) 오늘이 좋아요. 주말 같아요.

(11) 저녁에는 이 방은 술집 같아요.

(12) 이 구두를 작년에 샀어요. 그런데 새 구두 같아요.

(13) 이 모자는 그 것과 같아요.

Exercise (6): Fill in the Gaps and Translate

한테 On Sunday Sumi wrote a letter to me.

한테 So on Tuesday I called Sumi.

And we met yesterday.

와/하고/랑 Sumi came with Chaeho.

에서 We went for a walk together in the park.

는 Chaeho didn't have a lot of time. So he went quickly.

와/하고/랑 I went to the cinema with Sumi.

가 The movie was really interesting.

Exercise (7): Korean to English Translation

(1) I went to Seoul to go sight-seeing.

(2) The students all went out to smoke.

(3) Don't you want to go out today? No, I want to go to sleep early.

(4) It was really hot this morning. But on Tuesday it wasn't particularly hot.

(5) The movie wasn't particularly interesting. The movie theatre was too small.

(6) The teacher went out to rest for a minute.

(7) Is the movie finished? It's not finished yet.

(8) Do you want to make a phone call?

(9) Father went out to call a taxi.

(10) They went out to go for a walk in the park.

(11) The dog bit the cat.

(12) Did you eat supper in that new restaurant yesterday? Yes, but the food wasn't that tasty.

(13) I want to go to the bar upstairs.

(14) I did some economics research at university. But it wasn't very interesting.

(15) I went over to (play at) Mr. Yeon's house yesterday.

(16) Where did you go? or Where have you been? I've just come back from the post office.

(17) The movie just finished.

(18) Father, I want to go to the station to watch the trains.

(19) I want to rest a bit on the weekend.

(20) I want to go to the market for a minute.

(21) I spent a lot of money on these new shoes. [Literally: A lot of money went out on account of these shoes.]

(22) Are we there yet? No, we still have a long way to go.

Lesson Ten

Exercise (1): Find the Misfit

(1) 누구	(2) 지금	(3) 친구	(4) 남편
(5) 문	(6) 미국 사람	(7) 학생	(8) 다
(9) 산보해요.	(10) 물	(11) 약	(12) 분필

Exercise (2): Related Words

(1) 박사, 사장

(2) 대학교, 회사, 백화점, 도서관, 식당

(3) 저녁, 밤, 날

(4) 아래, 밖

(5) 캐나다, 중국, 한국, 일본, 호주, 독일

(6) 어머니, 아이, 부모

(7) 마셔요, 이를 닦아요, 학교에 가요

Exercise (3): Fill in the Blanks

(1) 는/에서/을
(2) 는/에서
(3) 가/이
(4) 에/은
(5) 에/에서/을/를
(6) 에서/을/하고(과)/를
(7) 에서/는/을

(8) 못
(9) 에/와
(10) 한테서/가
(11) 이/에/에
(12) 에서/이/을
(13) 에/을/못
(14) 하고(와)

Exercise (5): Questions and Answers

(1) 정치학을 공부해요? 아니오. 정치학 공부를 안 해요.
(2) 친구를 기다려요? 아니오, 친구를 안 기다려요.
(3) 자요? 아니오, 안 자요.
(4) 혼자서 살아요? 아니오, 혼자서 안 살아요.
(5) 러시아말을 배워요? 아니오, 러시아말을 안 배워요.
(6) 한국 사람 많이 있어요? 아니오, 많이 없어요.
(7) 양말을 찾아요? 아니오, 양말을 안 찾아요.
(8) 일때문에 왔어요? 아니오, 일때문에 안 왔어요.
(9) 집에 있어요? 아니오, 집에 없어요.
(10) 영화구경을 해요? 아니오, 영화구경을 안 해요.
(11) 의사에요? 아니오, 의사가 아니에요.
(12) 무역 회사에서 일 해요? 아니오, 무역 회사에서 일을 안 해요.
(13) 명함을 많이 받아요? 아니오, 많이 못 받아요.
(14) 와인을 마셔요? 아니오, 와인을 안 마셔요.
(15) 일본말을 해요? 아니오, 일본말을 못해요.
(16) 선생님이에요? 아니오, 선생님이 아니에요.
(17) 여기 계세요? 아니오, 여기 안 계세요.
(18) 값이 좀 내렸어요? 아니오, 값이 안 내렸어요.
(19) 술집에 자주 가요? 아니오, 술집에 자주 안 가요.
(20) 지금 은행에서 일을 해요? 아니오, 은행에서 일을 안 해요.
(21) 텔레비전을 너무 많이 봐요? 아니오, 너무 많이 안 봐요.
(22) 알아 들어요? 아니오, 못 알아 들어요.
(23) 청바지를 자주 입어요? 아니오, 청바지를 자주 안 입어요.
(24) 많이 알아요? 아니오, 많이 몰라요.
(25) 방이 깨끗해요? 아니오, 방이 안 깨끗해요.
(26) 부산에 언제 도착 해요?

Exercise (6): Questions and Answers (Honorific)

(1) 텔레비젼을 보세요?
(2) 방금 나가셨어요?
(3) 아이하고 자주 노세요?
(4) 부모님과 같이 사세요?
(5) 일찍 일어나세요?
(6) 영화를 보러 자주 가세요?
(7) 지금 회사에 계세요?
(8) 주말을 재미 있게 보내셨어요?
(9) 한국 분이세요?
(10) 대사관으로 전화를 거셨어요?
(11) 중국말을 공부하세요?
(12) 차를 파셨어요?
(13) 어디 다녀 오셨어요?
(14) 가수세요?
(15) 보통 늦게 주무세요?
(16) 사립대학교에서 일을 하세요?
(17) 영어를 배우세요?
(18) 다른 외국어도 하세요?
(19) 명함을 주셨어요?
(20) 일찍 집에 들어오세요?
(21) 공원에서 만나세요?
(22) 보통 회사에 늦게 가세요?

Exercise (8): Opposites

(1) 건물이 커요? 아니오, 작아요.
(2) 문을 열어요? 아니오, 닫아요.
(3) 학생이 많아요? 아니오, 적어요.
(4) 김 선생님한테 돈을 줘요? 아니오, 김 선생님한테서 돈을 받아요.
(5) 한국어를 가르쳐요? 아니오, 한국어를 배워요.
(6) 스웨터를 입었어요? 아니오, 스웨터를 벗었어요.
(7) 일어나요? 아니오, 자요.
(8) 음식은 맛이 있었어요? 아니오, 맛 없었어요.
(9) 차를 팔았어요? 아니오, 차를 샀어요.
(10) 선생님의 말을 잘 들어요? 아니오, 말을 잘 안 들어요.
(11) 장갑이 비쌌어요? 아니오, 쌌어요.
(12) 보통 집에 있어요? 아니오, 집에 없어요.
(13) 일을 해요? 아니오, 쉬어요.
(14) 방금 떠났어요? 아니오, 방금 도착 했어요.

Exercise (9): Opposites (Honorific)

(1) 건물이 크세요? 아니오, 작으세요. [but odd]
(2) 문을 여세요? 아니오, 닫으세요.
(3) 학생이 많으세요? 아니오, 적으세요.
(4) 김 선생님한테 돈을 주세요? 아니오, 김 선생님한테서 받으세요.
(5) 한국어를 가르치세요? 아니오, 한국어를 공부하세요.
(6) 스웨터를 입으셨어요? 아니오, 스웨터를 벗으셨어요.

Answer Key / 386

(7) 일어나세요? 아니오, 주무세요.

(8) 음식은 맛이 있으셨어요? 아니오, 맛 없으셨어요. [but odd]

(9) 차를 파세요? 아니오, 차를 사셨어요.

(10) 선생님의 말을 잘 들으세요? 아니오, 선생님의 말을 잘 안 들으세요.

(11) 장갑이 비싸셨어요? 아니오, 싸셨어요. [but odd]

(12) 보통 집에 계세요? 아니오, 집에 안 계세요.

(13) 일을 하세요? 아니오, 쉬세요.

(14) 방금 떠나셨어요? 아니오, 방금 도착하셨어요.

Exercise (10): Korean to English Translation

(1) It's time. Let's start.

(2) Is that person a teacher? No, he's a student.

(3) What are you doing (now)? I'm watching the news.

(4) Whose ring is this? It's my ring. Please give it to me.

(5) Where do you study Korean? At Korea University.

(6) Are you going to a restaurant? I'm going to [Literally: play at] a friend's house.

(7) Do you study in the evenings? Yes, sometimes.

(8) I couldn't understand. Please say it in English.

(9) These days I usually get up quite late. And I always go to bed late.

(10) Did you find the house easily? No, it was a little difficult.

(11) Were they all Koreans? No, some foreigners came too.

(12) Do you usually go to bed early? Yes, I usually go to sleep early.

(13) I came as an exchange student. Really? Which country are you from?

(14) Do you speak Japanese as well? I want to learn a bit of Japanese, too.

(15) Aren't you busy this afternoon? I have a favor to ask.

(16) Is it far from here? No, it's not that far. I'll go with you.

(17) Isn't he American? No, he's English.

(18) Is Korean difficult? Yes, it's hard.

(19) Isn't she Manho's girlfriend?

(20) Do you teach Korean? No, I teach English.

(21) Where do you teach? I teach at the Cathedral/Catholic church.

(22) There are lots of trees outside my house. They are really pretty.

(23) Who sleeps in the next room?

(24) Is the building next door a restaurant? No, it seems to be a bar.

(25) Do you usually study at school or at home? I study at home. I can't really study at school.

(26) Do you have a dog? Yes, we do. It's very good. We have a cat as well.

(27) Is your father home now? Yes, he is. Please wait a moment.

(28) Where are the children? They are playing in front of the house.

(29) I can't go and watch a movie today. I'm sorry.

(30) Do you usually eat lunch in the school cafeteria? No, the food is bad (tasting) there.

(31) Did you buy a ticket? No, I didn't buy [haven't had a chance to buy] one yet. Where is the ticket booth?

(32) When does the Chonju train leave? And how many hours does it take?

(33) Where have you been? I've been to buy new shoes.

(34) How long does it take? It takes two hours.

(35) Where did you learn Russian? I learned it in Russia. Really? How long were you in Russia?

(36) Do you like foreign languages? Yes, I want to learn many foreign languages.

(37) Ewha University, Yonsei University and Sogang University are all in Shinch'on. They are rather far from Seoul National University. They are far from Korea University, too.

(38) Do you usually get up early on Sundays? No, I get up late on Sundays.

(39) Is there a shoe store in this area? Yes, there's one over there across from the front gate of the university.

(40) Our car is always clean. So it's like new.

(41) Who are you waiting for? I am waiting for my father and mother.

(42) Usually I go straight home from school.

(43) In the afternoon I'm meeting a friend in front of the post office.

(44) Excuse me, but I have a favor to ask. Yes, go ahead.

(45) Did you eat? No, I haven't eaten yet.

(46) Take your time (go slowly). You still have lots of time.

(47) Between the market and the post office there are a lot of inns.

(48) Do you usually return home late in the evenings? No, I don't return late. Usually I come home early.

(49) On Sunday morning I read a book in the garden.

(50) I can't drink alcohol. And I can't smoke either. Really? I didn't know.

Exercise (11): English to Korean Translation

(1) 한국말 선생님이 어디 계세요? 교실에 계세요.

(2) 미국분이세요? 아닌데요. 영국 사람이에요.

(3) 여기서 무엇을 하세요? 영국 무역회사에서 일해요.

(4) 도서관에 한국 신문이 있어요? 네, 있어요.

(5) 부인이 한국에 같이 안 가세요? 아니오, 같이 가요.

(6) 일본말을 배우세요? 네. 일때문에 일본에 자주 가요.

(7) 담배가 있어요? 네, 담배도 성냥도 제 책상 위에 있어요.

(8) 너무 재미 있었어요. 시간이 빨리 갔어요.

(9) 저녁에 잡지와 책을 읽으세요? 보통 신문을 먼저 읽어요.

(10) 누구한테서 들었어요? 정말이에요. 남동생한테서 들었어요.

(11) 부모님하고 같이 살아요? 아니오, 시청 근처에 친구하고 살아요.

(12) 펜이 있어요? 미안합니다. 펜도 연필도 없어요.

(13) 무엇을 하세요? 제 명함을 찾아요.

(14) 김 선생님은 담배를 안 피우세요. 술도 안 마시세요.

(15) 오늘 저녁에 영화구경을 같이 못 가요. 너무 바빠요.

(16) 저녁에는 보통 집에 있어요. 그리고 일찍 자요.

(17) 한국에는 정원하고 공원이 많이 있어요? 네, 있어요. 그런데 영국에는
더 많아요.

(18) 김 선생님은 미국에서 외교관들한테 한국말을 가르치셨어요. 그렇지만
지금은 서울에서 사세요.

(19) 학교에서 일본말을 배워요? 아니오, 중국말을 배워요. 그렇지만 말을
아직 잘 못 해요.

(20) 가방에는 종이 있어요? 네, 여기 있어요.

(21) 성냥도 담배도 없어요. 있어요?

(22) 집이 크세요? 아니오, 별로 안 커요. 그렇지만 좋아요.

(23) 어제는 아주 즐거웠어요. 다시 가고 싶어요.

(24) 고양이 있어요? 아니오, 개도 고양이도 없어요.

(25) 낮에는 은행에서 일을 해요. 그리고 밤에는 호텔에서 일을 해요. 일
때문에 항상 바빠요.

(26) 저녁에는 이 가게 앞에서 제 친구를 만나요. 그리고 영화구경을 가요.

(27) 보통 공원에서 혼자서 산보를 해요? 아니오, 보통 제 친구하고 해요.

(28) 아침을 아주 일찍 먹어요. 그리고 학교에 가요.

(29) 물을 많이 마셔요. 그건데 고기는 많이 안 먹어요.

(30) 점심을 먹으러 식당에 가요.

(31) 약을 먹었어요?

(32) 어느 것이 더 좋아요? 이 것이 더 좋아요.

(33) 오늘 저녁에는 시간이 좀 있어요.

(34) 친구한테 전화를 걸고 싶었어요.

(35) 그런데 나갔어요.

(36) 가끔 정원에서 일을 해요.

(37) 그래서 전화를 못 받아요.

(38) 지금 바로 집에 가고 싶어요.

(39) 극장 안에는 너무 더웠어요. 그래서 스웨터를 벗었어요.

(40) 이를 닦고 싶었어요. 그런데 시간이 없었어요.

(41) 오늘 아침에 어디에 갔다왔어요? 새 청파지를 사러 시장에

잤다왔어요.

(42) 자전거로 가고 싶어요. 자전거로는 못 가요. 너무 멀어요.

(43) 아침에는 보통 빵과 우유를 먹어요? 아니오. 밥을 좋아해요.

(44) 동생에게 돈을 주고 싶었어요. 그런데 돈이 없었어요.

(45) 내일 일찍 일어나고 싶어요.

Lesson Eleven

Exercise (2): Numerals and Counters

(1) 일곱시, 여덟시 정각, 일곱시 오분, 일곱시 오분 전, 여섯시 반쯤

(2) 여섯명, 잡지 아홉 권, 개 두 마리, 건물 열한 채, 자동차 네 대

(3) 열한시, 열시 사십 오분, 열한시 십분, 아홉시 반, 열두시

(4) 이불, 신문 두 개, 책 열 권, 개 두 마리, 종이 열다섯 장

(5) 두 시간, 오일, 십사일, 여덟 시간 반, 십분

(6) 이일, 십일, 이 주간, 삼개월/세달/석달, 여섯 해

(7) 여덟시 십칠분, 여덟시 사십 칠분, 여덟시 칠분 전/일곱시 오십 삼분,
    일곱시 이십 오분, 일곱시 정각

Exercise (3): Answer the Questions

(4) 십이월에 있습니다.

(6) 여덟시간 반쯤 일했습니다.

(7) 일월달에 시작합니다.

(8) 마흔 한살입니다.

(9) 석달쯤 쉽니다.

(10) 열시부터 일을 시작합니다.

(11) 스물네 시간입니다.

Exercise (4): Fill in the Missing Particles

(1) 마다/쯤

(2) 부터

(3) 마다

(4) 만

(5) 부터/까지

(6) 쯤

(7) 부터/까지

(8) 마다/쯤

(9) 정각에

(10) 마리/상자/병

Exercise (5): Formal Style

Part One: Easier Verbs
 (1) 여기 앉습니다, 앉습니까?, 앉으십시오, 앉읍시다.
 (2) 늦게 떠납니다, 떠납니까?, 떠나십시오, 떠납시다.
 (3) 거기 있습니다, 있습니까?, 있으십시오, 있읍시다
 (4) 친구를 기다립니다, 기다립니까?, 기다리십시오, 기다립시다.
 (5) 애기한테 음식을 줍니다, 줍니까?, 주십시오, 줍시다.
 (6) 빨리 시작합니다, 합니까?, 하십시오, 합시다.
 (7) 술집에 갑니다, 갑니까?, 가십시오, 갑시다.
 (8) 편지를 씁니다, 씁니까?, 쓰십시오, 씁시다.
 (9) 교회에 나갑니다, 나갑니까?, 나가십시오, 나갑시다.
 (10) 전화를 받습니다. 받습니까?, 받으십시오, 받읍시다.
 (11) 십분만 쉽니다, 쉽니까?, 쉬십시오, 쉽시다.

Part Two: Trickier Verbs
 (1) 라디오를 듣습니다, 듣습니까?, 들으십시오, 들읍시다.
 (2) 택시를 부릅니다, 부릅니까?, 부르십시오, 부릅시다.
 (3) 사장님한테 전화를 겁니다, 겁니까?, 거십시오, 겁시다.
 (4) 고기를 굽습니다, 굽습니까?, 구우십시오, 구웁시다.
 (5) 즐겁습니다, 즐겁습니까?, (absent), (absent).
 (6) 오늘은 참 덥습니다, 덥습니까? (absent), (absent).
 (7) 나는 이사람을 잘 압니다, 압니까?, 아십시오, 압시다.
 (8) 한국 음식은 아주 맵습니다, 맵습니까? (absent), (absent).
 (9) 밖에 좀 춥습니다, 춥습니까? (absent), (absent).
 (10) 내 동생은 서울에서 삽니다, 삽니까?, 사십시오, 삽시다.

Exercise (6): English to Korean Translation

 (1) 하루에 세번씩 이를 닦습니다.
 (2) 오늘부터 아주 바쁩니다.
 (3) 언제까지 있습니까?
 (4) 산보를 하러 나갑시다.
 (5) 사람마다 다릅니다.
 (6) 언제 만나고 싶습니까?
 (7) 아르바이트를 찾으러 왔습니다.
 (8) 학생마다 그 선생님을 좋아합니다.
 (9) 토요일까지 그 여관에 있었습니다.
 (10) 왜 늦었습니까? 죄송합니다.

(11) 몇 시쯤 갑니까?

(12) 금년도 아내의 생일을 잊어버렸습니다.

(13) 만원씩 주십시오.

(14) 아홉시부터 시작을 합시다.

(15) 언제쯤 서울로 떠납니까?

Lesson Twelve

Exercise (1): Manipulating -지만

(1) 택시를 불렀지만 아직 안 왔어요.

(2) 아기는 자지만 어머니는 못 주무세요.

(3) 음악회는 가지 않지만 연극에는 가요.

(4) 내 나이가 여든살이지만 오십년은 더 살고 싶어요.

(5) 점심때까지 일을 마치고 싶었지만 손님이 갑자기 왔어요.

(6) 맥주는 좋지만 소주는 싫어요.

(7) 지금 잡지를 보고 싶지 않지만 만화는 보고 싶어요.

(8) 양주는 비싸지만, 소주는 싸요.

(9) 우리 오빠는 결혼했지만 아직도 술집에 다녀요.

(10) 선생님을 만나고 싶지만 시간이 없어요.

(11) 돈은 있지만 사고 싶지 않아요.

(12) 나는 영화구경을 가끔 가지만 동생은 잘 가지 않아요.

(13) 나는 돈이 적지만 친구는 많아요.

(14) 김 사장은 아들은 없지만 딸은 둘이 있어요.

(15) 오빠는 일찍 왔지만 동생은 늦게 왔어요.

(16) 그분의 아버님은 우체국에서 일을 하시지만 편지를 많이 안 쓰세요.

(17) 나는 전에는 학생이었지만 지금은 선생이에요.

(18) 내 약혼자는 나한테 꽃을 주었지만 나는 꽃을 좋아하지 않아요.

(19) 어머니는 부산에 사시지만 달마다 서울에 한 번씩 오세요.

(20) 우리집은 크지 않지만 좋아요.

(21) 아침마다 수영을 하지만, 건강하지 못합니다.

(22) 학생들은 많지만 학교는 작아요.

Exercise (2): Suggestions and Tentative Questions

(1) 집에 돌아갈까요? *Shall we go home?*

(2) 그 책을 읽을까요? *Shall we read that book?*

(3) 춤을 출까요? *Shall we dance?*

(4) 길에서 옷을 벗을까요? *Shall we take off our clothes on the road?*

(5) 걸어갈까요? *Shall we go by foot?*

(6) 음악회에 같이 갈까요? *Shall we go to the music concert together?*

(7) 소주 시킬까요? 아니면 생맥주 시킬까요? *Shall we order soju? Or, shall we order draft beer?*

(8) 언니가 그 남자와 결혼할까요? *Do you suppose my older sister will marry that man?*

(9) 그 이야기를 다시 한번 들을까요? *Shall I listen to that story one more time?*

(10) 어머니가 백화점에서 어떤 옷을 샀을까요? *What clothes do you suppose mother bought at the department store?*

(11) 김 선생님은 여자 친구하고 같이 오실까요? *Do you suppose Mr. Kim will come with his girlfriend?*

(12) 한국 옷을 입을까요? *Shall we wear Korean clothes?*

(13) 다른 집에서 살까요? *Shall we live in a different house?*

(14) 택시를 부를까요? *Shall I call a taxi?*

(15) 크림 넣을까요? 아니면 프리마 넣을까요? *Shall I add cream? Or shall I add non-dairy creamer?*

Exercise (3): The *wanna* Form

(1) 술 마실래요? *Do you feel like drinking?*

(2) 테니스 칠래요? *Do you feel like playing tennis?*

(3) 내일 극장에 갈래요? *Do you feel like going to the movies tomorrow?*

(4) 한국 신문을 읽을래요? *Do you feel like reading a Korean newspaper?*

(5) 우리 집에 갈래요? *Do you want to go to our house?*

(6) 한국 노래를 들을래요? *Do feel like listening to a Korean song?*

(7) 햄버거나 빨리 먹을래요? *Do you feel like eating a hamburger quickly or something?*

(8) 한국 담배를 피울래요? 양담배를 피울래요? *Do you feel like smoking Korean cigarettes? Or Western cigarettes?*

(9) 학교 식당에서 나를 기다릴래요? *Do you feel like waiting for me in the school cafeteria?*

(10) 토요일에 은행 앞에서 만날래요? *Do you feel like meeting in front of the bank on Saturday?*

(11) 이게 힘이 들어요. 좀 도와줄래요? *This is difficult. Do you feel like helping me?*

(12) 내일 떠날래요? 아니면 모레 떠날래요? *Do you feel like leaving tomorrow? Or, the day after tomorrow?*

Exercise (4): Long Negatives

(1) 그 여자의 언니는 학교에서 공부를 하지 않았어요. *Her sister did not study at school.*

(2) 이 상자는 여자에게는 너무 무겁지 않아요? *Isn't this box too heavy for a woman?*

(3) 애들 때문에 피곤하지 않으세요? *Aren't you tired because of the kids?*

(4) 나는 일본서 오지 않았어요. *I did not come from Japan.*

(5) 언니는 나를 많이 기다리지 않았어요? *You didn't wait long for me?*

(6) 언니는 담배를 피우지 않아요. *My older sister doesn't smoke.*

(7) 나는 한국말을 한국에서 배우지 않았어요. *I did not learn Korean in Korea.*

(8) 저 아저씨는 부자 동네에서 살지 않아요. *That man does not live in a rich neighborhood.*

(9) 아들은 춤을 추지 않았어요. *My son did not dance.*

(10) 아이들은 날마다 학교에 가지 않아요. *The children do not go to school every day.*

(11) 그 여자는 그 남자와 약혼하고 싶어하지 않아요. *That woman does not want to be engaged to that man.*

(12) 수미씨는 오빠와 같이 라디오를 듣지 않아요. *Sumi does not listen to the radio with her brother.*

(13) 일요일에 나는 성당에 나가지 않아요. *I do not go to church on Sundays.*

(14) 커피에 설탕이랑 크림을 타지 않아요? *Don't you take sugar and cream in your coffee?*

Exercise (5): Negative Commands

(1) 책을 보지 마세요. *Don't look at the book.*

(2) 여자 친구를 만나지 마세요. *Don't meet your girlfriend.*

(3) 술을 많이 마시지 마세요. *Don't drink a lot of alcohol.*

(4) 담배를 피우지 마세요. *Please don't smoke.*

(5) 그 의자에 앉지 마세요. *Don't sit in that chair.*

(6) 얼음 넣지 마세요. *Don't add ice.*

(7) 설탕 타지 마세요. *Don't add sugar.*

(8) 늦게 들어오지 마세요. *Don't come back late.*

(9) 날마다 술집에 다니지 마세요. *Don't go to bars every day.*

(10) 그 남자랑 춤 추지 마세요. *Don't dance with that man.*

(11) 모레 떠나지 마세요. *Don't leave the day after tomorrow.*

(12) 걸어가지 마세요. *Don't go by foot.*

(13) 혼자 다니지 마세요. *Don't go alone.*

(14) 내년에는 은퇴하지 마세요. *Don't retire next year.*

(15) 그 사람한테 전화번호를 주지 마세요. *Don't give (that person) him your phone number.*

(16) 이 샤쓰에 풀을 먹이지 마세요. *Don't starch this shirt.*

(17) 이 바지를 세탁하지 마세요. *Don't wash these pants.*

Exercise (6): English to Korean Translation

(1) 다방에도 술집에도 가지 마십시오. (2) 아이스크림을 먹고 싶지 않았지만 오빠가 하나 줬어요. (3) 벌써 오후 일곱시에요? 그러면 여기 계시지 마세요. 집에 가십시오. (4) 작년에 한국에 돌아갔지만 좋아하지 않았어요. (5) 커피에 설탕을 넣으세요. (6) 위스키를 마실래요? 아니면 소주를 마실래요? (7) 술을 마시지 않아요. 선생님도 술을 드시지 마세요! (8) A. 야구를 합시다. B. 하지 않을래요. 위층에서 쉴래요. (9) 요즘 우리 오빠가 일찍 돌아오지 않아요. (10) 아들도 딸도 똑똑하지 못 합니다.

Exercise (7): Korean to English Translation

(1) Mr. Nam does not like music. My wife does not like it either.

(2) I'm thinking of going for a walk or something in that park over there.

(3) These things are very heavy. Do you feel like helping me?

(4) When did you return home?

(5) I cooked the meat cooked deliciously, but no one ate any.

(6) Yesterday our dog suddenly bit my father.

(7) This cream is expensive, but it is not at all tasty. Do not eat it!

(8) Teacher Kim is pretty like a movie actress.

(9) A. Would you like a cola? Or would you like ice water?

 B. I don't like either one. Could you give me a beer?

(10) I'm thinking of going to Pusan tonight. Would you like to go with me (together)?

(11) I called many times, but no one answered.

(12) A. What would you like to buy?

 B. I do not want to buy anything.

(13) You speak Korean well. About how many years did you study?

(14) I'm bored. Shall we go to a *tabang* or something?

(15) A. Do you suppose whiskey and *soju* are bad for your health?

 B. I'm not sure. Let's not eat them.

Lesson Thirteen

Exercise (1): Sequentials in -(으)니까

(1) 밤에 눈이 왔으니까 골프를 못 칠거에요. *It snowed last night so I won't be able to play golf.*

(2) 저희 어머니가 항상 집에 있으니까 걱정 마세요. *Don't worry— my mom is always at home.*

(3) 한국말이 너무 어려우니까 다른 외국어를 할래요. *Korean is so difficult, I would like to do a different foreign language.*

(4) 오늘 좀 바쁘니까 내일 만날까요? *I am a bit busy today, so shall we meet tomorrow?*

(5) 나는 중국사람이 아니니까 중국말은 못 가르칩니다. *I am not Chinese, so I can't teach Chinese.*

(6) 영화관 앞으로 나가니까 친구가 벌써 기다리고 있었어요. *When I went out to the front of the theatre, my friend was already waiting.*

(7) 방 안으로 들어가니까 아무도 없었어요. *When I entered the room, there was no one there.*

(8) 밖에 나가니까 눈이 오고 있었어요. *When I went outside, I fount that it was snowing.*

(9) 연구실에서 편지를 쓰고 있으니까 일본에서 전화가 왔어요. *While I was writing a letter in my [research] office, I got a phone call from Japan.*

(10) 서울역에 도착하니까 벌써 밤이었습니다. *When I arrived at Seoul station, it was already night.*

Exercise (2): -(으)ㄹ거에요 as Probable Future

(1) 동생은 교회에 갈거에요. *My brother is going to go to church.*

(2) 시아버님은 일주일동안 계실거에요. *My father-in law is going to stay for a week.*

(3) 선생님은 넥타이를 맬거에요. *The teacher is going to wear a tie.*

(4) 할아버지는 모자를 쓰실거에요. *Grandfather is going to wear a hat.*

(5) 내일 숙제가 많을거에요. *There will be a lot of homework tomorrow.*

(6) 내일 비가 올거에요. *It is going to rain tomorrow.*

(7) 오늘 밤에 조카가 올거에요. *Tonight my nephew will come.*

(8) 나는 한국에서 영어를 가르칠거에요. *I'm going to teach English in Korea.*

(9) 아저씨는 이번 겨울에 가족을 만날거에요. *He will meet his family this winter.*

(10) 형은 군인이 될거에요. *My brother will become a soldier.*

(11) 내일 아침부터 눈이 올거에요. *It is going to snow from tomorrow morning.*

(12) 나는 이번 가을에는 일본에 갈거에요. *I am going to go to Japan this autumn.*

(13) 조카한테 뭘 줄거에요? *What are you going to give to your nephew?*

(14) 김 선생님이 내년에 결혼할거에요. *Mr. Kim is going to get married next year.*

(15) 내 약혼자는 이번 가을에 졸업할거에요. *My fiance is going to graduate this autumn.*

Exercise (3): -(으)ㄹ거에요 as Probable Present

(1) 외삼촌은 중국에 살고 계실거에요. *My uncle is probably living in China.*

(2) 장인어른은 지금 주무실거에요. *My father-in-law is probably sleeping now.*

(3) 밖이 추울거에요. *It's probably cold outside.*

(4) 영국은 날씨가 별로 안 좋을거에요. *The weather in England is probably not that good.*

(5) 우리 시어머니는 교회에 나가실거에요. *My mother-in-law will probably go to church.*

(6) 그 아이가 아직 어릴거에요. *That child is probably still young.*

(7) 그 부모님들이 젊으시지 않을거에요. *His parents are probably not young.*

(8) 그 상점이 가까울거에요. *That store is probably close.*

(9) 영화관은 너무 멀거에요. *The movie theatre is probably too far.*

(10) 우리 시아버님은 돈이 많으실거에요. *My father-in-law probably has a lot of money.*

(11) 우리 며느리는 영어를 잘 할거에요. *Our daughter-in-law probably speaks English well.*

(12) 선생님의 약혼자는 꽃을 좋아 하실거에요. *The teacher's fiance probably likes flowers.*

(13) 내 사위가 미국사람이지만 한국말을 좀 할거에요. *My son-in-law is an American, but he probably speaks a little Korean.*

(14) 아저씨는 남동생 집에서 사실거에요. *He probably lives in his brother's house.*

(15) 선생님의 아드님이 졸업했을거에요. *The teacher's son has probably graduated.*

(16) 오빠가 운동하고 있을거에요. *My brother is probably exercising.*

(17) 고모부가 그거 모르실거에요. *My uncle probably won't know that.*

(18) 할아버지가 일찍 주무셨을거에요. *Grandfather probably went to bed early.*

(19) 영화가 인제 끝났을거에요. *The movie is probably finished now.*

(20) 조카가 그 편지를 이틀 전에 받았을거에요. *My nephew probably received the letter two days ago.*

Exercise (4): Kinship terms and Honorifics

(1) 남동생은 봄에는 골프를 치지만 여름에는 테니스를 쳐요. 아버님께서는 봄에는 골프를 치시지만 여름에는 테니스를 치셔요.

(2) 남동생은 어제 밤에 일찍 잤지만 오늘 아침에는 일찍 일어나지 않았어요. 아버님께서는 어제 밤에 일찍 주무셨지만 오늘 아침에는 일찍 일어나시지 않았어요.

(3) 남동생은 고기도 잘 안 먹고 물도 잘 안 마셔요. 아버님께서는 고기도 잘 잡수시지 않고 물도 잘 드세요.

(4) 남동생은 늙었지만 마음은 젊어요. 아버님께서는 연세가 많으시지만 마음은 젊으세요.

(5) 남동생은 며느리를 안 좋아하지만 사위는 좋아해요. 아버님께서는 며느리를 좋아하시지 않지만 사위는 좋아하세요.

(6) 남동생은 어제 오후에는 집에 없었지만 지금은 있어요. 아버님께서는 어제 오후에는 집에 안 계셨지만 지금은 계세요.

(7) 남동생은 낮에는 일을 열심히 해요. 밤에는 쉬어요. 아버님께서는 낮에는 일을 열심히 하세요. 밤에는 쉬세요.

(8) 남동생은 작년에 대학교에서 영어를 가르쳤지만 지금은 안 가르쳐요. 아버님께서는 작년에 대학교에서 영어를 가르치셨지만 지금은 가르치시지 않아요.

(9) 남동생은 호텔에서 한 시간동안 기다렸지만 친구가 안 왔어요. 아버님께서는 호텔에서 한 시간동안 기다리셨지만 친구가 오시지 않았어요.

(10) 어제 남동생은 여동생에게 돈을 줬어요. 어제 아버님께서는 여동생에게 돈을 주셨어요.

(11) 어제 밤에 남동생은 두 시간동안 라디오를 들었어요. 어제 밤에 우리 아버님께서는 두 시간동안 라디오를 들으셨어요.

Exercise (5): English to Korean Translation

(1)　　A. 우리 가족은 커요. 식구가 많아요.
　　　　B. 호철씨, 형제가 몇 명이세요?
　　　　A. 남동생 네명 하고 여동생 한 명 있어요.
　　　　B. 형님이나 누님이 없으세요?
　　　　A. 네, 없어요. 형도 누나도 없어요.
　　　　B. 호철씨, 자녀분이 있으세요?
　　　　A. 네, 이제 아들 하고 딸이 있어요.

(2)　　A. 여기서 뭘 하고 있어요?
　　　　B. 여자친구를 기다리고 있어요.

(3)   A. 애가 지금 뭘 하고 있어요?
       B. 자고 있어요.
(4) 선생님이 넥타이를 매고 계세요.
(5) 우리 고모부가 구두를 신고 계세요.
(6) 졸업을 하자마자 일본에 가고 싶어요.
(7) 영화가 끝나자마자 다방에 갔어요.
(8) 우리 이모부가 카나다에서 돌아오자마자 눈이 왔어요.
(9) 부산에 도착하자마자 집에 전화를 걸었어요.
(10) 전화번호를 찾자마자 전화를 걸었어요.
(11) 값이 좀 올라가자마자 차를 팔았어요.

Exercise (6). Korean-to-English Translation

(1) That man was probably a soldier.

(2) I'm going to do some sight-seeing in Seoul tomorrow.

(3)   A. Are you going to meet Mrs. Lee this evening?
       B. But she already left for Seoul, didn't she?

(4) It probably snowed last night.

(5) Our grandparents are living in Taegu.

(6) I am going to graduate this spring.

(7) A. How old is your son? B. He is twenty-four.

(8) That woman is probably divorced.

(9)   A. I majored in economics.
       B. Really? But it's boring, don't you think?

(10)   A. Shall we go to the stadium to do some exercise?
       B. But it's raining!

(11) My sister is writing a book.

(12) Our granddaughter always wears a hat.

(13) I have many members in my family. I have five younger brothers and two older
     sisters.

(14)   A. Sujan speaks Korean really well now.
       B. She studies hard all the time, doesn't she.

(15)   A. There are always lots of customers in this restaurant.
       B. Well, the food is delicious (isn't it).

(16) It's cold, so let's not go outside.

(17) This program is really boring, so don't watch it.

(18) When I went outside, it was cold.

(19) I telephoned just now, but no one answered.

(20) The movie is probably finished now.

Exercise (7): More Practice with Sequentials

(1) 집에 돌아가니까 아무도 없었어요. *When I returned home there was no one there.*

(2) 밖에 나가니까 아주 더웠어요. *When I went outside, it was very hot.*

(3) 산에 올라가니까 참 추웠어요. *When I went up the mountain, it was very cold.*

(4) 다시 한번 보니까 외삼촌이었어요. *When I looked again, it was my uncle.*

(5) 누님한테 전화 거니까 받지 않았어요. *When I called my sister, no one answered.*

(6) 양복을 입으니까 다른 사람 같아요. *With a suit on you look like a different person.*

(7) 은퇴를 하니까 갑자기 심심해요. *Now that I have retired, all of a sudden I feel bored.*

(8) 맥주 한잔 마시니까 노래를 부르고 싶어요. *Now that I've had a glass of beer, I want to sing.*

(9) 그 여자랑 데이트 하니까 부모님이 싫어하셨어요. *When I went on a date with that girl [I discovered] my parents didn't like her.*

(10) 택시 타니까 아저씨가 영어를 잘 했어요. *When I got into the taxi [I discovered that] the taxi driver spoke English well.*

(11) 좀 피곤하니까 오늘은 나가지 맙시다. *We're a bit tired, so let's not go out today.*

(12) 한국은 겨울에 추우니까 봄에 갑시다. *It's cold in Korea in the winter, so let's go in the spring.*

(13) 선교사니까 한국말을 잘 할거에요. *He's a missionary, so he probably speaks Korean well.*

(14) 나이가 많으니까 너무 빨리 걷지 말아요. *He's old, so don't walk too quickly.*

(15) 내일 눈이 올거니까 다음 주일에 합시다. *It's probably going to snow tomorrow, so let's do it next week.*

(16) 사장님께 말씀 드렸으니까 걱정하지 마십시오. *I told the company president, so don't worry.*

(17) 장마가 시작됐으니까 비가 많이 올겁니다. *The rainy season has started so it will rain a lot.*

(18) 한국사람이니까 김치를 좋아해요. *He's Korean, so he likes kimchee.*

(19) 커피가 없으니까 홍차로 할까요? *There's no coffee, so shall we have tea?*

(20) 댁에 혼자 계시니까 심심하실겁니다. *He is staying home alone, so he is probably bored.*

(21) 부자동네에 사니까 돈이 많을거에요. *They live in a rich neighborhood, so they probably have a lot of money.*

Exercise (8): Practice with -고 있어요

(1) 동생은 넥타이를 매고 있어요. *My brother is wearing a tie. or My brother is putting on a tie.*

(2)　A. 뭐 하고 있어요? *What are you doing?*
　　B. 냉커피 마시고 있어요. *I'm drinking iced coffee.*

(3) 순희씨는 째즈 음악을 듣고 있어요. *Sunhui is listening to jazz.*

(4) 사장님은 손님하고 이야기를 하고 계세요. *The president is speaking with a customer/guest.*

(5)　A. 아까 그 학생이 어디 갔어요?
　　　Where did that student just go?
　　B. 지금 복도에서 기다리고 있을거에요.
　　　He's probably waiting in the hallway.

(6)　A. 아직도 시청 근처에 살고 계세요?
　　　Are you still living in the vicinity of city hall?
　　B. 아니오, 지금은 친척 집에서 살고 있어요.
　　　No, I am living at my relative's house now.

(7) 내 노트를 찾고 있어요. 못 봤어요? *I'm looking for my notebook. Haven't you seen it?*

(8) 언니하고 오빠는 지금 테니스를 치고 있어요. *My older sister and brother are playing tennis now.*

(9)　A. 언니는 어디 갔어요?
　　　Where did she go?
　　B. 저기서 춤을 추고 있잖아요?
　　　That's her dancing over there (isn't it~don't you know).

(10) 요즘 왜 안경을 안 쓰고 있어요? *Why aren't you wearing your glasses recently?*

Exercise (9): Vocabulary Drill

(1) 아내-남편/ 형-오빠/ 조카/ 할머니/ 장모-시어머니한테서 편지를 받았습니다.

(2) 우리 아버지/ 고모-이모/ 누나-언니/ 부모님/ 할아버지 은/는 돈을 조금 주셨습니다.

(3) 제 친구가 남동생/ 형/ 장인/ 조카/ 부인 옆에 앉습니다.

(4) 제 친구는 부모님/ 장인/ 손주/ 고모-이모/ 형하고같이 삽니다.

(5) 내 여동생은 공원에서 남편/ 아버지/ 우리 딸/ 며느리/이모와~과/
   개와 같이 산보를 하고 있습니다.

Lesson Fourteen

Exercise (1): Future-Presumptives in -겠-

(1) 나는 우체국까지 가겠어요. *I will go as far as the post office.*
(2) 나는 서울대학교에서 공부하겠어요. *I will study at Seoul National University.*
(3) 선생님은 무엇을 하시겠어요? *What will you do?*
(4) 내일까지 집에 돌아오겠어요. *I will return home by tomorrow.*
(5) 기차를 타고 시내에 가겠어요. *I will take the train downtown.*
(6) 나는 한국에서 영어를 가르치겠어요. *I will teach English in Korea.*
(7) 점심 값을 내가 내겠어요. *I'll pay for lunch.*
(8) 김 선생님이 자동차를 파시겠어요? *Are you going to sell your car, Mr. Kim?*
(9) 다방 앞에서 기다리겠어요. *I will wait in front of the tabang.*
(10) 나는 이번 가을에 일본에 가겠어요. *I will go to Japan this autumn.*

Exercise (2): Suppositives in -지요

(1) 선생님이 매일 술값을 내지요. *Our teacher pays for drinks every day, you know.*
(2) 복동씨의 할아버님은 연세가 많으시지요? *Poktong's grandfather is really old, isn't he?*
(3) 할머님은 벌써 삼년 전에 돌아가셨지요. *My grandmother passed away already three years ago, you know.*
(4) 언니는 우리와 같이 살지 않지요. *My older sister doesn't live with us, you know.*
(5) 일본에 돌아가고 싶지요? *I imagine you want to go back to Japan (don't you)?*
(6) 그 사람은 지금 쉬고 있겠지요. *I suppose he's resting now.*
(7) 동생 옷이 예쁘지요. *My sister's clothes are pretty, you know.*
(8) 조금 더 걸어가지요. *Let's walk a little more (OK)?*
(9) 그 사람을 매일 만나지요. *I meet him every day, you know.*
(10) 화장실에 내 우산이 없었지요? *My umbrella wasn't in the bathroom, was it?*
(11) 머리가 아프지요? *You have a headache (don't you)?*

Exercise (3): English to Korean Translation

(1) 음악회를 좋아하지요? 네, 영화는 좋아하지 않지만 음악회는 좋아해요.

(2) 그럼, 오늘 밤에 음악회에 같이 갈까요? 좋지요.

(3) 지금 몇시지요? 모르겠어요.

(4) 날씨가 너무 좋지요? 공원에서 산보를 할까요?

(5) 그 노래를 어떻게 배웠지요? 라디오에서 들었어요.

(6) 어제 밤에 눈이 많이 왔지요?

(7) 그 시디를 서점에서 샀어요? 아니오! 서점에서는 시디를 안 팔잖아요!

(8) 기차가 세시까지 도착 할까요? 도착하겠지요!

(9) 테레비젼을 보고 있겠지요?

(10) 형님이 두명만 있어요. or 형님이 두명밖에 없어요.

(11) 김 선생님이 텔레비전에서 나오셨지요?

(12) 작년에 서울에서 살지 않았어요?

(13) 자동차로 올께요.

(14) 값이 십오불쯤 하겠습니다.

(15) 편지를 벌써 썼겠지요?

(16) 한국에 갔어요.

(17) 그 할아버지께서는 벌써 돌아가셨겠지요?

(18) 여기서 잠깐 기다릴께요.

(19) 엘리베이터를 타고 올라왔어요.

(20) 동대문에서 만날까요?

(21) 가방 속에 돈이 있었어요?

(22) 그저께 일을 많이 했지만 돈은 못 받았어요.

Exercise (4): Practice with -겠지요

(1) 장 선생님은 공부하고 계시겠지요. *Mr. Chang is probably/must be studying.*

(2) 밖이 춥겠지요. *It must be cold outside.*

(3) 오빠가 기분이 좋겠지요. *My brother is probably/ must be in a good mood.*

(4) 학생들이 일찍 학교에 오겠지요. *The students will probably come to school early.*

(5) 그 아이가 어리겠지요. *That child is probably be young.*

(6) 부모님들이 젊으시겠지요. *His parents are probably/ must be young.*

(7) 그 상점은 굉장히 비싸겠지요. *That store is probably/ must be extremely expensive.*

(8) 영화관은 너무 멀겠지요. *The movie theatre is probably/ must be too far away.*

(9) 시험이 어렵겠지요. *The exam will probably be difficult.*

(10) 선생님의 약혼자는 꽃을 좋아하시겠지요. *The teacher's fiance will probably/ must like flowers.*

(11) 선생님의 따님이 예쁘겠지요. *The teacher's daughter will probably be/ must be pretty.*

(12) 내일 아침부터 눈이 오겠지요. *It will probably snow from tomorrow morning.*

Exercise (5): *only*

(1) 저희 학교에는 여자는 많지만, 남자는 한 명밖에 없어요.

(2) 지금은 방학이에요. 학교에는 학생 몇 명밖에 없어요.

(3) 어제 두 사람밖에 안 왔습니다/ 오지 않았습니다.

(4) 맥주 몇 병 사셨어요? 한 병밖에 안/못 샀어요.

(5) 돈 얼마나 있으세요? 조금밖에 없어요.

(6) 어제 밤에는 네 시간밖에 못 잤어요. 그래서 굉장히 피곤하지요.

(7) 지난 달에는 영화구경을 두 번밖에 가지 않았어요.

(8) 크리스마스에는 선물을 많이 받으셨어요? 아니오, 몇 개밖에 안 받았어요.

(9) 이건 빨리 합시다. 시간이 조금밖에 없어요.

(10) 한국말 잘 하세요? 아니오, 한 학기밖에 못 배웠어요.

Exercise (6): Korean-to-English Translation

(1) A. Chinho, don't you smoke?
   B. I used to smoke, but I quit.

(2) A. Who all came to the last party?
   B. My friends from the dormitory and my church friends came.

(3) A. Sujin goes to the swimming pool nowadays to learn how to swim.
   B. Really? I used to go there, too.

(4) A. Eric speaks Korean well, doesn't he?
   B. Yes, he couldn't speak a word a year ago, but now he speaks really well.

(5) A. Chinho, are you dating that girl these days?
   B. No, until one month ago we met often, but I'm dating another girl now.

(6) A. The weather is hot, isn't it?
   B. Yes, it's really hot.

(7)   A. You like *pulgogi*, right?

        B. Yes; how many portions should we order?

(8)   A. These shoes are much too big for me.

        B. Then give them to me. I'll wear them.

(9)   A. You're going to change into a suit, right?

        B. Yes; I'll change quickly.

(10)   A. You're going to quit drinking now, right?

        B. Yes. I'll quit smoking, too.

Lesson Fifteen

Exercise (1): Matching Synonyms

(1) 좋아요 – 괜찮아요

(2) 주어요 – 드려요

(3) 한 주간 – 일주일 (4) 일년 – 열두달

(5) 읽어요– 봐요

(6) 교수 – 선생

(7) 거기 – 그 곳

(8) 세 명 – 세 사람

(9) 날마다 – 매일

(10) 백화점 – 상점

(11) 대학 – 학교

(12) 공부해요 – 배워요

Exercise (2): Matching Opposites

(1) 전에 – 후에

(2) 추워요 – 더워요

(3) 여름 – 겨울

(4) 일해요 – 쉬어요

(5) 딸 – 아들

(6) 일어나요 – 누워요

(7) 가을 – 봄

(8) 손자 – 손녀

(9) 이야기해요 – 들어요

(10) 내일 – 어제

(11) 할아버지 – 할머니

(12) 싸요 – 비싸요

(13) 오전 – 오후

(14) 밤 – 낮

(15) 사요 – 팔아요

(16) 서요 – 앉아요

(17) 시작해요 – 마쳐요

(18) 여동생 – 남동생

Exercise (3): Picking the Misfits

(1) 개가 나와요
(2) 교회
(3) 전화를 걸어요
(4) 시내
(5) 심어요
(6) 머리가 아파요

Exercise (4): Particle Manipulation

(1) 내년까지 결혼을 하고 싶어요.
(2) 기차로 갈까요?
(3) 기차도 지하철도 괜찮아요.
(4) 이 옷밖에 없어요.
(5) 비싸겠지만 새 옷을 사겠어요.
(6) 모자도 신발도 샀어요.
(7) 열 명쯤 파티에 왔어요.
(8) 아침마다 신문을 읽어요.
(9) 서울에서 부산까지 기차로 몇 시간 걸려요?
(10) 하루에 한 번쯤 지하철을 타요.
(11) 오늘 비가 오지만 나는 영화를 보러 시내에 갈거에요.
(12) 시간이 얼마나 있어요? 십분만 있어요.
(13) 오늘 고기밖에 안 먹었어요.
(14) 선생님한테 전화 두 번 걸었지만 집에 안 계셨어요.
(15) 일년에 몇 번씩 음악회에 가세요?
(16) 오늘 오전 여덟 시에서 오후 열 시까지 일을 했어요.
(17) 어제 눈이 오지 않았어요. 그리고 비도 오지 않았어요.

Exercise (7): Change to Formal Style

(1) 영국분이십니까? *Are you English?*
(2) 나는 영국사람이 아닙니다. *I am not English.*
(3) 그럼, 어디서 오셨습니까? *Then, where are you from?*
(4) 미국에서 왔습니다. *I came from America.*
(5) 미국은 한국에서 멉니까? *Is America far from Korea?*
(6) 가깝지 않습니다. 대단히 멉니다. *It's not close. It's very far.*
(7) 미국에서는 무슨 일을 하셨습니까? *What kind of work did you do in America?*
(8) 학교에서 경제학을 가르쳤습니다. *I taught economics at school.*
(9) 지금 저희 학교를 좀 구경하시겠습니까? *Would you like to have a look at my school?*
(10) 네, 학생들을 만나고 싶습니다. *Yes, I'd like to meet the students.*

(11) 우리 학교는 작지만, 학생은 많습니다. *Our school is small but we have a lot of students.*

(12) 담배를 하나 피우시겠습니까? *Would you like to smoke a cigarette?*

(13) 고맙습니다. 나는 담배를 너무 좋아합니다. 늘 피웁니다. *Thank you. I really like cigarettes, I always smoke.*

(14) 학생들이 어디서 점심을 먹습니까? *Where do the students eat lunch?*

(15) 학생들의 집들이 다 가깝습니다. 그래서, 집에서 점심을 먹지요. *The student's houses are all close. So they all eat lunch at home, you see.*

(16) 선생들은 좋습니까? *Are the teachers good?*

(17) 여기가 우리 교실입니다. *This is our classroom.*

(18) 교실이 참 큽니다. *The classroom is really large.*

(19) 교실이 크지만, 책이 많지 않습니다. *The classroom is big but there are not many books.*

(20) 저희 학교는 돈이 없습니다. 그래서, 책을 많이 못 삽니다. *Our school doesn't have any money. So, we can't buy many books.*

Exercise (8): Numerals and Counters

(1) 어제 저는 여섯 시간, 열 시부터 네 시까지, 사십분만, 일곱 시 십오분 전부터 한 시 십오분까지, 세 시간 일을 했어요.

(2) 지난주에 서울에서 친구 세 명, 극장 네 군데, 미국 의사 선생님 열 분, 만명쯤, 건물 열여덟 채 봤어요.

(3) 교실에서 신문 세 장, 책 오십 권쯤, 학생 사십 명, 선생님 세 분, 창문 여섯개하고 문 두 개 있어요.

(4) 중국어를 삼년동안, 오주일만, 몇 달, 천 구백 팔십 칠년에, 이월부터 유월까지 공부했어요.

(5) 내 남동생이 두 살, 한 살, 네 살, 마흔 살, 스무 살.

(6) 우체국 앞에 자전거 두 개, 자동차 열두 대, 개 네 마리, 의사 선생님 다섯 분(계세요) 있어요.

(7) 저는 이십일년 전에, 천 구백 사십년 사월 일일에, 천 구백 육십 육년 구월 삼십일에, 천 구백 이십 팔년 오월 이십칠일에, 천 구백 사십 오년 일월 십사일에 태어났어요.

(8) 기차는 오후 여섯 시 십팔분에, 오전 네 시 사십이분에, 오후 일곱 시 삼십칠분에, 오후 다섯 시 오분에, 오전 한 시 십구분에 떠나요.

Exercise (9): Translate into English

(1) That movie was really boring. I wanted to leave in the middle.

(2) Six years ago I wore glasses, but nowadays I wear contact lenses, you know.

(3) I put that book on top of the desk yesterday. I suppose someone is reading it.

(4) Until yesterday I wanted to go to Japan, but now I want to go to Korea.

(5)　　A. Have you brushed your teeth?

　　　B. I'm brushing them now (aren't I?).

(6) I will give you three questions each. But, can you solve them?

(7) I only study political science at university. Sometimes I do six hours of homework per day. Then after that I rest.

(8) You haven't met anyone this morning? No. I haven't been out yet, have I!

(9) Tomorrow is the beginning of school. I am going to study hard this year.

(10) I will study hard, but my brother will most likely be mainly playing (having fun).

(11) I don't want to go out. I want to drink coffee at home.

(12) This food doesn't taste very good. Shall we eat something else?

(13) How much is that book? I'll get some money out of the bank.

(14) Yesterday I went out to find our cat, but I couldn't find him.

(15) I'm doing well thanks to my boss.

(16)　　A. I can't solve this problem.

　　　B. Then I'll do it.

(17) Hurry up and go to sleep. It's really late, (isn't it?)!

(18) Do you suppose it will be cold tomorrow? I don't know.

(19) Shall we go to school? But it's Sunday today!

(20) That's my shirt, isn't it? Please give it to me quickly!

(21) Let's go and drink coffee in a tabang on Thursday.

(22) On the fifth floor they sell gloves and wallets.

(23) Would you like to play tennis?

(24) I go to church twice a month.

(25) I drank all the coffee but it didn't taste good.

(26) Has the boss arrived already? Then give him a glass of beer.

(27) What country are you from? I'm from Russia, but I came here ten years ago, you see.

(28) These books are all different. And what's more, they are all interesting. Which book store did you buy them from?

(29) My daughter is smart, but she doesn't study very hard.

(30) I don't like that story. Tell another one.

(31) The weather is bad today, but I'm in a good mood.

(32) Don't eat that bread!

(33) I'm thinking of finishing this work by next week.

(34) He doesn't live with us, but of course he wants to live with us.

(35) Shall we sit on the grass?

(36) I am looking for a girlfriend, but I don't want to get married yet.

(37) In London both the subway and the buses have lots of problems.

(38) This semester I am studying political science, economics, and Korean language.

(39) How many people are there in your family?

(40) My father goes to church, but my younger brother doesn't go.

(41) I don't have a chance to read any books these days.

(42) Last summer my professor came to my house.

(43) My nephew is still a bachelor, but I suppose he will get married sometime.

(44) Does Grandfather give you a lot of money?

(45) I'm thinking of seeing a play downtown this evening.

(46) Do they sell flowers in the book store? Of course they don't sell them.

(47) My younger cousin is a soldier in the States.

(48) How many siblings do you have?

(49) Would you like coffee? No, I want to go to bed early.

(50) He probably learned some Russian in the United States.

Exercise (10): Translate into Korean

(1) 벌써 오셨을거에요. or 벌써 왔겠지요. or 벌써 왔겠어요.
(2) 그 학생은 브라운 선생님을 기다리고 있어요.
(3) 삼천원밖에 없어요. 그래서 이 물건을 다 못 사겠어요.
(4) 그 자전거를 자주 타세요?
(5) 십오분만 공부를 할거에요.
(6) 이번주에 아버님한테서 돈을 못 받을거에요.
(7) 박 선생님의 조카가 내년에 졸업할거에요?
(8) 몇 시지요?
(9) 공원에서 같이 산보를 할래요?
(10) 그 여자는 형의 약혼자일거에요.
(11) 실례하지만, 잠깐 위층에 갈께요.
(12) 모레 장 선생님의 누님을 만날거에요.
(13) 지금 이 옷을 좀 입을래요?
(14) 기분이 좋으세요?
(15) 머리가 몹시 아파요.
(16) 여름에 시험이 많이 있을 거에요.
(17) 버스 정류장이 어디 있습니까?
(18) 어제 봤지만 몰라요.
(19) 머리를 빗으세요!
(20) 집에 계실까요? 물론 계시겠지요!